T5-CVN-086

THE FATHERS OF THE CHURCH

A NEW TRANSLATION

VOLUME 7

THE FATHERS OF THE CHURCH

Founded by
LUDWIG SCHOPP

NICETA OF REMESIANA

WRITINGS

Translated by
GERALD G. WALSH, S.J.

SULPICIUS SEVERUS

WRITINGS

Translated by
BERNARD M. PEEBLES

VINCENT OF LERINS

COMMONITORIES

Translated by
RUDOLPH E. MORRIS

PROSPER OF AQUITAINE

GRACE AND FREE WILL

Translated by
J. REGINALD O'DONNELL, C.S.B.

New York
FATHERS OF THE CHURCH, INC.
1949

NIHIL OBSTAT:

JOHN M. A. FEARNS, S.T.D.
Censor Librorum

IMPRIMATUR:

✠ FRANCIS CARDINAL SPELLMAN
Archbishop of New York

October 25, 1949

The Nihil obstat and Imprimatur are official declarations that a book or pamphlet is free of doctrinal or moral error. No implication is contained therein that those who have granted the Nihil obstat and Imprimatur agree with the contents, opinions or statements expressed.

Lithography by Bishop Litho, Inc.
Typography by Miller & Watson, Inc.
U. S. A.

CONTENTS

NICETA OF REMESIANA

SULPICIUS SEVERUS

WRITINGS OF NICETA OF REMESIANA

Translated

by

GERALD G. WALSH, S.J., M.A. (Oxon), Ph.D., S.T.D.
Fordham University

IMPRIMI POTEST
JOHN J. McMAHON, S.J.
Praep. Prov.

Neo Eboraci
die 17 Sept., 1948

INTRODUCTION

THE RESTORATION to name and fame of Niceta of Remesiana (*c.* 335-*c.* 415), whose extant and authentic works appear here for the first time in an English dress, constitutes one of the most romantic stories in the history of patristic research. For centuries a misspelt 'Niceas of Romatiana' was given credit for half a dozen long-lost Instructions for Converts.[1] A still worse spelt 'Nicha' was known to have been addressed in a letter of 366 A. D. by his fellow-bishop, Germinius of Sirmium (near Mitrovicza, on the Save, in modern Jugoslavia).[2] In the third quarter of the sixth century, the saintly and scholarly ex-Senator Cassiodorus praised the 'compendious brevity' and the 'clarity of heavenly doctrine' in a summary of the doctrine of the Trinity to be found in a work on Faith by 'Nicetus.'[3]

Meanwhile, although the works were lost, there was an all but full-length picture of the saintly, scholarly, lovable personality of Niceta contained in a letter and two poems written by the poet-saint, Paulinus of Nola (*c.* 354-431), an almost exact contemporary of St. Augustine of Hippo (354-430). In the letter, Niceta appears as a 'venerable' bishop, a man of eminent learning, *doctissimus,* who had come from

1 Gennadius, *Catalogus virorum illustrium,* cap. 22 (cited in A. E. Burn, *Niceta of Remesiana,* p. 137).
2 Burn, *op. cit.,* pp. 138-141.
3 *Ibid.,* p. 155.

Dacia to Rome and had 'deservedly won the admiration of all.' The two poems are inspired by immense affection. 'Go, if you must, but leave your heart behind you' (*I memor nostri remaneque vadens*),[4] Paulinus pleads in a well-turned Sapphic verse, when Niceta had to return in 398 to his heroic missionary work among the half-barbarian frontiersmen in the valleys and on the mountains of what is now Jugoslavia. Two minds and hearts and spirits, the poem says, were one. First, the journey is described—from Calabria in Italy to Epirus (modern Albania), then by sea to Thessalonica, up the Vardar valley to Scupi (now Skoplje), then by the Morava valley to Naissus (Nisch) and so to his home town of Remesiana (now called Bela Palanka, 'Whitby' or 'Whiteboro,' as we might say). With a pardonable mixture of genuine affection and rhetorical affectation, Paulinus says he loves the roads that brought Niceta to him, but hates them, as they take him home. What pleased Paulinus most was the thought of his fellow poet, the hymn writer, Niceta, captivating the hearts of the rough sailors by his songs. Oh! for the wings of a dove, Paulinus cries, that he might join in the singing himself! Even the dolphins, lured by the lovely sounds, will follow in the wake of the ship!

But, poetic fancy aside, what stirred Paulinus most of all was the heroism of his friend's missionary work among the wild inhabitants of those frontier regions and the still wilder invaders. Even the Bessi, whose hearts were harder than the ice on their mountain tops, have been tamed, he sings, and led like sheep into the peaceful fold of Christ,

et sua Bessi nive duriores
nunc oves facti, duce te, gregantur
pacis in aulam.

4 The relevant parts of the letter and poems of Paulinus are given in Burn, *op. cit.*, pp. 141-155.

Warriors have been turned into monks and pillagers into apostles of peace. A land of blood has been turned into a fertile field of Christian life. The once barbarous voices, now tamed by Christian virtue and in tune with Roman peace, make that silent region re-echo with the Name of Christ.

Orbis in muta regione per te
barbari discunt resonare Christum[5]
corde Romano placidamque casti
vivere pacem.

At the end, Paulinus begs Niceta to remember that God meant him to be a link between East and West, a master of more than one people, a citizen of both Dacia and Rome, a shepherd of his new people and a lover of his old friends.

In a second song, written (not in Horatian Sapphics but in Virgilian hexameters) on the occasion of another visit to Rome in 402, Paulinus praises the purity of Niceta's priestly heart and the clarity of his scholarly mind. The same admiration and the same affection break through these Latin verses. And you can feel, above all, their common devotion to the cause of Christ.

There were hints enough in these poems that Niceta was, perhaps, the author of the *Te Deum* or, at least, of the work on Liturgical Song which appeared in a number of manuscripts. The fact is that Irish manuscripts of the *Te Deum* did attribute it to 'Niceta' or 'Nicetius,' and some manuscripts of the work on Liturgical Song bore the name Niceta, too. However, when the latter work was printed by Luc d'Achéry in 1659, it was attributed to Nicetius of Trier (d. 566). Scholars like Sirmond and Labbe protested, but the wrong

5 The words *resonare Christum,* taken from St. Paulinus' poem, appear on the coat of arms of Bishop John Wright of Boston. The sermon preached on the occasion of Bishop Wright's consecration, June 29, 1947, and dealing with the relations of Niceta and Paulinus, was published in the *Congressional Record,* July 8, 1947.

attribution was maintained. There was a chance in 1799 of giving Niceta his due in regard to the Instruction on the Creed. But the manuscript unearthed by Cardinal Borgia bore the name of a Nicetas who was Bishop of Aquileia from 454 to 485. In 1802, some fragments attributed to 'Nicetas' were published by M. Denis, and, in spite of the arguments of J. P. Zabeo, an extremely long dissertation of P. Braida in 1810 won the day for Nicetas of Aquileia.[6]

So it remained even in 1827. In that year, a newly discovered manuscript containing the Sermons on Faith, the Power of the Holy Spirit, and the Names and Titles of Christ was published by Cardinal Mai. Nicetas of Aquileia, however, was given the credit of authorship. The result was that Migne, in the *Patrologia Latina,* published the works on Faith, the Holy Spirit, the Names of Christ, the Sermon on the Creed and Six Fragments under the name of the Bishop of Aquileia,[7] and the works on Vigils and Psalmody under the name of Nicetius of Trier.[8]

The Benedictine scholar, Dom Morin, finally tried to solve the question. In a series of articles in the *Revue Bénédictine,* beginning in 1894, he argues with much cogency that the *Te Deum* belonged to Niceta of Remesiana. Great scholars like Cagin and Blume were not fully convinced, but, at least in regard to the works here translated, all doubts have now been dissipated. In 1905, the English scholar A. E. Burn published a critical text on the basis of all the manuscript evidence then available. Some needed corrections to this text of two of the works were supplied by C. H. Turner in the *Journal of Theological Studies* in 1921 and 1923. Of these, of course, I have availed myself, but for the most part

6 The dissertation is printed in Migne, *PL* 52.875-1134.
7 Migne, *PL* 52.837-876.
8 *Ibid.,* 68.365-576.

the present translation follows the text of the *editio princeps* prepared by A. E. Burn.

Niceta (*Niketes* is the Greek form) seems to have been born in Remesiana, on the imperial road connecting East and West, about 335. The first mention of his name—'Nicha' is, of course, a copyist's mistake for Niceta—is in the letter of Bishop Germinius, already alluded to, written in the winter of 366-367. It seems very likely that the remarkable meditation on the Names and Titles of Christ was written shortly after the reception of this letter. It is at least possible that Bishop Niceta was present at the Synod of Rome called by Pope Damasus in 371. Other councils were called by Pope Damasus in 374 and 376 and there may be echoes of the decisions of these councils in Niceta's Sermons on Faith and the Holy Spirit. As against Burn, who dates these sermons 370-375, Patin has argued for a date later than 381.[9]

Either at the beginning of the reign of Theodosius in 379 or, as seems to some scholars more probable, at the end in 395, the ecclesiastical province of Illyria, which was attached to the patriarchate of Rome, passed under the political control of the Eastern Empire. Niceta knew Greek well enough, as one can see from his quoting of the Greek text of St. Paul, and still more from his knowledge of such a work as the *Catechetical Instructions* of St. Cyril of Jerusalem; yet his spirit was thoroughly Latin and he reveals a complete mastery of the Latin language. His close friendship with Paulinus implies frequent visits to Nola, but we are quite sure only of the visits of 398 and 402. It is tempting to suggest that Niceta may have visited St. Ambrose in Milan shortly after the latter's introduction of community hymn singing in 386 or thereabouts. The two men, at once poetical, practical and

9 W. A. Patin, *Niceta, Bischof von Remesiana, als Schriftsteller und Theologe* (Munich 1909) 33ff.

pastoral, could easily have become friends. The last mention of Niceta's name occurs in a letter of Pope Innocent I in 414.[10]

The century in which Niceta lived was one of bold innovation. Theological speculation, especially in the East, was magnificently constructive and the theological lexicon was filled with all the new words which were found necessary to silence the subtleties of the heretics. In regard to worship, there was a battle between the conservative puritans who wanted none of the new-fangled 'Oriental' noisiness of congregational singing and the forward-looking realists who understood the spiritual value of the innovation. Niceta fought the old-timers in regard to both ascetical and liturgical practice. His instructions on Vigils and Psalmody are the evidence of his victory.

The man who emerges from these writings may not have been a profoundly speculative genius, but he was certainly a lovable, hard-working, highly cultivated, courageous, deeply spiritual, thoroughly contemporary pastor of souls.

10 Migne, *PL* 20.526ff.

SELECT BIBLIOGRAPHY

A. E. Burn, *Niceta of Remesiana, His Life and Works* (Cambridge 1905).

C. H. Turner's text of *De Vigiliis* and *De utilitate hymnorum* based on *Cod. Vatic. Reg. lat.* 131, saec. 9-10. *Journal of Theological Studies,* 22, 24.

W. A. Patin, *Niceta, Bischof von Remesiana, als Schriftsteller und Theologe* (Munich 1909).

Dom Morin in *Revue Bénédictine,* 1894, 49-77; 337-345; 1907, 108-223.

THE NAMES AND TITLES
OF OUR SAVIOUR

(De diversis appellationibus)

IN THE HOLY SCRIPTURES there are many names and titles which are applied to our Lord and Saviour, Jesus. He is said to be the Word; He is called Wisdom, Light and Power; right hand, arm and angel; man and lamb, sheep and priest. He is the Way, the Truth, the Life; a vine, Justice and Redemption; bread, a stone and doctor; a fount of living water; peace and judge and door. Yet, for all these names—which are to help us grasp the nature and range of His power—there is but one and the same Son of God who is our God.

These, then, are His names; but what are the meanings of these names? He is called the Word, first, to imply that He was begotten of the Father with no more passivity or substantial diminution in the Father than there is in a person who utters a spoken word; second, for the obvious reason that God the Father has always spoken through Him both to men and angels. The name Wisdom tells us that in the beginning all things, through Him, were ordered wisely. He is the Light, because it was He who brought light into the primordial darkness of the world and who, by His coming among men, dissipated the darkness of their minds.

Power is one of His names, since no created thing can ever overcome Him. He is a right hand and arm, for through Him all things were made and by Him they are all sustained. He is called an angel of great counsel, because He is the announcer of His Father's will. He is said to be the Son of man, because on account of us men He deigned to be born a man. He is called a lamb, because of His perfect innocence; a sheep, to symbolize His passion. For two reasons He is called a priest: first, because He offered up His body as an oblation and victim to God the Father for us; second, because, through us, He condescends day after day to be offered up. He is the Way along which we journey to our salvation; the Truth, because He rejects what is false; the Life, because He destroys death. He is a vine, because He spread out the branches of His arms that the world might pluck in clusters the grapes of consolation[1] from the Cross. His is called Justice, because through faith in His name sinners are made just; and Redemption, because He paid the price in His blood to buy us back—we who had been so long lost. He is called bread, because by His Gospel He fed the hunger of our ignorance;[2] and a stone, both because on Him the serpent left no trace and because He afforded us protection. He is the doctor who came to visit us and cured our weakness and our wounds; the fount of living water, because by the 'bath of regeneration'[3] He cleanses sinners and gives them life. He is peace, because He brought together those who lived apart, and reconciled us to God the Father. He is the Resurrection, because He will raise all bodies from

---

1 *Magnum . . . dulcedinis . . . fructum,* literally, 'the great fruit of sweetness' or 'much sweet fruit.'

2 *Famem scientiae,* literally, our 'hunger for knowledge.' Cardinal Mai's text in Migne, *PL* 52.865, reads: *famen gentium,* 'the hunger of the Gentiles.'

3 Titus 3.5.

their graves; and the judge because it is He who will judge both the living and the dead. He is the door, because it is by Him that those who believe enter the kingdom of heaven.

These many names and titles belong to one Lord. Take courage, therefore, O man of faith, and plant your hope firmly in Him. If you would learn of the Father, listen to this Word. If you would be wise, ask Him who is Wisdom. When it is too dark for you to see, seek Christ, for He is the Light. Are you sick? Have recourse to Him who is both doctor and health.[4] Would you know by whom the world was made and all things are sustained? Believe in Him, for He is the arm and right hand. Are you afraid of this or that? Remember that on all occasions He will stand by your side like an angel. If you find it hard to meet face to face the high majesty of the Only-begotten,[5] do not lose hope. Remember, He was made man to make it easy for men to approach Him. If you are innocent, like a lamb He will join your company. If you are saddened by pagan persecution, take courage. Remember that He Himself went like a lamb to the slaughter, and, priest that He is, He will offer you up as a victim to the Father. If you do not know the way of salvation, look for Christ, for He is the road for souls. If it is truth that you want, listen to Him, for He is the Truth. Have no fear whatever of death, for Christ is the Life of those who believe. Do the pleasures of the world seduce you? Turn all the more to the Cross of Christ to find solace in the sweetness of the vine that clustered there. Are you a lost sinner? Then you must hunger for justice and thirst for the Redeemer, for that is what Christ is. Because He is bread, He takes away all hunger. If you are stumbling, fix your

---

4 *Virtus,* literally, 'strength,' 'power.'

5 The Latin reads: *accedere ad tantam unigeniti maiestatem.*

foot firmly on Him, for He is a rock;[6] and like a wall He will protect you. Are you weak and sick? Ask for a medicine from Him, because He is a doctor. Especially, if you are still unbaptized, you may suffer from the ardors of passion. Then hurry to the well of life to put out the flame and to gain for your soul eternal life. If anger is tormenting you and you are torn by dissension, appeal to Christ, who is peace, and you will be reconciled to the Father and will love everyone as you would like[7] to be loved yourself. If you are afraid that your body is failing and have a dread of death, remember that He is the Resurrection, and can raise up what has fallen. When sinful pleasure tempts you and the flesh is weak, recall that you are in the presence of a just judge, severe in weighing the evidence and one who is making ready everlasting fire. Then, sinner as you are, you will lose your taste for sin. In your hour of death, brother, should you lose hope of obtaining a just reward in heavenly glory, be bold in faith to remember that He is the door, and through Him, once you are raised from the dead, you will enter the mysteries of heaven, join the company of angels, and hear the longed-for words: 'Well done, good and faithful servant; because thou hast been faithful over a few things, I will set thee over many; enter the joy of thy master . . . take possession of the kingdom prepared for you from the foundation of the world.'[8] Amen.

---

6 *Lapis,* in the text.

7 Burn accepts the reading *diligendum* [*judicas*], which was suggested by Cardinal Mai. There is, in fact, a space for one word left in the best MSS. Considering how careful Niceta is in the matter of cadenced *clausulae,* we suggest that he was more likely to have written *diligendum judicaris* or *putaveris.*

8 Matt. 25.23,34.

AN INSTRUCTION ON FAITH[1]

(*De ratione fidei*)

Once men have been reborn and made holy by faith, according to the Gospel form, 'In the name of the Father and of the Son and of the Holy Spirit,' this profession gives them hope of the kingdom of heaven. For such men, as the Apostle has said, nothing is more useful than to give themselves to good works; so he writes to Titus: 'I desire thee to insist, that they who believe in God may be careful to excel in good works. These things are good and useful to men. But avoid foolish controversies and genealogies and quarrels and disputes about the Law; for they are useless and futile.'[2]

When the blessed Apostle wrote this, he already foresaw that there would be men who would neglect good works.

1 The title most commonly given to this work is *De ratione fidei*. However, this work and the next, *De Spiritus sancti potentia*, taken together, constitute the third of the 'six books of instruction' (*instructionis libellos sex*), mentioned by Gennadius of Marseilles (*De viris illustribus* 22) and which he attributes to *Niceas, Romacianae civitatis episcopus*.

2 Titus 3.8,9. The Latin text used by Niceta was earlier than the Vulgate of St. Jerome. I have used the Confraternity of Christian Doctrine translation from the Vulgate, since in most cases there is very little difference in the general sense. Here, however, in place of *curent bonis operibus praeesse*, 'to excel in good works,' Niceta's text reads *curam habeant bonorum*, 'should have a care for good [works].'

They would be preoccupied by curious and useless questions, and thus lose the peace which the Lord had bequeathed to His Church. The fact is that men who look for lofty wisdom are often puzzled by the simplest problems. They forget what the Apostle said, 'Be not highminded, but fear.'[3] Seeking what is unlawful, they lose what is lawful. They pretend to weigh and grasp the very Author and Maker of heaven and earth.[4] Yet, they are unable to perceive and grasp what God has made even with their senses.[5] In the presence of the magnitude and multitude of God's works, their single and simple duty should be to adore. Yet, they choose to doubt. The nature and immensity of God are matters of mystery. Yet, they debate the questions: How big is the Father? What kind of a Son is there? And what sort of a Holy Spirit? Imagine a mere man, without full knowledge even of himself, daring to set limits to God.

(2) I need only mention Sabellius the Patripassian.[6] He had the folly and presumption to assert that the Son was one and the same person as the Father and the Holy Spirit, that the Trinity was not a reality but a name, that there were three names but not three persons. He muddled the whole matter by saying that it was the Father who assumed a body and suffered.

---

3 Rom. 11.20.

4 *Ipsum conditorem et fabricatorem Deum capere et mensurare.*

5 *Sensu colligere et capere.*

6 The heresy of Sabellianism consists in the idea that the three 'Persons' are merely three 'modes' in which one God acts, or three 'parts' which He plays in the drama of Creation, Incarnation and Sanctification. When Calvin rejected the Catholic doctrine of real immanent relations in God, he prepared the way for modern forms of Sabellianism.

7 Bishop Photinus of Sirmium in Pannonia died in 376. His anti-Trinitarian views were condemned in 344 by the Synod of Antioch and again in 345 by the Western bishops at Milan. He was deposed at the Synod of Sirmium in 351.

Nor need I dwell on Photinus.[7] He knew of the Incarnation, the abasement and saving passion of the Only-begotten Son of God, but looked upon Him as nothing but a man. He denied the divinity which His works should have forced him to admit. He forgot that the Apostle had said that, though Christ was in the form of God, He took the form of a servant so as to give true liberty to us who were slaves of sin.[8] So, too, to the Corinthians: 'For you know the graciousness of Our Lord Jesus—how, being rich, he became poor for your sakes, that by his poverty you might be rich.'[9] If I say no more concerning Sabellius and Photinus, it is because practically every church has already rightly condemned their error.

(3) What you really want of me is to say something of the heresy which is here and now assailing the Catholic faith, namely, the heresy started by Arius.[10] He was not content with the explicit mention, in the Gospels and the writings of the Apostles, of the Father and the Son and the Holy Spirit. Nor was he humble enough to believe, as he ought to have done, that the Father has a Son and the Son really has a Father. Unfortunately, he wanted to go further and

---

8 Cf. Phil. 2.6.

9 2 Cor. 8.9.

10 The denial by Arius (A.D. 256-336) of the divinity of the Word was condemned by a synod in Alexandria in 320 and by the ecumenical Council of Nicaea in 325. However, under the Emperor Constantius II (350-361), the Arian movement regained strength. In 357, the second formula of Sirmium declared the Word unlike (*anómoios*) the Father—hence, Anomaeanism. Moderate Arians, Homoiousians, accepted the formula that the Word was of 'like substance' with the Father (*homoioúsios*). The fourth formula of Sirmium triumphed in 359. No mention was made of the substance, *ousía,* but the Word was declared 'like in all things' (*hómoios katà pánta*). However, with the nomination of St. Ambrose as Bishop of Milan in 374, and with the continued activity of St. Athanasius and the Cappadocians—St. Basil and St. Gregory Nazianzen—the Nicene formula became more and more universally accepted.

ask how and in what sense God could be a Father. Not understanding how—since no one can understand this—he fell into the error of denying both the Father and the Son. He denies the Father by saying that He could not beget of Himself a real and proper Son. He denies the Son by saying that the Son was not begotten, but was of another origin, being made out of nothing, and that He was merely a special kind of creature whose love merited for Him the name of Son. He was not really a Son begotten by the Father. Hence, Arius imagined that the Son was of some other substance and by no means to be thought of as the true Son of the Father.

It was to combat this perverse novelty in doctrine that the Nicene Council was assembled. There, after all the texts of Scripture had been compared and discussed, the truth was made clear and a creed was composed. Arius had said that the Son had some other origin, not of the Father, not of the substance of the Father, that is, not of that very substance which is God. Therefore, our holy Fathers proclaimed that the Son was 'born of the Father, that is, of the substance of the Father, God of God, light of light, true God of true God, begotten not made, of one substance with the Father.' Thus, there is nothing in the Son to make Him other than God. In reality, if He is the true Son of God and was truly begotten of God the Father, we cannot believe He is of some other substance than that of Him whose Son He is. Thus, as the Father is God, so the Son is God; and, as the Father is light, so the Son is light.

(4) However, a number of people take offense at this profession—that the Son is of the same substance. Consequently, the holy profession is twisted to a false meaning. Some take the expression, 'of one substance,' to imply that we divide the Father, as though the Son were a part

of the Father and that God the Father suffered a diminution in the Son; or, at least that the Son retains the unity of the paternal substance only by being an outflowing or emanation from the Father. May God forbid that Christians should think of or even listen to such things—let alone believe them! What we believe is that the Son is one substance, in this sense, that the Father, who is eternally perfect and unchangeably impassible, begot the Son without suffering any diminution of His nature or majesty. Himself perfect, He begot of Himself a perfect Son, a true Son, likewise omnipotent by whom 'all things were made and without whom nothing was made.' Thus we believe that the Father is truly Father of His only begotten Son, and the Son is truly Son of the Father, each distinct and without confusion. The Son has in Himself all that the Father has, as He says in the Gospel: 'All things whatsoever the Father has are mine.'[11] If we ask what these things are, the answer is: Perfection, certainly, and the power, the goodness, the incorruption, the glory and the eternity that are the Father's. For, of course, if this were not so, I am afraid I should have to say that the Father, apparently, had degenerated in the Son. But, if it is true that the Son is to be reckoned as less than the Father, how can there be the same honor which our Lord Himself speaks about: 'That all men may honor the Son even as they honor the Father.'[12] This is what the Lord asks for and this is what the faithful do. They find no difficulty in the humility of the Son and Saviour, nor in the words which He spoke as man, nor in His sufferings which He deigned to accept for the salvation of the world. Rather, they feel that they owe all the more gratitude and honor to Christ; so much so, that, even though it were not commanded in the Gospel to honor

11 John 16.15.
12 John 5.23.

the Son as they honor the Father, the truly faithful would do this of their own accord. It would have been fitting to exalt Him just because He had humbled Himself, for it is written: 'He who humbles himself shall be exalted.'[13]

(5) When we hear the Father saying: 'This is my Son; hear you Him,'[14] and the Son asking 'that all men may honor the Son even as they honor the Father,'[15] is it not shortsighted to pass over the honor and play up the sufferings? Are we not likely to forget our hope if we keep thinking of Christ as weak, inferior and contemptible, when it is He who made us strong and great and heirs of glory? This was the will of His Father. The fact is, the Son's honor is the Father's glory. The more you give to the Only-begotten, the more you glorify the Father. The Father is too good to envy the glory of the Son, and, in any case, what is given to the Son redounds to the glory of the Father. This is the Catholic sense, the feeling of the faithful, the mind of the saints. This is why they so think and speak of all that was said and done by the Saviour. Nor is their love the least bit lessened because of certain expressions which the Lord chose to use, such as, 'The Father is greater than I,'[16] and 'I came not to do my will,'[17] or 'The Son can do nothing of himself,'[18] and so on. Such texts in no way lessen nor depreciate the Son. They merely distinguish Him from the Father. In any case, to make sure that His true divinity should not be denied, these other things were said: 'I came out from the Father';[19] 'I in the Father and the Father

13 Luke 14.11.
14 Matt. 3.17; Luke 9.35.
15 John 5.23.
16 John 14.24.
17 John 6.38.
18 John 5.19.
19 John 16.28.

in me';[20] 'I and the Father are one'; 'He who sees me sees also the Father';[21] and 'For as the Father raises the dead, and gives them life, even so the Son also gives life to whom he will.'[22]

(6) Nor is the mind of the faithful scandalized by what is said of the Lord's thirsting and sleeping and weeping; of being sad unto death; of the cross, passion, and burial. Such things were said or done to prove His patience and help us to acknowledge the reality of His Incarnation. What is said of the Lord's thirsting implies the assumption of a true body, just as what is said of feeding the five thousand with five loaves and two fishes implies His real divinity. Certainly, when He says: 'I am the bread that comes down from heaven,'[23] it does not occur to us to think that the Bread hungered for bread. So, too, we understand His sleep. Just as we recognize the reality of His body in His sleep, so is His divinity proved by the fact that He commanded the winds and the waves. As to the tears He shed for Lazarus, they remove all suspicion that He was merely an appearance, since tears can flow only from a body that is real. On the other hand, when He said: 'Lazarus come forth,'[24] and one who was already corrupting emerged alive from the opening grave, He gave a clear indication of divinity. At the same time, from this resurrection of Lazarus we shall know how to understand the words, 'My soul is sorrowful

20 John 10.30,38.
21 John 14.9.
22 John 5.21.
23 John 6.41. It has been pointed out by Cardinal Mai (Migne *PL* 52.851 fn. f) that we have in this passage an imitation of the thirty-fifth Discourse of St. Gregory Nazianzen. It may be added that the five theological discourses, pronounced by St. Gregory at Constantinople in 380, contain more than one point that resembles those of Niceta.
24 John 11.43.

even unto death.'[25] While His divinity had no fear of death, His human feeling was revealed by the sadness of His soul. It only takes one or two sayings of the Lord to show that the cross, passion and burial imply no lack of power or any weakness. Thus, when He said to the Jews: 'Destroy this temple' (meaning His body), He added: 'and in three days I will raise it up.'[26] And, again, He says: 'I have power to lay down my life, and I have power to take it up again.'[27] If, then, He raises up the temple of His body, if He has power to lay down His life by the passion and take it up again by the resurrection, surely the obvious greatness of this power makes it impossible to imagine that Christ was weak.

(7) Thus, we need the understanding of faith. We must bring reverence to all such discussions. Both natures are to be admitted in the Lord—both the form in which He existed from eternity and 'the form of a slave' which He accepted for the sake of us slaves. We must believe both His passion according to the flesh and His impassibility inasmuch as He was God. In this way, no one can blame us for lacking either faith or gratitude. Only a heretic will deny that the Son of God is impassible as God, or assert that He is unlike God the Father. And only one who is ungrateful will refuse to confess His sufferings according to the flesh. Let us, then, glory in the Cross of Christ, as Paul was accustomed to do. 'God forbid that I should glory save in the cross of our Lord Jesus Christ.'[28] Let us confess our oneness with Christ, lest we be separated from Him. In the words of the Apostle: 'If we have died with him we shall also live with

25 Matt. 26.38.
26 John 2.19.
27 John 10.19.
28 Gal. 6.14.

him. If we endure we shall also reign with him. If we disown him, he also will disown us.'[29] If we do not believe what he said, 'I and the Father are one,'[30] 'he remains faithful, for he cannot disown himself.'[31] The reason is that He is in the glory of God the Father, and lives with the Father, and reigns with the Father in one and the same lordship. When the Apostle said that 'no fornicator or unclean or covetous person has any inheritance in the kingdom of Christ and of God,'[32] he spoke of one kingdom 'Of Christ and of God,' because of one will of the Father and the Son, one co-operation, one grace, one lordship. So, too, the same teacher of the Gentiles writes: 'Grace be to you, and peace from God our Father, and from the Lord Jesus Christ.'[33] Again, he writes: 'May God our Father and our Lord Jesus Christ direct [*dirigat*] our way unto you.'[34] He did not say 'they direct' [*dirigant*], lest he should imply any difference between the Father and Son either in will or in power. He said 'may he direct' [*dirigat*], so as to bring out the unity. In this same faith, therefore, and in these same words, let us pray that the one grace, one peace, one lordship of Father, Son and Holy Spirit may ever protect and direct us.

Since you asked me to write to you, I could not refuse you this little tract. I trust that, brief as it is, it may bring to your believing souls abundant joy in God.

---

29 2 Tim. 2.11,12.
30 John 10.30.
31 2 Tim. 2.13.
32 Eph. 5.15.
33 Phil. 1.12.
34 1 Thess. 3.11.

him. If we endure we shall also reign with him. If we disown him, he also will disown us.[8] If we do not believe what he said: 'I and the Father are one,'[9] he remains faithful, for he cannot disown himself.[10] The reason is that He is in the glory of God the Father, and lives with the Father, and reigns with the Father in one and the same lordship. When the Apostle said that the [illegible] without God,[11] [illegible] Christ and [illegible] "Grace be to you, and peace from God our Father, and from the Lord Jesus Christ."[12] Again, he writes: "May God our Father and our Lord Jesus Christ direct (*dirigat*) our way unto you."[13] He did not say "they direct" (*dirigant*), lest he should imply any difference between the Father and Son either in will or in power. He said "may he direct" (*dirigat*) [illegible] the unity [illegible] in this same [illegible] that the [illegible] peace, the [illegible] of Father, Son and Holy Spirit may ever protect and direct us.

Since you asked me to write to you, I could not refuse you this little tract. I trust that, brief as it is, it may bring to your believing souls abundant joy in God.

8 2 Tim. 2.12.
9 John 10.30.
10 2 Tim. 2.13.
11 Eph. 2.12.
12 Rom. 1.7.
13 1 Thess. 3.11.

THE POWER OF THE HOLY SPIRIT

(De spiritus sancti potentia)

MY NEXT TASK is to explain, as far as I can, what I hold in regard to the third Person, the Holy Spirit. I understand that many have difficulties on this subject. Perhaps it is rash to discuss the Person associated with the Father and Son in the Creed which is according to the tradition of our Lord and to the profession we make in baptism. Nevertheless, I feel it a duty to give some account of the matter, since there are so many differing opinions and since you have asked me to do so. My single appeal will be to the Holy Scriptures. And yet, I am sure that it will be hard to gain entrance to ears and minds already filled, unfortunately, with a prejudiced opinion. It is not easy for human nature to renounce a fixed opinion, even with the help of good instructors. It is like discounting unfounded gossip about a good man, once we have been told a lie, before we hear the truth. This, I am afraid, is the case with many who have been led by their teachers into the error of believing that the Holy Spirit is a creature, worthy of no more respect than a slave. However, let us return to the main point.

(2) In the formula of the Creed of the Council of Nicaea it is said: 'We believe also in the Holy Spirit.' This was sufficient for the faithful, since the main question in debate at that Council concerned not the Holy Spirit, but the Son.

And would to heaven that those who later on raised an issue in regard to the Holy Spirit could have believed in all simplicity in the Holy Spirit along with the Father and the Son according to tradition. Take, for example, the Macedonians[1] and those who share their doubts. When they asked whether the Holy Spirit was born or created, and what, whence and how great He is, they merely raised another schism among the people. As the Apostle puts it, their contribution to the Church is an 'endless'[2] controversy. They once believed that the Holy Spirit was by His nature holy. Surely, it was right for such people to honor Him with the Father and Son rather than to rank Him as a creature. But they raised further difficulties, trying with tortuous questions to rob simple believers of their faith. I think there can be no doubt that a wily question can lead an ignorant and unwary person into heresy. This is what Paul had in mind when he wrote: 'See that no one deceives you by philosophy and vain deceit.'[3] Those who are opposed to the Holy Spirit ask: 'Was He born or was He unbegotten?' What is that but to set traps both to the right and the left of a man. On whichever side you place the foot of your reply, you are caught. If you say He was born, you will be told: 'It follows that the Son of God is not the "only-begotten," since there is another who is born.' If you say He was not born, you will be told: 'Therefore, there must be a second unbegotten Father; hence, there is not one God the Father from whom all else flows.' Once the dilemma has blocked the road of

1 Macedonius (d. 362) was the leader of the Semi-Arians in Constantinople from 342 to 346 and again from 351 to 360. Tixeront (*Histoire du dogme de la Trinité* II 58) considers it difficult to prove that Macedonius was opposed to the divinity of the Holy Spirit. The Deacon Marathonius, whom Macedonius named Bishop of Nicomedia, may be the Macedonian whom Niceta has in mind.

2 1 Tim. 1.4.

3 Col. 2.8.

reply on both sides, the heretic leads you straight into the ditch by saying: 'If, therefore, the Spirit is neither born of Father nor unbegotten, nothing is left but to say that He is a creature.'

(3) How does the faith of the Church face this dilemma? Must it bow to a trick of logic and believe, in the face of the whole witness of Old and New Testaments, in which the Spirit is never described as a creature, that the Holy Spirit of God was created? Of course not. It is obviously better to despise such human conclusions and insidious questions, and turn to the words of the Lord. He tells us in the Gospel whence the Holy Spirit came. He put an end to this endless debate. He told the Apostles: 'I will send you from the Father [the Paraclete] the spirit of truth.'[4] But whence, then, is He? If you do not know, but wish to know, listen to what the Lord adds: '. . .who proceeds from the Father.' What, then, my brothers, are we to do? Should we pay heed to Christ or to men? Christ says neither that the Spirit was born nor that He was made, but only that He proceeds from the Father. Those who oppose us say that He was made and created. I should think that it is better to believe what Christ revealed rather than what human presumption has imagined. When we in our turn ask them how they can prove that the Holy Spirit was made, they can produce no certain and evident witness in Scripture. Instead, they have recourse to these words of the Gospel: 'All things were made through him and without him was made nothing that was made.'[5] They argue thus: If all things were made through Him, we must believe that the Holy Spirit was made along with all other things. There is here no proof of the point in debate—nothing but a careful selection of

4 John 15.26.
5 John 1.3.

texts. Just ask the question: In what Spirit did John speak when he uttered these words? Did he not speak in the Holy Spirit? And if he spoke in the Spirit, it was the Spirit Himself who spoke. He spoke of these things because through Him was made everything in the manifold order of creatures. The Spirit did not include Himself, in the sense that we should believe that He, too, was among the creatures made out of nothing.

(4) The Apostle Paul bears witness to the same truth when he points out, one by one, the things which were made through Christ. 'In him,' he says, 'were created all things in the heavens and on the earth, things visible and things invisible, whether Thrones or Dominations, or Principalities or Powers. All things have been created through and unto him.'[6] He does not mention the Holy Spirit among any of these things which are in heaven or on earth. Surely, he would have mentioned the Holy Spirit in the very first place, if he knew that the Holy Spirit had been either made or created like the rest. And if one is to understand the words, 'all things were created by him,' so literally as not to exclude the Holy Spirit, what is one to think about the expression the Prophet David addressed to the Lord, 'all things serve thee'?[7] Are we to say that the Holy Spirit is among all those things that serve? Are we to give the name of slave to one who, so far from being slave, is the Lord liberating the creature from servitude? That the Holy Spirit is the Lord, we see clearly enough from what St. Paul wrote to the Thessalonians: 'May the Lord direct your hearts into the love of God and the patience of Christ.'[8] Without doubt, the same Spirit is here called Lord of whom our Saviour told the Apostles

6 Col. 1.16.
7 Ps. 108.91.
8 2 Thess. 3.5.

that 'he will teach you all truth.'[9] To make this point even more obvious, St. Paul tells us that 'the Lord is the Spirit; and where the Spirit of the Lord is, there is freedom.'[10] So, too, to the Romans he says: 'Now you have not received a Spirit of bondage so as to be again in fear, but you have received a Spirit of adoption as sons.'[11] If He is the Spirit of adoption and makes men sons of God, how can He be considered a slave—since no slave can legitimately make another free? 'And because you are sons, God has sent the Spirit of his Son into our hearts, crying: Abba, Father. So that he is no longer a slave, but a son; and if a son, an heir also through God.'[12] If, then, the Spirit makes me free and a son and in a true sense an heir of His divinity, it ill becomes me to call One who has made me free a slave. How little the Spirit is a slave is clear from what the Apostle says: 'But all these things are the work of one and the same Spirit, who divides to everyone according as he will.'[13] Where there is a question of freely dividing, it is impossible to talk of servile condition. Yet, in a creature we must imply the condition of a slave, as in the Trinity there is only Lordship and liberty. Therefore, it follows that if the words of the psalm, 'all things serve thee,' apply to creatures and not the Holy Spirit, then the 'all' in the other dictum, 'all things were created by him,' does not include the Holy Spirit. Nowhere, in fact, do we read that He who proceeds from the Father was either made out of anything or created out of nothing.

(5) It is enough, then, for the faithful to know that, while

---

9 John 16.13.
10 2 Cor. 3.17.
11 Rom. 8.15.
12 Gal. 4.6,7.
13 1 Cor. 12.11.

the Son was begotten, the Spirit proceeds from the Father.[14] Let us use the very words which the Scripture of God wishes us to use. No one who loves life and knows the Author of life and has received in baptism the sacrament of the Three Names with equal honor will look for any limit in One in whom, he believes, there was no beginning. Hence, we believe that the Holy Spirit proceeds from the Father and is neither the Son nor the Son of the Son—as is sometimes foolishly pretended—but the Spirit of Truth, the manner and measure of whose procession it is given to no one to understand. That there is much about the Holy Spirit we cannot understand is clear from the Gospel: 'The wind [*spiritus*] blows where it will, and thou hearest its sound but dost not know where it comes from or where it goes.'[15]

We know that this Spirit is a Person in the proper and true sense of the word. He is the source of sanctification, the light of souls, the distributor of graces. The Spirit sanctifies; He is not sanctified. He illumines; He is not illumined. No creature, without this Spirit, reaches eternal life or can be properly called holy. I make bold to add that the very temple of the Lord, that is, the body which He received from the Virgin, was the work of this Spirit. The Angel Gabriel said to Mary: 'The Holy Spirit shall come upon thee and the power of the Most High shall overshadow thee. And therefore what shall be born is of the Holy Spirit.'[16] Thus we see that the very temple in which the Word, the Lord, dwelt was made holy by the Spirit. It is true that the Lord says of Himself: 'whom the Father has made holy and sent

---

14 It will be noted that Niceta says 'proceeded from the Father,' not 'from the Father and the Son.' The *Filioque* is absent, too, in his *Explanation of the Creed*. There was at this early date no controversy in the matter.

15 John 3.8.

16 Cf. Luke 1.35. Niceta's text differs from the Vulgate.

into the world,'[17] 'and for whom I sanctify myself.'[18] For, of course, the Son of God can make His body or anything else holy. Nevertheless, in order to manifest to the world the power appropriate to the Holy Spirit,[19] He received the Holy Spirit in the form of a dove on His body at the time of His baptism. Thus, it could be truly said by the Apostle that 'in him dwells all the fullness of the Godhead bodily.'[20] It was from this fullness that the Apostles later received 'grace for grace,'[21] when the Lord breathed into the face of the Apostles and said: 'Receive the Holy Spirit; whose sins you shall forgive, they are forgiven them; and whose sins you shall retain, they are retained.'[22] And, although it is written: 'Who can forgive sins, but God only,'[23] here we have the Apostles reported as forgiving sins through the power of the Spirit. Hence, we can realize how much the Spirit can do, when we notice, first, what He did in regard to the Body of our Lord and, second, that the power is no less apparent when the Spirit forgives sins.

(6) We may now turn to the other powers and works of the Holy Spirit. These will help us to realize His nature and greatness. It is only by their works that we know the Father and the Son—'believe the works,'[24] said the Lord. In the same way, we shall not fully know the nature of the Holy Spirit unless we know how wonderful are His works. And so, let no one feel annoyed if I summarize the powers of the Holy Spirit, nor close his ears when I set down the words of divine revelation. One should believe heavenly witnesses

17 John 10.36.
18 John 17.19.
19 *...virtutem et proprietatem sancti Spiritus.*
20 Col. 2.9.
21 John 1.19.
22 John 20.22.
23 Luke 5.21.
24 John 10.38.

rather than human fictions. My only point in this is to draw attention to the undoubted tradition of the Lord. If it is not enough to be baptized in the name of the Father and the Son, without the Holy Spirit, neither are we made holy and started on the way to eternal life without the Holy Spirit. My purpose is to show that it is not only in baptism, but in all other things, that the Holy Spirit has worked and will ever work with the Father and the Son.

(7) As a matter of fact, it ought to be enough merely to show the co-operation of the Holy Spirit in the sacrament of baptism, because we can argue from this that nothing was created without the Holy Spirit. What kind of a faith would it be to believe that man's sanctification and redemption depended on the Holy Spirit, but that his formation and creation did not? Can anyone doubt that the sacrament of baptism calls for more than the beginning of a creature calls for? Eternal life springs from baptism, whereas from Adam in our beginning what came was the reign of death. Remember what the Prophet David said of our creation: 'By the word of the Lord the heavens were established, and all the power of them by the spirit of his mouth.'[25] By the 'word' we must here understand the Son, through whom, as St. John declares, 'all things were made.'[26] And what is 'the spirit of his mouth' if not the Spirit whom we believe to be Holy? Thus, in one text, you have the Lord, the Word of the Lord and the Holy Spirit making the full mystery of the Trinity. Some people, of course, have been rash enough to say that this Word by which the heavens were made was nothing but the voice of God commanding and that the Spirit was nothing but a passing breath of air. This position leads inevitably to Judaism, since, like Photinus, the Jews deny that

25 Ps. 32.6.
26 John 1.3.

anything was made by a subsistent Word [*verbum substantivum*] or by the Spirit.

(8) One may concede that, in regard to the Word, it is clear that He created, but have doubts in regard to the Spirit. My reply to this is the testimony of Job, the righteous man of old, who wrote: 'The spirit of God made me.'[27] So, too, David in one of his psalms says to God: 'Thou shalt send forth thy spirit, and they shall be created; and thou shalt renew the face of the earth.'[28] But, if creation and renewal are to be attributed to the Spirit, certainly the beginning of creation did not occur apart from the Spirit. However, those who are opposed to the truth resort to the evasion of saying that, wherever there is mention of the Spirit as creator, the name and person of the Spirit belong to the Son. The Son is a Spirit, they say, just as the Father is a Spirit. This is a fallacy that should deceive no one. It is enough merely to remember that David clearly distinguishes the Son, whom he calls the Word of the Lord, from the Holy One, whom he calls the Spirit. It is the Word who 'makes the heavens'; it is the Spirit who 'adorns' them, who gives them their power. Anyone who reads these words must believe—else, if he insists on being obstinate, why does he bother to read? Let no one imagine that, somehow, our faith dims the glory of the Father. Rather, it adds to the glory of the Father to refer the creation of all things to a Word of which He is the Father or to a Spirit of which He is the source. The fact remains that when His word and Spirit create, it is He who creates all things.

(9) The Trinity, then, creates. We must next show that the Trinity gives life. First, in regard to the person of the Father—the Apostle says: 'I charge thee in the sight of God,

27 Job 33.4.
28 Ps. 103.30.

who gives life to all things.'[29] Christ, too, gives life, for He says: 'My sheep hear my voice . . . And I give them everlasting life.'[30] Finally, we are given life by the Spirit, as we may see from our Lord's words, 'It is the Spirit that gives life.'[31] So, too, Paul to the Romans: 'He who raised Christ from the dead will also bring to life your mortal bodies because of his Spirit who dwells in you.'[32] You can see here the clear demonstration that one and the same giving of life belongs to the Father and Son and Holy Spirit.

(10) To God belongs foreknowledge of all that will happen and knowledge of all that is hidden. No Christian is unaware of this; yet, if need be, it can be proved from Daniel: 'God knoweth hidden things, who seeth all things before they come to pass.'[33] This same foreknowledge belongs to Christ, according to the Evangelist: 'For Jesus knew from the beginning who they were who did not believe and who it was who should betray him.'[34] It is clear, too, that He had knowledge of what is hidden, when He revealed the hidden plans of the Jews: 'Why do you harbor evil thoughts in your hearts?'[35]

(11) In the same way, God made it clear that the Spirit has foreknowledge of all things. For He said to the Apostles: 'When he the Spirit of truth has come, he will teach you all the truth . . . and the things that are to come he will declare to you.'[36] I take it that when one is reported as foretelling the future, there can be no doubt about his foreknowledge of all things. For 'he searches the deep things of God' and

29 1 Tim. 6.13.
30 John 10.37.
31 John 6.64.
32 Rom. 6.11.
33 Dan. 13.42.
34 John 6.65.
35 Matt. 9.4.
36 John 16.13.

has knowledge of all that belongs to God. He reveals, too, the secrets of God, according to the witness of Daniel: 'He is the God of gods and Lord of kings, and a revealer of hidden things.'[37] All things are revealed by Christ. For He tells us Himself: 'No one knows . . . who the Father is except the Son, and him to whom the Son chooses to reveal him.'[38] In the same way, all revelation belongs to the Spirit, according to the testimony of Paul: 'But to us God has revealed them through his Holy Spirit.'[39] Thus, there is one Revelation common to the Trinity, which is God.

(12) That God is everywhere present and fills all things, we have the witness of Isaias: 'I am God drawing nigh, and not God from afar.'[40] 'If a man should be hidden in a hiding place, shall I not see him? Do I not fill heaven and earth?'[41] The same is true of the omnipresence of our Saviour, Christ. Does He not say in the Gospel: 'Wheresoever two or three shall be gathered in my name, there I shall be in the midst of them'?[42] And that He fills all things, the Apostle bears witness: 'He who descended he it is who ascended also above the heavens, that he might fill all things.'[43] It is equally true that the Spirit is everywhere. Thus, the Prophet, speaking in the person of the Lord, says: 'I am with you . . . and my Spirit stands in the midst of you.'[44] So, too, Solomon says: 'The Spirit of the Lord filled the whole earth.'[45]

God dwells among His saints, according to the promise He made: 'I will dwell and move among them.'[46] Recall,

37 Dan. 2.47.
38 Luke 10.22.
39 1 Cor. 2.10.
40 Isa. 30.27.
41 Jer. 23.24.
42 Matt. 18.20.
43 Eph. 4.10.
44 Ag. 2.5,6.
45 Wisd. 1.7.
46 2 Cor. 6.16.

too, what the Lord says in the Gospel: 'Remain in me and I in you.'[47] The same point is proved by Paul: 'Do you not know yourselves that Christ Jesus is in you?'[48] Now, this same inhabitation is realized in the case of the Spirit, as John reminds us: 'And from this we know that he abides in us, by his Spirit whom he has given us.'[49] The same point is made in similar words by St. Paul: 'Do you not know that you are the temple of God and that the Spirit of God dwells in you.'[50] And again he says: 'Glorify God and bear him in your body.'[51]

(13) It can be proved, too, that just as the Father and Son judge, so does the Holy Spirit. For in Psalm 49 it is written: 'To the sinner God hath said: Why dost thou declare my justices?' And a few verses later: 'I will reprove thee and set it before thy face.'[52] In the same way, David in prayer to God says: 'O Lord rebuke me not in thy indignation.'[53] God will come to convict all flesh. So, too, we find the Saviour in the Gospel saying in regard to the Holy Spirit: 'When the Comforter has come he will convict the world of sin, and of justice, and of judgment.'[54] David, who foresaw this, cried out to the Lord: 'Whither shall I go from thy Spirit? or whither shall I flee from thy face?'[55] And St. Paul makes clear that there is to be but one judgment—that by God through Christ: 'God will judge the hidden secrets of men through Jesus Christ.'[56] And speaking of His person,

---

47 John 15.4.
48 2 Cor. 13.5.
49 1 John 3.24.
50 1 Cor. 3.16.
51 1 Cor. 6.20.
52 Ps. 49.16,21.
53 Ps. 6.2.
54 John 16.8.
55 Ps. 138.7.
56 Rom. 2.16.

the Apostle makes equally clear that the Holy Spirit is to judge the Antichrist, '. . .whom the Lord Jesus will slay with the spirit of his mouth.'[57] If the Antichrist is slain by the breath [*spiritus*] of His mouth, it follows that every creature will be judged by the Spirit according to the witness of Solomon: 'A mighty wind [*spiritus virtutis*] shall stand up against them, and as a whirlwind shall divide them.'[58]

(14) It can be proved, too, that just as the Father is good and the Son is good, so the Holy Spirit is good. Of the Father, the Only-begotten speaks in the Gospel: 'One there is who is good, that is God.'[59] Of Himself He says: 'I am the good shepherd.'[60] So, too, of the Holy Spirit, David in his psalms says to the Lord: 'Thy good spirit shall lead me into the right land.'[61] Just as it is said of the Son: 'The word of the Lord is right,'[62] so of the Holy Spirit it is said: 'Renew a right spirit within my bowels.'[63]

(15) How could anyone be silent in regard to the divine authority of the Holy Spirit? The ancient Prophets cried out: 'These things say the Lord.' When Christ came, He also used this word 'say' in His own person: 'But I say unto you.' Listen now to what the Prophets of the New Testament proclaim. Take the Prophet Agabus in the Acts of the Apostles: 'Thus says the Holy Spirit.'[64] So, too, Paul to Timothy: 'Now the Spirit expressly says . . .'[65] Paul also speaks of himself as called and commissioned by God the Father and by Christ: 'Paul, an apostle sent not from men,

57 2 Thess. 2.8.
58 Wisd. 5.24.
59 Matt. 19.17.
60 John 10.11.
61 Ps. 142.10.
62 Ps. 32.4.
63 Ps. 50.12.
64 Acts 21.11.
65 1 Tim. 4.1.

not by man, but by Jesus Christ and God the Father.'[66] Yet, in the Acts of the Apostles it is said that he was set apart and called by the Holy Spirit: 'The Holy Spirit said: "Set apart for me Saul and Barnabas unto the work to which I have called them." ' And it is added: 'So they, sent forth by the Holy Spirit, went down to Seleucia.'[67]

(16) Let no one think less of the Holy Spirit because He is called the Comforter. Advocate or Comforter is simply the translation of the Greek, *Parácletos.* This name belongs equally to the Son of God, as we see from St. John: 'These things I write to you in order that you may not sin. But if you should sin, we have an advocate with the Father, Jesus Christ the just.'[68] So, too, when our Lord said to the Apostles: 'the Father will send you another advocate,' by speaking of 'another' He made clear that He, too, was a comforter. This same name, Paraclete, is not inappropriate even for the Father—not, of course, to describe His nature, but rather His goodness. We have Paul writing to the Corinthians: 'Blessed be the God and Father of our Lord Jesus Christ, the Father of mercies and the God of all comfort who comforts us.' The Greek for 'God of all comfort' is *theòs páses parakléseos.*[69] Hence, the Father is called comforter, and the Son is called comforter, and the Holy Spirit is called comforter. But, of course, it is one and the same comfort which the Trinity gives to us, as we see from the words: 'You have been washed, you have been sanctified, you have been justified in the name of our Lord Jesus Christ, and in the Spirit of our God.'[70]

---

66 Gal. 1.1.

67 Acts 13.2,4.

68 1 John 2.1.

69 2 Cor. 1.3. This is the only direct citation from the Greek New Testament in the extant writings of St. Niceta.

70 1 Cor. 6.11.

(17) However, it is possible that these benign and beneficent qualities do not rouse our mind to an understanding of the power of the Holy Spirit. Let us turn, then, to aspects more terrifying. It is written in the Acts of the Apostles that the disciple Ananias sold his possessions and by fraud kept back part of the price, and, bringing the rest in place of the whole, laid it at the feet of the Apostles. He offended the Holy Spirit whom he had thought to deceive. Now, what did St. Peter without hesitation say to him? 'Ananias, why has Satan tempted thy heart, that thou shouldst lie to the Holy Spirit?' Then he added: 'Thou hast not lied to men, but to God.'[71] And being struck by the power of Him whom he had hoped to deceive, he expired. What does St. Peter here mean by the Holy Spirit? He clearly gives the answer when he says: 'Thou hast not lied to men, but to God.' It is clear that one who lies to the Holy Spirit lies to God; therefore, one who believes in the Holy Spirit believes in God. The wife of Ananias, who connived at the lie, also joined him in his death.

The Lord shows us something as terrifying, if not more so, when He says in the Gospel: 'Every kind of sin and blasphemy shall be forgiven to men; but the blasphemy against the Spirit will not be forgiven . . . either in this world or in the world to come.'[72] Terrible judgment! He says that the sin of one who blasphemes against the Holy Spirit is unpardonable. Compare with this judgment what is said in the Book of Kings: 'If one man shall sin against another, God may be appeased in his behalf, but if a man shall sin against the Lord, who shall pray for him?'[73] Thus, it is one and the same sin whether we blaspheme against the Holy

71 Acts 5.3,4.
72 Matt. 12.32.
73 1 Kings 2.25.

Spirit or against God, and it is inexpiable.[74] Hence, the nature of the Holy Spirit begins to dawn in our intelligences.

(18) It would be easy to adduce more proofs from the Divine Scriptures to show a Trinity of single power and operation in accord with [the form[75] of words in] the sacrament of baptism. But, since the wise understand these things well enough, I may stop here. I shall be content with a short recapitulation. The Holy Spirit proceeds from the Father; He makes us free; He sanctifies; He is the Lord in the sense which the Apostle explains; He creates along with the Father and the Son; He gives life; He has foreknowledge just like the Father and the Son; He makes revelations; He is everywhere; He fills the whole world; He dwells in the elect; He convicts the world; He judges; He is good and just; it is proclaimed of Him: 'The Holy Spirit says these things'; He constituted Prophets; He commissioned Apostles; He is the Comforter; He cleanses and justifies; He strikes down those who seek to deceive Him; anyone who blasphemes against Him is pardoned neither in this world nor in the world to come—something that can be said only of God

If—or, rather, because—all this is true, why should I be asked to explain the nature of the Holy Spirit? Does He not prove what He is by the great things He does? How, then, can He be other than divine, if He is not different from the Father and Son in the power of operation? It is futile to deny Him the name of God, since His power cannot be doubted. It is vain to prohibit my venerating Him

74 Cardinal Mai (Migne, *PL* 52.861) suggests that Niceta here uses words that are harsher than the meaning he wishes to convey. God Himself (and, therefore, the Holy Spirit) can forgive even 'inexpiable' sins.

75 This bracket has been added in virtue of Niceta's expression in the beginning of the *Instruction on Faith: secundum evangelii formam in nomine Patris, et Filii, et Spiritus sancti.*

along with the Father and the Son, since I am bound in very truth to confess Him along with the Father and the Son. If, along with the Father and the Son, He gives me the remission of my sins, and gives me grace and eternal life, I should indeed be ungrateful if I refused to glorify Him along with the Father and the Son. On the other hand, if He is not to be adored with the Father and the Son, He is not to be confessed with Them in baptism. But He most certainly is to be confessed according to the word of the Lord and the tradition of the Apostle—if faith is to be more than half-hearted.[76] Who, then, can keep me from worshipping Him? I am commanded to believe in Him; I shall pay Him due honor with all my heart.

(19) Therefore, with one and the same veneration I shall adore the Father, adore the Son, and adore the Holy Spirit. If any find this hard, let them remember how David exhorts the faithful to the worship of God: 'Adore his footstool.'[77] If it is religious to adore His footstool, it is surely still more religious to adore His Spirit. Remember, this is the Spirit whom St. Paul exalted so highly when he said: 'And now the angels can satisfy their eager gaze; the Holy Spirit has been sent from heaven.'[78] If the angels desire to look upon Him, should not men be all the more afraid to despise Him? We ought to be afraid lest it be said of us what was said to the Jews: 'You always oppose the Holy Spirit; as your fathers did.'[79]

(20) If, however, so many strong arguments fail to move you to adore the Holy Spirit, there is one still stronger.

---

76 ...*ne semiplena sit fides.*

77 Ps. 98.5.

78 1 Peter 1.12. The translation by Msgr. Knox has been used in this instance. The text used by Niceta says that the Apostles 'preached to you the Holy Spirit sent from heaven, upon whom the angels desire to look.'

79 Acts 7.51.

Listen to the way in which Paul instructs the prophets of the Church, in whom and through whom the Spirit Himself spoke: 'If while all are prophesying there should come in an unbeliever or uninstructed person, he is convicted by all, he is put on trial by all; the secrets of his heart are manifest, and so, falling on his face, he will worship God, declaring that God is truly among you.'[80] Of course, he supposed that it was the Holy Spirit that spoke by the Prophets. The unbelievers fall on their faces and adore, in fear, the Holy Spirit, and they confess, unwillingly, compelled by the greatness of what has been done, namely, the outflowing of spiritual grace. If this is so of unbelievers, should not believers voluntarily and with all their hearts be still more ready to adore the Holy Spirit?

(21) Of course, the Holy Spirit is not adored as a separate God, after the fashion of the pagans, just as the Son who sits on the right hand of the Father is not adored as a separate God. When we adore the Father, we believe that we are adoring at the same time the Son and the Holy Spirit. When we invoke the Son, we believe that we are invoking the Father. And when we ask of the Father we believe we are answered by the Son, according to the promise of the Lord: 'Whatsoever you shall ask of the Father in my name, I will do; that the Father may be glorified in the Son.'[81] So, when the Spirit is adored, He, too, is adored whose Spirit it is we adore.

(22) No one is unaware of the fact that human supplications can neither add to nor take away anything from the Divine Majesty. Still, each of us, according to our purpose, can gain merit by our faithful veneration or be confounded if we obstinately resist the Holy Spirit. Certain it is that cap-

---

80 1 Cor. 14.24.
81 John 14.13.

tiousness and pride bring about damnation; while giving honor can look for the reward of devotion. How, then, can any of the faithful fail in giving full honor to the Trinity to whom, as they hope, they belong, in whose name they were baptized, and from whom they rejoice to have taken their name? They are called men of God from the name of the Father, just as Elias and Moses were called men of God, as Timothy was called a man of God by Paul. In the same way, from the name of Christ they are called Christians. They are also called spiritual—because of the Holy Spirit. If you are called a man of God and are not a Christian, you are nothing. So, too, if you are called Christian and are not spiritual, do not be too confident of your salvation. And so, according to the profession of our saving baptism, let our faith be in the whole Trinity. Let there be singleness of devotion in our filial piety. Let us have no thought of separate powers or of any creature in the Trinity, as though we were pagans. And still less should we deny God's Son or refuse worship to His Spirit, and thus succumb to what is a scandal for the Jews. Rather, let us adore and magnify the perfect Trinity and let us keep in mind what we proclaim aloud in the Mysteries: 'One is holy [the Spirit], one is the Lord, Jesus Christ, in the glory of God the Father, Amen,'[82] because the worship of the Trinity is one. Finally, let us pursue peace and love and abound always in good works. And let us give ear to what the Corinthians heard in the second epistle: 'The grace of our Lord Jesus Christ, and the Charity of God and the fellowship of the Holy Spirit be with you all. Amen.'[83]

---

82 These words are quoted from the Byzantine and Syrian Greek liturgy as it appears in the *Apostolic Constitutions* and in St. Cyril of Jerusalem: *heis hágios, heis Kúrios Iesoûs Christòs eis dóxan Theoû patrós.*

83 2 Cor. 13.13.

AN EXPLANATION OF THE CREED

(*De symbolo*)

A BELIEVER in Christ is one who follows Him as a leader toward the true life, much as the people of Israel followed Moses and entered the land of promise. One who trusts in the leadership of Christ renounces the Enemy and his angels, that is to say, all manner of magical superstition which depends on the emissaries of Satan. Moreover, the Christian renounces all the Devil's works—cults, idols, omens, auguries, pomps and shows, robberies and fraud, sins of the flesh and drunkenness, dancing and lying. Such things—not to mention much else—separated you from the Lord and allied you with the devil. They are the chains of the Serpent, loaded on the souls of men to lead them to the prison of hell. Only when a man has rid himself of these evils, and cast off these chains from his back and thrown them, so to speak, in the face of the Enemy, can he proclaim his act of faith with sincerity.

(2) *I believe in God, the Father Almighty, creator of heaven and earth.* The confession begins, as it should, with a firm 'I believe,' for so St. Paul has put it: 'With the heart a man believes unto justice, and with the mouth profession of faith is made unto salvation.'[1] And so you believe

1 Rom. 10.10.

in God the Father Almighty—an unbegotten God, because He had no origin or beginning outside Himself; an invisible God, whom no bodily eye is able to look upon; an incomprehensible God, who comprehends all else; an immutable God, who does not change with time nor age with years but ever remains the same, who never began nor will ever cease to live, nor will ever be succeeded by another; a good and just God, the creator of heaven and earth. You confess Him as God, but you likewise confess Him as Father, and, therefore, the Father of His Son, since no one is father unless he have a son. He is the Father by reason of the Son, having, of course, a Son of whom He is Father. This, then, is devout faith in God, not merely to know Him as God, after the manner of the Jews, but as a Father, 'the Father of the living Word, of his own power and wisdom,'[2] who before the world began, before anything began, before there was any time, begot of Himself His Son, as Spirit begets Spirit, and God, God. 'For in him were created all things in heaven and on the earth, things visible and things invisible,' as Paul teaches us.[3] And this is confirmed by John: 'All things were made through him and without him was made nothing that was made.'[4]

(3) And so, the moment you believe in God the Father, you confess that you believe also in *Jesus Christ, His Son.* This is the Son of God, Jesus Christ. 'Jesus,' in the language of the Hebrews, means 'saviour.' 'Christ' is a name to indicate royal majesty. One and the same Christ Jesus is both saviour

---

2 It has been pointed out by A. E. Burn (*Niceta of Remesiana,* p. 40) that these words are taken from an old Latin translation of the Creed of Gregory Thaumaturgus. Gregory had written *dunámeos aïdíou,* 'everlasting power,' but both the old Latin translation and that of Rufinus seem to suppose a reading *idíou* rather than *aïdíou.*

3 Col. 1.16.

4 John 1.3.

and king. For our salvation, He descended from the Father in heaven and took on a body like ours.

He was born of the Holy Spirit and the Virgin Mary, and in this no man had any part. Body of her body, He was born by the power of the Holy Spirit. Continuing to be God, He became man, so that men might see Him, learn of Him, and be saved by Him. In no other way, save by the assumption of a visible body, could divinity be borne by men.

(4) And so He was born of the holy and immaculate Virgin[5] to initiate a holy rebirth in us. His birth had been foretold by the Prophet: 'Behold a virgin shall be with child and shall bring forth a son; and you shall call his name Emmanuel, which is translated, God with us.'[6] Our faith, therefore, is that He who was born of the Virgin is God with us, God from the Father before all ages, a man born of the Virgin for the sake of men. He was truly born in the flesh, not in mere seeming. Certain heretics, erroneously ashamed of the Mystery of God, say that the Incarnation of the Lord was effected in a phantom, and that what was seen had no real existence but was an illusion in men's eyes. This is far indeed from God's truth. For, if the Incarnation is unreal, the salvation of men will be an illusion. On the other hand, if there is real salvation in Christ, then the Incarnation is equally real. Each really existed—the man who was seen, the God who was not seen, a visible man and that of the invisible God. As a man, He would hunger, but, because He was God, He would feed five thousand men with five loaves of bread. He felt thirst, as a man, but, as God He gave us the water of life. As man, He slept in the ship, but, as God, He commanded the wind and the waves. As man, His hands were nailed to the cross, but,

5 . . .*ex sancta et incontaminata virgine.*
6 Matt. 1.23; Isa. 7.14.

as God, He promised paradise to the thief who confessed Him. As man, He put aside for a time His body and accepted death, but, as God, He raised from the grave a man who was four days dead. So, we must believe both: Christ is God and Christ is man. If He is seen as a man in His sufferings, in His divine works He is recognized as God. Hence, you have an answer for the teachers of fallacies. If anyone tries to beguile your ears with the idea that Christ was only a man, tell him that He who was made a man for the sake of our sins is seen to be God in His works and His words. It was the Saviour Himself who declared to the Jews: 'If you are not willing to believe me, believe the works, that you may know and believe that the Father is in me and I am in the Father.'[7]

(5) The next point is that you believe in the Lord's passion. You confess that Christ *suffered, was crucified* by the Jews, according to what had been foretold by the Prophets. Make sure that you are not ashamed of the passion of your Lord. If, by any chance, some trace of Jewish unbelief or pagan folly should tempt you to minimize the greatness of the Cross of Christ, always remember what our Lord has said: 'Therefore, everyone who acknowledges me before men, I also will acknowledge him before my Father in heaven.'[8] And, indeed, you have nothing to feel ashamed of, if only you will understand the mystery of Christ's sufferings. He did not suffer in His divinity, but in His flesh. God, of course, can never suffer. He suffered 'in the flesh,' as the Apostle teaches,[9] so that from His wounds might flow salvation to mankind. And this the Prophet Isaias had foretold: 'He was wounded for our iniquities . . . and by his bruises we

7 John 10.38.
8 Matt. 10.32.
9 1 Pet. 4.1.

are healed.'[10] Christ suffered for our sins, so that grace might be given to us.

Suffered under Pontius Pilate. The time is indicated—when Pontius Pilate was Governor of Syria and Palestine. It is well to have this set down, because a number of the heretics, who have been fooled by the Devil's deceptions, prattle about more than one Christ. You are taught the time of the Passion so that you may confess, not someone else who happened to suffer, but Christ, who truly suffered under Pontius Pilate for the salvation of the world. And Christ *died* that He might destroy the rights of death.

(6) *The third day He rose again alive from the dead,* or in the words of the Prophet, He was 'free among the dead.'[11] For Christ could not have been held captive by death, since He has full power over death and life.

He ascended into heaven, whence He had descended. 'No man has ascended into heaven, but he that descended from heaven, the Son of man who is in heaven.'[12] *He sits at the right hand of the Father,* according to what was said to David, typifying God the Father speaking to His Son: 'Sit thou at my right hand until I make thy enemies thy footstool.'[13] *Thence He shall come to judge both the living and the dead.* Believe that Christ Himself, our God, will come with the angels and virtues of heaven to judge both the living and the dead, to give to each according to his works, that is, to award eternal life to the just and to subject the wicked to eternal punishment.

(7) *And in the Holy Spirit.* This Spirit is one and sanctifies all. He proceeds from the Father, and He alone pene-

10 Isa. 53.5.
11 Ps. 87.6.
12 John 3.13
13 Ps. 109.1.

trates the mysteries and depths of God. In the shape of a dove He came down from heaven to Christ. This Holy Spirit is one in Himself, but manifold in powers and operations. He divides the gift of graces 'to everyone according as he will.'[14] He appointed the Prophets and inspired the Apostles. At the time of baptism He makes holy the souls and bodies of those who believe. Without his co-operation, no creature can come to eternal life, and upon His glory 'angels desire to look.'[15] By His majesty He makes holy the Thrones and Dominations[16] and all the Powers of heaven. And, as the Lord proclaimed: 'He that shall speak against the Holy Spirit it shall not be forgiven him, neither in this world nor in the world to come.[17]

(8) Make strong in your hearts, my brothers, this faith in the Trinity, believing in one God the Father Almighty and in His Son, Jesus Christ our Lord, and in the Holy Spirit, the true light and sanctifier of souls, who is the pledge of our inheritance, who will lead us, if we will but follow, into all truth and will make us one with the citizens of heaven. This rule of faith the Apostles received from the Lord, so that they might baptize, 'in the name of the Father and of the Son and of the Holy Spirit, all peoples who would believe.'[18] May this faith remain in you. O beloved, 'keep that which is committed to your trust, avoiding profane novelties of words and the oppositions of knowledge falsely so called.'[19]

(9) If the pagans urge you to worship once more many Fathers, keep to your holy profession, to the confession of

14 1 Cor. 12.11.
15 1 Pet. 1.12.
16 . . *sedes et dominationes.*
17 Matt. 12.32.
18 Matt. 28.19.
19 1 Tim. 6.20.

one Father who is God. After all, not even nature permits a man to have more than one father. If a Jew tries to persuade you not to believe that Christ is the Son of God, treat him as a foe to be fought, if you are well armed with the Scriptures, or else avoid him. If any heretic, claiming to be a Christian, teaches you that Christ is a creature or that the Holy Spirit is not one with the Father and the Son in glory, let him be to you as a 'gentile and a publican,' as one leading you to idolatry by urging you to worship a creature. If he tries to tangle you up in the meshes of debate, have recourse to the wall of your faith and say to him, in the words of the Apostle: 'I have been washed, I have been sanctified, I have been justified in the name of our Lord Jesus Christ, and in the Spirit of my God.'[20] I shall not risk my salvation nor weaken my faith by giving up a single word of this profession of the Trinity.

(10) After the confession of the Blessed Trinity, you profess faith in the *Holy Catholic Church*. The Church is simply the community of all the saints. All who from the beginning of the world were or are or will be justified—whether Patriarchs, like Abraham, Isaac and Jacob, or Prophets, whether Apostles or martyrs, or any others—make up one Church, because they are made holy by one faith and way of life,[21] stamped with one Spirit, made into one body whose head, as we are told, is Christ. I go further. The angels and virtues and powers in heaven are co-members in this one Church, for, as the Apostle teaches us, in Christ 'all things whether on the earth or in the heavens, have been reconciled.'[22] You must believe, therefore, that in this one

20 1 Cor. 6.11.
21 . . .*una fide et conversatione sanctificati, uno Spiritu signati.*
22 Col. 1.18,20. In the sentence that follows, we have one of the first references to the Communion of Saints as an article of the Creed.

Church you are gathered into the *Communion of Saints.* You must know that this is the one Catholic Church established throughout the world, and with it you must remain in unshaken communion. There are, indeed, other so-called 'churches' with which you can have no communion: for example, those of the Manichaeans, the Cataphrygians, the Marcionites and other heretics and schismatics.[23] These 'churches' ceased to be holy, because they were deceived by the doctrines of the Devil to believe and behave differently from what Christ commanded and from the tradition of the Apostles.

Next, you believe in the *forgiveness of sins.* This is the grace by which those who believe in and confess God and Christ receive in baptism the remission of all their sins. We call it a rebirth, because it makes a man more innocent and pure than when he is born from his mother's womb.

Further, you believe in the *resurrection of the body and life everlasting.* In truth, if you do not believe this, your faith in God is vain. It is because of our resurrection that we believe all that we believe. Otherwise, 'if with this life only in view we have had hope in Christ, we are,' as the

23 These three sects started during the second century. All three were inspired by a fear of the physical and the natural. The followers of Mani accepted the idea of a double divinity, one of Light and one of Darkness. The followers of Montanus, called Cataphrygians because they were active mainly in Phrygia (*hoi katà Phrúgas*), looked on their founder as the Organ of the Paraclete, thought of themselves as 'pneumatic' or 'spiritual' and not merely as 'psychic,' like ordinary Catholics, and they looked for the coming of the Age of the Holy Spirit. The Marcionites emphasized free grace at the expense of good works, distinguished the God of mere 'justice' in the Old Testament from the God of 'love' revealed in the New. The Manichaeans reappear in the medieval Cathari; the Montanists' ideas appear in medieval apocalypticism as popularized by Joachim of Flora; the Marcionite 'puritanism' and 'spiritualism' resembles that of the pre-Reformers. It is opposition to the organized, visible Church, in the name of a so-called purer, more ascetic, spiritual, invisible Church, which Niceta seems to have in mind.

Apostle says, 'of all men the most to be pitied.'[24] The fact is that it was precisely for this that Christ assumed human flesh, that He might confer on our mortal substance a share in immortal life.

(11) There are, indeed, many heretics who distort this faith in resurrection. They claim that salvation is only for the soul and deny the resurrection of the body. But you who believe in Christ profess the resurrection of your body. 'For to this end Christ died and rose again; that he might be Lord both of the dead and of the living.'[25] Nor do you believe this without foundation. You have authorities enough. Take the Prophet Isaias, who clearly proclaimed that 'the dead men shall live and my slain shall rise again: awake and give praise, ye that dwell in the dust.'[26] And you have the Lord of the Prophets promising in the Gospel: 'I am the resurrection and the life: he who believes in me, even if he die, shall live.'[27] And, in another place: 'Amen I say to you . . . the hour is coming in which all who are in the tombs shall hear the voice of the Son of God. And they who have done good shall come forth unto resurrection of life: but they that have done evil unto resurrection of judgment.'[28] You have St. Paul, who assures us: 'This corruptible body must put on incorruption; and this mortal body must put on immortality.'[29] You know that we exist in a double substance: in body and soul. The body is mortal, but the soul is immortal. When a man departs from this life, he does not die in soul, but, when the soul goes, only the body

24 1 Cor. 15.19.
25 Rom. 14.9.
26 Isa. 26.19. Niceta's translation reads: 'The dead men shall rise again, and those in the grave shall rise, and those who dwell in dust shall give praise.'
27 John 11.25.
28 John 5.28,29.
29 1 Cor. 15.53.

dies. While the body rots in the earth, the soul is kept in a place of light or in a place of darkness according to its deserts, so that, in the day of the coming of the Lord from heaven, when He comes with His holy angels, all will come to life and the souls will be recalled to their bodies and there will be a just separation of the good and the evil. 'Then the just will shine forth like the sun in the kingdom of their Father.'[30] The impious and the wicked will depart to the darkness of hell, where, as we are told, 'there will be weeping and gnashing of teeth.'[31]

(12) To remove all doubt about the resurrection of the body, take a single illustration from the course of nature. The Apostle reminds us: 'What thou thyself sowest is not brought to life, unless it dies.'[32] Here you have a grain of wheat, dead and dry and sown in the earth. It is softened by the rain from heaven. Only when it decays does it spring to life and begin to grow. I take it that He who raises to life the grain of wheat for the sake of man will be able to raise to life the man himself who has been sown in the earth. He both can and wills to do this. What the rains do for the seed, the dew of the Spirit does for the body that is to be raised to life. Thus Isaias cries to Christ: 'Thy dew is health for them,'[33] true health, since, once the bodies of the saints have been raised to life, they feel no pain, they fear no death. They will live with Christ in heaven, who lived on earth according to the words and ways of Christ. This is the eternal and blessed life in which you believe. This is the fruit of all our faith and holy works. This is the hope on acount of which we are born, believe and are reborn. It was on account of this that the Prophets, Apostles and martyrs sustained such

30 Matt. 13.43.
31 Matt. 13.42.
32 1 Cor. 15.36.
33 Cf. Isa. 26.19.

endless toil and accepted death with joy. This is a life which neither a pagan nor an unbelieving Jew may have and possess—nor, for that matter, any Christian who is a slave to his vices and sins. It is a life prepared only for those who both believe and live without blemish.

(13) These things being so, beloved, persevere in the tradition which you have learned. Be true to the pact you made with the Lord, to the profession of faith which you made in the presence of angels and of men. The words of the Creed are few—but all the mysteries are in them. Selected from the whole of Scripture and put together for the sake of brevity, they are like precious gems making a single crown. Thus, all the faithful have sufficient knowledge of salvation, even though many are unable, or too busy with their worldly affairs, to read the Scriptures.

(14) And so, beloved, whether you are walking, resting or at work, whether you are asleep or awake, let this salutary confession be ever in your hearts. Let your soul be ever in heaven, your hope in the resurrection, your longing fixed on what is promised. Let the Cross of Christ and His glorious Passion be proclaimed with confidence. And whenever the Enemy tempts your mind with fear or greed or anger, answer him boldy with words: 'I have renounced and shall continue to renounce you and your works and emissaries, because I believe in the living God and in his Son and Spirit and, stamped as I am, I no longer fear death.' Thus will the hand of God protect you and the Spirit of Christ guard the entrance to your soul, now and forever, so long as, with minds fixed on Christ, you say to one another: Brothers, whether we wake or sleep, let us live with Christ, to whom be glory forever and ever. Amen.

THE VIGILS OF THE SAINTS

(*De vigiliis servorum Dei*)

IT IS ALTOGETHER right, fitting and becoming, my brothers, for me to speak to you about holy vigils, seeing how solicitous you have been in asking for a night talk. You know that night is a physical darkness which impels men and other living creatures to sleep in order to restore their strength and wake up ready for the burdens of the day. The good God who foresaw this need so arranged that man, who was to 'go forth to his work and to his labor until the evening,'[1] should have a second period in which to rest after the hard work and great fatigue. Thus, He made the day for work, the night for rest. For this, as for all else, we should thank Him who has arranged it so.

Nevertheless, you also know that many men set aside a part of the night for some special task. Some do this to please their parents; others, for some profit to themselves. They think it pays to rob their rest for the sake of something that is to be done. Solomon praises the valiant woman who rose in the night for her spinning and weaving and whose lamp was not put out. And he adds that, as a result, her husband was 'honorable in the gates' and much praise was given him.[2] Far from being blamed, people are praised for

1 Ps. 103.23.
2 The reference is to Prov. 30.13,23.

vigils of this sort, which have no purpose higher than the merely physical need of food or clothing. Yet, I am astonished to find that there are some who consider sacred vigils, which produce such spiritual fruit and are filled with prayers, hymns and holy reading, to be superfluous, otiose or, what is worse, unbecoming.

(2) Not, of course, that we need be surprised if men who are far from our faith should feel that way. Why should we expect the profane to like what is religious? Indeed, if they did, they would join us and be what we are, namely, Christians. But there are some among ourselves who take offense at the practice of salutary vigils. I can only hope that they are suffering from nothing worse than laziness or sleepiness or, what is much the same, old age or infirmity. If it is laziness, they should be ashamed of themselves, and listen to the words of Solomon: 'Go to the ant, O sluggard, and consider her ways.'[3] If the trouble is drowsiness, let them be wakened with the words of Scripture: 'How long wilt thou sleep, O sluggard? When wilt thou rise out of thy sleep? Thou wilt sleep a little, thou wilt slumber a little, thou wilt fold thy hands a little to sleep. And want shall come upon thee, as a traveler, and poverty as a man armed.'[4] If you are an old man, no one will force you to keep awake—although, for that matter, your years should be enough to keep you awake. If, finally, you are too weak to stand, and think you are unable, you have no right to recruit to your own torpor those who are young and strong. You must remember youth has many temptations and should mortify itself with appropriate vigils. Nor, if you are weak in body, should you criticize what you cannot yourself do; rather, you

3 Prov. 6.6.
4 Prov. 6.9-11.

should weep in bed, saying: 'If I have remembered thee upon my bed.'[5] And you can always ask those who are keeping vigils to help you with their prayers, so that with God's grace you may be able, on your bed of sorrow, to sing and even say: 'I will meditate on thee in the morning, because thou hast been my helper.'[5] Certainly, it is foolish and strange to hold back those who run merely because we are unable to run ourselves. Unable as we are we should congratulate rather than envy those who can. For, just as we shall be punished with the wicked, if we have consented to their sin, so may we hope for a share in the glory of those whose virtues we approved. Some men are rewarded for what they do; others, because of good will.

(3) Even for those with delicate bodies, does it seem too much or too hard to give, twice in the week, that is, on Saturday and Sunday, a portion of the night to the service of God? This is the least we can do to purify, as it were, the five days or nights in which our bodies have been sunk in sloth, our spirits defiled by worldly ways.

Surely, no one need be ashamed of doing what is holy, if sinners are not ashamed of doing what is foul. It is well that in the Scriptures the Book of the Preacher reminds us: 'There is a shame that bringeth sin';[6] for, it is as much a sin to be ashamed of doing good as it is wicked not to be ashamed of doing wrong. If you are in grace, love vigils so that by your vigils you may guard your treasure and keep yourself in holiness. If you are in sin, hurry to be cleansed by watching and praying. Keep beating your breast and crying out: 'From my secret sins cleanse me, O Lord, and from those of others spare thy servant.'[7] Once a man longs

5 Ps. 62.7.
6 Eccli. 4.25.
7 Ps. 18.13,14.

to be cleansed of his hidden sins, he loses all joy in being soiled by such things.

(4) And, now, beloved, I ought to say a word about the antiquity of the tradition and utility of vigils.[8] It is easier to begin a work if we keep before our eyes how useful it is. The devotion to vigils is very old. It has been a household tradition among the saints. It was the Prophet Isaias who cried out to the Lord: 'My soul hath desired thee in the night. Yea, and with my spirit within me in the morning early I will watch to thee.'[9]

David, who was doubly anointed both as king and prophet, thus broke into song: 'O Lord, the God of my salvation, I have cried in the day, and in the night before thee.'[10] And again he says: 'In the night I have remembered thy name, O Lord, and have kept thy law.'[11] Perhaps you think he was in bed when he sang these psalms. And, indeed, some of the lazier sort do think it enough if one prays in bed and mutters a psalm or so. Of course, there is nothing wrong in that, since it is good for the soul to think of God at any time and anywhere. However, to prove that it is better to get up before putting oneself in the presence of God, here is a third expression of the same Prophet which reveals the time, place and manner of prayer: 'In the nights lift up your hands to the holy places and bless ye the Lord.'[12] Lest you should think he had in mind only the early hours, he hastens to add: 'I rose at midnight to give praise to thee; for the judgments of thy justification.'[13] Here you have

---

8 Niceta's words are: *de auctoritate vigiliarum et antiquitate.*

9 Isa. 26.9. Niceta's text reads: 'Thy soul watches for thee in the night, O God, for your laws are a light over the earth.'

10 Ps. 87.2.

11 Ps. 118.55.

12 Ps. 133.2.

13 Ps. 118.62.

the time of rising expressed no less clearly than the solicitude with which we should confess to God.

(5) The more I meditate on the mind of the saints, the more I am reminded of something that is high and hard and beyond the powers of human nature. Call to mind what the same psalmist has said: 'If I shall go up into the bed wherein I lie; if I shall give sleep to my eyes, or slumber to my eyelids, or rest to my temples; until I find out a place for the Lord, a tabernacle for the God of Jacob.'[14] Who would not be amazed at such a love of God, such dedication of soul, that a king and prophet should deny himself all sleep—the very essential of bodily vigor—until he should find a place to build a temple to the Lord? This fact should be a strong admonishment to us who long to be a dwelling place of the Lord and to be considered His tabernacle and temple forever. 'You are,' as St. Paul reminds us, 'the temple of the living God.'[15] Let us, then, be moved by the example of the saints to love vigils to the utmost of our power. And let it not be said of us what is said in the psalm: 'They have slept their sleep and . . . found nothing.'[16] Rather, let each of us be glad to say: 'In the day of my trouble I have sought God and with my hands lifted up to him in the night, and I was not deceived.'[17] The reason is that 'It is good to give praise to the Lord, and to sing to thy name, O most High; to show forth thy mercy in the morning, and thy truth in the night.'[18] These and many other such thoughts the saints have left us in song and other writings, so that we who are their heirs may be moved by such examples to celebrate at night the vigils of our salvation.

---

14 Ps. 131.3-5.
15 1 Cor. 3.16.
16 Ps. 75.6.
17 Ps. 76.3.
18 Ps. 91.2,3.

(6) Let us turn now from the old to the new, from the ministers of the Law to the ministers of the Gospel. For the grace of vigils is vouched for in the New Testament, too. It is written in the Gospel that Anna the daughter of Phanuel, a holy widow serving the Lord with prayers and fasting, never left the temple night or day.[19] It was while the holy shepherds were keeping watch over their sheep by night that they were rewarded by being the first to see the angels in glory and to hear of the birth of Christ on earth.[20] It is the same, too, with the teaching of our Saviour. He was ever rousing His hearers to watching. Take what He says in the parable of the sower: 'while men were asleep, an enemy came and sowed weeds among the wheat, and went away.'[21] The presumption is that, had they not been asleep, the enemy could not have sown the weeds. Or, take His other words: 'Let your loins be girt about and your lamps burning, and you yourselves like men waiting for the master's return from the wedding . . . Blessed are those servants whom the master, on his return, shall find watching . . . And if he comes in the second watch and if in the third, and finds them so, blessed are those servants . . . You must also be ready, because at an hour that you do not expect, the Son of Man is coming.'[22] In regard to watching, what He taught in words He confirmed also by example. The Gospel bears witness to the fact that 'Jesus spent the whole night in the prayer of God.'[23] The Lord kept this nightly vigil, not for Himself, but that His servants who are poor and weak might know what to do, seeing that the Lord who was rich in prayer, of which He had no need, was so resolute the whole

19 Cf. Luke 2.36ff.
20 Cf. Luke 2.8-14.
21 Matt. 13.25.
22 Luke 12.35-40.
23 Luke 6.12.

night long in prayer. So it was that He chided Peter at the time of the passion: 'Could you not watch one hour with me.' And then to all He said: 'Watch that you may not enter into temptation.'[24] And now, I ask you, is there any one whom words and examples like these could not rouse even from a sleep deep enough to look almost like death?

(7) The blessed Apostles, taught by words like these and strengthened by such examples, kept watch themselves and ordered vigils. When Peter was in prison, he was awakened by an angel, and, when the iron gate was opened, he came to the house of Mary, 'where many had gathered together' and were praying—not, I need hardly say, snoring.[25] It is Peter who puts these words into his epistle: 'Be sober, be watchful! For your adversary, the devil, as a roaring lion, goes about seeking someone to devour.'[26] It is related that, when Paul and Silas were in the public prison, they were praying at midnight, singing a hymn while the prisoners were listening to them: suddenly, the foundations of the prison were shaken by an earthquake, and the doors flew open, and everyone's chains were unfastened.[27] The same blessed Apostle, when he was about to depart from Troy, 'prolonged his address until midnight,' so that they lit 'the many lamps in the upper room.' And a young man named Eutychus, overcome with drowsiness, as Paul addressed them at great length, went fast asleep and fell from the third-story window to the ground and was picked up dead. And as soon as he was restored to life, Paul went on with his sermon 'even till daybreak,' and then, with the help of God, departed.[28] In writing to the Thessalonians, St. Paul is no less full and ex-

24 Matt. 26.40,41.
25 Acts 12.7ff.
26 1 Pet. 5.8.
27 Cf. Acts 16.25,26.
28 Cf. Acts 20.7-11.

plicit in his exhortation to the practice of vigils: 'Therefore let us not sleep as do the rest, but let us be wakeful and sober. For they who sleep, sleep at night, and they who are drunk, are drunk at night. But let us, who are of the day, be sober.' Then he ends with these marvelous words: 'Whether we wake or sleep, we should live together with him.'[29] To the Corinthians he writes: 'Watch, stand fast in the faith, act like men, be strong.'[30]

(8) I hope I have said enough about the ancient and authentic tradition of vigils.[31] I must turn now to the next point, as I promised, and say a word about their usefulness —although this can be better learned by experience than expressed in words. It would seem that we must ourselves 'taste,' as the Scripture has it, 'how sweet is the Lord.'[32] Only one who has tasted understands and feels how great a weight is taken from our heart, what sloth is shaken from our minds when we watch, what light floods the soul of one who watches and prays, what a grace and presence fills every member with joy. By watching, all fear is cast out and confidence is born, the flesh is weakened, vices waste away and charity is strengthened, folly disappears and prudence takes its place, the mind is sharpened, error is blunted, the Devil, the instigator of our sins, is wounded by the sword of the Spirit. Is there anything we need more than we do such advantages, any profit greater than such gains, anything sweeter than this joy or more blessed than this happiness? I need only call to witness the Prophet who in the beginning of his psalms describes the happy man and indicates his supreme felicity in this verse: 'If he meditates on the

29 1 Thess. 5.6-10. Niceta's text reads: '. . . as, who are of God's (*Dei* in place of *diei*).

30 1 Cor. 16.13.

31 ...*de antiquitate et auctoritate vigiliarum.*

32 Ps. 33.9.

law of the Lord day and night.'[33] Meditation during the day is, of course, good; but that at night is better. During the day, there is the clamor of our many cares, the mental distraction of our occupations. A double preoccupation divides our attention. The quiet and solitude of the night make it a favorable time for prayer and most suitable for those who watch. With worldly occupations put aside and the attention undivided, the whole man, at night, stands in the divine presence.

I need not add that the Devil is always skillful in imitating divine things. He has given to his followers not only fasts but vain virginity and baptisms without validity. So, too, he has copied this holy service and given nightly watchings to his sorry followers [*commiseronibus*]. However, those of us who are not moved, by all they have learned, to practice holy vigils, should at least not pretend that vigils are opposed to the service of God, because they can be travestied by the Devil. The truth is that he would not copy these things for the deception of his followers unless he realized how pleasing to God they were and how rich in blessings for those who practice them.

(9) Only, dear brothers, if one is to keep awake with his eyes, let him watch also with his heart; if he prays with his lips, let him pray also with his mind. It is of little avail to keep one's eyes open, if the soul is asleep. The very opposite is the truth, as the Scripture bears witness, speaking in the name of the Church: 'I sleep but my heart is awake.'[34] And, needless to say, no one who intends to watch should have his stomach loaded with too much food or drink. Belching and hiccoughing is not only personally unpleasant, but it makes us unworthy of the grace of the Spirit. One of the

33 Ps. 1.2.
34 Cant. 5.2.

outstanding bishops of our days has said: 'Belchings with undigested food turns away the favors of the Holy Spirit just as smoke puts the bees to flight.'[35] Therefore, like men about to perform a divine function, we must prepare ahead of time by fasting, so that we may be ready to watch with all our wits about us. And if the prayer of the watcher is not to be 'turned to sin,' as the psalm[36] puts it, every evil thought must be put away. Some watching is the work of the Devil, as we may see from the Book of Proverbs: 'For they sleep not except they have done evil; and their sleep is taken away unless they have made some to fall.'[37] May all such watching, brothers, be far from this congregation. Rather, let the heart of those who watch be closed to the Devil and open to Christ, so that the Name on our lips may be close to our heart. Only then will our vigils be agreeable to Christ and our night of prayer bring us grace, if with becoming diligence and sincere devotion, our ministry is offered in the sight of God.

So much, then, for the dignity, antiquity and spiritual value of vigils. I would be glad to add a word here on how pleasing and acceptable to God is the practice of the singing of hymns and psalms. But what I have to say would take another volume. I shall do this, God willing, in my next sermon. 'May the grace of our Lord, Jesus Christ, be with you all. Amen.'[38]

35 St. Basil, Homily on Fasting, Migne, *PG* 31.184b.
36 Ps. 108.7.
37 Prov. 4.15. Niceta's text reads: 'Wherefore, their sleep is taken from their eyes, for they sleep not except they have done evil.'
38 2 Cor. 13.14.

LITURGICAL SINGING

(*De utilitate hymnorum*)

MAN who keeps a promise pays a debt. I remember promising at the end of my sermon on the spiritual value[1] of vigils that, in the next sermon, I would speak of the ministry of hymns and psalms.[2] That promise I shall fulfill, God willing, in this sermon; for I do not see how any better time can be found than this, in which the sons of light think of the night as day, in which silence and quiet are being offered to us by the night itself and in which we are engaged in the very thing which my sermon is to speak about.[3] The proper time to exhort a soldier is when he is just about to begin the battle. So for sailors—a rollicking song best suits them when they are bending to the oars and sweeping over the sea. So with us. Now is the very best time to keep my promise to speak of liturgical singing—now that the congregation has come together for this very purpose.

(2) I am aware that there are some among us, and some in the Eastern provinces, too, who hold that there is something superfluous, not to say, suspicious, about the singing of hymns and psalms during divine service. Their idea is

1 . . .*de gratia et utilitate* . . .

2 *Laudum,* lit., 'praises.'

3 The Latin text of this paragraph as given by Burn (p. 68) has been rejected in favor of the text published by C. H. Turner in the *Journal of Theological Studies,* vol. 24.

that it is unrestrained to utter with the tongue what it is enough to say with the heart. They base their opinion on a text from the Apostle's Epistle to the Ephesians: 'Be filled with the Spirit, speaking to one another in psalms and hymns and spiritual songs, singing and making melody in your hearts to the Lord.'[4] There, they say, you have the Apostle stating that we should sing in our hearts, and not make a noise with musical notes—like people on the stage.[5] For God, 'who searches the heart,'[6] it is enough, they insist, if our song be silent and in the heart. I take a different view. There is nothing wrong, of course, with singing in the heart. In fact, it is always good to meditate with the heart on the things of God. But I also think that there is something praiseworthy when people glorify God with the sound of their voices.

I shall prove this by adducing many texts of Holy Scripture, but, first, I must appeal to the very text of the Apostle to refute, by what it precribes, the folly of all those who find there a condemnation of vocal singing. It is true, of course, that the Apostle said: 'Be filled with the Spirit, speaking to one another in psalms.'[7] But it is no less true that he meant us to open our mouths and move our tongues and loosen our lips—for the simple reason that no one can speak without these organs. Speaking and silence are as different as hot and cold. Notice, the Apostle says: 'speaking in psalms and hymns and canticles.' Surely, he would not have mentioned canticles if he wanted to imply that the person singing was completely silent. The simple fact is that no one can both sing and keep complete silence at the same

4 Eph. 5.18,19.
5 ...*non more tragoediae vocis modulamine garriendum.*
6 Rom. 8.2.
7 Eph. 5.19.

time. When he says 'in your hearts,' the Apostle wants to warn us not to sing solely with our voice, without any feeling in our hearts. So, too, in another text, 'I will sing with the spirit, but I will sing with the understanding,'[8] he means with both voice and thought.

The objection to singing is the invention of heretics. When their faith grows cold, they think up reasons for rejecting song. They cloak their hatred of the Prophets and, particularly, of the prophecies concerning the Lord and Creator. Under the pretext of piety, they silence the words of the Prophets and, above all, the heavenly songs of David.

(3) Beloved, we have been brought up in all the teachings of the Prophets, the Gospels, and the apostolic writings. Let us keep before our eyes all that has been said and done by those to whom we owe all that we are. Let us appeal to the authority of those who have spoken from the beginning to prove how pleasing to God are spiritual canticles.

If we ask who was the first to introduce this kind of singing, the answer is: Moses. He sang a remarkable song to God after Egypt had been afflicted by the ten plagues, Pharoah had been drowned, and the people [of Israel] moved toward the desert, filled with joy by the miraculous passage through the [Red] Sea. He sang: 'Let us sing to the Lord, for he is gloriously magnified.'[9] (In passing, I must warn you against the book entitled *The Revelation of Abraham,*[10] with its fictions about the singing of animals, fountains

8 1 Cor. 14.15.

9 Exod. 15.1.

10 Niceta's title, *Inquisitio Abrahae,* may stand for *Análepsis Abraám* (Acceptance or, possibly, Ascension of Abraham), which is mentioned in Pseudo-Athanasius (Migne, *PG* 28.432b), or for an *Apokálupsis Abraám,* alluded to by Epiphanius (*PG* 41.671d). St. Jerome speaks of *fictas revelationes omnium patriarchum.* See note in A. E. Burn, *Niceta of Remesiana,* p. 70. *Acquisitio* would have been a Latin equivalent for *Análepsis,* and may have been the original reading.

and the elements. The work is neither credible nor authentic.) Thus, the first to institute choirs was Moses, the leader of the tribes of Israel. Separating the men and women into two choirs, with himself and his sister as leaders, he taught them to sing a song of triumph to God. Somewhat later, Debbora, a lady of some distinction mentioned in the book of Judges, is found performing the same ministry.[11] Moses, again, when about to depart from this life, sang a fear-inspiring canticle in Deuteronomy.[12] He left the song as a sort of testament to the people of Israel, to teach them the kind of funeral they should expect, if ever they abandoned God. And woe to those who refused to give up unlawful superstitions, once they had heard such a clear denunciation.

(4) After this, you will find plenty of men and women, filled with a divine spirit, who sang of the mysteries of God. Among these was David. As a boy, he was given a special call to this office, and by God's grace he became the prince of singers and left us a treasury of song. He was still a boy when his sweet, strong song with his harp subdued the evil spirit working in Saul.[13] Not that there was any kind of power in the harp, but, with its wooden frame and the strings stretched across, it was a symbol of the Cross of Christ. It was the Passion that was being sung, and it was this which subdued the spirit of the Devil.

(5) You will find in David's psalms everything that can help edify and console men and women of every class and age. Children will find milk for their minds; boys, material to praise God; youths, corrections for their ways; young women, a model to follow; and old men, food for prayer. Women can learn modesty. Orphans will find in David a father;

---

11 Judges 5, the Canticle of Debbora and Barac after victory.
12 Deut. 32.
13 1 Kings 16.14-23.

widows, a vindicator; the poor, a protector; strangers, a guardian. Rulers and magistrates learn lessons in fear. A psalm consoles the sad, tempers the joyous, calms the angry, consoles the poor and stirs the conscience of the rich. A psalm offers medicine for all who will receive it—including even the sinner, to whom it brings the cure of holy penance and tears.

The Holy Spirit makes ample provision so that even the hardest and most recalcitrant hearts may, little by little, be glad to receive the medicine of these revealed words. Ordinarily, human nature runs away from what is hard, even though it is salutary, rejecting such things or, at least, taking them only when they seem to be tempting. Through David his servant, the Lord prepared a medicine, powerful enough to cure the wounds of sin, yet sweet to the taste by reason of the melody. For, when a psalm is sung, it is sweet to the ear. It enters the soul because it is pleasant. It is easily retained if it is often enough repeated. Confessions that no severity of law could extort from the heart are willingly made under the sweet influence of song. There is contained in these songs, for those who meditate on them, all that is consoling in the Law, the Prophets and even the Gospels.

(6) God is revealed and idols are scorned; faith is accepted and infidelity rejected; justice is recommended and injustice forbidden; mercy is praised and cruelty blamed; truth is demanded and lies are condemned; guilt is accused and innocence commended; pride is cast down and humility exalted; patience is preached; the banner of peace is unfurled; protection from enemies is prayed for; vindication is promised; confident hope is fostered. And what is more than all the rest, the Mysteries of Christ are sung. The Incarnation is clearly indicated and, even more so, His rejection by an ungrateful people and His welcome among the Gen-

tiles. The miracles of the Lord are sung; His venerable Passion is depicted; His glorious Resurrection made clear; and mention is made of His sitting at the right hand of the Father. In addition to all this, the coming of the Lord in a cloud of glory is declared and His terrible judgment of the living and the dead is revealed. Need more be said? There is, likewise, a revelation of the sending forth of the Creating Spirit and the renewal of the world which is to be followed by the eternal kingdom of the just in the glory of the Lord and the everlasting punishment of the wicked.

(7) Such are the songs which the Church of God sings. These are the songs with which we here in this congregation are filling our throats. For the singer they are not only a recreation but also a responsibility. They put out, rather than excite, the passions. There can be no doubt that such songs are pleasing to God, since everything about them is directed solely to the glory of the Creator. And the same psalmist who says: 'Let every spirit praise the Lord'—thus urging everyone and everything to praise God who is the ruler of them all—likewise says: 'I will praise the name of God with a canticle, and I will magnify him with praise'[14] —thus promising to give praise himself. He adds: 'And it shall please God better than a young calf that bringeth forth horns and hoofs,' to bring out something still more excellent, a spiritual sacrifice that is greater than all sacrifices of victims. This is as it should be. In such sacrifices the blood of irrational animals was shed, but from the soul and a good conscience rational praise is offered up. Rightly did the Lord say: 'The sacrifice of praise shall glorify me, and there is the way by which I will show him the salvation of God.'[15] Praise, then, the Lord in your life, offer to Him

14 Ps. 150.6; 68.31.
15 Ps. 49.23.

the sacrifice of praise, and thus show in your soul the way by which you come to His salvation.

(8) Praise issuing from a pure conscience delights the Lord, and so the same psalmist exhorts us: 'Praise ye the Lord because a psalm is good; to our God be joyful and comely praise.'[16] With this in mind, aware of how pleasing to God is this ministry, the psalmist again declares: 'Seven times a day I have given praise to thee.'[17] To this he adds a further promise: 'And my tongue shall meditate thy justice, thy praise all the day long.'[18] Without doubt, he had experience of the good to be derived from this work, for he reminds us: 'Praising I will call upon the Lord, and I shall be saved from my enemies.'[19] It was with such a shield to protect him that as a boy he destroyed the great power of the giant Goliath and, in many other instances, came out victorious over the invaders.

(9) I must not bore you, beloved, with more details of the history of the psalms. It is time to turn to the New Testament to confirm what is said in the Old, and, particularly, to point out that the office of psalmody is not to be considered abolished merely because many other observances of the Old Law have fallen into desuetude.[20] Only the corporal institutions have been rejected, like circumcision, the sabbath, sacrifices, discrimination in foods. So, too, the trumpets, harps, cymbals and timbrels. For the sound of these we now have a better substitute in the music from the mouths of men. The daily ablutions, the new-moon observances, the careful inspection of leprosy are completely

16 Ps 145.1.
17 Ps. 118.164.
18 Ps. 34.28.
19 Ps. 17.4.
20 Translation is based on C. H. Turner's suggestion, *pessum data.* I have followed his text for the passage beginning: *Cessaverunt plane...*

past and gone, along with whatever else was necessary only for a time—as it were, for children. Of course, what was spiritual in the Old Testament, for example, faith, piety, prayer, fasting, patience, chastity, psalm-singing—all this has been increased in the New Testament rather than diminished. Thus, in the Gospel you will find, first of all, Zachary the father of the great John, after his long silence uttering a prophecy in the form of a hymn.[21] Nor did Elizabeth, who had been so long sterile, cease to magnify God in her soul when the son of promise had been born.[22] And when Christ was born on earth, the army of angels sang a song of praise: 'Glory to God in the highest and on earth peace to men of good will.'[23] The children in the Temple raised their voices to sing: 'Hosanna to the Son of David'[24]—only to make the Pharisees more angry. However, the Lord rather opened than closed the mouths of the little ones when He said: 'Have you never read, Out of the mouth of infants and sucklings thou hast perfected praise.'[25] If these keep silence, the stones will cry out.'[26] But I must be brief. The Lord Himself, our teacher and master in words and deeds, showed how pleasing was the ministry of hymns when He went out to the Mount of Olives only after a hymn had been sung. With such evidence before him, how can anyone go on doubting the religious value of psalms and hymns? For here we are told that He who is adored and sung by the angels in heaven sang a hymn along with His disciples.

21 Luke 1.67-79. This, of course, is the *Benedictus*.

22 Here and at the end of Chapter 11 (according to the reading of the eighth-century Cava MS), it is supposed that Elizabeth, and not Mary, sang the *Magnificat*. The great weight of MS authority, including all Greek and Syriac texts, is in favor of Mary.

23 Luke 2.14.

24 Matt. 21.15.

25 Matt. 21.16.

26 Luke 19.40.

(10) And we know that later on the Apostles also did this, since not even in prison did they cease to sing. So, too, Paul speaks to the Prophets of the Church: 'When you come together, each of you has a hymn, has an instruction, has a revelation, has a tongue, has an interpretation. Let all things be done unto edification.'[27] And again, in another place: 'I will sing with the spirit, but I will sing with the understanding also.'[28] So, too, James sets down in his Epistle: 'Is any one of you sad? Let him pray. Is any one in good spirits? Let him sing a hymn.'[29] And John in the Apocalypse reports that, when the Spirit revealed himself to him, he saw and heard 'a voice of the heavenly army, as it were the voice of many waters and as the voice of mighty thunders, saying, Alleluia.'[30] From all this we may conclude that no one should doubt that this ministry, if only it is celebrated with true faith and devotion, is one with that of the angels, who, as we know, unhindered by sleep or other occupation, cease not to praise the Lord in heaven and to bless the Saviour.

(11) These things being so, brothers, let us have full confidence in carrying out our ministry of song. Let us believe that we have been given a great, a very great, grace by God who has granted to us to sing the marvels of the eternal God in the company of so many and such great saints, prophets and even martyrs. We confess to Him, with David, that 'He is good.' And, with Moses, we sing in these great canticles the glory of the Holy and Divine Spirit. With Anna, who is a symbol of the Church—once sterile and now fecund—we strengthen our hearts in the praise of God. With Isaias, we keep our night watch. We join Habacuc in

27 1 Cor. 14.26.
28 1 Cor. 14.15.
29 James 5.13.
30 Apoc. 19.6.

song. With the holy fathers, Jonas and Jeremias, we join song to prayer. With the three children in the flames, we call on every creature to bless the Lord. With Elizabeth our soul magnifies the Lord.

(12) Can any joy be greater than that of delighting ourselves with psalms and nourishing ourselves with prayer and feeding ourselves with the lessons that are read in between? Like guests at table enjoying a variety of dishes, our souls feast on the rich banquet of lessons and hymns.

(13) Only, brothers, let us please God by singing with attention and a mind wide awake, undistracted by idle talk. For so the psalm invites us: 'Sing ye wisely, for God is the King of all the earth.'[31] That is, we must sing with our intelligences; not only with the spirit (in the sense of the sound of our voice), but also with our mind. We must think about what we are singing, lest we lose by distracting talk and extraneous thoughts the fruit of our effort. The sound and melody of our singing must be suitably religious. It must not be melodramatic, but a revelation of the true Christianity within. It must have nothing theatrical about it, but should move us to sorrow for our sins.

Of course, you must all sing in harmony, without discordant notes. One of you should not linger unreasonably on the notes, while his neighbor is going too fast; nor should one of you sing too low while another is raising his voice. Each one should be asked to contribute his part in humility to the volume of the choir as a whole. No one should sing unbecomingly louder or slower than the rest, as though for vain ostentation or out of human respect. The whole service must be carried out in the presence of God, not with a view to pleasing men. In regard to the harmony of voices we

31 Ps. 46.8.

have a model and example in the three blessed boys of whom the Prophet Daniel tells us: 'Then these three, as with one mouth, praised and glorified and blessed God in the furnace, saying: Blessed art thou, O Lord the God of our fathers.'[32] You see that it was for our instruction that we are told that the three boys humbly and holily praised God with one voice. Therefore, let us sing all together, as with one voice, and let all of us modulate our voices in the same way. If one cannot sing in tune with the others, it is better to sing in a low voice rather than drown the others. In this way he will take his part in the service without interfering with the community singing. Not everyone, of course, has a flexible and musical voice. St. Cyprian is said to have invited his friend Donatus, whom he knew to be a good singer, to join him in the office: 'Let us pass the day in joy, so that not one hour of the feast will be without some heavenly grace. Let the feast be loud with songs, since you have a full memory and a musical voice. Come to this duty regularly. You will feed your beloved friends if you give us something spiritual to listen to. There is something alluring about religious sweetness; and those who sing well have a special grace to attract to religion those who listen to them.'[33] And if our voice is without harshness and in tune with the notes of well-played cymbals, it will be a joy to ourselves and source of edification to those who hear us. And 'God who maketh men of one manner to dwell in His House'[34] will find our united praise agreeable to Him.

When we sing, all should sing; when we pray, all should

---

32 Dan. 3.51,52.

33 Cyprian, *Epist. ad Donatum* 16. The entire passage, 'Not everyone, of course,... listen to them,' is not found in five of the extant MSS. It appears, however, in the *Codex Cavensis,* in *Codex Vaticanus 5729* (The Bible of Farfa), and in the Codex used by C. H. Turner,

34 Ps. 67.7.

pray. So, when the lesson is being read, all should remain silent, that all may equally hear. No one should be praying with so loud a voice as to disturb the one who is reading. And if you should happen to come in while the lesson is being read, just adore the Lord and make the Sign of the Cross, and then give an attentive ear to what is being read.

(14) Obviously, the time to pray is when we are all praying. Of course, you may pray privately whenever and as often as you choose. But do not, under the pretext of prayer, miss the lesson. You can always pray whenever you will, but you cannot always have a lesson at hand. Do not imagine that there is little to be gained by listening to the sacred lesson. The fact is that prayer is improved if our mind has been recently fed on reading and is able to roam among the thoughts of divine things which it has recently heard. The word of the Lord assures us that Mary, the sister of Martha, chose the better part when she sat at the feet of Jesus, listening intently to the word of God without a thought of her sister.[35] We need not wonder, then, if the deacon in a clear voice like a herald warns all that, whether they are praying or bowing the knees, singing hymns, or listening to the lessons, they should all act together. God loves 'men of one manner' and, as was said before, 'maketh them to dwell in his house.'[36] And those who dwell in this house are proclaimed by the psalm to be blessed, because they will praise God forever and ever. Amen.

---

35 Cf. Luke 10.42.
36 Ps. 67.7.

WRITINGS
OF
SULPICIUS SEVERUS

Translated

by

BERNARD PEEBLES, Ph. D.

The Catholic University of America

INTRODUCTION

It is most often the case with biographies that their authors remain far less well known than their subjects, and this is eminently true with Sulpicius Severus. If in the course of fifteen hundred years there have been few literate Christians who have not heard of St. Martin of Tours and have not had some acquaintance with one or more episodes of his life, there have been a great many to whom even the name of his first and most widely read biographer is unknown. Even the fact that Sulpicius was one of the first Christian Latin writers to compose a biography and wrote in a style that even a Gibbon[1] could call 'not unworthy of the Augustan age' has not saved him from an obscurity which few besides specialists in literary history care to penetrate. While some hints about the character and stature of the man may be drawn from the scanty materials concerning him which have survived, these are far too meager to furnish a basis for a reliable judgment. It may well be that there was little in Sulpicius himself to merit personal fame and that, apart from such spiritual heroism as was required for his renunciation of worldly honors, his only great achievement was to produce the portrait of the indefatigable pastor of souls, missioner, monk, and worker of miracles whom, chiefly through the pen of Sulpicius, the world knows as Martin of Tours.

1 *Decline and Fall,* Chap. 27, n. 61 (ed. J. B. Bury [London 1897] 3.155).

High merits indeed would have been required to make him conspicuous among the great Christian Latin writers who were his contemporaries—St. Ambrose, St. Jerome, and St. Augustine. Theirs was a brilliance that might have darkened even a far brighter luminary than Sulpicius ever was. Of these three, only St. Jerome mentions Sulpicius Severus:[2] he calls him 'our Severus,' with an appropriate intimacy, since, if the two men were not known to one another through mutual correspondence, they had more than one acquaintance in common. What is more, it was a reading of Sulpicius's *Dialogues* that led St. Jerome to speak of him, a work which contains an enthusiastic appreciation of the great Doctor of Bethlehem.[3] In Sulpicius, St. Ambrose twice receives brief mention;[4] St. Augustine, none at all. On their side, there is reason to believe that each may have known of Sulpicius, and their failure to speak of him—or of St. Martin either—is regrettable.

As basic sources for the life of Sulpicius we are confined to the statements he himself makes, to the thirteen letters addressed to him by St. Paulinus of Nola,[5] and to a brief chapter in the work of Gennadius of Marseilles (d. before 500), *On Famous Men.*[6]

Sulpicius Severus—called Severus by his contemporaries, but Sulpicius in his own *Dialogues*[7]—was born about 360 into

---

2 Cf. below, n. 58.

3 *Dial.* 1.7-9.

4 Cf. *Dial.* 1.25, n. 11.

5 Selected writings of St. Paulinus will be translated elsewhere in this series. The Latin text of his letters is found in *PL* 61 and *CSEL* 29.

6 Chap. 19 (*PL* 58.1072); also in Halm's edition of Sulpicius Severus, *CSEL* 1.xiii. A translation by E. C. Richardson is found in *A Select Library of the Nicene and Post-Nicene Fathers,* Second Series, 3 (New York 1892) 389f.

7 The two names are joined in the salutation of the *Letter to Bassula.*

a distinguished Aquitanian family.[8] He was educated at Bordeaux during the best period of the Gallic schools of rhetoric. Presumably in the course of his studies there he formed an intimate friendship with Meropius Pontius Paulinus, a native of Bordeaux and a pupil of one of its most distinguished teachers, the poet Ausonius. While still young, Sulpicius attained celebrity in the practice of law and saw his worldly fame increased by marriage with the daughter of a certain Bassula, high-born and wealthy. The early death of his wife may have helped to turn the mind of Sulpicius from the secular honors in which he was so rich toward a life of renunciation. About the year 390 the two friends, Paulinus and Sulpicius, had been baptized together. A few years later, to the amazement and regret of some of his contemporaries, Paulinus foreswore his own riches and secular renown, and Sulpicius soon followed his example. It appears that he had already made the acquaintance of Martin, the powerful and ascetic Bishop of Tours, for, in his *Life* of the bishop, Sulpicius tells how enthusiastically Martin commended to his imitation Paulinus's rejection of the allurements and empty burdens of the world.[9] Paulinus, after being ordained priest in Barcelona, passed the rest of his life in Italy, near the Campanian town of Nola, ultimately as its bishop. It was only through letters and visits of common friends that he kept in touch with Sulpicius, who remained in Gaul.

After spending some time at Eluso (the present Elsonne, near Toulouse), Sulpicius transferred the seat of his retirement to a place which Paulinus calls Primuliacum, an uncertain site fixed by some scholars near Béziers, by others near

8 The present passage is based largely on Gennadius, *loc. cit.*, and on the letters of Paulinus, especially *Epist.* 5. The year 360 is a mere approximation, based on the fact that Paulinus, who was somewhat older than Sulpicius, was born in 353 or 354.

9 *Life* 25.

Périgueux.[10] It is presumably at Primuliacum that the scene of Sulpicius's *Dialogues* is laid. There is little description of background in that work and nothing to suggest the interesting architectural arrangements which were to be found at Primuliacum. Fortunately, a letter[11] of Paulinus indicates that there were two basilicas and a baptistery. On the walls of the baptistery Sulpicius had two murals: one representing Martin, the other Paulinus. The humble ascetic of Nola could only deplore the juxtaposition, but acceded to his friend's request for verses to be inscribed under the portraits. While no trace of these murals has been discovered, their subjects show how clearly Sulpicius recognized a double debt: one to the somewhat older, somewhat bolder friend of his youth; the other to the venerable bishop of Tours, whom he deemed worthy of comparison with the Apostles.[12] As may be concluded from his own writings, Sulpicius had remained in close association with Martin up to his death and, later, with several of Martin's disciples. The knowledge he so gained clearly qualified Sulpicius to turn his well-trained literary talents to a biography of his saintly mentor.

His literary activity—not least of all the research that his *Chronicles* required—must have given Sulpicius adequate

10 For Eluso, see Paulinus, *Epist.* 1.11; for Primuliacum, *Epist.* 31.1. The latter is located near Béziers by F. Mouret, *Sulpice Sévère à Primuliac* (Paris 1907), near Périgueux by E.-Ch. Babut, in *Annales du Midi* 20 (1908) 457-468; Jullian, in *REA* 25 (1923) 249f., suggests it should be looked for farther north, near Bourges.

11 *Epist.* 32 (*Epist.* 30 and 31 are also relevant). Cf. the work of Gold-Schmidt (cited *Dial.* 3.17, n. 3) 36.

12 Cf. *Life* 7 and the other references cited in n. 4 there. (Babut 37f. notes a *crescendo* in Sulpicius's successive eulogies of St. Martin.) In his *De servorum Dei beatificatione* etc. (3rd ed., Rome 1747-1751), IV.ii.xi.1, Prospero Cardinal Lambertini (later Pope Benedict XIV) considers the question whether St. Martin is to be held equal to the Apostles; after quoting Sulpicius and Odo of Cluny for the affirmative, he refers to a passage in St. Thomas Aquinas (*In epist. ad Ephes.*, lect. 3), where such comparison is declared to be a temerity, if not an actual error.

occupation during the years he spent at Primuliacum. It is reasonable to suppose that there was abundant recreation as well—reunions with intimate friends, for example, like that described in the *Dialogues;* when Sulpicius withdrew from the world, he did not shake off a certain lovable attachment to its more wholesome values. It is not known where he died or when—a date around 420 is probable. Gennadius calls him a priest (*presbyter*). While nothing in the writings either of Sulpicius himself or of Paulinus confirms this, the statement of Gennadius should not be ignored. The same writer is also alone in relating another biographical detail. He tells us that Sulpicius, in his old age, fell victim to the heresy of the Pelagians, and, to apply the appropriate correction to the loquacity he considered the cause of his fault, maintained silence to the end of his days. Here, also, there may be some truth in the report of Gennadius; if there is, and if the *Dialogues* do not exaggerate the pleasure Sulpicius took in conversation, his self-imposed silence was a heavy penance indeed.

Until Pope Urban VIII (1623-1644) expunged his name, certain printings of the *Roman Martyrology* listed Sulpicius among the saints of January 29, and the Bollandists could not refrain from considering his merits in the *Acta Sanctorum* for that date. The appearance of Sulpicius Severus in the *Martyrology* was due to a confusion with an unquestioned saint of January 29, another Sulpicius, Archbishop of Bourges (584-591), likewise called Severus.[13]

13 Cf. *Acta Sanctorum,* Jan. III (Brussels 1863) 531, 583-4. Alban Butler included a relatively long life of our Sulpicius in his *The Lives of the Saints;* cf. the edition of Herbert Thurston, S.J., 1 (London 1926) 375-378. The famous church of Saint-Sulpice in Paris is dedicated to another Archbishop of Bourges, Sulpicius Pius (626-647), and it is from this church that the Sulpician Fathers are named. For further comment on our Severus and Bourges, see Jullian, *loc. cit.* (above, n. 10); also, below, *Dial.* 1.27, n. 2.

Of the writings which Gennadius ascribes to Sulpicius, most have survived. Naturally, there were letters, and it is here that time has taken a heavy toll. Making no specific mention of the three letters which do survive and which are a kind of appendix to the *Life of St. Martin,* Gennadius speaks of many letters written by Sulpicius to a sister, exhorting her to the love of God and the renunciation of the world, and also of letters to Paulinus of Nola and to others. Gennadius speaks of only two letters to Paulinus, but it appears from those of Paulinus to Sulpicius—none earlier than 394 or later than 404 is preserved—that Sulpicius must have written at least eleven.[14] Among seven letters ascribed to a Severus in various manuscripts (one of them addressed to 'Saint Paulinus'),[15] two might appear to be among the spiritual letters to his sister which Gennadius mentions; if they are such, her name was Claudia. But these letters, as well as the other five, are generally viewed by scholars as falsely attributed to Sulpicius; some have been recently declared to be the work of Pelagius.[16]

Sulpicius's longest work is listed by Gennadius without the slightest comment: 'He also composed the *Chronicles.*' As their introduction makes clear, the two books of the *Chronicles* contain an abridged presentation of sacred history from the creation of the world down to the author's own time, with careful attention to chronology. The author's recasting of

14 So P. Reinelt, *Studien über die Briefe des hl. Paulinus von Nola* (Diss., Breslau 1904) 57.

15 Edited by Halm in his edition of Sulpicius, *CSEL* 1.219-256. English translation by Roberts (cf. below, p. 98 in Select Bibliography). In Halm, the title to No. 3 should show *Paulinum* instead of *Paulum;* this letter is the most probably genuine of the lot.

16 Hyltén 156f. denies them to Sulpicius and also holds the single authorship of all seven letters unlikely. For Pelagius as the author of the first two, see G. de Plinval, *Pélage, ses écrits, sa vie et sa reforme* (Lausanne etc.: Payot 1943) 31-45; *ibid.* 42 n.4 for possible Pelagian authorship of a third.

Old Testament history occupies all of the first book and half of the second. He thought it would be unfitting to reduce to a summary the narrative contained in the *Gospels* and the *Acts*; hence, he omits it.[17] In the remainder of his work Sulpicius traces the history of the persecutions and other events in Church history down to the first consulship of Stilicho (A.D. 400).[18] Sulpicius's handling of a contemporary event, the affair of the heretical Priscillian, is a valuable source-document and furnishes his history with a stark and shocking ending.[19] One section of this narrative reveals Martin as playing an important role; this is translated below as an Appendix to the *Dialogues*. In the latter half of his second book Sulpicius draws his material from a variety of sources. In one instance St. Paulinus supplies him with the facts—those relating to the finding of the True Cross by St. Helena.[20] The letter from Nola containing this material was written in 402 or 403. It was after this date, then, that the *Chronicles* of Sulpicius were finished and published. To call the *Chronicles,* as Bardenhewer does,[21] the 'pearl' among the surviving writings may well involve an injustice to Sulpicius's works on St. Martin. Still, it is in the *Chronicles* that the author's style is, in many respects, seen at its best, a result in large measure of his sedulous study of Sallust and Tacitus and, to a less degree, of Livy and Velleius Paterculus. (Sulpicius's knowledge of the pagan classics was extensive, as his Martinian writings also show.) The stylistic merits of the *Chronicles* doubtless commended the book to many of the well-schooled

17 *Chron.* 2.27.3. For the *Chronicles* the title *Sacred History* is also frequently used.

18 *Chron.* 2.9.7 and 27.5 (cf. 33.1) show at least that Sulpicius was using Stilicho's consulship as a terminus for chronological reference.

19 The passage in question is *Chron.* 2.46-51.

20 *Chron.* 2.33ff. Cf. Paulinus, *Epist.* 31.

21 O. Bardenhewer, *Gesch. d. altkirchl. Literatur* 3 (Freiburg im Breisgau 1923) 422.

contemporaries of its author, but its refinements were lost on the less literate reading public of the period following the barbarian invasions. Traces of its existence in the Middle Ages are few, and only one manuscript (of the tenth or eleventh century) has survived to modern times.

The writings which remain to be mentioned are precisely those which comprise the new translation into English here furnished: the *Life of St. Martin,* three *Letters,* and the *Dialogues.* In this group of works, representing three different literary forms, it was the author's chief intention to relate the life and miracles of St. Martin of Tours, a task which he accomplished 'to the advantage of many,' as Gennadius justly observed. Sulpicius might have organized all of his material in one single *Vita,* but he chose to do otherwise. After the publication of the *Life* proper, various situations arose which led him to add to the material he had presented there, and these circumstances produced the biography in the five (or six) parts which we know.

How and why Sulpicius came to write the *Life* is best read in the author's own words in Chapters 1 and 25. While the work was probably, in large part, composed during Martin's lifetime, the text as we now have it presupposes the bishop's death. Certain phrases in Chapter 1 and the whole tone of the characterization of Martin found in Chapters 26 and 27 are incompatible with any other assumption than that Martin was no longer living. Doubtless, these sections were added when the author, after Martin's death, agreed to the publication of the work—reluctantly, if the prefatory letter to Desiderius is to be taken at face value. That a copy soon found its way to Nola and was joyfully received there is shown by the eleventh letter of Paulinus.

Sulpicius's second and third *Letters* are probably next in order of composition, both occasioned by Martin's death;

they may well have been published along with the *Life*. The second is addressed to a certain Aurelius, deacon then but later a priest, and probably a disciple of St. Martin. It was written, Sulpicius says elsewhere,[22] from Toulouse, that is, in all likelihood, Eluso. It contains express mention of the *Life*.[23] The third makes a clear reference to the second,[24] and is addressed to Bassula, the mother of Sulpicius's deceased wife. Where Bassula was when her son-in-law composed the letter is not clear—perhaps still at Trèves, where an unauthorized copy of the letter to Aurelius reached her. In the letter to Bassula the playful raillery against his mother-in-law (it is with traditionally typical mother-in-law conduct he charges her) is abruptly followed by one of the most eloquent passages in all hagiographical literature, the moving description of Martin's last days, his death and burial. The prayer of the dying Martin—and especially his expression of willingness to continue with his earthly work if God so willed, his *Non recuso laborem*—has often been repeated by other saints.[25] The first *Letter* of Sulpicius seems to be latest in date, for it states that the *Life of St. Martin* was already being widely read.[26] The priest Eusebius addressed here by Sulpicius had become a bishop when the *Dialogues* were composed.

The most sizeable additions to Martin's biography as contained in the *Life* are found in the *Dialogues*. Are we to speak

22 *Epist.* 3 (cf. below, p. 00).
23 Cf. below, p. 00.
24 Cf. below, p. 00.
25 The future Benedict XIV, *op. cit.* (above, n. 12) III.xxxviii.18, refers to a similar expression used by St. Thomas de Villanova. St. Francis de Sales on his deathbed was asked to use St. Martin's prayer, but declined, declaring that he was a 'useless servant, useless, useless.' When St. Jean Marie Vianney was eager to abandon his exhausting apostolic work for a life of cloistered retirement, his disciples used the example of St. Martin's *non recuso laborem* to dissuade him.
26 Cf. below, p. 00.

of the *Dialogues* as two or as three? Nearly all the manuscripts and printed editions show a three-fold division and it is this that is preserved in the present translation. Yet, a division into two reported by Gennadius is probably the original arrangement. The actual two-fold grouping found in a few of the manuscripts[27] has a very natural basis and may well represent Sulpicius's intentions. The conversations related in the *Dialogues* occupy two days, and this division is such that the transactions of the first day are contained in the first *Dialogue,* those of the following day in the second. There is basis, however, for a further division, and this is found in the subject matter of the work.

The dominant figure in the early part of the *Dialogue* is Sulpicius's friend Postumianus, who is just back from a trip to Egypt and Palestine and who relates his experiences and the wonders he saw and heard of there. But, while quite willing to tell these wonder-stories of the East to Sulpicius and Gallus—a disciple of Martin who is with them—Postumianus is eager to hear more about St. Martin than Sulpicius had included in his 'little book,' a work that had admittedly left much unsaid. It falls to Gallus to relate further stories about Martin, and his report occupies the second half of the first day and all of the second. It is precisely at the point where his narrative begins that the second part in the more-current three-fold division of the *Dialogues* opens, the third part being identical with the second *Dialogue* of the apparently original grouping.

Whatever may be true as to how the *Dialogues* came to show two systems of internal division, they seem to date, if

27 Notably *V, D, B*; cf. below, Select Bibliography.

considered as a single work, from about 404.[28] They are manifestly a supplement to the *Life,* and both that work and the *Letter* to Eusebius are mentioned in them.[29] Sulpicius's use of the dialogue-form as a vehicle for biography is striking and altogether effective. The similar procedure followed in the *Dialogues* of St. Gregory the Great is almost certainly based on Sulpicius's example. Just as Sulpicius foresaw, the conversational exchanges which are interspersed between the stretches of narrative enliven the book and allow scope for the author's salty Gallic wit. Precisely for this reason the *Dialogues* have been called 'one of the earliest instances of the idiosyncrasy of French prose, although the words are Latin.'[30]

For any readers of Sulpicius's biography who, knowing how to use it best, are content to follow the narrative simply for the pleasure and edification it can supply, it is idle to enquire into the trustworthiness of Sulpicius as an historian or his accuracy in such a matter as chronology. Since these may be important considerations for others, however, a word on both points may not be out of place.

A tendency among some of the author's contemporaries to doubt the truth of Martin's miracles and to make a low estimation of his merits is noted by Sulpicius himself.[31] This

28 Postumianus's three-year journey (*Dial.* 1.1) took him early to Egypt, where he seems to have arrived shortly after Theophilus's expulsion of the Origenistic monks in August 401 (cf. *Dial.* 1.6 n.1). This places the dramatic date of the *Dialogues,* if not that of their composition, in about 404. Cf. *Dial.* 2.14 n. 3 for a supporting argument.

29 *Dial.* 2.9.

30 Helen Waddell, *Beasts and Saints* (London 1934) xiv. The first two stories in Miss Waddell's collection are an admirable translation from Sulp., *Dial.* 1.13,14.

31 Cf. esp. *Life* 27, *Epist.* 1 (opening), *Dial.* 3.5,6. For Sulpicius's sensitivity to a charge of falsification, cf. *Life* 1 (end), *Dial.* 1.26, *Dial.* 2.13, *Dial.* 3.2. The regular naming of witnesses in *Dial.* 3 is noteworthy (cf. *Dial.* 3.5).

skepticism, which, perhaps, has never been wholly absent among critical readers, gained its fullest expression early in the present century, in an important book by Ernest-Charles Babut, *Saint Martin de Tours* (Paris 1912). Babut's thesis, in part, is briefly this: Martin, far from being the influential figure painted by Sulpicius, was constantly thwarted by hostility on the part of the clergy and his fellow bishops and ended by falling into almost general disfavor. A number of outbursts of indignation voiced by Sulpicius against unnamed enemies—especially, it seems, among the higher clergy—are advanced in proof of this.[32] Contemporary literature of Gaul, moreover, ignores Martin, and the universal renown that he was later to enjoy was due to one single fact—the literary excellence and extraordinary popularity of Sulpicius's biography. This biography, or, rather *'vie merveilleuse,'*[33] is in large measure a work of fiction and represents heavy and substantial borrowings from a variety of sources, oral and written, notably the *Life of St. Anthony* by St. Athanasius as translated into Latin shortly before by Evagrius.[34]

There is no place here for a lengthy discussion of Babut's provocative thesis. He was killed fiighting in Belgium in 1916, and, for a time, opponents of his conclusions (and of some of his methods) were reluctant to offer a rebuttal. After a while, this hesitancy was overcome, and careful replies to Babut's arguments were made by two scholars who had a special right to be heard: Camille Jullian,[35] then the leading

32 In addition to some of the passages listed in the foregoing note, cf. *Life* 9,26; *Dial.* 1.2,26; *Dial.* 3.11, 13, 15, 16, 18.

33 Babut 89. On Martin's reputation as based on this *'vie merveilleuse,'* cf. Babut 21: [la] 'gloire [de saint Martin] est d'origine littéraire; elle est sortie des petits livres de Sulpice Sévèré.'

34 *PG* 26.837ff. The translation was made some time after 362.

35 In a series of articles in *Revue des études anciennes;* see Select Bibliography.

Gallo-Romanist of France, and Hippolyte Delehaye, S.J.,[36] a scholar of the deepest integrity and unsurpassed in the study of hagiography. Few have spoken since then in Babut's support,[37] and it would appear that the general judgment of scholars has pronounced his position untenable, even if high praise is due him for his masterly assembly of evidence.

One feature of the *Martiniana* of Sulpicius which tends to lower their value as an historical document is the weakness of his chronology of the life of Martin and especially of Martin's early years. This weakness is all the more striking when we consider the exactness in the matter of dates which his *Chronicles* generally exhibit. The chronological data supplied by Sulpicius in the *Life* and *Dialogues*—at least in the text as we have it—are not only inconsistent among themselves, but do not fully agree with those given by Gregory, Bishop of Tours, who had at his disposal the official records of the see that had also been Martin's. Various attempts to solve the problems of Martinian chronology have been made, none wholly successful. Since the resolutions proposed by Père Delehaye in his answer to Babut are the most convincing, it may be useful to record here his principal results:[38]

November 11, 397	Martin's burial; the fundamental date in the entire chronology, known from the traditions of the Church at Tours
July 4, 371 (or 370)	His consecration as bishop
385	His presence at the court of Trèves
Ca. 315	His birth.

36 In *Analecta Bollandiana* 38 (1920) 5-136.

37 The present writer knows only M. Bloch, in *Revue d'histoire et de littérature religieuses,* N. S. 7 (1921) 44-57.

38 *Anal. Boll.* 38.31 (cf. 19-33). Attention is called in the notes to the present translation to certain passages in Sulpicius of special interest for the chronology.

The last date follows from the statement in *Dial.* 2.7 that Martin was already a septuaginarian when he was present at the court of Maximus, and must of necessity be approximate, since the description 'septuaginarian' is itself not precise. If 315 be the date of Martin's birth, the following additional dates can be reached from statements made in Chapters 2-4 of the *Life*:

325 The beginning of Martin's catechumenate
330 His conscription
334 His entrance on active military service
337 His baptism
339 His withdrawal from the army.

While, as we have seen, everything tends to show that the *Chronicles* of Sulpicius were not widely read until post-Renaissance times, the case is altogether different with his writings on St. Martin. Even if we take with some reservation the account of their popularity given by Sulpicius himself,[39] there is abundant external evidence, beginning from the end of the fourth century and continuing throughout the Middle Ages, to establish the wide dissemination and manifold influence that Sulpicius's biography of St. Martin enjoyed.[40] Only a few points can be touched on here. Without doubt, St. Paulinus of Nola and such well-traveled friends of his as St. Niceta of Remesiana promoted the circulation of copies of the *Life* and its sequels.[41] An early reader and imitator was Paulinus of Milan, who, about 399, at St. Augustine's re-

39 *Epist.* 1 (p. 141); *Dial.* 1.23. These passages refer only to the *Life* (and to the *Letters,* if they formed an attachment to it). *Dial.* 3.17 shows that Sulpicius is hopeful that the *Dialogues* will enjoy an equally wide circulation.

40 For an admirable assembly of a great deal of the evidence, cf. Lecoy de la Marche 557ff.

41 Cf. *Dial.* 1.23 and 3.17, n. 2.

quest, wrote a life of St. Ambrose, and names Sulpicius's *Life of St. Martin* as a model.[42] Similar is the case of a letter on the death of St. Paulinus of Nola, written by a disciple of the saint, the priest Uranius.[43] As we have seen, St. Jerome, in Bethlehem, had occasion to read the *Dialogues;* they reached him prior to 414.[44] Just before the middle of the fifth century, we find that Sozomen, writing in Greek, probably at Constantinople, gives an important place to St. Martin in his *Ecclesiastical History* and summarizes the early chapters of Sulpicius's *Life*.[45] Shortly afterwards, in Gaul, Paulinus of Périgueux paraphrased Sulpicius's *Martiniana* in six books of hexameters,[46] and a similar work was produced about a century later by a better poet, Venantius Fortunatus.[47] This writer's verse-setting of Sulpicius was prompted by Bishop Gregory of Tours, who himself greatly extended the report of St. Martin's miracles in his *History of the Franks* and especially in his four books *On the Miracles of St. Martin*;[48] evidence of his close familiarity with the writings of Sulpicius is found throughout. Gregory makes the interesting statement that the *Life* of St. Martin was publicly read in

42 Latin text in *PL* 14.27ff., and also in Catholic University of America Patristic Studies 16 (Washington 1928), by Sister M. Simplicia Kaniecka, who adds an English translation and commentary.

43 Latin text in *PL* 53.859ff.

44 Cf. below, n. 58.

45 *Hist. eccl.* 3.14 (*PG* 67.1081); English translation by C. D. Hartranft in *A Select Library of the Nicene and Post-Nicene Fathers,* Second Series 2 (New York 1890) 294.

46 Latin text in *PL* 61.1009ff.; *CSEL* 16.17ff. Cf. the works of Huber and Chase cited in the Select Bibliography.

47 Latin text in *PL* 88.363ff.; *Monumenta Germaniae Historica,* Auctores antiquissimi 4.1.293ff.; also Chase, *op. cit.*

48 Latin text in *PL* 71; *Mon. Germ. Hist.,* Scriptores rerum merovingicarum, Parts 1 (*Hist. Franc.*) and 2.584ff. (*De virt. sancti Martini*). For the *History of the Franks* (cf. below, *Letter to Bassula,* n. 15), there is the excellent translation (with notes) by O. M. Dalton (Oxford 1927).

church at celebrations of his feast.[49] The official cult of St. Martin, established earlier at Tours, dates at Rome from the pontificate of Pope Symmachus (498-514)[50] and early Sacramentaries from various centers contain propers for St. Martin's feasts (November 11 and July 4). Liturgical requirements no doubt produced a heavy demand for copies of Sulpicius's writings on St. Martin (or at least of parts of them) and were responsible in no small measure for the multiplication of manuscripts. Among the still uncounted hundreds of manuscripts of Sulpicius that are to be found in European and American libraries, the oldest is a venerable book of the Verona Chapter Library, written in 517 by a certain Ursicinus, *lector* of that city.[51]

The various uses to which Sulpicius's *Martiniana* were put in the first two centuries after their composition continue without break during the entire mediaeval period and after. The use of the *Life* as a model for biography, secular as well as ecclesiastical, is even more frequent. When, as often, we find a mediaeval biography beginning abruptly with the word *Igitur* ('therefore' 'then'), it is fair to guess that its prototype, immediate or remote, is Sulpicius's *Life of St. Martin*. The *Igitur* is used in slavish imitation of the opening of the second chapter of Sulpicius.[52] His work is a source of much of the

---

49 *De virt. sancti Martini* 2.29,49.

50 Cf. Ildefonso Cardinal Schuster, *The Sacramentary* (*Liber Sacramentorum*) 5 (London 1930) 266.

51 For a facsimile, description, and bibliography, see E. A. Lowe, *Codices Latini antiquiores* 4 (Oxford 1947) no. 494. For an interesting fifteenth-century manuscript of American ownership and used by G. Da Prato (below, n. 63) for his edition of 1741, cf. the present writer's *Saibantianus*. Facsimile pages from a number of fine copies written in the very foundations at Tours which St. Martin had planted (cf. below, *Life* 10, n. 3) may be found in E. K. Rand, *A Survey of the Manuscripts of Tours* (text and volume of plates, Cambridge, Mass. 1929); cf. his Index, p. 230, *s. v. 'Martinellus.'*

52 Cf. Babut 8, n. 1.

homiletic literature produced in honor of St. Martin; notable examples are sermons by St. Peter Damiani,[53] St. Bernard of Clairvaux,[54] and St. Lawrence Giustiniani.[55] The chapter on St. Martin in the *Golden Legend* of Jacobus da Voragine is taken largely from Sulpicius. Renaissance scholars often found his writings to their taste. Petrarch was proud to own a copy of the *Life of St. Martin*,[56] and Coluccio Salutati of Florence had the Martinian writings of Sulpicius and Gregory of Tours copied in a magnificent volume which later belonged to Cosimo de' Medici and to the Dominicans of San Marco.[57] Sulpicius's *Martiniana* were first printed (Milan *ca.* 1479) in the *Sanctuarium* of Boninus Mombritius. There are several other incunable editions and a neat pocket-size Aldine printing of 1501. The subsquent bibliography is very extensive.

In one matter the *Dialogues* ran afoul of censure. In the final chapter of the second *Dialogue* is a report of St. Martin's teaching about the coming end of the world. Various features of his doctrine, as Sulpicius reports Gallus stating it, were unacceptable to St. Jerome. His condemnation of the passage is found in the *Commentary on Ezechiel*,[58] and it is here that he makes the mention of Sulpicius, already referred to. St. Jerome's condemnation seems not to have been without effect, for in the manuscripts we frequently find the offending passage

---

53 Latin text in *PL* 144.815ff.

54 Latin text in *PL* 183.489ff.

55 *Sermo* 33. San Lorenzo, Patriarch of Venice (d. 1455); feast day, September 5.

56 Cf. his *Epistulae de rebus senilibus* 8.6, as quoted by P. de Nolhac, *Pétrarque et l'humanisme* (Paris 1907) 2.211, who adds that Petrarch had a very special admiration for Sulpicius (that is, for the Martinian writings—he does not appear to have known the *Chronicles*).

57 The manuscript is now in the Biblioteca Nazionale of Florence (*Conv. soppr. I.VI.18*); cf. the present writer's *Da Prato* 38, n. 3.

58 *Comm. in Ezech.* 11.36 (*PL* 25.339). The composition of the *Commentary* fell between the years 410 and 414 (or 415).

omitted.[59] Nor was St. Jerome alone in taking exception. A portion of a decree traditionally ascribed to Pope Gelasius I (492-496) is, in some sense, the first 'Index of Prohibited Books.'[60] The writings there listed are to be 'avoided by Catholics,' and include *Opuscula Postumiani et Galli apocrypha*—surely, the *Dialogues* of Sulpicius, even if Postumianus and Gallus are apparently named as authors rather than as speakers in a conversation recorded by Sulpicius. Gennadius's statement that Sulpicius was won over in his old age to the Pelagian heresy may have caused the listing of his *Dialogues* in the 'Gelasian Decree,' but it is still more likely that St. Jerome's criticism prompted their inclusion. It is universally agreed, however, that Pope Gelasius is not the author of the decree that bears his name; who composed that portion of it that contains the list of 'Books Not to be Received' is uncertain, as is also, in consequence, the precise juridical force of the list at the time of its issue. What is clear is that, both before the date of the list and since, the *Dialogues*, like the other works of Sulpicius on St. Martin, have been consistently read by responsible Catholics and have provided teachers of Catholic morality, among them Pope Benedict XIV (1740-1758),[61] with more than one outstanding example of Christian perfection.

The present translation is based primarily on the text

59 Cf. Babut 301ff. and Chase 60. Cf. the frequent omission (or displacement) of a section in *Dial.* 3 (cf. *Dial.* 3.15 n. 1).

60 Latin text in *PL* 59 (col. 163B for the relevant entry; cf. col. 161C and 162A); or in the edition of E. von Dobschütz, in A. Harnack *et al.* (eds.), *Texte und Untersuchungen* . . ., 38, 4 (Leipzig 1912) 11f. (cf. 312). Cf. H. Denzinger-J. B. Umberg, *Enchiridion symbolorum* . . . ed. 21-23, Freiburg im Breisgau 1937) nos. 162-166 (esp. no. 166); at p. 79, n. 1 the statement that the section of the decree dealing with 'Books Not to be Received' is, as it were (*quasi*), the first 'Index.'

61 *Op. cit.* (above, n. 12), III.xli.14, III.xli.16, IV.i.xxix.8, etc.

edited by Halm (1866) in the first volume of the *Corpus scriptorum ecclesiasticorum Latinorum.* Halm's text has been generally pronounced as far from definitive and a number of scholars have proposed improvements. Among these suggestions, the translator has attempted to consider all that would substantially affect the essential meaning of the text, whether the proposed reading be a conjecture or a neglected manuscript variant. Indication has been made in the notes whereever the translation rests on a reading other than that adopted by Halm. Like other students of Sulpicius's text, the translator is especially indebted to the doctoral dissertation (Lund 1940) of Per Hyltén, *Studien zu Sulpicius Severus.* Hyltén has turned to good use the complete *index verborum* which he prepared as a basis for his studies and which it is to be hoped he will publish, and his examination of the *clausulae* of Sulpicius has furnished scholarship with a helpful criterion for distinguishing among variant readings.

The most recent published English translation of Sulpicius made directly from the Latin is that of Roberts in the *Nicene and Post-Nicene Fathers.*[62] Aside from being very conscientiously done, it has the merit of including with the writings on St. Martin both the *Chronicles* and the seven doubtful letters. The present translator has frequently consulted, and with profit, the German rendering of P. Pius Bihlmeyer, O.S.B., and the especially skillful French rendering of Paul Monceaux.

The notes owe not a little to those of P. Bihlmeyer, but most to the all but inexhaustible commentary of the Oratorian, Girolamo Da Prato,[63] an eighteenth-century scholar of Verona,

62 The English translation of Mary Caroline Watt (London 1928) is based on the French of Paul Monceaux and is bowdlerized.

63 On Da Prato's manuscripts and editorial procedure, see the present writer's *Da Prato* (p. 60f. for notes on Da Prato's life, to which add *Saibantianus* 231, n. 3).

whose work on Sulpicius Severus, taken in all its parts, has never been surpassed.

SELECT BIBLIOGRAPHY

Editions of the Latin Text:

Sulpicii Severi libri qui supersunt recensuit . . . Carolus Halm (*CSEL* 1, Vienna 1866).

Sulpicii Severi opera . . . studio et labore Hieronymi de Prato (2 vols. Verona 1741, 1754). Generally cited below as 'Da Prato, *ed. Sulp.*' Da Prato's edition, less nearly all of its valuable apparatus, was reprinted in A. Gallandus, *Bibl. vet. patrum* (Venice 1772) 8.392ff. and passed thence into *PL* 20.79ff.

A. Lavertujon, *La Chronique de Sulpice Sévère* (2 vols., Paris 1896, 1899). An elaborately annotated edition of the *Chronicles* only.

Translations:

Die Schriften des Sulpicius Severus über den heiligen Martinus . . . übersetzt von P. Pius Bihlmeyer, O.S.B.; in *Bibliothek der Kirchenväter* 20 (Kempten and Munich n. d.).

Saint Martin. Récits de Sulpice Sévère mis en francais avec une introduction par Paul Monceaux (Paris 1927). For an English translation made from the French of Monceaux, see above, Introduction n. 62.

A Select Library of the Nicene and Post-Nicene Fathers, Second Series 11 (New York 1894) 1-122; an English translation of all the writings of Sulpicius Severus by Alexander Roberts.

Manuscripts (*mentioned in the notes to this translation*):

V—Verona, Chapter Library, MS. XXXVIII (36); of the year 517.

D—Dublin, Trinity College, MS. 52 (*Liber Ardmachanus*); of *ca.* 807. Type facsimile in J. Gwynn, *The Book of Armagh* (Dublin 1913); pp. cclxvii-cclxxv contain valuable discussion of the text by Babut.

B—*Codex Brixianus* of Da Prato; identified by Peebles (*Da Prato* 39ff.) with Brescia, Civic Library, MS. *A.VII.13 (of the 15th cent.).

Studies relating primarily to the text:

A. H. Chase, 'The metrical lives of St. Martin of Tours . . .,' *Harvard Studies in Classical Philology* 43 (1932) 51-76.

J. Fürtner, *Textkritische Bemerkungen zu Sulpicius Severus* (Programm, Landshut 1884/1885).

A. Huber, *Die poetische Bearbeitung der Vita S. Martini des Sulpicius Severus durch Paulinus von Périgueux* (Programm, Kempten 1901).

P. Hyltén, *Studien zu Sulpicius Severus* (Diss., Lund 1940).

B. M. Peebles, 'Girolamo Da Prato and his manuscripts of Sulpicius Severus,' *Memoirs of the American Academy in Rome* 13 (1936) 7-65.

———'Da Prato's *Saibantianus* of Sulpicius Severus and its humanistic connections.' *Classical and Mediaeval Studies in Honor of E. K. Rand*, ed. L. W. Jones (New York 1938) 231-244.

J. Zellerer, *Palaeographicae et criticae de Sulpicio Severo Aquitano commentationes* (Diss., Munich 1912).

Other Works:

E.-Ch. Babut, *Saint Martin de Tours* (Paris n. d.); first issued as a series of articles in the *Revue d'histoire et de littérature religieuses,* N. S. 1 (1910)—3 (1912). See also above under *Manuscripts*: *D.*

J.-M. Besse, *Les moines de l'ancienne France* (Archives de la France monastique 2) (Paris 1906).

M. Bloch, 'Saint Martin à propos d'une polémique,' *Revue d'histoire et de littérature religieuses,* N. S. 7 (1921) 44-57.

F. Cabrol-H. Leclercq, *Dictionnaire d'archéologie chrétienne et de liturgie* (Paris 1924—). (*DACL.*)

R. P. Coleman-Norton, 'The use of dialogue in the *Vitae Sanctorum,*' *Journal of Theological Studies* 27 (1925-1926) 388-395.

Corpus scriptorum ecclesiasticorum latinorum (Vienna 1866—). (*CSEL.*)

L. H. Cottineau, O.S.B., *Répertoire topo-bibliographique des abbayes et prieurés* (2 vols., Macon 1935, 1937).

H. Delehaye, S. J., 'Saint Martin et Sulpice Sévère,' *Analecta Bollandiana* 38 (1920) 5-136.

L. Duchesne, *Fastes épiscopaux de l'ancienne Gaule* (3 vols., Paris: 1 [2nd ed. 1907], 2 [2nd ed. 1910], 3[1915]).

E. S. Duckett, *Latin Writers of the Fifth Century* (New York 1930).

Pierre Fabre, *Essai sur la chronologie de l'oeuvre de saint Paulin de Nole* (Paris 1948). Available too late to be used.

T. R. Glover, *Life and Letters in the Fifth Century* (Cambridge 1901; New York 1924) 278-303.

K. P. Harrington, 'The place of Sulpicius in miracle literature,' *Classical Journal* 15 (1919-20) 465-474.

C. Jullian, *Histoire de la Gaule* (8 vols., Paris 1908-1926).

———, 'Remarques critiques sur les sources de la vie et l'oeuvre de Saint Martin,' *Revue des études anciennes* 24 (1922) 37-47, 123-128, 229-235, 303-312; 25 (1923) 49-55, 139-143, 234-250.

P. de Labriolle, *Histoire de la littérature latine chrétienne* (2nd ed., Paris 1924) 508-516; (3rd ed. [revised and enlarged by G. Bardy], Paris 1947) 566-574. There is an English translation by Herbert Wilson (New York 1925).

A. Lecoy de la Marche, *Saint Martin* (3rd ed., Tours n. d.).

A. Longnon, *Géographie de la Gaule au VIème siècle* (Paris 1878).

J. P. Migne, *Patrologiae cursus completus*: *Series Graeca* (161 vols., Paris 1857-1886). (*PG.*)

————, ——— *Series Latina* (221 vols., Paris 1844-1864). (*PL.*)

A. Pauly—G. Wissowa—W. Kroll, *Real-Encyclopädie der classischen Altertumswissenschaft* (Stuttgart 1894—). (PWK.)

E. M. Pickman, *The Mind of Latin Christendom* (New York 1937).

E. K. Rand, 'St. Martin of Tours,' *Bulletin of the John Rylands Library* 11 (1927) 101-109.

Revue des études anciennes (Bordeaux 1899—). (*REA.*)

A. Vacant—E. Mangenot, *Dictionnaire de théologie catholique* (Paris 1903–). (*DTC.*)

LIFE OF SAINT MARTIN, BISHOP AND CONFESSOR[1]

Severus to his beloved brother Desiderius[2]

As to the little book I wrote on the life of St. Martin, I had decided for my part, brother of my soul, to confine it to the paper it was written on and not let it go beyond the walls of my own house. Since I am of a very weak disposition, I wanted to avoid the judgments of men. I was afraid that readers would probably not like the somewhat unpolished style of the book, and that everyone would find me gravely at fault for having had the impudence to usurp a subject which should be reserved for eloquent writers. But I was unable to refuse your insistent requests. (For what expenditure is there which I would not make for love of you, even if it meant a loss to my modesty?) However, I have released the book to you, trusting in my belief that you will reveal it to no one, as you promised. Even so, I am afraid you may prove a door of escape for the book, which, once sent forth, could never be recalled.[3] If this should happen and you should see it being read by anyone, I beg you kindly to ask its readers to weigh its matter rather than its words, and to be patient if its faulty diction jar, perhaps, upon their ears.

1 For the date and other circumstances of composition, see above, p. 86.

2 Not surely identifiable. Probably the addressee of St. Jerome's 47th letter (*PL* 22.492; *CSEL* 54.345) and of the 43rd letter of St. Paulinus of Nola (*PL* 61.382; *CSEL* 29.363). See Seeck in PWK 9.250.

3 The Latin (*emissus semel revocari non queat*) is reminiscent of Horace, *Satires* 1.18.71: *et semel emissum volat irrevocabile verbum.*

It is not upon eloquence that the kingdom of God depends, but upon faith.[4] And let them also remember that the gospel of salvation was preached to the world, not by orators—though, surely, if this had been profitable, the Lord could have managed this as well—but by fishermen.[5] Because I thought it wrong that the virtues of so great a man should lie hidden, I determined, when first I put my mind to writing,[6] not to be ashamed of offenses against rules of grammar. I had never attained to any great knowledge of these matters; whatever smattering I might have once acquired from their study I had totally lost through long disuse. Nevertheless, so that we may be spared so irksome an excuse, suppress the name of the writer, if you are agreeable to this, and let the book be released. To do this, erase the title at the front, so that the page, its voice muted, may speak of its subject matter—that is enough—while being silent as to its author.[7]

Chapter 1

Many people,[1] vainly dedicated to study and worldly renown, have sought to perpetuate the memory of their names

4 Cf. 1 Cor. 4.20.

5 Cf. Paulinus, *Epist.* 5.6. (*PL* 61.170; *CSEL* 29.28f.) : *piscatorum praedicationes Tullianis omnibus et tuis litteris praetulisti.* The letter is addressed to Sulpicius.

6 The Latin closely imitates the opening line of the prologue of Terence's *Andria*: *Poeta quom primum animum ad scribendum adpulit.*

7 The beginning of this sentence is quoted by Remigius of Auxerre, *In artem Donati minorem commentum* 1 (p. 1 Fox) . See also C. Weyman, *Beiträge zur Geschichte der christlich-lateinischen Poesie* (Munich 1926) 211 (imitation by Hucbald) .

1 The Latin (*Plerique mortales studio et gloriae saeculari inaniter dediti*) closely imitates Sallust, *Bellum Catilinae* 2.8: *multi mortales dediti ventri atque somno,* etc. Various other details in this introduction of Sulpicius suggest the early chapters of Sallust's essay. For example, in each an *igitur* ('therefore') opens the sentence in which the exact subject to be discussed is named. On Sulpicius as borrower from Sallust, see Hyltén 4.

through glorifying by their pens the lives of famous men. Although, of course, this has not satisfied the hope of immortality they had conceived, it has none the less achieved some small result. Not only has their own memory been extended (however uselessly), but, through the presentation of exemplary actions of great men, no small degree of emulation has been aroused in their readers. Nevertheless, these labors of theirs have had nothing to do with the eternal and happy life. What profit has come to the authors themselves from the renown of their writings, destined as it is to perish with this world? And as for posterity, what gain has it made through reading of the conflicts of Hector or the disputations of Socrates? Not only is it folly to imitate these men, it is madness not to oppose them with all eagerness. Judging human life only by deeds of the moment, they have consigned their hopes to fables and their souls to the tomb. They have felt obligated to a self-perpetuation which looks solely to the memory of men, when, actually, it is a man's duty to seek eternal life rather than an abiding place in that memory, and this not through writing or fighting or philosophizing, but through living a pious, holy, and God-fearing life. This faulty human reasoning, transmitted in writings, has gained such power that there are now many men completely emulous of an empty philosophy or of that foolish ideal of valor.

Consequently, I thought it would be worth while[2] if I wrote down the life of a very holy man, to serve in turn as an example to others. In this way, readers will be spurred on to true wisdom, to the heavenly warfaring, and to Godlike virtue. In this I am also taking account of my own advantage;[3]

---

2 The Latin (*facturus mihi operae pretium videor*) reflects the beginning of Livy's *History*: *Facturusne operae pretium sim,* etc.

3 Sulpicius may have had in mind a phrase of Cicero's: *non ullius rationem sui commodi ducit* (*Pro Roscio Amerino* 44.128).

yet it is not a place in the vain memory of men that I expect, but an eternal reward from God. Even though my own life has not been such as to permit it to be an example to others, I have taken pains to see that one who is worthy of imitation should not remain in obscurity.

It is, then, the life of St. Martin that I shall begin to write, both what preceded his episcopate and what happened during it, though I surely shall not be able to embrace all the particulars of his career. Indeed, as to those events of which he himself was the sole witness, we are completely in ignorance. Looking for no praise from men, he would have wished to conceal all his miracles,[4] insofar as he could. Even so, among those acts of which I have learned, I have omitted many, thinking it sufficient if only the outstanding ones should be noted. Consideration for my readers required me at the same time to see to it that an excessive mass of material should not weary them. I beg those who will read this to give their trust to what has been written, and to believe that I have set down nothing without full knowledge and proof. Rather than tell falsehoods, I should have preferred to be silent.

Chapter 2

To begin, Martin was a native of Sabaria,[1] a town of the Pannonians, but was reared in Italy, in Ticinum.[2] His parents were not of lowly rank according to worldly standards,

4 Lat. *virtutes*, a word constantly used by Sulpicius to mean miracles. The singular, *virtus*, sometimes designates the saint's miracle-working power.

1 Probably the Savaria of the Roman inscriptions, a city in Upper Pannonia raised to the status of a Roman colony by the Emperor Claudius; generally identified today with Szombathely (German: Steinamanger) in western Hungary. For another identification (Szent Marton near the Benedictine abbey of Martinsberg) and a discussion of the problem, see Lecoy de la Marche 66ff.; Babut 172 n. 4.

2 The present-day Pavia in Italy (prov. Pavia).

but were pagans. His father was first a simple soldier and afterwards military tribune. Martin himself, entering the military service in his youth, served in the cavalry of the imperial guard[3] under Emperor Constantius,[4] and subsequently under Emperor Julian.[5] Yet, this was not of his own accord, for, from almost his first years, he aspired rather to the service of God, his saintly childhood foreshadowing the nobility of his youth. When he was ten years old, against the wish of his parents, he took refuge in a church and demanded to be made a catechumen. With a complete and remarkable dedication to the work of God,[6] he longed, at the age of twelve, for the desert, and would indeed have satisfied his wish if the weakness of his years had not stood in the way. With his spirit, none the less, ever drawn toward monasteries or the Church, he even then in boyhood was reflecting upon what later his devotion was to fulfill. But, when an imperial edict was issued, requiring sons of veterans to be enrolled for military service, he was handed over by his father, who was hostile toward his spiritual actions. Martin was fifteen years old when, arrested and in chains, he was subjected to the military oath. He satisfied himself with the service of a single slave. Yet, by a reversal of roles, it was the master who was the servant. This went so far that Martin generally took off the other's boots, and cleaned them himself. They would

3 Lat. *inter scolares alas*: elite palace troops with no fixed garrison and available to the emperor for special assignments. See art. 'Scolae palatinae' in PWK, 2te Reihe 3.621-624; C. Jullian, in *REA* 12 (1910) 267-270 (a discussion of Martin's military service) and also his *Histoire* 7.256 n. 1.

4 Constantius II, Emperor 337-361.

5 Julian the Apostate, Emperor 361-363. Ch. 4, below, recounts a meeting between Martin and Julian.

6 An early appearance of the phrase *opus Dei* ('God's work'), which here, as also elsewhere in Sulpicius, must mean the whole duty of a Christian; cf. below, Ch. 26. The special meaning ('divine office') found often in the *Rule* of St. Benedict (e.g., Ch. 7) is a natural development.

take their meals together, Martin, however, usually doing the serving.

He was three years under arms before his baptism, yet free from those vices in which such men are commonly involved. His kindness toward his fellow soldiers was great, his charity remarkable, and his patience and humility surpassed human measure. There is no need to praise his temperance; it was such that even then he was considered not a soldier, but a monk. These traits served so to attach his fellows to him that their remarkable affection for him amounted to veneration. None the less he had not yet been reborn in Christ, but was serving a sort of candidacy for baptism through his good works: assisting the sick, bringing help to the wretched, feeding the needy, clothing the naked, reserving nothing from his army pay beyond his daily sustenance. With no thought for the morrow,[7] he even then was not listening with deaf ears to the words of the Gospel.[8]

Chapter 3

One day, at the gate of the city of Amiens,[1] Martin met a poor man who was naked. Martin's clothing was reduced to his armor and his simple military cloak. It was the middle

7 Cf. Matt. 6.34.

8 The Latin phrase, *evangelii non surdus auditor,* also occurs in the previously cited letter of Paulinus to Sulpicius (*Epist.* 5.6: *PL* 61.170; *CSEL* 29.28). Each of these writers has been declared the borrower; see C. Weyman, in *Rheinisches Museum* 53 (1898) 317; E.-Ch. Babut, in *Annales du Midi* 20 (1908) 26. Possibly, both authors were using a current expression (Delehaye 57). Independent derivation from Rom. 2.13 and James 1.22, suggested by Bihlmeyer (22 n. 3), seems unlikely.

1 In the sixth century, the site was marked by an oratory (Gregory of Tours, *De virt. S. Mart.* 1.17) and was subsequently not forgotten; see Longnon, *Géographie* 419.

of a winter which had been more severe than usual, and, indeed, many had perished from the extreme cold. Those who had passed that way had been begged by the pitiable pauper to have compassion on him, but all had gone by. Martin, however, filled with God's grace, saw that it was for him, when others had denied their mercy, that the suppliant was being reserved. Yet, what should he do? He had nothing except the cloak he was wearing; he had already devoted the rest of his clothing to similar purposes. Then, drawing the sword which he was wearing, he cut the cloak in two;[2] one part he gave to the pauper; in the other he again dressed himself. Meanwhile, some of the bystanders began to laugh, for it was an inelegant figure Martin cut, dressed in half a garment. Yet, many, of saner mind, sighed deeply. When they, who had more to give, might have clothed the pauper without making themselves naked, they had done nothing of the sort.

When night had come and he was deep in sleep, Martin beheld Christ, clothed in that part of his own cloak with which he had covered the pauper. He was bidden to look attentively upon the Lord and to recognize the garment he had given. And soon, to the throng of angels standing about, he heard Jesus saying in a clear voice: 'Martin, still a catechumen, has covered me with this cloak.' The Lord, in declaring that it was He who had been clothed in the person of the pauper, was truly mindful of His own words uttered

2 Certainly, the sword and perhaps the cloak were long after believed to have survived as relics. In 1425, a distinguished jurist of Verona, Maggio Maggi, testified that he had seen and touched the sword (see my arts. *Da Prato* 19-22, 59 and *Saibantianus* 263ff.). It is well known that in France, in the early middle ages, a garment (*cappa*), claimed as St. Martin's, was preserved in the royal treasury (see Leclercq in *DACL* 3.1.381-390), but it is uncertain whether the *cappa* was taken to be (part of?) the garment here in question or that which is featured in *Dial.* 2.1, below.

long ago: 'As long as you did it to one of these my least, you did it to me.'[3] Further, to strengthen the evidence of such a good deed, He deigned to show Himself in the very garment the pauper had received.

The blessed man was not puffed up with human pride because of this vision. Rather, recognizing God's goodness in his own act, he was baptized without delay. (He was then eighteen.[4]) But he did not immediately renounce military service, won over by the prayers of his tribune, whom Martin accompanied on terms of intimate friendship. This officer promised that he would renounce the world upon the completion of the term of his tribunate. Held in suspense by this expectation, Martin, for about two years after his baptism, remained a soldier, though only in name.

Chapter 4

In the meantime, the barbarians were invading the Gallic provinces. Assembling an army at the city of the Vangiones,[1] Emperor Julian prepared to distribute a bonus[2] to his troops. The men were called up in the customary manner, one by one, until Martin's turn came. He recognized that moment as a suitable time to ask for his discharge, and he did not think it would be honest for him to accept the bonus when he did not intend to fight. 'I have fought for you up to this point,' he

---

3 Matt. 25.40.

4 Excellent MSS. (*V, D*) fix Martin's age at twenty-two, instead. This passage contributes to the confusion which surrounds the chronology of St. Martin's life. See above, pp. 91-92.

---

1 Worms. Jullian dates the episode in 356: *REA* 12 (1910) 264; *Histoire* 7.256 n. 2. In one solution of the chronological problem presented by Martin's career (see above, p. 92) the event here narrated is dated much earlier, in the reign of Constans (337-350). See Delehaye 25f.

2 Lat. *donativum.*

said to Caesar. 'Now let me fight for God. As for your bonus, let someone who is going to join the battle receive it. I am a soldier of Christ: combat is not permitted me.'[3] Confronted with this speech, the tyrant fumed and said it was fear of the battle which was to occur the next day that was causing him to refuse participation, not any religious motive. Martin undismayed, was made all the bolder by the attempt to intimidate him. 'If my act is set down to cowardice rather than to faith,' he said, 'I shall stand unarmed tomorrow before our lines. In the name of the Lord Jesus and protected only by the sign of the cross, without shield or helmet, I shall penetrate the enemy's ranks and not be afraid.' The order was given that he should be put under guard: he was to make good his promise to be exposed, unarmed, to the barbarians.

The next day, the enemy sent an embassy to sue for peace, handing over themselves and all that was theirs. From this can anyone doubt that the victory was due to the blessed man—a grace granted to prevent his being sent unarmed into combat? True, the Lord, in His goodness, could have preserved His soldier even among swords and spears. Yet, to prevent the gaze of the saint from being outraged even by the death of others, He removed the need of the battle. This was exactly the kind of victory Christ ought to have granted for His soldier's sake—a capitulation of the enemy in which no one died and no blood was shed.

Chapter 5

Upon leaving military service, Martin sought out St. Hilary, the bishop of the city of Poitiers, a man conspicuous at that

3 Apparently, Martin wished to avoid having to shed human blood. His legal and moral position in this case has been the subject of extended discussion: see Leclercq in *DACL* 11.1150-1152; E. Vacandard, *Etudes de critique et d'histoire religieuses,* 2ème Série (Paris 1910) 164, 253-263.

time in the things of God and renowned for his steadfast faith.[1] While Martin remained with him for a while, Hilary attempted to impose the office of deacon upon him, and thus join him more closely to himself and win him to the divine ministry. But Martin insisted upon his unworthiness and repeatedly resisted. Then the bishop, a man of deep insight, realized that the one way to compel him was to impose upon him an office which would seem to involve some measure of humiliation. Accordingly, he bade him be an exorcist. This grade Martin did not refuse, lest he seem to despise it as too humble for himself.[2]

Not long after that, he was advised in his sleep to go to his native land and in a spirit of religious zeal to visit his parents, who were still pagans. He set out with the consent of St. Hilary, but obligated by the bishop's repeated and tearful urging to return. The report is that he was sad as he began that pilgrimage. He called the brothers to witness that he would experience many adversities—a prediction borne out by subsequent events.

First of all, following a by-road in crossing the Alps, he fell among highwaymen. One of them had his axe poised for a blow upon Martin's head, when another checked the assassin's hand. None the less, his arms tied behind his back, Martin was turned over to one of the highwaymen, who was to guard and strip him. He led Martin to a retired spot and began asking him who he was. Martin replied he was a Christian. The other then asked him whether he was afraid,

1 Martin's meeting with St. Hilary (Bishop of Poitiers, *ca.* 350-367) occurred before the latter was banished to Phrygia by order of Constantius (356); see Jullian in *REA* 12 (1910) 270-272. Hilary's return (below, Ch. 6) took place in 360 or 361.

2 As members of the lower clergy, exorcists are known at Rome from the third century on. The hierarchy of the minor orders (as finally fixed in the West) is as follows, beginning from the lowest: porter, lector, exorcist, acolyte. A lector appears in Ch. 9, below.

to which Martin with great firmness declared he had never been so safe, knowing that the Lord's mercy would be found especially in moments of trial; the grief he felt was rather for his captor, who, in practising brigandage, was unworthy of the mercy of Christ. Then, through an explanation of the Gospel, he began preaching the word of God to the highwayman. To make the story short, the highwayman believed. He went with Martin and put him again on his road, begging that he pray to the Lord for him. Later, this same man led a God-fearing life. In fact, what I have just related is told as heard from his own mouth.

Chapter 6

When Martin, continuing his journey, had gone past Milan, the Devil, in human form, met him on the way and asked him where he was going. When he had received from Martin the answer that he was going to where the Lord was calling him, the Devil said to him: 'Wherever you go or whatever you attempt, the Devil will oppose you.' Then Martin answered, in the words of the Prophet: 'The Lord is my helper: I will not fear what man can do unto me.'[1] And instantly, the enemy vanished from his sight.

To continue, he delivered his mother from the error of paganism, fulfilling the hope his heart and mind had conceived. Though his father persevered in unbelief, Martin brought salvation to many through his example.

At this time, the Arian heresy was gaining strength throughout the whole world, but especially in Illyria.[2] Against the errors of the bishops, Martin was almost alone in making

1 Ps. 117.6.

2 Of high importance in the history of Arianism in this period are synods held in the (secular) 'Diocese' of Illyricum: at Sardica (343) and at Sirmium (five: 347-359).

determined opposition; in return, he was subjected to many punishments: he was publicly scourged with rods and finally compelled to abandon the city.[3] He proceeded again to Italy. He found that St. Hilary had been forced into exile by the violence of the heretics and that, at his departure, the Church in the Gallic provinces also was in great trouble. Consequently, he established for himself a monastery in Milan. Here also, Auxentius,[4] leader and chief of the Arians, bitterly persecuted him, and, after inflicting many injuries, drove him from the city. And so, Martin decided he should yield to the circumstances. He retired to an island named Gallinaria,[5] accompanied by a priest, a man of very great virtues. Here he lived for a while on the roots of herbs. It was during this time that he ate some hellebore, a plant generally considered poisonous. But, when he felt the power of the poison working within him and death near at hand, he repulsed the imminent peril through prayer, and at once all the pain left him.

Not long afterwards, he learned that the emperor's change of heart had permitted St. Hilary to return.[6] Martin sought to meet him at Rome and set out for the city.

Chapter 7

Since Hilary had already gone ahead, Martin followed after. He was welcomed by the bishop most graciously. Not far from the town he set up a monastery for himself.[1] It was

3 Presumably, Martin's native Sabaria.

4 Arian bishop of Milan 355-374, for two decades the mainstay of Arianism in the West.

5 A rocky island off the Ligurian coast, nearly opposite the city of Albenga (prov. Savona). Named for the fowl (*gallinae rusticae*) which inhabited it (Varro, *De re rustica* 3.9.17; Columella, *De re rustica* 8.2).

6 See above, Ch. 5 n. 1.

1 The later Monasterium Locogiacum; now Ligugé, near Poitiers; bibliography in Cottineau, *Répertoire* 1613.

at this time that there joined him a catechumen eager to be instructed by the discipline of so holy a man. A few days later, the catechumen was seized with faintness and fell sick with a violent fever. Martin happened to be away at the time and after three days' absence returned to find a lifeless body. Death had come so suddenly that the catechumen had expired without being baptized. The body had been laid out and the sorrowing brothers were busily performing their sad duties upon it, when Martin came running up, weeping and lamenting. Then his whole mind was suffused with the Holy Spirit. He told all the others to leave the cell in which the body lay. He barred the door and stretched himself upon the lifeless body of the dead brother.[2] For some time he gave himself to prayer and perceived through the Spirit that the virtue of the Lord was present. Lifting himself up somewhat and with his gaze fixed upon the face of the dead man, he awaited with confidence the outcome of his own prayers and of the mercy of the Lord. Hardly two hours had elapsed before he saw all the limbs of the dead man move little by little and his eyes quiver as they opened, once more to see. Then, turning to the Lord with a loud voice and giving thanks, Martin filled the whole cell with his cry of joy. On hearing this, those who had been standing outside the door at once rushed in. Wonderful spectacle: they saw alive one whom they had abandoned as dead.[3]

The catechumen, restored to life, at once received baptism and lived for many years afterwards: he, indeed, was the first to furnish us proof or tangible evidence of Martin's miracles. The same man used to tell what happened to him when he was stripped of his body. He had been led to the Judge's tribunal and had received a sentence that destined

---

2 Martin's action here and in the similar case described in the next chapter recalls those of Elias and Eliseus in 3 Kings 17.21, 4 Kings 4.34.

3 Sulpicius records two other cases in which Martin raised the dead; see the following chapter and *Dial.* 2.4.

him with the vulgar crowd to regions of darkness. Then, word was brought to the Judge by two angels that this was the man for whom Martin was praying. Consequently, the two angels were ordered to have him led back, restored to Martin, and re-established in his former life. From this time on, the reputation of the blessed Martin rose in brilliance. Already held to be a saint, he was now regarded as powerful in wonders and truly apostolic.[4]

Chapter 8

Not long afterwards, while Martin was going across the property of a certain Lupicinus,[1] a man of distinguished worldly position, the grief-stricken cries of a throng of mourners caught his ear. Martin was concerned at this, and approached. Asking what the mourning was, he was told one of the household, a young slave, had taken his own life by hanging. On learning this, Martin entered the cell where the body lay. He cleared the room of the thronging spectators and, stretching himself upon the body, prayed for a while. Soon, life began to return to the features of the dead man, as his still languid eyes were lifted to look into the face of Martin.[2] Forcing himself slowly to rise and grasping the hand of the blessed man, he stood up. Then, accompanied by Martin as the whole crowd looked on, he walked to the vestibule of the house.

---

4 The same impressive claim is made in the *Chronica* 2.50 (see below, p. 253) and in *Epist.* 1 and 2 (below, p. 142 and 149); cf. *Dial.* 2.5; also above, Introduction, p. 82 n. 12.

---

1 Possibly identical with a Lupicinus who was consul in 367 (PWK 26.1844), but see Da Prato, *ed. Sulp.*, 1.333f.

2 'Still languid eyes': I have used the reading *marcentibus oculis.* On the doubtful text, see Hyltén 132.

Chapter 9

At about this time, Martin was sought as bishop for the church in Tours. Since he could not easily be attracted away from his monastery, one of the men of Tours, a certain Rusticius,[1] pretending that his wife was ill, threw himself at Martin's knees and thus prevailed on him to set out. Groups of citizens had already been placed at intervals along the route, so that it was under something resembling a guard that he was brought to the city. An incredibly large number of people—not only from Tours but from nearby localities —had assembled to voice their vote.[2] Among them all there was one single will, one prayer, one judgment: Martin was the most worthy to be bishop; the church would be fortunate which had such as he for its head. Yet, there were a few men —among them some of the bishops who had been called together to ordain the future prelate—who set up an unscrupulous opposition. He was a contemptible person, they said; a man so unpresentable in his appearance, shabbily dressed, with unkempt hair, was unworthy of the episcopate. This stupid opposition was laughed down, however, by the general public, whose judgment was saner. The attempts to revile the illustrious man only served to extol him. And the only course that lay open to them was to do what the populace, inspired by the Lord's will, thought best.

Now, among the bishops who were present, a certain Defensor[3] is said to have been most bitter in his opposition. It was this fact which brought people to notice how he was

1 The name is uncertain. The MSS. show also *Rusticus, Ruritius, Ruricius.*

2 The role of laymen in the election of bishops was at that time large; see Leclercq in *DACL* 4.2618ff.

3 Bishop of Angers. Cf. Duchesne, *Fastes épiscopaux* 2.356.

infamously branded by a reading from the Prophets.[4] It happened that the lector whose turn it was to recite the lesson that day had been blocked by the congregation and was not at his place. The ministers were thrown into confusion. While the absent lector was awaited, one of the bystanders seized the psalter and pounced upon the first verse he found. And the psalm was this:[5] 'Out of the mouth of infants and of sucklings thou hast perfected praise, because of thy enemies, that thou mayst destroy the enemy and the defender' [*defensorem*]. At this reading the congregation lifted up its voice; the party of the opposition was confounded. It was held that the Divine Will had caused that psalm to be read, so that a judgment upon his work might be heard by Defensor: when the praise of the Lord had been perfected in the person of Martin, it was he who, out of the mouth of infants and of sucklings, had been both denounced as the enemy and destroyed.

Chapter 10

It is not within our power to describe the quality and grandeur of Martin's life, once he had assumed the office of bishop.[1] What he had been before, he firmly continued to be.

---

4 Evidence that in the rite followed at Tours at this time there was a lesson from the Old Testament in addition to the two lessons drawn from the New.

5 Ps. 8.3. The text quoted varies from the Vulgate chiefly in the last word, the key of Sulpicius's story. Here we find *defensorem* instead of *ultorem* ('avenger') or *vindicatorem*. St. Augustine, *Enarrationes in psalmos* 102.14 (*PL* 37.1328), reports *defensorem* as the reading of certain psalters and in fact uses the word in his *Enarratio* of Ps. 8 (6; *PL* 36.111). *Defensorem* is the reading of the *Psalterium Romanum* (*PL* 29.130) and the word is found in two quotations made by Paulinus of Nola from Ps. 8.3: *Epist.* 23.27 and 24.22 (*PL* 61.275, 299; *CSEL* 29. 184, 222).

---

1 As to the date of Martin's ordination as bishop, while there is no reason to question July 4 as the day of the month (Gregory of Tours, *Hist. Franc.* 2.14), the year is uncertain: 371 or 370 according to Delehaye (p. 31), 372 according to Duchesne (*Fastes épiscopaux* 2.302).

There was the same humility in his heart, the same poverty in his dress. Lacking nothing in authority and grace, he fulfilled the dignity of a bishop, yet did not abandon the virtuous resolve of a monk. So, for a while he used a cell attached to the church. Then, unable to bear up under the distraction caused by throngs of visitors, he set up for himself a monastery some two miles outside the city.[2]

This location was so sheltered and remote that it could have been a desert solitude. On one side it was hedged in by the sheer rock of a high mountain; on the other the plain was closed in by a little bend of the River Loire. Approach was possible by a single path, and that a very narrow one. Martin himself occupied a cell built of wood. While many of the brothers had similar shelters, the majority fashioned lodgings for themselves carved out of the rock of the overhanging mountain. The disciples numbered about eighty, all forming themselves after the model of their blessed master. No one there had anything as his own; all property was brought together for common holding. It was illicit to buy or to sell anything (as is the practice of many monks). No art was practised there except that of the copyist,[3] and to this work only the more youthful were assigned; the elders had their time free for prayer. Rarely was anyone found outside his own cell, except when they came together at the place of prayer. All had meals in common and after the hour of fasting. All abstained from wine, except when compelled by illness. The majority were dressed in camel's hair; the use of any softer

---

2 The later *Maius monasterium,* Marmoutier, across the Loire from the old city of Tours, bibliography in Cottineau, *Répertoire* 1762ff. A visit to the site furnishes even today an instructive commentary on the present chapter.

3 An early start for the fine tradition of book-copying maintained at Tours. The importance of this provision of the rule followed at Marmoutier was duly noted by Ludwig Traube, *Vorlesungen und Abhandlungen* 2 (Munich 1911) 127.

clothing was held a serious offense. This must be regarded as all the more remarkable, in that many of the monks were thought to be nobles who, after a far different upbringing, had constrained themselves to such practices of humility and patience. A number of them we later saw as bishops.[4] And what city or what church would not have wished for itself a bishop from Martin's monastery?

Chapter 11

Now I come to treat of other miracles of his, those he performed while bishop. Not far from the town and very close to the monastery was a place[1] which enjoyed a certain sanctity because of the mistaken opinion that martyrs were buried there. Even an altar was maintained, erected there by former bishops. But Martin was disinclined to believe what was uncertain. He kept asking those who were older, priests and clerics alike, to reveal the name of the martyr and the date of his martyrdom. He felt, he said, considerable scruple in the matter, since nothing certain had been handed down by any reliable report from his predecessors. He himself abstained from visiting the place for a while: he neither disparaged the cult, since his own position was uncertain, nor granted the populace the support of his authority, lest he fortify a superstition. One day, taking a few of the brothers

4 On the disciples of St. Martin, see Lecoy de la Marche 351ff. Dom J.-M. Besse, Benedictine of Ligugé, has an excellent chapter on St. Martin's monks in his *Les moines de l'ancienne France* 1-33.

1 The place in question—a village called Calitonnum—is named in the relevant section of a group of chapter-headings for Sulpicius's *Life of St. Martin* found in a number of MSS. of which the earliest date from the eighth and ninth centuries. The locality is probably identical with a *vicus* of nearly identical spelling named by Gregory of Tours, *Hist. Franc.* 10.31, for which see Longnon, *Géographie* 267 f.; Lecoy de la Marche 207 n. 5. The exemplary value of Martin's action in the episode described in this chapter is noted by an anonymous Bollandist in *Analecta Bollandiana* 20 (1901) 340.

with him, he went to the place. He stood upon the tomb itself and prayed to the Lord to reveal who was buried there and what his merits were. He then turned to the left and saw standing near him a grim, unclean spirit. He ordered him to speak out his name and his deserts. The spirit announced his name and confessed his criminal life: formerly a brigand, he had been executed for his crimes and was receiving veneration through the mistaken opinion of the populace; he had nothing in common with the martyrs—heavenly glory was their portion; punishment, his. Strange wonder: those who were with Martin heard the voice, yet saw no one. Martin then recounted what he had seen and ordered the altar which had been in that place to be removed. Thus he freed the people from the error of that superstition.

Chapter 12

Somewhat later, while he was making a journey, it chanced that he met the funeral procession of a pagan. While the body was being carried to the tomb with superstitious rites, he saw the attendant throng approaching from a distance. Not knowing what it was, he halted for a while. The distance between was some five hundred paces, so that it was hard to distinguish what he saw. Still, because it was a band of peasants, and cloths laid over the body were flapping in the breeze, he concluded that pagan rites of sacrifice were being celebrated. (For it was a custom of the Gauls of the countryside to cover images of demons with white cloths and carry them around their fields amid frenzied lamentation.) Martin then raised his hand and made the sign of the cross in the direction of the oncoming peasants, ordering them to stand firm and to lay down their load. Then you could have seen a wonderful thing: the wretched folk first stiffen as into stone, then, bending all their efforts to advance but unable to move, whirl about in place, executing ridiculous pirouettes. Overcome in the end, they laid down the body they were carrying. They were amazed and, looking at one another in silence, wondered what could have happened to them. The blessed man, however, on learning that the company were concerned with a funeral, not with sacrifices, raised his hand once more and thus gave them power to advance and carry off the body. We see then that, when he wished, he compelled them to halt, and, when it pleased him, he permitted them to go on their way.

Chapter 13

At another time, Martin had destroyed a very ancient temple in a certain village. And when he attempted to cut down a pine tree which was near the shrine, the priest[1] of the place and the rest of the band of pagans began to oppose him. These same men, who, by the will of the Lord, were quiet during the demolition of the temple, could not endure the cutting down of the tree. Martin's urging was diligent: there was no religious value in a tree trunk; rather, let them follow the God whose servant he was; the tree was dedicated to a demon and so deserved to be cut down. Then, one of the crowd, bolder than others, said: 'If you have any faith in this God of yours whom you say you worship, we ourselves will cut down the tree, provided you stand under and receive the fall. If your Lord is with you, as you say, you will escape.' Martin, steadfastly trusting in the Lord, promised he would do so. And to this arrangement that entire company of pagans agreed: they were resigned to the loss

1 Halm's reading of the singular *antistes* has been retained, but see Hyltén 134, who supports the plural.

of their tree, if only through its fall they could destroy the enemy of their rites.

Since the tree leaned to one side, so that there was no doubt in what direction it would crash when cut, Martin was bound and placed at a point chosen by the peasants and where no one doubted the tree would fall. They themselves then began hewing down their own pine tree with joy and gladness. At a distance stood a crowd of wondering bystanders. Now, little by little, the pine began swaying and threatening ruin by its fall. From their distant stand the monks grew pale, and, as the peril came nearer, in their terror they lost all hope and faith, expecting nothing other than the death of Martin. But, he waited with steadfast confidence in the Lord. The pine cracked as it finally was cut through. It now began to fall, it now began to crash upon him, when he finally raised his hand and made the sign of salvation in its direction. The tree—and you would have likened its backward action to a tornado—crashed in just the opposite direction, so that it all but overwhelmed the peasants who, as they thought, had taken places of safety. The pagans, stupified by the miracle, raised a great shout to heaven, while the monks wept for joy; all joined in exalting the name of Christ. It is generally agreed that salvation came to that region on that day. There was almost no one, out of the vast number of pagans who inhabited it, who failed to receive the long-awaited laying-on of hands[2] and, abandoning the error of impiety, to believe in the Lord Jesus. Yet in fact, before Martin came, very few in those parts, or, rather, almost none, had received the name of Christ. Through Martin's miracles and example, the faith gained such strength that you can now find no place without its many monasteries or much-frequented churches.

---

2 Whereby they became catechumens; cf. *Dial.* 2.4. end.

For it was Martin's custom, wherever he destroyed pagan shrines, to replace them with churches or monasteries.[3]

Chapter 14

At about this same time, he performed a similar, but no less impressive, miracle. In a certain village he had set fire to a very ancient and celebrated shrine. Globes of flame, driven by the wind, were being carried to a dwelling which was near by, or, rather, attached. When Martin perceived this, he ran quickly, scaled the roof of the house, and set himself in the path of the oncoming flames. Then, in a completely marvelous way, you could have seen the fire turn back upon itself, in direct opposition to the driving force of the wind; there seemed to be a conflict among the very elements as they strove against one another. Through Martin's miraculous power the force of the fire operated only where it was bid.

In a village named Leprosum[1] there was a temple which superstitious devotion had erected in great splendor. When, as before, Martin wished to overturn it, he was resisted by a crowd of pagans. Indeed, he was repulsed, and not without injury. He withdrew to a place near by and, covering himself with sackcloth and ashes, applied himself for three days to fasting and prayer. Because human hands had not succeeded in overturning the temple, he prayed the Lord to

3 A chapter (7) of nearly a hundred pages in Lecoy de la Marche is devoted to churches dedicated to St. Martin; see also his Appendix 2. While a number of these foundations doubtless date from the bishop's own vigorous apostolate, the warning of Delehaye (p. 115) against an exaggerated use of such evidence is in order.

1 *Leprosum* (spelling doubtful) may be the present-day Levroux, situated between Châteauroux and Valencay (dep. Indre) (Lecoy de la Marche 277), but the identification is questioned by Babut 208 n. 1.

use divine power to destroy it. Suddenly, two angels appeared before him, armed, in the manner of the heavenly host, with spears and shields. They had been sent by the Lord, they said, to put the peasant throng to rout and to lend aid to Martin, so that there would be no resistance while the temple was being destroyed; he was to go back and devoutly achieve the work he had begun. So, he returned to the village and, with the pagan crowds quietly looking on, demolished the profane edifice to its foundations, reducing all its altars and images to dust. The peasants, seeing this, realized that it was the Divine Will that had brought stupor and fear upon them, to prevent them from opposing the bishop. Nearly all believed in the Lord Jesus, making an open confession as they cried aloud that Martin's God should be worshipped and that their idols, unable to help themselves,[2] should be abandoned.

Chapter 15

I shall now relate what happened in the country of the Aedui.[1] Here, also, when Martin was beginning to overturn a temple, a frenzied crowd of pagan peasants rushed upon him. As one of their number, bolder than the others, was making for him with a drawn sword, Martin threw off his mantle and extended his bared neck to the blow. The pagan showed no hesitation about striking, but, in raising his arm somewhat too high, he fell over backwards. Thrown into consternation by divinely inspired fear, he begged for mercy.

The following incident was similar. As Martin was destroy-

2 The reading commonly followed before Da Prato's edition, *sibi adesse non possent*, has been restored. Apparently supported by Babut 229 and Delehaye 55, it has the almost universal support of the MSS., and Da Prato's conjecture, adopted by Halm, was based on a misreading of the old Verona MS. (*V*), which shows *nec sibi adesse non posset.*

1 The chief city of the region was Augustudunum, the present Autun.

ing some idols, someone tried to strike him with a knife. While the man was in the very act of delivering the blow, the weapon flew out of his hands and disappeared.

Often, however, when the peasants opposed his efforts to destroy their shrines, Martin's saintly preaching so softened the hearts of the pagans that the light of truth was revealed to them and they themselves overturned their temples.

Chapter 16

In the matter of healing, Martin had such a power of grace within him that hardly anyone who was sick approached him without at once recovering health. A clear example will be found in the following incident.[1]

At Trèves, a girl lay ill in the grip of a fearful paralysis. For a long time she could make no use of her body for the needs of human life. Already dead in all her members, her body breathed feebly and barely pulsed with life. Her kin were standing by, awaiting only her funeral, when suddenly the news was brought that Martin had come to that city. When the girl's father learned this, he ran breathlessly to beseech him on behalf of his daughter. As it happened, Martin had already entered the church. There, under the eyes of the people and in the presence of many other bishops, the old man, waiting, embraced his knees and said: 'My daughter is dying from a terrible kind of sickness. Her condition is more cruel than death itself: it is only through breathing that she lives; in her flesh she is already dead. I beg you to come to her and bless her, for I have faith that she can be restored to health through you.' These words confused and astonished Martin, and he drew back, saying that the grace required for

1 What appears to be another version of the miracle which follows is found in *Dial.* 3.2; see n. 4 there.

such an act was not his. The old man's judgment had misled him, he said; he was unworthy to be an agent for the manifestation of the Lord's power. The father persisted, weeping more bitterly and praying him to visit the lifeless girl. Finally, the bishops who stood about compelled him to go, and he went down to the girl's house. A great crowd was waiting before the door to see what the servant of God would do. Using the means which were familiar to him in situations of this kind, he first prostrated himself upon the floor and prayed. Then he looked at the sick girl and asked that some oil be given him. He blessed the potent and sanctified fluid and poured it into the girl's mouth. At once, her voice was restored to her. Then, at his touch, her members one by one began gradually to regain life, until, with the people there to witness it, strength returned to her limbs and she arose.

Chapter 17

In the same period, a slave of a certain proconsul, Taetradius,[1] had been possessed by a demon and was suffering terrible torture. Martin, asked to lay his hand upon him, ordered that the man be brought to him. The evil spirit, however, could in no way be brought out of the little room where he was; against those who came near he raged and bared his teeth. Then, Taetradius threw himself at the knees of the blessed man and begged him to go down to the house where the possessed man was. At this, Martin said that he could not come to the house of a profane and pagan person (for Taetradius was at that time still entangled in the error of paganism). So, Taetradius promised to become a Christian

1 Da Prato (*ed. Sulp.* 1.340) suggests possible identification of this Taetradius with the addressee of a poem of Ausonius (18.11) or with a person of the same name addressed in Sidonius, *Epist.* 3.10 and also named by the same author in *Carm.* 24.81.

if the demon should be driven out of the boy. Martin then laid his hand upon the boy and expelled the unclean spirit. When Taetradius saw this, he believed in the Lord Jesus. He was made a catechumen at once and not long afterwards was baptized. Since it was to Martin that he attributed his salvation, he always showed him a wonderful affection.

In the same town and at about the same time, Martin, on entering the dwelling of a certain householder, halted at the very threshold, saying that he saw a horrible demon in the vestibule of the house. When Martin ordered him to depart, he took possession of the householder's cook,[2] who stayed in the inner part of the house. The wretched man madly began to bite and to lacerate whoever confronted him. The household was alarmed, the slaves thrown into confusion, the people reduced to flight. Martin threw himself before the maniac and, first, ordered him to stand still. When the other gnashed his teeth and, with mouth agape, threatened to bite him, Martin thrust his fingers into his mouth. 'If you have any power,' he said, 'bite these.' Then, as if he had taken a white-hot iron in his throat, the possessed man drew back his teeth so as to avoid touching the fingers of the blessed man. The pains and tortures he was suffering were forcing the demon to leave the possessed body, yet he could not get out through the mouth. So, leaving behind a track of filth, he was expelled in a discharge from the bowels.

Chapter 18

Meanwhile, the city[1] was thrown into confusion by a sud-

2 The well-attested reading *cocum patris familiae* has been adopted; it is favored by Zellerer (58f.) and by Chase, in *Harvard Studies in Classical Philology* 43 (1932) 69.

1 Probably, Trèves.

den rumor that the barbarians were on the move and would attack. Martin had a possessed man brought to him and ordered him to declare whether the report was true. The maniac confessed that he had ten demons with him who had spread the rumor among the people, hoping that fear of the attack, if nothing else, would drive Martin from the city; nothing was farther from the minds of the barbarians than an invasion. This confession, made by the unclean spirit in the middle of the church, freed the city from the fear which was then troubling it.

At Paris, while Martin, accompanied by vast crowds, was entering a gate of the city,[2] he saw a leper. The others all were moved to horror by the leper's lamentable appearance, but Martin kissed him and blessed him. Instantly, he was completely cleansed, and the next day, his skin glistening clear, he came to the church and gave thanks for the recovery of his health. Mention also should be made of the fact that threads removed from Martin's clothing or hair shirt worked frequent cures upon the sick. Twisted about the fingers or placed on the neck, these fibres frequently expelled illness from diseased bodies.

Chapter 19

Arborius,[1] the former prefect, a pious and God-fearing man, had a daughter who suffered gravely from the burning heat of a quartan fever. A letter of Martin's had been brought to him by chance. This letter, when the fever was again intense,

2 The Porte-Saint-Martin seems to have been named in commemoration of this episode. The site of the miracle was marked by a chapel in the sixth century (Gregory of Tours, *Hist. Franc.* 8.33).

1 Magnus Arborius of Bordeaux, nephew of the poet Ausonius, in 380 *praefectus praetorio* at Rome: Seeck in PWK 2.420. Arborius is named as a witness in *Dial.* 3.10.

he placed on the girl's chest; instantly, the fever departed. The event had such an effect on Arborius that he at once promised the girl to God and dedicated her to perpetual virginity. He then went to Martin and presented to him the girl who had been cured through him, even though he was absent—a visible witness of his miraculous powers. Arborius would not have it otherwise than that she should receive the habit of virginity from Martin himself and be consecrated by him.

Paulinus,[2] a man whose example was destined to be very powerful, was undergoing severe pain in one of his eyes, the pupil already covered by a thick film. Martin touched his eye with a little sponge. The pain passed completely away and he was restored to his former health.

One day, Martin chanced somehow or other to fall from an upper story. Tumbling down the rough steps of the stairway, he injured himself in several places. He lay nearly lifeless in his cell under the tortures of excessive pain. In the night he saw an angel wash his wounds and anoint the bruises on his mangled body with a healing ointment. On the day following, he had been so restored to health that you would have thought he had received no harm at all.

But it would be tedious to relate the miracles one by one. Let these suffice, even though they be few among many. And we must be satisfied if, in presenting the more outstanding, we have not detracted from the truth and have at the same time avoided being tedious by offering too many.

Chapter 20

To such impressive examples we shall now add others of

2 On the distinguished Paulinus (of Nola), see above, p. 81f; also below, Ch. 25 and *Dial.* 1.23, 3.17.

less moment—although, given the character of our times, in which there is universal degradation and corruption, it seems almost an extraordinary thing for the firmness of a bishop not to sink to adulation of an emperor. To the court of Emperor Maximus[1]—a man of ferocious temper and full of pride through his victory in the civil wars—there had come together numerous bishops from many parts of the world. Conspicuous in them all was their disgraceful flattery of the prince; yielding to a degenerate weakness, episcopal dignity was subordinated to patronage of the emperor. In Martin alone apostolic authority remained firm. If it fell to him to intercede with the emperor on behalf of anyone, he commanded rather than pleaded. Further, though frequently invited, he abstained from the imperial table. He said that he could not share the same board with one who had deprived one emperor of his kingdom, another of his life. In reply, Maximus affirmed he had not taken the empire upon himself voluntarily; the soldiers, by divine command, had compelled him to rule and he had simply defended his position with armed force. Nor, he continued, did God's favor seem lacking to one to whom victory had come so absolutely contrary to expectation. And, finally, none of his opponents had fallen except on the field of battle. At last, overcome either by argument or supplication, Martin came to the table of the emperor, who was overjoyed that he had had his way.

1 Magnus Maximus, a native of Spain. Proclaimed Emperor by troops in Britain, Maximus crossed over to Gaul and overthrew Gratian (383). Theodosius, Gratian's colleague, was forced to allow Maximus supreme authority in Gaul, Spain, and Britain, provided Valentinian II ruled Italy and Illyricum. In 387, Maximus drove Valentinian from Italy. The latter gained the support of Theodosius, who overcame the forces of Maximus and, at Aquileia, captured and beheaded Maximus himself (388). *Dial.* 2.6 and 3.11 supply other glimpses of Maximus, as also of his pious wife. The latter passage, with *Chronica* 2.49-51. (cf. below, p. 252), deals with the part played by Maximus in the trial of Priscillian.

The guests were summoned as though for a festival. Most distinguished and illustrious men were among them: Evodius,[2] who was at once prefect and consul and a man of unexcelled justice, and two *comites*[3] who held positions of the highest authority, namely, the emperor's brother and his paternal uncle. Between these two reclined Martin's priest, while Martin himself sat in a chair placed next to the emperor. At the customary moment, about the middle of the meal, a servant presented a cup to the emperor. He ordered that it be given first to the holy bishop, from whose hand it was his expectation and aim that he should have it back. But Martin, when he had drunk, passed the cup to his priest, convinced that there was no one more worthy to drink immediately after himself, and that it would not be proper to prefer to a priest either the emperor himself or those who were next in rank to the emperor. Martin's act so astonished the emperor and all who were then present that the very deed by which they were humiliated won their approval. It was a matter for enthusiastic praise throughout the palace that, at a banquet of the emperor, Martin had done something which none of the bishops had done even at the tables of the lowest officials.

To this same Maximus, Martin, long before the event, predicted what would happen if he should move into Italy, where he desired to go to wage war against Emperor Valen-

2 Flavius Evodius, *praefectus praetorio* as well as consul in 386. Cf. Seeck in PWK 6.1153. 386 should, then, be the year of the banquet here described, but Martin's relations with Maximus after the execution of Priscillian (385) were presumably such that he would not have shared the emperor's board in 386. Quite possibly, as Delehaye suggests (p. 22), Sulpicius is simply giving Evodius the title of consul prior to the event. See below, p. 254, for Evodius's connection with the case of Priscillian.

3 One of these, the emperor's brother, Marcellinus, was overcome by Theodosius at Paetovio in 388, prior to Maximus's capture.

tinian.[4] In the first attack he would be victorious, but would perish shortly thereafter. We have lived to see this occur. Immediately upon the arrival of Maximus, Valentinian took to flight, but then, about a year later, assembled fresh forces, imprisoned Maximus within the walls of Aquileia, and slew him.

Chapter 21

It is well established that Martin frequently enjoyed the vision even of angels; not only this, but that they spoke and conversed together.[1] The Devil also was plainly visible to the bishop's eyes. Sometimes he would confine himself within his proper substance, at other times transform himself into a variety of shapes of spiritual wickedness.[2] Whatever form he took, he was discovered by Martin. Knowing that he could not escape him, the Devil would frequently taunt him with insults because he could not deceive him by his wiles.

One day, holding a bloody ox horn in his hand and making a loud roar, he rushed into Martin's cell. He showed him his blood-stained hand and boasted of the crime he had just committed: 'Where, Martin, is your power? I have just killed one of your men.' Then Martin called the brothers together and reported what the Devil had announced. He told them to go hurriedly from cell to cell to find out to whom this misfortune had occurred. The report was made that none of the monks was missing, but that a peasant, hired to haul wood in a cart, had gone into the forest. Martin ordered some of the monks to go to meet him. The peasant was found, almost dead, not far from the monastery. As he drew his last

---

4 Valentinian II, brother of Gratian and Emperor 375-392.

---

1 On Martin's relations with angels, see *Dial.* 1.25; 2.5,12,13; 3.11,13.
2 Lat. *spiritalis nequitiae;* cf. Eph. 6.12.

breath, he revealed to the brothers the cause of his mortal wound. After he had yoked his team and was tightening the loose thongs, one of the oxen had tossed its head and driven its horn into his groin. Not long afterwards, he died. It is for you to see why the Lord gave such power to the Devil. What was remarkable with Martin—and the example just related is but one of many similar instances—was that, when anything happened, he would foresee it long before or, learning of it by revelation, would announce it to the brothers.

Chapter 22

In the course of his attempts to make sport of the holy man by a thousand devices of harm-doing,[1] the Devil frequently showed himself to Martin under a great diversity of forms. Sometimes he assumed the mask of Jupiter and often that of Mercury;[2] often, too, he presented himself transfigured under the features of Venus or Minerva. When confronting him, the ever-fearless Martin would protect himself with the sign of the cross and the shield of prayer. The insults with which a crowd of demons would insolently upbraid him were often heard, but Martin would not be moved by these taunts, recognizing them all as false and vain.

Some of the brothers would testify that they had heard the Demon inveighing insolently against Martin. Detailing the individual crimes of certain of the brothers who, through a variety of faults, had at one time lost the grace of baptism, he demanded why Martin, upon their conversion, had received them into the monastery. Martin, standing up to the Devil, had firmly replied that former faults are washed

---

1 Lat. *mille nocendi artibus,* quoted from Virgil, *Aeneid* 7.338. Paulinus also cites this line of Virgil: *Epist.* 4.2 (*PL* 61.165; *CSEL* 29.20).

2 Cf. *Dial.* 2.13, 3.6; also Acts 14.12.

away by conversion to a better life, and that, through the Lord's mercy, absolution from sin is to come to those who stop sinning. The Devil countered by saying that pardon does not apply to criminals and that, to men who have once lapsed, the Lord is incapable of granting clemency. Then, they said, Martin cried out in these words: 'If you yourself, wretched one, should stop pursuing mankind and, even now, when the day of judgment is near, should repent of your deeds, my confidence in the Lord Jesus Christ is such that I would promise you mercy.' What holy presumption on the loving kindness of the Lord! Even if Martin could not produce an authority for his promise, it at least showed his generous charity.

Now that we are talking about the Devil and his cunning, it seems proper to relate another incident, even if it be unconnected with our subject. It both belongs to the story of Martin's wonder-working and, since it was the occasion for a miracle, deserves to be put on record as an example of something to avoid, should any such thing ever happen in the future.

Chapter 23

A certain Clarus[1]—a youth of noble birth, later a priest, and now, after a holy death, blessed—gave up everything and joined Martin. In a short time he rose brilliantly to the perfection of faith and all the virtues. Not far from the monastery of the bishop, he established for himself a cell, and many brothers lived with him. There was a young man named

1 *Epist.* 2 (below, p. 148) records that Clarus died shortly before his master, Martin. Paulinus has left us inscriptions composed by himself for the tomb of Clarus at Primuliacum: *Epist.* 32.6 (*PL* 61.333f.; *CSEL* 29.280); he elsewhere pairs Martin and Clarus as examples of virtue: *Epist.* 23.3, 27.3 (*PL* 61.258, 308; *CSEL* 29.160, 240). Clarus is commemorated in the *Roman Martyrology* (November 8).

Anatolius, whose life as a monk was an outright counterfeit of humility and innocence. He came to Clarus and for a while lived in common with the others. Then, as time went on, he kept saying that angels frequently conversed with him. No one believed his story until Anatolius, by using certain signs and wonders, compelled many to do so. Finally, things went so far that he announced that messengers ran to and fro between himself and God, and at last he wished to have himself considered as one of the Prophets. Clarus, however, could not be persuaded, though Anatolius threatened him with the wrath of the Lord and immediate punishment for being unwilling to believe a saint. Finally, they say, Anatolius burst out with these words: 'Behold, this night the Lord will give me from heaven a white garment and, dressed in it, I shall move in the midst of you. And this shall be for you a sign that I, who have been endowed with God's vestments, am the power of God.'[2] This announcement aroused great expectation among all. About midnight, there came a noise, as of men tramping the earth, which seemed to shake the whole monastery. In the cell in which the young man was you could have seen a constant flashing of light, while there resounded from it the sound of steps moving here and there and a kind of murmur of many voices. Then, all was quiet. Anatolius called one of the brothers[3] to him and displayed the tunic in which he was dressed. The brother was amazed at the sight and called the others together. Even Clarus himself came running up. A light was brought, and they all carefully examined the garment. It was extremely soft, uncommonly white, and bordered with glittering purple, yet they could not distinguish the kind or texture of the material. However, when carefully examined by the eye or touch, it

2 Reading, with Zellerer (61f.), *me Dei esse virtutem;* cf. Acts 8.10.
3 Some of the MSS. here add 'Sabbatius by name.' Cf. *Dial.* 3.1 n. 8.

seemed nothing other than a garment. Meanwhile, Clarus admonished the brothers to pray fervently that the Lord should more clearly reveal to them what it was. The remainder of the night was given to singing hymns and psalms. When day broke, Clarus took Anatolius by the hand and wished to bring him to Martin, certain that no device of the Devil could deceive the latter. At this, the wretched man began to resist and protest, declaring that he had been forbidden to show himself to Martin. When they compelled him to go against his will, the garment vanished under the very hands of those who were dragging him. Can there be any doubt? Here, again, the miraculous power of Martin was such that the Devil, when his delusion was to be submitted to Martin's eyes, could no longer disguise or conceal it.

Chapter 24

We should note the fact that there was in Spain at about this time a young man who had made a name for himself through many signs and wonders. His pride reached such a pitch that he gave himself out to be Elias. When many had rashly come to believe this, he went further and said that he was Christ. His deception was so successful that a certain bishop named Rufus[1] adored him as God, a fact which, as we have seen, later caused his removal from the episcopate. Again, many of the brothers reported to us that at this time, in the East, someone boasted that he was John. From the appearance of pseudo-prophets of this kind we can conjecture that the coming of the Antichrist is imminent, those

1 Da Prato argues well (*ed. Sulp.* 1.347f.) that the Rufus here in question is probably distinct from the Rufus named in *Chronica* 2.50 (below, p. 254). Presumably valueless is an entry in the forged *Chronicle* of Dexter recording, under the year 424, the removal from office of a Spanish bishop Rufus who for some years had been following a pseudo-Christ: *PL* 31.559-560.

persons serving as advance agents for him of the mystery of iniquity.[2]

A point we should not pass over is the extreme cunning used by the Devil at about this time in tempting Martin. One day, as Martin was praying in his cell, he stood by him, preceded[3] and surrounded by a purple light, since the glittering of this added brilliance would assist his delusion. He was clothed in a royal garment and crowned with a diadem of gold and precious stones; his shoes were gilded, his face serene, his mien joyous. There was nothing he resembled less than the Devil. Martin, on first seeing him, was stupefied; both maintained a deep silence[4] for a long while. Then the Devil took the lead and said: 'Recognize, Martin, him whom you see. I am Christ. Descending upon the earth, I wished to reveal myself first to you.' When, at this, Martin was silent and made no reply, the Devil made bold to repeat his presumptuous declaration: 'Why, Martin, do you hesitate to believe,[5] since you see? I am Christ.' Then Martin received a revelation of the Spirit and through it understood that it was the Devil, not the Lord. 'It was not clad in purple,' he said, 'nor with a glittering diadem that the Lord Jesus foretold that He would come. Except in that clothing and in that form which were His when He suffered, and unless the stigmata of the cross be worn, I shall not believe that Christ has come.' At these words, the other instantly vanished like smoke, filling the cell with such a stench as to leave no doubt that it was the Devil. This incident, just as I have related it, I learned from Martin's own mouth. I mention this, lest someone may think it a fable.

---

2 Cf. 2 Thess. 2.7.

3 For *prece* (Halm) I read with Zellerer (62) *prae se.*

4 The text is uncertain (Hyltén 139), but the meaning is in little doubt. For Halm's *multum* it appears likely that *mutum* should be read.

5 Halm's reading retained, but see Hyltén 139f.

Chapter 25

When I had heard Martin's faith, his career, and miraculous power spoken of for a considerable time, and I was consumed with a longing to know him, I was very glad to undertake a long journey to go and see him. Further, because I already had an ardent desire to write his life, I informed myself by searching out the facts, partly from Martin himself (insofar as he could be questioned), partly from those who had shared his experiences with him or knew about them.

One cannot imagine the humility and kindness with which he received me at that time. He congratulated himself and greatly rejoiced in the Lord that my esteem of him had been such that I had undertaken a long journey to seek him out. Imagine my distress when—I almost dare not confess it—he deigned to invite me to his own saintly board, poured water himself upon my hands and at evening washed my feet. I had not the courage to resist or oppose him. His authority so overwhelmed me that I thought it a sacrilege not to yield to him. In his conversation with me he talked only of the need of abandoning the seductions of the world and the burdens of this present age so that we might follow the Lord Jesus, free and unimpeded. As the most outstanding example of these times he brought forward that of the illustrious Paulinus, who has been named above.[1] Casting away an incomparable fortune and following Christ, he, almost alone in these times, had carried out the precepts of the Gospel. It was he, he declared, whom we should follow and whom we should imitate. Our present age was happy in having had such a lesson in faith and virtue. Following the Lord's saying,[2] one who was rich and of many possessions had sold all and had

1 In Ch. 19.
2 Luke 14.33; Matt. 19.21.

given to the poor. What had seemed impossible to achieve he had made possible through his example.

And in Martin's words and conversation what seriousness, what dignity! How penetrating, how forceful he was, how quick and at ease in resolving questions from the Scriptures! And because I know that many are incredulous on this point (since I have noticed that they did not believe when I myself was telling them about it), I call to witness Jesus and our common hope of salvation that I have never heard from any other mouth words so full of wisdom and of so sound and pure an eloquence. To be sure, in comparison with Martin's virtues, this is but a small commendation, except that it is remarkable that not even this merit was lacking in a man untrained in letters.

Chapter 26

But now, our book demands an ending; our recital must come to a close. It is not that I have exhausted all that could be said about Martin. Rather, like unskillful poets who become negligent at the end of their work,[1] we are overcome by the mass of our material and leave off. An attempt to speak of his deeds might or might not be successful, but it is otherwise with his interior life, his daily manner of living, the constant direction of his spirit to heaven. As to these things, I speak the simple truth when I say that no possible form of speech can ever unfold them. His perseverance and temperance in fasts and abstinence, his power in vigils and prayers, nights spent by him as if they were days, with never a moment withdrawn from the work of God,[2] no allowance made for leisure or business, nor even for

1 With the Lat. (*ut inertes poetae extremo in opere neclegentes*) cf. Cicero, *De senectute* 2.4: *extremum actum tamquam ab inerti poeta esse neglectum.*

2 Cf. above, Ch. 2 n. 6.

food or sleep, except insofar as natural necessity compelled him—all this, in very truth, not Homer himself could describe, even if, as they say, he should rise from the dead.[3] So true it is that with Martin everything is too big for words to be able to express it.

An hour, a moment never passed without Martin being absorbed in prayer or busy in reading. Even in the midst of reading or whatever he happened to be doing, he never relaxed his spirit from prayer. Even as blacksmiths, in the midst of their work, try to find some alleviation of their toil by constant striking of the anvil, so Martin, even when he seemed to be doing something else, was always praying. O truly happy man, in whom there was no guile,[4] who judged no one, who condemned no one, who returned to no one evil for evil! He showed such patience toward all kinds of injury that, though he was highest in dignity, a bishop, even the lowest clergy could abuse him with impunity. Yet, he never on this account removed such men from their posts or, so far as it rested with him, banished them from his love.

Chapter 27

He was never seen to be angry, never violent, never sorrowing, never laughing. Always one and the same, he seemed, somehow beyond the nature of man, to show a heavenly gladness in his countenance. In his speech, only Christ was ever to be found; in his heart, only love, peace, and mercy.[1]

He would often weep even for the sins of those who had

3 A similar expression is used by St. Jerome, *Vita Hilarionis,* prol. (*PL* 23.29).
4 Cf. John 1.47.

1 Hilary of Arles, *Vita Honorati* 8.37 (*PL* 50.1270), has a similar turn of phrase. Less striking resemblances between the two authors are listed by Babut 16 n. 1 (Delehaye 133f.).

shown themselves his detractors, who used poisoned tongues and viper's teeth to slander him in the quiet of his retreat. Indeed, we have seen at work some who were envious of his virtue and mode of life, who hated in him what they did not see in themselves and could not imitate. And it is a horrible thing, grievous, and lamentable, that there were named as his persecutors—very few though these be—almost no others than bishops. There is no need to mention any by name, even if most of them will bark out their rage against me. If any of them read this and recognize themselves, it will be enough for me if they are ashamed. If they become angry, that in itself will be an admission that my words concern them, when, perhaps, I was thinking of others. Yet, I do not shrink from having any persons of this sort make me, along with such a man as Martin, the object of their hate.

Of one thing I am reasonably confident, that this little book will find favor with all who are truly faithful.[2] But if anyone reads these things with other than the eyes of faith, the sin will be his own. For myself, I am sure that what led me to write was belief in the story and love of Christ. I am sure, also, that I have related attested facts and spoken the truth. The reward which I hope has been made ready by God will be won, not by him who has read, but by him who has believed.

---

2 Lat. *omnibus sanctis*: as Bihlmeyer suggests (53 n. 1), it is probable that monks are especially intended.

THE LETTER TO EUSEBIUS[1]

Yesterday, a number of monks came to see me. We had a long conversation and told one story after another. Mention was made of the little book I wrote on the life of the blessed man, Martin the bishop. They said, to my satisfaction, that many people were reading it with great pleasure. In this connection, I was told of a remark someone had made under the influence of the evil spirit. Martin, he observed, had resurrected the dead and driven flames from burning houses. Why, then, was he himself, some time ago, put in peril of his life through being burned in a fire?

Wretched man, whoever he is! In his words we recognize the incredulity of the Jews, who, when the Lord hung upon the cross, flung at Him this rebuke: 'He saved others: himself he cannot save.'[2] Whoever that man is who now in like manner blasphemes against a saint of the Lord, he ought to have been born in those ancient times, so that he could have used those words against the Lord.[3]

---

1 For the addressee of the letter and the circumstances of its composition, see above, p. 86f.

2 Matt. 27.42.

3 The text varies in the MSS. I have followed Halm's reading in the light of Hyltén's remarks (p. 76f.). The Dublin MS. shows a fuller text which yields the following translation: 'In truth, that man, whoever he is, had he been born in those times, would surely have uttered that speech against the Lord. He who in like fashion blasphemes against a saint of the Lord would certainly not have been lacking in will towards treachery.' See E.-Ch. Babut, in *Le moyen âge* 19 (1906) 207; Zellerer 47f., Hyltén, *loc. cit.*

What is it you are saying, whoever you are? Is Martin not powerful and not holy just because a fire endangered him?

Blessed Martin, in everything like the Apostles, even in respect to these reproaches! That is just what we are told the Gentiles thought of Paul, too, when the viper bit him. 'This man,' they said, 'must be a murderer; though he has been saved from the sea, the fates have not permitted him to live.'[4] But Paul shook off the viper into the fire and was not hurt. The Gentiles thought he would at once fall down and quickly die. When they saw that no harm was coming to him, they changed their minds and said he was a god. The example of these Gentiles surely ought to have caused you, most unhappy of men, to convict yourself of incredulity. If you were offended to see Martin touched by the flame, you ought to attribute to his merits and virtue the fact that, when he was hemmed in by fire, he did not die.

Something you do not know, wretched man, and must learn is this: Almost all the saints have especially distinguished themselves by miracles worked when they were in danger. I see Peter, powerful in faith, overcoming the force of nature by walking upon the sea, impressing his footprints upon the unstable waters.[5] The Apostle of the Gentiles was swallowed up by the waves and spent three days and three nights in

4 Acts 28.4. The text varies significantly from the Vulgate (see the Wordsworth-White *Novum Testamentum Latine* III 1 [Oxford 1905], *ad. loc.*) and represents, according to P. Sabatier, *Bibl. Sacr. Lat.* III (Paris 1751) 587, the *'Antiqua versio.'* The three sentences that follow in Sulpicius are partly a transcript, partly a paraphrase of Acts 28.5-6.

5 Cf. Matt. 14.29f.

the deep before the surging sea brought him out.[6] Yet, I do not consider him inferior to Peter on that account; perhaps it is even a greater thing to have lived in the deep than to have passed over it upon the surface. But you, fool that you are, have not read this, I suppose, or, if you have read it, have not comprehended it. It was part of the divine plan that the blessed Evangelist brought forward in the Sacred Scriptures an example of this kind. The human mind was thereby to be taught the meaning of disasters caused by shipwrecks and serpents and[7] of those other dangers mentioned by the Apostle,[8] who glories in nakedness and in hunger and in perils from robbers. All these disasters are the common lot of the saints, who must suffer them. It is in enduring them and in overcoming them that the virtue of the just has always been conspicuous. With invincible strength they have defied all trials; the heavier the sufferings they endured, the more courageous were their victories.[9]

This shows that the example proposed in proof of Martin's weakness is abundant evidence of his merit and glory, for it was a grave danger that tried him, and he came out victorious. Yet, no one should be surprised that I omitted this episode

---

6 According to 2 Cor. 11.25, St. Paul passed only a day and a night *in profundo maris*. The three-day duration spoken of by Sulpicius and his language in general suggests rather the Prophet Jonas's experiences (cf. Matt. 12.40) than any of St. Paul's. As Da Prato suggested (*ed. Sulp.* 1.39 on line 18), something may have fallen out of Sulpicius's text with the result that what now is said of St. Paul originally related to Jonas. Da Prato quotes from an anonymous sermon for the feast of Sts. Peter and Paul ([Augustine], *Sermo* 203.3: *PL* 39.2123) which joins the experiences of the two Apostles as Sulpicius does and names Jonas in connection with those of St. Paul. Verbal parallels noted by Da Prato make it in fact likely that one of the texts is an imitation of the other.

7 This involved passage has been translated in the light of the punctuation and interpretation proposed by Fürtner (35f.).

8 Cf. 2 Cor. 11.26f.

9 Cf. James 1.12.

in the book I wrote about his life. I said there I had not embraced all he had done.[10] If I had chosen to write down everything, the volume offered my readers would have been immense. And his deeds are so many[11] that one could not include them all in a narrative. However, I shall now bring to light the incident about which the question arose, relating it in its entirety, just as it happened. Since it could be used to the disparagement of the blessed Martin, I do not wish to seem to have passed over it intentionally.

Martin had arrived in a certain parish,[12] following the practice bishops have of making regular visits to their churches. It was about the middle of winter. The clergy of the church had prepared lodging for him in the sacristy, and under its thin and rudely constructed flooring had kindled a sizeable fire. They had laid out a bed generously stuffed with straw. Now, Martin was accustomed to sleep on the bare ground, with a single covering of camel's hair over him. So, when he had put himself to bed, he was terrified by the enticement of the unaccustomed soft straw. Acting as if some injury had been done him, he cast aside all the straw bedding, and, as it happened, heaped up a part of the rejected straw over the furnace.[13] He then went to sleep on the bare floor, as was his practice, succumbing to the fatigue of his journey. Around midnight, the fire had eaten through the flooring—which was faulty, as has been said, and caught the dry straw. Martin was aroused from his sleep. Taken without warning, uncertain in the face of danger, and, most of all, as he re-

10 Chs. 1 and 26.

11 Reading *neque enim sunt tam pauca* (*pauca,* Da Prato's emendation of *parva*).

12 Lat. *dioecesim.* The word regularly means parish in these writings of Sulpicius.

13 Like a *hypocaustum* in a Roman bath establishment, the sacristy seems to have been heated by fire burning below the floor. The floor, we are told, was imperfect.

ported, surprised by the Devil, who had him in ambush and was pressing him hard, Martin was slower than he should have been to take refuge in prayer. His first concern was to break out of the room, and he struggled long and hard with the bolt which held the door. Flames had consumed his clothing, so intense was the fire by which he saw himself surrounded. At last he came to his senses. His safeguard, he realized, was not in flight, but in the Lord. In the midst of the flames he seized the shield of faith[14] and prayer and turned himself wholly to the Lord. As he prayed, the divine power dispelled the fire and rendered harmless the flames which encircled him. The monks were outside. They heard the crackling and gasping of the flames. Breaking open the bolted door, they beat down the fire and brought Martin out of the midst of the flames, although they feared that he would be entirely consumed by a fire that had burned so long.

In what follows, the Lord is witness to my words. Martin himself gave me the account. He confessed, and not without groaning, that the Devil's cunning had deceived him in this instance. He had no idea of combatting the danger through faith and prayer when first aroused from his sleep. As long as he tried in his confusion to burst open the door, the fire raged about him. But, when he again took up the standard of the cross and the arms of prayer, the flames retreated from the center out. The flames from whose burning he had suffered now seemed to bathe him in dew.[15]

Anyone who reads this should understand that, if this danger put Martin to the test, he came out of it tried and true.

14 Cf. Eph. 6.16.
15 Cf. Dan. 3.50.

THE LETTER TO THE DEACON AURELIUS[1]

AFTER YOU LEFT me early this morning, I was sitting alone in my cell. Thoughts came to me which often occupy my mind: the hope of things to come and the weariness of this present life, fear of the judgment, and dread of its punishments. These led to what had started me to meditate—recollecting my sins—and this left me saddened and worn out. My anguish of mind had wearied my body, so I went to bed. As often happens when one is sorrowful, sleep stole upon me. Sleep in the morning hours is different from other sleep. It is lighter and uncertain, it spreads itself through the body in tenuous suspense. This makes you feel you are sleeping, when, in fact, you are almost awake.

Suddenly, I seemed to see the holy bishop Martin. He wore a white toga, his countenance gleamed, his eyes were like stars, his hair was bathed in purple. He was showing himself to me in that figure and form which I knew, yet—and it is hard for me to express it—I could not look at him, though I could recognize him. He was smiling gently at me, and in his right hand was carrying the little book I had written about his life. I embraced his sacred knees and, as was my custom,[2] asked for his blessing. As I felt the touch of his hand upon my

1 For the addressee of the letter and the circumstances of its composition, see above, p. 86f.

2 The Lat. phrase, *pro consuetudine,* is omitted in the oldest MS (*V*) and bracketed by Halm.

head, it was like a caress. He pronounced the appointed words of benediction, repeating the name of the cross that his lips knew so well. My eyes were fixed upon him, yet I could not satisfy my desire for the sight of his face. Suddenly, he was lifted aloft and I had his company no more. As he passed through the empty reaches of the air, borne up by a fast-moving cloud, I could follow him with my eyes. Then the heavens opened up and received him, and he could no longer be seen. A little later, I saw the holy priest, Clarus,[3] Martin's disciple, recently dead, ascending by the same path his master took. I conceived the daring desire to follow them. While I was making strenuous exertions to rise in the air, I woke up.

Aroused from sleep, I began congratulating myself upon the vision I had seen, when one of the household servants came in. His face was uncommonly sad; it was as if he wished to speak and to weep at the same time. 'What is the sad message you wish to give me?' I asked. 'Two monks have just arrived from Tours,' he replied. 'They bring word that Martin[4] is dead.' I collapsed, I am frank to admit. Tears sprang to my eyes and I wept copiously. In fact, my dear brother, even as I write these words, my tears are flowing. My grief has overmastered me and admits no consolation.

When the news reached me, I wished to let you share my sorrow—you who shared my love for Martin. So, come to me at once so that we may both mourn for him whom we both love. I know, of course, that there ought to be no mourning for Martin. After overcoming the world and triumphing over its pomps and vanities, he has received the crown of justice.[5] Yet, my will cannot control my grief. True, I have

3 See *Life of St. Martin,* Ch. 23 n. 1.

4 Lat. *domnum Martinum*—as a present-day Italian might say 'Don Martino.'

5 Cf. 2 Tim. 4.8.

sent a heavenly patron ahead of me, but I have lost what gave me solace in this present life.

If only my grief would let my reason operate, my part would be to rejoice. Martin has joined the ranks of the Apostles[6] and the Prophets, and in that company is second to none of them—may there be no displeasure among the saints at my saying this. What I hope most of all and confidently believe to be true is that he has been enrolled among those who have washed their robes in blood, and that now, free from all defilement, he follows the Lamb and accompanies Him.[7] Given the condition of the times, martyrdom was not possible for him, but he will not lack a martyr's glory. So far as his desire and virtue are concerned, he could have been and wished to be a martyr. Suppose he had lived in the age of Nero or of Decius and could have taken part in the struggles of those times.[8] I swear by the God of heaven and earth he would have mounted the rack of his own accord; no one would have been needed to throw him into the fire. Like the Hebrew youths, in the midst of the rolling flames and the fiery furnace,[9] he would have sung a song of praise to the Lord. Perhaps the persecutor would have chosen for him the

6 See *Life,* Ch. 7 n. 4.

7 Cf. Apoc. 7.14; 14.4.

8 The reign of Nero (54-68) and especially that of Decius (249-251) were marked by persecution of Christians. In this passage, Sulpicius must have had in mind St. Hilary's *Contra Constantium* 4 (*PL* 10.580f.). We there find Hilary expressing a wish that his life had been spent 'in the age of Nero or of Decius' and listing a variety of punishments which, in God's mercy, he might then have endured. Sulpicius's catalogue of tortures resembles Hilary's.

9 Cf. Dan. 3.51ff.

famous torture of Isaias.[10] Fully a match for the Prophet, he would not have feared to see his limbs cut away by the saw or the knife's edge. If the frenzy of the infidels had chosen to cast his blessed body from precipitous rocks or sheer mountain crags—I am confident this is true—he would have thrown himself over of his own accord. Suppose that Martin, like the Doctor of the Gentiles,[11] had been condemned to the sword and been led out, as often happened, with other victims. He would have compelled the executioner to strike him before the others, so that he might be the first to grasp the bloody palm of martyrdom. Whatever are the painful punishments to which men's weakness has most often succumbed, he would have withstood them unshaken, never denying his faith in the Lord. Joyous in his wounds, happy in pain, he would have smiled no matter what torture racked him.

Of course, he did not experience any of these things, yet he did fulfill a bloodless martyrdom. In his hope of eternal life, is there any bitterness of human suffering he did not endure[12]—hunger, vigils, nakedness, fastings, envious insults, vicious persecution, worry for the sick, anxiety for those in danger? Who grieved and he did not grieve? Who was scandalized and he was not consumed with fire? Who perished and he did not groan? Further, there were his daily struggles of many kinds against the great wickedness of men and evil

---

10 The tradition that Isaias met his death by being cut in two with a saw is at least as old as Tertullian (*De patientia* 14: *PL* 1.1270; *CSEL* 47.21. References to other early texts in *Catholic Encyclopedia* 8.180f. and in F. Vigouroux, *Dictionnaire de la Bible* 3.944f. See the *Roman Martyrology* (July 6); also Potamius (Bishop of Lisbon; died *ca.* 360), *Tractatus de martyrio Esaiae prophetae* (*PL* 8.1415; ed. A. C. Vega, *Scriptores ecclesiastici Hispano-Latini veteris et medii aevi,* fasc. 2 [Escorial 1934] 35f.).

11 Cf. *Roman Martyrology* (June 29) for St. Paul's death by the sword.

12 In this passage Sulpicius emphasizes the apostolic virtues of St. Martin by closely imitating the language of St. Paul (2 Cor. 11.27-30).

spirits.[13] Strength to win, patience to wait, evenness of temper to withstand—these were always in him and overcame the temptations which attacked him. A man unique for his virtues, which cannot be described: piety, mercy, and charity. When charity, in this chilly world, was growing cold[14] even in holy men, in him it increased day by day and lasted to the end.

I profited in a special way from his goodness, for, in spite of my faults and unworthiness, he had a particular affection for me. Now, again, my tears are flowing and a sigh rises from my innermost heart. After this, where will there be a man in whom I can find such repose, from whose charity I can derive such consolation? Wretched, unhappy man that I am. If I continue to live, can I fail to grieve that I have survived Martin? After this, will life be joyous, will any day or hour be free from tears? When I am with you, beloved brother, shall I be able to mention his name without weeping? Or, in conversations with you, shall I be able to speak of anything else?

But why make you weep and sigh? I, who cannot console myself, desire to see you consoled. Martin will not, believe me, will not be absent from us. He will be among us when we converse about him, he will be standing by when we pray. The favor he did me today will not be unique: he will often show himself in his glory, that we may see him. As he did a little while ago, he will always be shielding us with his blessing. Again, to deal with the rest of my vision, he has shown us that heaven is open to those who follow him. He has taught us the path to take, the end our hope should aim for, the goal for which our spirit should strive.

Nevertheless, my brother, what will happen? I shall be

---

13 Lat. *adversum vim humanae spiritalisque nequitiae;* cf. Eph. 6.12.
14 Cf. Matt. 24.12.

unable to climb that steep path and pursue it to the end: of this I am quite sure. My irksome burden weighs me down too heavily.[15] I am sunk under the mass of my sin. This forbids me to ascend to the stars and leads me in my wretchedness to the dread abyss of Hell. Yet, hope remains, one single, last hope: that what we cannot obtain of ourselves we may secure through the merits of Martin's prayers for us.

But why, brother, occupy you longer with a wordy letter and delay your coming? Also, the page is full and will hold no more. Yet, I did have a reason for prolonging this communication. When it was my letter that would announce to you your sorrow, I wished that the same sheet of paper would somehow effect a conversation between us and so bring you consolation.

15 With this passage Bihlmeyer compares Paulinus, *Epist.* 24.1 (*PL* 61.287; *CSEL* 29.201f).

THE LETTER TO BASSULA[1]

Sulpicius Severus greets Bassula, his venerable mother

If it were permissible to call one's parents to justice,[2] I should surely charge you with pillage and larceny. In the justice of my resentment I should hale you before the praetor's tribunal. Why should I not complain of the wrong you have done me? In my house you have left me no scrap of paper, no book, no letter, so complete has been your thievery, so thorough your dissemination. I have only to write something in a familiar letter to a friend or perhaps, as a pastime, dictate some would-be secret, for everything to reach you almost before it is written or dictated. No wonder! You have got my secretaries bribed to rèveal to you the trifles of my thought. Yet, I cannot be irritated with them, if they do what you wish. It is largely through your generous expenditure that they are at my disposition, and, naturally, they regard themselves as yours rather than mine. My charge is directed only against you. The fault is entirely yours. It is through your plotting against me and your deceptive treatment of them that my writings fall into your hands without being submitted to any selection—familiar letters as well as things I have carelessly tossed off, quite without revising or

1 For the writer's relations with Bassula, see above, pp. 81, 86f.

2 Revelant legislation is found in the *Digest* 2.4 (*Corpus Iuris Civilis* I [15th ed., Berlin 1928] 43).

polishing them. I shall ask you about one case and let the others go. That letter I recently wrote to the deacon Aurelius[3]—how did it manage to reach you so quickly? I was at Toulouse. You were at Trèves, drawn far from home through worry over your son. How, then, did you contrive to steal that letter of mine, written to a friend? Yes, I have received your message. You write that, in the same letter in which I mention St. Martin's death, I ought to have detailed the circumstances in which the blessed man passed away. As if I sent that letter for any other than its own addressee to read, or as if mine were the enormous task of publishing, by my own hand, everything that should be known about Martin. If you want to learn about the holy bishop's death, the people to ask are those who were present. I have determined not to write you a line, so that you may not broadcast my words. However, if you promise to read this to no one,[4] I shall write a few words to satisfy your wish. That is the condition on which I am letting you share the facts I have ascertained.

Martin foresaw his death long before it occurred, remarking to the brothers that the dissolution of his body was imminent.[5] At that time, an occasion arose for his visiting the parish of Candes.[6] There was a dispute among the clergy of that church and he wished to restore peace. He well knew the end of his days was close, yet he would not refuse to make the trip on that account. He thought it would be a fitting crown to his life of virtue to re-establish the church in peace and leave this as his legacy. So he set out, accompanied, as always, by a large band of holy disciples.

---

3 Above, pp. 147-152.

4 Cf. Sulpicius's letter to Desiderius prefixed to the *Life of St. Martin* (above, p. 101f.

5 Cf. 2 Tim. 4.6.

6 Candes is situated on the Loire, downstream from Tours, where the Vienne and the Loire join; cf. Longnon, *Géographie* 270ff.

On the river he saw some diving birds going after fish. Time and time again, the birds would make a capture and stuff their ravenous crops. 'Here,' he said 'is a picture of the demons. They ambush the unwary and capture them before they know it. They devour their victims, yet cannot satisfy their voraciousness.'

Then, with a mighty voice, he ordered the birds to leave the whirling waters where they were swimming and to go to some dry, deserted place. He addressed them with the same commanding tone he commonly used in putting demons to flight. The birds then formed a flock and together left the river, heading for the mountains and forests. Many of his disciples were amazed to see that Martin's power was so great that he could command even the birds.

He stayed for a short while in the village whose church he had come to visit. When peace was restored among the clergy, he thought about returning to the monastery. But he suddenly began to lose his strength. He called the brothers together and said he was going to die.

The grief and sorrow all made a single voice of lament: 'Why, father, do you abandon us? We are desolate, and to whom do you leave us? The ravenous wolves will invade your flock.[7] With the shepherd stricken,[8] who will defend us from their mouths? We know you are longing for Christ, but your rewards are safe; postpone them and they will not diminish. Have pity on us whom you abandon.'

Martin, absorbed in the Lord as always and overflowing with tender compassion,[9] was not unmoved by these lamen-

7 Cf. Matt. 7.15; Acts 20.29. In the preceding sentences Sulpicius may be recalling the words of St. Antony to Paul of Thebes: 'Why, Paul, do you forsake me? Why do you go away without letting me say farewell?' (Jerome, *Vita Pauli* 14: *PL* 23.27).

8 Cf. Matt. 26.31; Mark 14.27.

9 Lat. *misericordiae visceribus* (from Col. 3.12).

tations. It is said that he wept. He addressed himself to the Lord and only in this way replied to those who were weeping: 'Lord, if I am still necessary to your people, I do not refuse the toil: Thy will be done.'

It is no wonder that, torn between hope and affliction, he almost wavered in his choice. He wished neither to abandon his disciples nor to be separated any longer from Christ. He gave no place to his desire and left nothing to his will, committing himself wholly to the decision and power of the Lord. As he prayed, these were his words: 'It is hard, Lord, in Thy service to do combat in the flesh, and the battles in which I have engaged up to now are enough. Still, if Thou biddest me continue the toil and stand guard before Thy camp, I do not refuse and will not plead the exhaustion of age as an excuse. I will dedicate myself to fulfill the tasks Thou givest me. Under Thy standard I will serve as long as Thou biddest me. An old man would indeed desire his discharge after a laborious service, but courage knows no yielding[10] to old age and can overcome the weight of years. Yet, Lord, if in Thy good will Thou sparest my age, it is a kindness to me. Thou Thyself wilt watch over these men for whom I fear.'

Here was a man whose virtue you could not describe. Toil had not overcome him, nor would death be able to. Inclining neither one way nor the other, he neither feared to die nor refused to live.

For several days he suffered a violent fever, yet he did not desist from the work of God.[11] He spent the nights in prayer and vigil, forcing his exhausted limbs to obey his spirit. He lay on that noble bed of his, on sackcloth and ashes. When his

10 With the Lat. (*cedere nescius*) cf. Horace, *Odes* 1.6.6.

11 There is some doubt whether we should read *ab opere* ('from work') or, as in the above translation, *ab opere Dei;* cf. Hyltén 144. See *Life*, Ch. 2 n. 6.

disciples asked if they might spread at least a rough blanket under him, he refused. 'It is not fitting,' he said, 'for a Christian to die except in ashes. I should have sinned if I were to leave you any other example.' His eyes and hands directed always to heaven, his spirit unconquered, he prayed without relaxation. The priests who then had come together to see him asked him to rest his body by turning over on his side. 'Permit me, brothers,' he said, 'permit me to look at heaven rather than the earth. In this way my soul will be already started on the path that will take it to the Lord.' When he had said this, he saw the Devil standing close by. 'Why are you standing here, bloody beast?' he said, 'Fiend of destruction, in me you will find nothing.[12] The bosom of Abraham receives me.'[13]

With these words he gave up his spirit to heaven.[14] Those who were present have testified to me that they saw his face like the face of an angel. His body was white as snow; so much so that people remarked: 'Who could believe that he had ever worn sackcloth or been covered with ashes?' In fact,

12 Viz., 'nothing that is yours.' The dying saint adapts the words of Christ (John 14.30). Sulpicius's reading, *in me . . . nihil reperies,* reflects an early Latin version varying from the Vulgate (*in me non habet quicquam*). *The Codex Brixianus* (*f*) shows *non inveniet* for *non habet* (cf. Wordsworth and White, *ad loc.*) and St. Augsutine more than once quotes the phrase in the form *in me nihil inveniet,* e.g., *Sermo* 26.10 (*PL* 38.176).

13 Cf. Luke 16.22f.

14 The word *caelo* ('to heaven') is to be added to Halm's text after *spiritum.* It is probable that St. Martin died on Sunday, November 8, 397; see the following note. Halm's text for the remainder of the paragraph is based solely on the oldest MS., *V,* which in this passage differs widely from that represented by all other MSS. thus far reported. Whether or not the reading of *V* is closer to the intentions of the author, the widely dispersed text found in the other MSS. appears to be the only one known to most of Christendom until the publica-ion of Da Prato's edition in 1741 and therefore deserves not to be lost sight of (printed in Halm's critical note on 149.19 and in *PL* 20. 183f., left half of column); unfortunately, its interpretation is not altogether clear.

it seemed that the glory of the coming resurrection and the new nature of the transfigured body were already being displayed in him.

An unbelievably large crowd assembled for his funeral.[15] The whole city[16] rushed out to meet the bier. Everyone from the fields and villages was present, as well as many persons from the nearby cities. All were deeply grieved, and especially sorrowful were the lamentations of the monks. Of these, it is said that upwards of two thousand came together on that day—a tribute of honor especially appropriate to Martin; so many shoots had sprung from the tree his example had planted for the Lord's service. The shepherd was leading his flocks before him, those thronging ranks of holy men, pale of face and dressed in the pallium,[17] old men with long years of toil behind them or recruits newly professed to Christ's service.[18] Then came a chorus of virgins, abstaining from tears

---

15 Sulpicius passes immediately from the saint's death to his funeral. Gregory of Tours, *Hist. Franc.* 1.48 (43), relates an intervening episode, a spirited dispute between the people of Tours and the people of Poitiers as to which city should have for burial the body of the saintly bishop then lying at Candes, where representatives of the two cities had promptly assembled. The men of Tours removed the body by stealth, while the men of Poitiers slept, and conveyed it by boat to Tours, where it was buried. The burial occurred on November 11, 397 (the year is disputed, but Duchesne, *Fastes épiscopaux* 2.302, and Delehaye 31 agree on 397), probably three days after the saint's death.

16 Tours.

17 Lat. *pallidas turbas, agmina palliata.* Similar phrases descriptive of the appearance of monks in Paulinus, *Epist.* 22.2 (*PL* 61.254; *CSEL* 29.155) and in Salvian, *De gubernatione Dei* 8.4 (p. 231 of J. F. O'Sullivan's translation in this series). In the word *palliata* no reference is made, of course, to an archbishop's pallium, but to a simple outer garment commonly worn by St. Martin's monks; cf. Besse, *Les moines* 23f.

18 The Lat. phrase (*iuratos Christi in sacramenta tirones*), instead of referring to recently professed monks, might relate to persons who in baptism had lately sworn to serve as Christ's soldiers. In the present context, the latter interpretation seems the less likely, although *Dial.* 2.11 offers it some support.

through modesty, concealing their grief in holy joy. If faith forbade them to weep, in their love they still could not suppress a sigh. Just as there was holy exultation for Martin's glory, so was there tender sadness for his death. As they wept, you would have pardoned them; as they rejoiced, you would have wished them joy. Each man's grief was on his own account; each man's joy, on Martin's.

Singing hymns like those of heaven, this was the throng which solemnly accompanied the body of the blessed man to its burial place. For a comparison with secular throngs, one might think, I will not say of a funeral procession, but of a triumphant march of conquerors, if you please. Yet, could one there find anything like Martin's obsequies? If those conquerors as they rode led their captives before them, with hands bound behind their backs, Martin's body was escorted by such as had overcome the world through his leadership. If they were honored by the mad and confused applause of the populace, Martin had for his applause the psalms of God and was honored in heavenly hymns. They, after their triumphs, will be hurried into the horrors of Tartarus; Martin is received joyful in the bosom of Abraham. Martin, poor and humble here, enters into heaven a rich man. From there, as I hope, he keeps his watch, looking down on me as I write this; on you, as you read it.[19]

19 The final sentence, wanting in a number of MSS., is bracketed by Halm.

THE FIRST DIALOGUE[1]

Chapter 1

GALLUS[2] AND I had met together. He was a man very dear to me, both because of Martin's memory—for he was one of his disciples—and because of his own good qualities. We were joined by my friend Postumianus,[3] who had returned from the Orient to see me. (He had left his own country and gone there three years before.) I embraced my loving friend and kissed his knees and his feet. Together, with tears of joy in our eyes, we walked up and down a few times almost carried away by delight. Then we spread haircloth on the ground and sat down.

Postumianus was the first to speak. He looked at me and said: 'When I was in the remoter parts of Egypt, I decided to journey up to the sea. I found a merchant vessel there getting ready to set sail for Narbonne, laden with cargo. That night I seemed to see you in my sleep. You had grasped me with your hand and were forcing me to embark on that ship. When dawn dispelled the darkness, I rose from the place

---

1 On the date of composition and on the *Dialogues* in general, see above, pp. 87-89.

2 Apparently unknown outside of the *Dialogues*. The birthplace of Gallus may be indicated below (see Ch. 27 n. 2). Other biographical details in *Dial.* 2.1,2.

3 Represented as Aquitanian in origin (Ch. 27, below) and as having made a trip to the Orient (Ch. 8, below) before the one he now reports to Sulpicius and Gallus. One of the familiars of Paulinus of Nola was named Postumianus; see Babut 49 n. 2 and Delehaye 39.

where I had slept. I reflected on my dream and was suddenly seized with such a longing for you that I embarked on the ship without delay. On the thirtieth day I reached Marseilles and have arrived here[4] after a further trip of ten days. Such was the propitious journey which favored the loving desire of my heart. Please, then, put everything aside, and let me have you to embrace and enjoy. For it was on your account that I sailed over so many seas and traveled so far on land.'

'Even when you were staying in Egypt,' I said, 'I was always and wholly with you in mind and spirit. As I gave my thought to you day and night, your love then[5] quite possessed me, so do not suppose that now I shall be absent from you for an instant. As I look at you, I shall hang on your lips, I shall listen to you, I shall talk with you. Absolutely no one will be admitted to the private retreat with which this isolated cell provides us. I suppose you will not mind if my friend here, Gallus, is present. As you see, he is as drunk with joy at your arrival as I am.'

'Excellent,' said Postumianus. 'Your friend Gallus will remain in our company. Even if I do not know him well, the fact that he is very dear to you necessarily makes him dear to me, especially since he is a product of Martin's training. I am not at all averse to chatting with you, as you ask, at any length you please. The very reason why I came' —and here he put both his arms about me—'was to devote myself to the wishes of my friend Sulpicius, even if it meant that I should have to talk a lot.'

Chapter 2

'You surely have proved,' I said, 'how far loving affection will go. For my sake you have traveled here over so many

---

4 Presumably to Primuliacum (see above, p. 81f).

5 Reading *tunc* instead of Halm's *totum* (so *V*); cf. Hyltén 144.

seas and so much land, voyaging almost from the very rising of the sun to the place of its setting. We are all by ourselves here, with nothing to do, and we ought to be quite free to listen to you talk. So, please give us the full story of your travels. Tell us how the faith of Christ flourishes in the Orient, what peace reigns among the faithful, how monks are established there, what signs and wonders Christ works there among His servants. Here, in these parts, surely, given what we have to live through, we find life itself distasteful. So, we should be very glad to have you tell us whether in the desert at least one can live as a Christian.'

'I shall do what I see you want,' said Postumianus. 'But, first, may I please hear from you whether all those bishops I left here are still such as I knew them before I went away.'[1]

'Do not ask about those things,' I said. 'Either you know them, I suppose,[2] as I do, or, if you do not, it is better not to learn them. But there is one thing I cannot keep back. Those you ask about have not become any better than when you knew them. Not only that: the one who once loved me, in whom I would find relief from the attacks of the others, has been more unkind to me than he should have. But I shall not say anything harsh about him. I cultivated his friendship and I still loved him when he was thought to be my enemy. As I think about this in private, I experience a great grief that I have been all but deprived of the friendship of a wise and religious man. But this subject is full of sorrow. Let us leave it and listen to the story you just now promised us.'

'Agreed,' said Postumianus. When he had spoken, we all kept quiet for a little while. Then he moved the haircloth mat he was sitting on closer to me and began in this way.

1 Cf. *Life* 27 for earlier sharp criticism of bishops; also above, p. 90.
2 'I suppose': the phrase, omitted in *V*, is bracketed by Halm.

Chapter 3

'It was three years ago, Sulpicius, that I bade you farewell and went away. We weighed anchor at Narbonne and on the fifth day entered an African harbor. God had willed that the crossing be successful. I decided to go to Carthage, there to visit the places made holy by the saints, and, most of all, to pray at the tomb of the martyr Cyprian.[1] On the fifteenth day we returned to the harbor and put to sea, making for Alexandria. With the south wind opposing us, we were almost driven into the Syrtis.[2] The sailors foresaw the danger and took care to anchor the ship.

'The continent lay before our eyes. We put out in little boats and landed. When we found no trace anywhere of human habitation, I went on farther to make a more careful investigation of the region. Some three miles from the shore, I spied a hut in the middle of the sand. Its roof, shaped like those which Sallust[3] says resemble the hulls of ships, touched the earth and was built of quite strong planks. This was not because of any fear of rain—people did not even so much as speak of any precipitation in those parts—but rather of the winds. These blow with such violence that the least breeze, setting in even when the sky is quite clear, is of greater consequence there than a shipwreck at sea. Neither grass nor crops grow there. There is no firmness to the soil, since the dry sands yield to every motion of the winds. There are occasional promontories, however, turned away from the sea, which

1 St. Caecilius Cyprianus, Bishop of Carthage martyred 258 (*Roman Martyrology*, September 14).

2 The quicksands of two gulfs on the North African coast were much dreaded by seafarers of antiquity. The Syrtis Major, which seems to be here in question, is now the Gulf of Sidra, lying between Misurata and Bengasi. The Syrtis Minor is the present Gulf of Gabes. Cf. Acts 27.17.

3 Sallust, *Bellum Jugurth.* 18.8.

resist the winds. Here, the soil is somewhat firmer and can produce occasional rough herbs. Such are quite useful for nourishing sheep. The inhabitants live on milk. Those who are more skillful—or, so to speak, richer—have barley-bread, for barley is the only crop there. The soil causes such quick growth that it usually escapes destruction by the ravaging winds.[4] It is reported that it matures on the thirtieth day after sowing. The only reason the people have for staying there is that they are all exempt from tribute. These are, in fact, the extreme parts of Cyrenaica, touching on the desert which lies between Egypt and Africa. It was through this desert that Cato[5] once led his army, fleeing from Caesar.'

Chapter 4

'So I made for the hut I had seen from a distance. I there found an old man, dressed in skins and working a handmill. After our greetings, he gave us a kindly reception. We explained that we had been cast upon that shore and were prevented by the calm from being able at once to continue our course. Following the bent of human nature, we continued, we had landed in the hope of learning about the geography of the place and the manners of the inhabitants. We were, moreover, Christians, and especially eager to know whether there were any Christians in those lonely parts. Then, with tears of joy in his eyes, he cast himself at our knees. He kissed us again and again and invited us to pray. Then he spread his sheepskins on the ground and had us recline. He placed before us a truly sumptuous meal—half a loaf of barley-

4 On the doubtful text, cf. Hyltén 144f.

5 Marcus Porcius Cato the younger, 'Uticensis' (from his death at Utica in B. C. 46). Cato, after Pompey's death (B. C. 48), undertook the march in question in order to bring his forces into conjunction with those of Scipio. Sulpicius probably knew the extended narrative and description found in the ninth book of Lucan's *Bellum Civile*.

bread. We were four and he made a fifth. He added a little bunch of herbs. Its name has escaped me: it was similar to mint, exuberant in leaf, and had a taste like honey. We were delighted with its very sweet and pleasant taste and had our fill.'

At this I smiled and turned to my friend Gallus: 'What do you say, Gallus? Would you be happy lunching on a bunch of herbs and half a loaf of bread, with five men eating?'

Gallus, being very shy by nature, took my teasing with a bit of a blush. 'You are true to form, Sulpicius,' he said. 'Whenever the occasion arises, you never fail to rail at our good appetites. But it is an inhuman thing you do, to force us who are Gauls to live like angels. Still, my interest in eating makes me believe that the angels also eat. As for that half-loaf of barley-bread, I should be afraid to touch it even alone. Let it serve to satisfy that Cyrenian, whose hunger comes by necessity or else by nature. Or again, let it go to those travelers: they had lost their appetites, I suppose,. after being tossed about on the sea. But, we here are far from the sea and, as I have said to you, we are Gauls.[1] But, enough of that. Let Postumianus conclude the story about his Cyrenian.'

Chapter 5

'Very well,' said Postumianus. 'I shall be careful from now on to avoid praising anyone's abstinence. I do not wish any such strenuous example to offend our Gallic friends. To be sure, I had intended to speak of the dinner that Cyrenian offered us and of the banquets which followed, for it was seven days that we were with him. But I must refrain, so

1 Gallic love of good food and drink was, as now, almost proverbial in antiquity. Bihlmeyer cites Ammianus Marcellinus 15.12.4, 16.8.8 and Sidonius, *Epist.* 1.2.6. Chs. 8 and 9 below contain similar reference to Gallic fondness for eating; cf. Babut 135.

that Gallus will not think he is being teased. Well, the following day some of the inhabitants began to stream in to see us. We learned that our host was a priest, a fact he had been completely successful in hiding from us. Later, we went with him to the church, some two miles away and hidden from our view by an intervening mountain. It was constructed from the interlacing of rough branches, hardly surpassing in splendor the dwelling of our host, where you could not stand unless you bent over. By our inquiry into the customs of the inhabitants we learned one notable thing: they neither buy nor sell. What cheating or theft is they have no idea. And, as for gold and silver, which men value highest,[1] they neither have them nor wish to. When I offered our priest ten pieces of silver, he recoiled in horror, declaring in his profound wisdom that with gold one does not build up the Church but, rather, destroys it.[2] We presented him with various articles of clothing, which he kindly accepted.'[3]

Chapter 6

'When the sailors called us back to the sea, we took our leave. Good sailing brought us on the seventh day to Alexandria. Here, ugly battles were being waged between the bishops

---

1 The phrase is adapted from Sallust, *Bellum Jugurth.* 76.6.

2 With this judgment cf. *Chronica* 1.23.5 (*PL* 20.109; *CSEL* 1.26) and Ch. 21 below; also Jerome, *Vita Malchi* 1 (*PL* 23.53). Salvian seems to have had the present passage of Sulpicius in mind when writing the final paragraph of *Ad ecclesiam* 2.13 (p. 315 of J. F. O'Sullivan's translation in this series).

3 The final clause belongs, strictly, to the following chapter.

and the monks. The occasion or cause was as follows.[1] It seemed that the bishops, having met together in several well-attended synods, had decreed that no one was either to read the books of Origen or to own them. He had the reputation of being very expert as a commentator of the Sacred Scriptures. Nevertheless, the bishops listed from his books certain passages of unsound doctrine. His advocates did not dare defend them and preferred to say that they had been interpolated by heretics; consequently, what remained should not be condemned because of the parts that were justly censured. The faithful reader could easily distinguish, refusing to follow the falsified passages, while retaining those in which the discussion followed Catholic lines. It was no wonder that the falsification of heretics should have been at work in modern books of recent authorship,[2] when it had not hesitated even to assail the truth of the Gospels in a number of passages. Against these arguments, the bishops put up stubborn resistance. They used their power to force a blanket condemnation of Origen's works—the good along with the bad—and of the author himself. There already were more than enough books which had found acceptance with the Church; reading matter more likely to harm the foolish than help the wise should be altogether rejected.

'I myself made a rather careful investigation of certain

1 The brilliant writings of the Alexandrian theologian Origen (*ca.* 185-254/5) led at various times to vigorous controversies as to his orthodoxy. One such controversy, that described in Chs. 6 and 7, occurred at the end of the fourth century. The bishop of Alexandria mentioned near the end of Ch. 7 was Theophilus, who in 400 convened a council which solemnly condemned certain errors of Origen. It was also Theophilus who, in the following year, authorized the expulsion of the monks referred to in Ch. 7. For details, the reader might consult G. Fritz in *DTC* 11.1567-1588; P. de Labriolle, in A. Fliche-V. Martin, *Histoire de l'Eglise* 4 (Paris 1937) 31-46.

2 Lat. *in libris neotericis et recens scriptis.* On the meaning of *neotericus* here, see J. de Ghellinck, S.J., in *Bulletin Du Cange* 15 (1940-41) 114f.

of these books. I found many things very pleasing, but there were passages where I clearly saw that the author was in error, those passages where his defenders claim interpolation. I am amazed that one and the same man could differ so much from himself. In the part that is acceptable he has no equal since the Apostles, but in that which has justly been censured no one can be found who has made more disgraceful errors.'[3]

Chapter 7

'Among the many passages in Origen's books noted by the bishops and clearly contrary to the Catholic faith, there was one place that especially provoked hostility. Here it is said that the Lord Jesus, who had come in human flesh for man's redemption, endured the cross for man's salvation, and tasted death for man's eternal life, was also to redeem the Devil through an analogous passion. This, Origen added, befitted the goodness and charity of Christ: He who had reformed humankind when lost ought also to deliver the fallen angel.[1]

'When this passage and others like it were produced by the bishops, the animosity of the two parties led to dissension. When episcopal authority proved incapable of repressing

3 An apt and well-put judgment is quoted by Cassiodorus, *Institutiones* 1.1.8: *Ubi bene, nemo melius; ubi male, nemo peius* (ed. Mynors, Oxford 1937, p. 14), 'When he writes well, no one writes better; when he writes badly, no one writes worse' (tr. L. W. Jones, New York 1946, p. 77).

1 St. Jerome, *Epist.* 124.12 seems to have in mind the very passage Postumianus refers to here (*PL* 22.1070; *CSEL* 56.114); cf. the synodical letter of Theophilus (Jerome, *Epist.* 92.4: *PL* 22.767; *CSEL* 55.152). Among the anti-Origenist canons of a synod of 543 (its acts apparently confirmed by Pope Vigilius) one anathematizes those who hold that the punishment of demons and of impious men will come to an end; H. Denzinger, *Enchiridion Symbolorum* (ed. 21-23, Freiburg i. B. 1937) no. 211.

this, an unfortunate thing occurred:[2] the prefect was called in to direct the discipline of the Church. In terror, the brothers dispersed and the monks scattered and fled. Edicts were issued, preventing their remaining permanently in any place. One thing disturbed me greatly: the attitude of Jerome, a man eminently Catholic and very skilled in the sacred law. He was thought at first to be a follower of Origen; now he is eminent for having condemned the whole corpus of his writings.[3] When outstanding and very learned men were reported to disagree in this dispute, I certainly should not venture to give rash[4] judgment about anyone. What is in question may be a simple error—and this is my opinion—or else, as others think, a genuine heresy. In any event, the strenuous measures repeatedly taken by the bishops were unable to repress it. Surely, it could not have had so wide a spread unless dissension had served to increase it.

'Such, then, was the disturbance which was having its ups and downs when I came to Alexandria. The bishop of that city gave me a very kind welcome, a better one than I was expecting. He tried to keep me with him, but I had no heart to stay on where there was a fresh seething of hatred arising from the disaster of the brothers. It may seem that they ought to have obeyed the bishops. Yet, that was no reason why so vast a multitude, sharing belief in Christ, should have suffered affliction, especially at the hands of bishops.'

---

2 Sulpicius, *Chronica* 2.50 (below, p. 254) records St. Martin's sharp criticism, in the case of Priscillian, of permitting a secular judge to rule in an ecclesiastical case.

3 As late as 392, St. Jerome had only commendation for Origen; cf. Jerome, *De viris illustribus* 54 (*PL* 23.665). His association with the anti-Origenist party dates from the following year; cf. de Labriolle, *op. cit.* (above, Ch. 6 n. 1) 35. Even later Jerome could recognize that only certain parts of Origen's works deserved censure; cf. *Epist.* 61.1 (*PL* 22.517; *CSEL* 54.576).

4 The word, wanting in *V*, is bracketed in Halm.

Chapter 8

'So I left, and made for the town of Bethlehem. This lies six miles from Jerusalem and is separated from Alexandria by a journey of sixteen stages. The Church there is governed by the priest Jerome;[1] it is a parish of the bishop who has his seat at Jerusalem. I had already become acquainted with Jerome on my earlier journey, and he had easily secured my promise not to let anything stand in the way of my revisiting him. Aside from the merit of his faith and the quality of his virtues, he has such a fine training in letters, not only Greek and Latin, but Hebrew as well, that there is no science in which anyone dares to challenge him. I should be surprised if he is not also known to you through the many books which he has written and which are read throughout the world.'

'With us,' said Gallus, 'he is well known; indeed, too well known. Five years ago I read a book of his in which he violently maltreats and reviles our whole class of monks.[2] In consequence, it sometimes happens that our Belgian friend[3] gets very angry with him because he said that we stuff ourselves to the point of vomiting. For my part, I excuse him, believing that it was about the monks of the Orient rather than those of the West he was talking. For the Greeks, heavy eating is gluttony; for the Gauls, it is natural appetite.'

'That defense of your race, Gallus,' said I, 'was in the true style of the scholar. But tell me: that book of Jerome's, it was not only that one vice that it condemned in the monks?'

---

1 The great Doctor of the Church, Sophronius Eusebius Hieronymus (b. shortly before 350; d. 419). This chapter and the following justly evaluate the extent of his learning and the vigor of his moral strictures.

2 Gallus alludes to Jerome's long and widely read letter to Eustochium (*Epist.* 22: *PL* 22.394; *CSEL* 54.143-211).

3 This *Belgicus,* mentioned also in the following chapter, was probably one of the monks living with Sulpicius.

'By no means,' he said. 'There was absolutely nothing he failed to attack, tear apart, and expose. His principal reproach was against avarice and, equally, against vanity. He had much to say about pride and not a little about superstition. To be quite frank, I thought he depicted the vices of a great many people.'

Chapter 9

'Again, when he dealt with the intimacies of virgins with monks and even with clerics, he spoke with truth and great power. That is why we hear that he is not loved by certain persons, whom I decline to name. Our Belgian gets angry because we were reprimanded for heavy eating. Similarly, those persons, it is said, are enraged when in the little book in question they read this:[1]

"The virgin disdains her own brother, who is celibate, and for a brother seeks out a stranger." '

'You go too far, Gallus,' said I. 'Be careful that someone who recognizes this does not hear you; he will put you with Jerome and begin to dislike you. Because you are a scholar, it will not be inappropriate for me to quote as a warning to you that verse of the comic writer:[2] "Compliance begets friends; truth, hatred." But, Postumianus, continue as you began and resume your narrative of the Orient.'

'As I had intended to state,' he said, 'I spent six months with Jerome. His continuous, unrelenting warfare against evil men has aroused them to hostility against him. He is hated by the heretics because he never stops assailing them. He is hated by the clerics because he censures their vicious mode of life.[3] On the other hand, he has the admiration and

1 Jerome, *Epist.* 22.14 (*PL* 22.403; *CSEL* 54.162).
2 Terence, *Andria* 68.
3 Bihlmeyer cites Jerome, *Epist.* 130.19 and 52.7 (*PL* 22.1133, 539 f.; *CSEL* 56.199ff., 54.440f).

affection of all good men. Those who think he is a heretic[4] are mad. In all sincerity I assure you: his learning is Catholic, his doctrine is sound. He is always fully absorbed in reading and in books. Day and night he takes no rest. He is continually reading or writing something. Had my mind not been made up and my vow given to God to visit the desert as I had already planned, I should have been unwilling to leave the side of this great man for as much as an instant.

'I handed over and committed to him all my baggage and all my attendants. The latter had followed me against my wishes and their presence hampered me. As if a heavy burden had been lifted from my back, I was quite free. I returned to Alexandria and visited the brothers there. I then set off for the upper Thebaid, that is, the outer reaches of Egypt. There, in the broad-spreading desert wildernesses, a vast number of monks were said to live. It would take me a long time if I wished to relate all the things I saw. I shall deal briefly with only a few.'

Chapter 10

'Not far from the desert, on the banks of the Nile, there are many monasteries. The monks live together, most commonly in groups of a hundred. The chief point in their polity is to live under the rule of an abbot, to do nothing by their own will, to depend in everything on his command and authority.[1] Some among them, determined to achieve greater perfection, move to the desert to live a life of solitude, but they do not leave without the abbot's permission. For all the monks the chief virtue is to obey the order of another. When

4 In *Epist.* 61 (cited above, Ch. 7 n. 3) Jerome defends himself against a charge of heresy based on his attitude toward Origen.

1 A passage probably known to St. Benedict when he wrote Ch. 5 of his *Rule*.

they get to the desert, the abbot arranges for bread or some other food to be supplied.

'In the days immediately after my arrival in that region, the following incident occurred. One of the brothers had recently withdrawn to the desert and set up his dwelling not more than six miles from the monastery. The abbot had sent bread to him by two boys, the older fifteen years of age, the younger twelve. On their way back, they encountered a serpent of extraordinary size. The encounter brought them no alarm. When the serpent was in front of their feet, as if under a spell, it lowered its dark-blue neck[2] to the ground. The younger of the boys took it in his hand, wrapped it in his mantle, and carried it off. He returned to the monastery like a victor to meet the brothers. When all were looking on, he opened his mantle and put down the captive beast, not without boastful pride. The brothers extolled the faith and miraculous power of the boys. But the abbot, with his deeper wisdom,[3] was afraid that in the weakness of their youth they might become haughty. He beat them both with rods, reproving them for having revealed the deed the Lord had done through them. What had happened did not come from their faith, but from the divine power. They should learn to serve God in humility rather than pride themselves on signs and wonders; it was better to be conscious of one's weakness than to draw vainglory from miracles.'

Chapter 11

'The monk who had withdrawn heard all this: that the boys had been put in peril by encountering a serpent, and that, further, after their victory over the serpent, they had

2 The Lat. phrase *caerula colla* is found in Virgil, *Aeneid* 2.381.
3 Lat. *altiore consilio,* a phrase found in St. Benedict's *Rule* 63.

been soundly whipped. He pleaded with the abbot that from then on no bread or any food at all should be sent to him. Eight days had passed since the man of Christ had cut himself off, at the risk of dying through hunger. His limbs were dried up through fasting, but his mind was directed to heaven and could not tire. His body was faint from lack of nourishment, but his faith stood firm.

'Meanwhile, the abbot had been advised by the Spirit to visit his disciple. In his loving care he was eager to know what life-giving substance was nourishing the man of faith who had declined to have any fellow man supply him with bread. So, he set off himself to find him. The hermit saw from a distance the old man coming. He ran to meet him, gave thanks, and brought him to his cell. When the two entered together, they saw hanging[1] from a door post a basket made of palm branches and filled with warm bread. They first sensed the odor—the odor of warm bread; then, from touching it, they received the impression that it had been taken from the oven only a little while before. Still, the loaf they saw was not of the Egyptian shape. In amazement, they both recognized a gift from heaven. The hermit declared the gift had been made for the abbot's arrival, while the abbot ascribed it rather to the faith and virtue of the hermit. And so, together, in great gladness, they broke the heavenly bread. When the old man returned to the monastery, he reported the incident to the brothers. They all experienced such a great longing that each tried to outstrip the other in hastening to the desert and its sacred solitudes. They said they would be unhappy if they stayed any longer in a large community, where they had to tolerate relations with other men.'

---

1 Instead of Halm's *ante postem, de poste* has been read as proposed by Hyltén 147f.

Chapter 12

'In this monastery I saw two old men who were said to have lived there forty years without ever leaving it. What made me decide to mention them was the report of their virtues I had from the testimony of the abbot himself and the conversation of all the brothers, especially this—that the sun had never seen one of these two monks eating, nor the other angry.'[1]

On hearing this, Gallus looked at me and said: 'If only that friend of yours were now here—I refuse to give his name—I should greatly like him to hear this example, whose violent anger against many persons we have experienced too often. True, from what I learn he has recently forgiven his enemies. Still, if he could hear the example just given, he would become more and more confirmed in the belief that it is a wonderful virtue not to let yourself be stirred up by anger. I will not deny that he had just causes for his wrath, but, where the battle is hottest, there the crown of victory is most glorious. That is why, in my opinion, high praise is justly owed to a certain man whom you may recognize.[2] When an ungrateful freedman of his abandoned him, he pitied rather than reviled the runaway. He was not even angry with the man who apparently took this freedman off

---

1 The same statement is made about two other hermits by Cassian, *De instit. coenob.* 5.27 (*PL* 49.245; *CSEL* 17.103).

2 It may be that Sulpicius himself is meant. The freedman is probably The Pomponius that Sulpicius calls 'ours' in *Dial.* 3.18; see n. 2 there, with Babut's suggestion that the famous Vigilantius was the abductor.

with him. For my part,[3] if Postumianus had not brought forward that example of victory over wrath, I should be very angry about the fugitive's leave-taking. But, because anger is not permitted, let us stop talking about all those things that are painful to us. It is you, Postumianus, you we want to hear from.'

'I shall do what you wish, Gallus,' he said, 'since I see the two of you are so eager to listen. But remember, I am not depositing my story with you free of interest.[4] I gladly furnish what you demand, but on the condition that you will not deny my own demands a little later.'

'The two of us,' I said, 'have nothing with which to discharge our debt, even without interest. Still, demand whatever you choose, provided that you continue to satisfy our desires. We are utterly charmed with your narrative.'

'I shall not deceive your hopes,' said Postumianus. 'Now that you have learned about the virtue of one hermit, I shall tell you briefly of many more.'

---

3 In Halm's text, the words *Ego autem* are followed by a semicolon, to indicate that Sulpicius, the initial first-person narrator of the dialogue, is the speaker of the remainder of the paragraph. In the opening of the following paragraph, Halm reads the vocative *Sulpici* instead of the *Galle* of all the MSS. In all of this Halm follows Da Prato. In line with a suggestion made by Hyltén 78, I have replaced the semicolon after *Ego autem* with a comma (thus continuing Gallus as the speaker) and restored *Galle,* re-establishing the text in the form it had before Da Prato, e.g., in the edition of Giselinus (Antwerp 1574; cf. his note, p. 384). It is quite reasonable that Gallus, as a person friendly to Sulpicius, might have been inclined to anger at the abduction of the latter's freedman. The Da Prato-Halm text is indeed quite acceptable in itself, but the unsupported change to *Sulpici* is unwarranted since not absolutely required by the context.

4 The reader may be reminded of a passage in Cicero's dialogue, *Brutus,* in which Cicero acknowledges a debt to Atticus for the assistance he received from reading Atticus's *Liber Annalis* and promises repayment in full measure (Cicero, *Brutus* 4.15-5.20). The debt-motif in a dialogue reappears in St. Augustine, *De magistro* 7.19.

Chapter 13

'I had now come into the first stretches of the desert, about twelve miles from the Nile. As a guide, I had one of the brothers who had a good knowledge of the region. We arrived at the dwelling of an old man who lived at the foot of a mountain. Here, we found something that is very rare in those parts, a well. The old man owned an ox, whose work consisted entirely in turning a wheel for drawing water. The garden there was full of vegetables, contrary to what is usually the case in the desert. There, everything is parched, burned by the heat of the sun. Nowhere can the least root of any plant draw nourishment. That holy man owed his crop to the joint labor of himself and the ox and to his own diligence. What gave fertility to the sands was the repeated irrigation. As we saw, this caused the vegetables in that garden to be remarkably vigorous and fruitful. These were what the ox, along with his master, lived on, and from this same abundant supply the holy man gave us dinner. I saw there something you Gauls will perhaps not believe: the pot was filled with the vegetables that were being prepared for dinner and was boiling without any fire. The sun's heat is so great that there is no cook who would not find it sufficient even for preparing Gallic specialties.

'After dinner, when evening was coming on, our host invited us to go and see a palm tree, whose fruit he would eat from time to time. It was about two miles away. In the desert, palms are the only trees, and these are rare. Was it the industry of antiquity which provided them, or do they come about from the force of the sun? I do not know. Perhaps God foresaw that the desert was one day to be inhabited by His saints and provided these trees in advance for His servants. Of the people who have settled in those solitudes where there are no other plants, the greater part feed themselves on palm fruit.

'When we came to the tree to which our kind host was leading us, we met a lion there. My guide and I trembled at the sight of him, but the old man approached without hesitation. In spite of our fear, we followed him. The beast discreetly withdrew a short distance, as if under orders from God. He stopped while the old man picked the fruit that hung from the lower branches. He held out a handful of dates. The beast came running up and took the fruit more gently than any domestic animal. When he had eaten, he went away. As we watched this, still trembling, it was not hard for us to measure the great strength of the old man's faith and the extreme weakness of our own.'

Chapter 14

'We saw another man equally remarkable. He lived in a tiny hut not big enough for more than one. It was told of him that a she-wolf regularly attended him at dinner. The beast almost never failed to come running up at the regular mealtime. She would wait outside the door until the hermit would hand out whatever bread was left over from his meal. She would lick his hand and, as if having performed the proper courtesies and extended her greetings, go away.

'It once happened that the holy man had had a brother visit him and was accompanying him on his way home. In consequence, he was away some little while and failed to return until nightfall. Meanwhile, the beast had presented herself at the customary mealtime. She sensed that the cell was empty and that her familiar patron was not at home. She went in, making a careful search where the master could be. By chance, a palm-leaf basket hung near by, containing five loaves of bread. The wolf took one of these and devoured it.

After perpetrating this crime, she went away. On his return, the hermit saw that the basket was disarranged and did not contain the proper number of loaves. He realized there had been a theft from his supply and near the threshold found fragments of the loaf that had been eaten. He then had no uncertainty about the identity of the thief. In the following days, the beast did not come as usual. She was, no doubt, conscious of her presumptuous deed and was refraining from visiting the victim of her wrong-doing. On his part, the hermit was distressed at losing the comfort of the guest and companion of his meals. After seven days, recalled by the hermit's prayers, the wolf was there again, as before, for dinner. The embarrassment of the penitent was easy to see. The wolf did not presume to come close. In deep shame, she would not lift her eyes from the ground. It was plain that she was imploring some act of pardon. The hermit had pity on her confusion. He ordered her to come near and with a caressing hand stroked her sorrowful head. Then he refreshed the culprit with a double ration of bread. The wolf had received her pardon. She put her grief aside and renewed her habitual visits.

'I ask you to consider this very special aspect of Christ's charity. Through His grace even the brute is intelligent, even the savage beast is gentle. A wolf does acts of courtesy, a wolf recognizes the sin of theft, a wolf feels guilt and is ashamed. When summoned, she comes, she offers her head and perceives that forgiveness has been granted, just as before she had carried the shame of wrong-doing. This is the power, O Christ, of Thy charity; these, O Christ, are Thy miracles. For, whatever Thy servants do in Thy name, these things are Thine. And for this, indeed, do we grieve: that savage beasts perceive Thy majesty when men do not revere it.'

Chapter 15

'If anyone happens to find the foregoing story incredible, I have still greater marvels to tell. Faith in Christ is my witness that I am not inventing anything. I shall tell nothing that has been circulated from uncertain sources, and I shall confine myself to what I have learned through trustworthy men.

'There are a large number of men called anchorites who inhabit the desert without any huts to cover them. They live on the roots of herbs, and, out of fear of frequent visitors, they never remain fixed in any one spot. Wherever night finds them, that is their dwelling.[1] There was a man following this mode and rule of life whom two monks of Nitria[2] set out to find. They were, indeed, coming from a distant region, but they had once been the object of his special affection, when they all lived in a monastery, and they had heard subsequently of his miracles. After a long and intensive search, they finally found him, in the seventh month, living on the very edge of the desert, near Memphis.[3] It was said he had been inhabiting those solitudes for twelve years. In spite of his desire to avoid any meeting with man, he did not flee from the visitors when he recognized them. He even devoted him-

1 Cf. Sallust, *Bellum Jugurth.* 18.2

2 Nitria: a marshy wasteland west of the lower part of the Egyptian delta, the modern Wadi Natrun; an area of great importance in the history of monasticism in Egypt.

3 Da Prato, following the important MS. of Brescia (*B*), read *Blembis contiguum* ('near the Blembi') instead of *Memphis contiguum.* In Ch. 22. we read of military expeditions *contra Blembos.* If, as seems quite likely (cf. *Thes. Ling. Lat., s.v.* 'Blemyes'), *Blembi* is a variant of *Blemyes,* the speaker here had in mind a people of Ethiopian origin who were much given in the early centuries of our era to plundering southern Egypt; cf. Sethe in PWK 3.566ff. Their normal boundaries lay at a considerable distance from Nitria, whereas Memphis was relatively close. This and other arguments detailed by Da Prato make the reading *Blembis contiguum* more probable than the alternative.

self for three days to their friendly demands. On the fourth day, when they left, he went forward a short distance to accompany them. Suddenly, they saw a lioness of remarkable size coming toward them. The beast, though confronted with three men, had no hesitation as to which she would approach. She lay down at the feet of the anchorite. Lying there, she whimpered and whined and gave signs of grieving and at the same time of asking for something. All three men were moved, especially the anchorite, since the request was directed to him. The lioness went ahead and they followed. She stopped from time to time, and from time to time looked back, making it quite clear that what she wanted was that the anchorite should follow where she was leading. Why lengthen the tale? They came to the beast's cave. Here, the unfortunate mother nourished five cubs now well grown, who were born with closed eyes and had been blind ever since. One by one the mother brought them from the cave and laid them at the feet of the anchorite. At last, the saint saw what the beast was asking for. He called on God's name and with his hand touched the closed eyes of the cubs. At once, the darkness was dispelled, the beasts' eyes were opened, and the light long denied them shone in.[4]

'This done, the brothers returned. They had visited the anchorite they were eager to see and had received a very rich reward for their toil. They had become witnesses of a great miracle. As well as the saint's faith, they had seen Christ's glory, to which they were called on to testify. The story embraces still another miracle. After five days, the lioness returned to her benefactor, bringing him as a gift the skin of

4 Rufinus relates a similar story about a certain Macarius: *Hist. eccl.* 11.4 (ed. Mommsen in E. Schwartz's edition of Eusebius, *Hist. eccl.*: *Eusebius Werke* 2.2 [Leipzig 1908] 1006f.; or *PL* 21.512, where Bk. 11 is treated as Bk. 2) . Cf. Delehaye 50.

a rare animal. The saint would frequently wear this as a mantle, not declining to receive from the beast a gift he believed to have quite another source.'

Chapter 16

'Another anchorite of that region was very renowned. He lived in the part of the desert near Syene.[1] When he first came to the desert, where he intended to live on the roots of herbs (which grow in the sand and are sometimes very sweet and of an exquisite flavor), he was not skilled in distinguishing among plants and often gathered harmful ones. Nor was it easy to distinguish the nature of the roots by their taste. All were equally sweet, but many contained a hidden, poisonous liquid. As the anchorite was eating, he felt violent torture: all his vitals were racked by horrible pains; he vomited frequently from a stomach weakened to exhaustion; his sufferings were unendurable and threatened his very life. In dread of anything that was edible, he ate nothing for seven days. When his life's breath was failing, a wild beast approached him, an ibex. As it stood near, the anchorite threw it a bunch of herbs he had collected but had not dared to eat. The beast used its muzzle to put to one side the herbs that were poisonous and choose out those it knew were harmless. This example taught the anchorite what he should eat and what he should reject. He could now avoid poisonous herbs and thus escape the danger of hunger.

'But, to deal with all those who inhabit the desert, relating both what I saw myself and what I heard from others, would be a long story. I spent a whole year and almost seven months living in the desert. I could admire the virtue of

1 The modern Assuam, at the first cataract of the Nile; seat of a bishop as early as the fourth century.

others even when I could not undertake for myself a plan of life so arduous and difficult. Much of the time I passed with the old man who had the well and the ox.'

Chapter 17

'I visited two monasteries of the blessed Antony,[1] which are today occupied by his disciples. I even went to the place in which the very blessed Paul, the first hermit,[2] used to live. I saw the Red Sea and the mountain chain in which Sinai lies. The peak of Mount Sinai itself reaches nearly to heaven and is inaccessible.

'It was reported that an anchorite lived in the recesses of Mount Sinai, but, even after a long and intensive search, I failed to see him. He had cut himself off from human intercourse some fifty years before. He used no clothing. Covered only by the hairs of his own body, he was enabled by divine grace to ignore his nakedness. Whenever pious men tried to visit him, he ran to some inaccessible place and thus avoided human contact. It was said that he had let himself be interviewed only once, five years before, and that, I suppose, by a man whose strong faith had merited the privilege. The two had a long talk together. When the anchorite was asked why he so resolutely avoided men, it is said he replied that whoever receives visits from men cannot receive visits from angels. This remark led, not unreasonably, to the very general and widely circulated belief that this holy man often had angels as visitors.

1 St. Antony of the Desert (d. 356); *Roman Martyrology,* January 17. His life was written in Greek by St. Athanasius (*PG* 26.835ff.). The Latin translation made promptly by Evagrius (also in *PG, loc. cit.*) is held by Babut 75ff. to have been a principal source for Sulpicius's *Life of Saint Martin;* cf. above, p. 90.

2 St. Paul of Thebes (d. 347? at a reported age of 113), the founder, according to St. Jerome, of the monastic life; *Roman Martyrology,* January 10 and 15. St. Jerome's life of St. Paul is found in *PL* 23.17ff.

'As for me, when I left Mount Sinai, I went back toward the Nile. I covered both its banks and found them thick with monasteries. I saw that, for the most part, as I said a while back,[3] the monks live together in groups of a hundred. However, it is not unknown for two or three thousand to form a single community. You must not suppose that the monks who live together in large numbers are inferior in virtue to those men I have been speaking of, who have withdrawn themselves from human society. Among the former, the chief and outstanding virtue is obedience, as I have said.[4] Of such as come to the monastery only those are admitted by the abbot who have undergone probation: they must give evidence that they will never disobey an order of the abbot, however trying or difficult or intolerable it be.'

Chapter 18

'I shall relate two striking miracles of almost incredible obedience. My memory could supply a good many more; yet, when a few examples are not enough to excite emulation of virtue, there is no gain in multiplying them.

'A certain man who had renounced the active life of the world sought to be admitted into a monastery where the observance was very strict. The abbot proposed a number of things for him to consider: the discipline there was very trying; he himself was severe in his orders—there was no one whose patience could easily execute them; he ought to seek out another monastery, where the monks lived under an easier rule; he should not attempt to undertake what he could not fulfill. The candidate, however, was not disturbed by these terrifying prospects. He promised absolute obedience. Yes,

3 Ch. 10.
4 *Ibid.*

even if the abbot should order him to go into fire, he would not refuse. The master, hearing this promise, did not delay to put it to the test. As it happened, an oven stood near, heated by a roaring fire and ready for baking bread. Flame streamed out of its sides and, in the hollow chamber within, the fire raged unchecked.[1] The master ordered the newcomer to go in. The disciple instantly obeyed the command, entering unhesitatingly into the midst of the flames. So bold a faith could not be withstood. At his coming, the flames immediately receded, as they had long ago in the case of the Hebrew boys.[2] In the retreat of the flames, nature itself was conquered. It had been thought that the candidate would be burned; instead, he came out, to his own surprise, moistened, as it were, with a cooling dew. But, O Christ, why should we be surprised that the fire did not touch him, when the beginner being tried was Thine? So it resulted that the abbot did not have to repent his harsh command, nor the disciple regret his obedience. On the very day of his arrival, tried as being weak, he was found perfect. He deserved his happiness, he deserved his glory; tested in obedience, he was glorified in his suffering.'

Chapter 19

'The following incident occurred in the same monastery, where it was described as a recent happening. Another man had come to the same abbot to be admitted. The sovereign law of obedience was laid before him, and he promised a patience that would not fail under any test, however extreme. As it happened, the abbot was carrying in his hand a branch of storax that for some time had been dead. He set this into

1 With the Lat. (*totis habenis regnabat incendium*) cf. Virgil, *Aeneid* 5.662.

2 Cf. Dan. 3.50.

the ground and assigned the newcomer the task of caring for it. He was to water that rod until, contrary to all that was natural, the dry wood planted in dry soil should put forth leaves. It was a harsh order that the newcomer must obey. On his own shoulders he brought water daily, drawn from the Nile two miles away. When a whole year had passed, his labor continued and there seemed to be no hope for any result; still, the strength of his obedience resisted fatigue. The following year likewise only mocked the vain toil of the brother, who was now weakened. As time went by, a third year was running its course, and night and day the water-bearer did not fail in his work. Finally, the rod flowered. I have myself seen the shrub that grew from it. With its branches flourishing, it stands today in the court of the monastery, an abiding witness to the merits of obedience and the power of faith.[1]

'But the day would fail me before I could exhaust the various miracles I have learned of as proving the virtues of the saints.'

Chapter 20

'I still have two remarkable stories to tell. One supplies an impressive warning against being puffed up with miserable pride; the other is a striking lesson against false justice.

'There was a certain holy man endowed with an unbelievable power of driving out demons from the bodies of the possessed. Every day he worked unheard-of wonders. Neither his physical presence nor the sound of his voice was required. Possessed bodies were sometimes cured with shreds of his hair shirt or with letters he had sent. Consequently, he re-

1 A similar story is told by Cassian, *De instit. coenob.* 4.24 (*PL* 49.183f.; *CSEL* 17.636).

ceived an extraordinary number of visitors, who came to him from all over the world. Not to mention persons of lower station, there were often prefects and counts and officials of various ranks lying before his door. Most holy bishops also put aside their episcopal dignity and humbly begged to be touched and blessed by him. Not without reason, they thought they were sanctified and illumined by divine grace every time they touched his hand or his clothing. People believed that he was strictly abstaining from any kind of drink for the rest of his life and that, when it came to food—this, Sulpicius, I shall say in your ear, so that Gallus will not hear it—six dried figs[1] could sustain him. As time went by, the honor that came to the holy man from his miraculous power caused vanity to creep in. When he was first able to perceive within himself the progress of this evil, he tried long and hard to shake it off. But, while his power continued, he could not altogether dispel his vanity, even through the secret awareness of it that he had. His name was proclaimed everywhere by the demons. He was unable to keep away the throngs that flocked to him. With time, the latent poison crept deep into his soul. His simple nod was enough to drive the demons from the bodies of others, yet he could not purge his own self of secret thoughts of vanity.

'As the report runs, he turned to God with all the force of his prayers. He begged that for five months power be given to the Devil to make him like those persons he had cured. Why prolong the story? This man of extraordinary power, who was known throughout the Orient for his signs and wonders, to whose threshold there had come a stream of people, at whose door the highest powers of this world had

1 The figs are seven in number, according to some MSS. In the *Vita Pauli* 6 (*PL* 23.21) St. Jerome had told of a holy man of Egypt who could be sustained by five dried figs. Cf. Babut 49 n. 2; Delehaye 48.

lain prostrate, this man was seized by the Devil and held by his chains. When he had endured for five months all those sufferings which come to the possessed, he was cleansed—not of the Devil alone, but also of his vanity; a deliverance which he found more useful and desirable.'

Chapter 21

'As I tell all this, I can't help thinking of our own unhappiness[1] and our own weakness. Who of us, if he receives a humble greeting from some one wretched man or is commended with words of empty flattery by one mere woman, is not at once puffed up with pride and inflated with vanity? Even if he is fully aware that he has no sanctity, let him be called a saint through empty flattery or, perhaps, by some mistake, and he will think himself a paragon of holiness. If he is the recipient of frequent gifts, he will claim that it is the magnificence of God that is honoring him; even if he sleeps or takes his rest he will receive his necessities! If he experiences, even in a small matter, any sign at all of supernatural power, he will imagine himself an angel. Take someone quite inconspicuous either for deeds or virtues, and let him be made a cleric. He will at once broaden the fringes of his clothes, find pleasure in being spoken to, pride himself on the visits he receives, and gad about everywhere. Before, he used to go on foot or ride a donkey; now, he must be proudly drawn by foaming horses.[2] While once he lived happily in a mean and tiny cell, he now makes high the coffered ceilings and constructs room after room, has the doors

1 Lat. *infelicitas*. Hyltén 149, following Fürtner, makes out a plausible case for accepting instead the reading of *D* and *V*: *infidelitas* ('weakness of faith').

2 The Lat. phrase *spumantibus equis* may have been suggested by Virgil, *Aeneid* 6.881.

carved and the sideboards painted. Of rough clothing he will have none; it is on soft garments that his heart is set. He gets them as tribute from his dear widows and the virgins who are his familiars: this lady must weave him a nice thick raincoat, another a flowing mantle.[3] A more biting description of these things we must leave to the blessed man Jerome. Let us return to our subject.'

'I do not know what it is you have left to Jerome to discuss,' said my friend Gallus. 'In short compass, you have embraced all the practices of our compatriots. Those few words of yours, if they could be received without prejudice and pondered patiently, would do them so much good that I think they would have no further need to be corrected by the books of Jerome. But, please turn now to completing what you have begun. Give us that lesson you promised us against the dangers of false justice. To speak frankly with you, that is the most pernicious evil we suffer from in these Gallic regions.'

'I shall do so,' said Postumianus, 'and hola you in suspense no longer.'

Chapter 22

'A young man, of Asiatic origin, very rich, of distinguished parentage, married, and the father of a little son, was a tribune in Egypt. In a series of expeditions against the Blembi[1] he had reached various parts of the desert and had actually seen many of the rude huts of the holy hermits. From the blessed

3 The exact character of the two garments in question (*byrrus,* usually spelled *birrus*; *lacerna*) is uncertain. Da Prato's long discussion (*ed. Sulp.* 1.364-369) is full of curious detail.

1 On the Blembi (= Blemyes?) see Ch. 15 n. 3.

man John[2] he had received the message of salvation. Thereupon, he immediately despised as useless the military life and all its empty honors. He boldly entered the desert and became a shining example of perfection in all the virtues. He was mighty in fasting and outstanding for his humility. In his firm faith and zealous charity he easily equalled the monks of old times. Meanwhile, a thought crept into his mind, placed there by the Devil: it would be better for him to return to his native land and save his only son, his wife, and all his household. This, surely, would be more acceptable to God than being content with his own escape from the world; it would be a defect of charity for him to neglect the salvation of his own.

'He yielded to this pretext of justice, false though it was, and, after nearly four years, abandoned his cell and his hermit's vows. He came to the nearest monastery, inhabited by a large number of brothers. When they questioned him, he revealed the cause of his withdrawal and the plan he had in mind. All of them, especially the abbot, opposed his project, yet could not dislodge the firm intention to which his mind so unfortunately clung. So, the poor obstinate fellow rushed out and left the brothers, to the sorrow of all. He had hardly gone out of their sight when a demon took possession of him. With bloody foam issuing from his mouth, he began tearing his own body with his teeth. The brothers of that monastery brought him back on their shoulders. Since they could not restrain the unclean spirit which possessed him, they were compelled to put him in irons, his feet bound to his hands. The fugitive's punishment seemed not undeserved; when faith

---

2 St. John of Lycopolis, Egyptian hermit of the fourth century (*Roman Martyrology,* March 27). Cf. Da Prato *ad loc.* also Palladius, *Lausiac History* 35 (ed. C. Butler [*Texts and Studies,* ed. J. A. Robinson 6.2 (Cambridge 1904)] 100; with Butler's note 61, p. 212).

could not restrain him, it only remained for chains to do so. After two years, the prayers of the saints obtained his release from the unclean spirit. He at once returned to the desert which he had left. Through his own correction, he was to serve as a lesson to others, that one should not be deceived by any false semblance of justice or let restlessness or frivolity force him to abandon what had once been undertaken.[3]

'Here, then, is what I had to tell you about the Lord's miracles as worked in his servants, showing us now what we should imitate, now what we should dread. I hope this is enough. Now that I have given satisfaction to your ears, or rather, more than satisfaction (for I probably have been wordier than I should have), it is up to you.' (It was then to me he was speaking.) 'Pay off that interest you owe. Following your custom, tell us more about your dear Martin. I have eagerly desired this for a long time.'

Chapter 23

'Tell me,' I said, 'are you not satisfied with the book I wrote about Martin? You know well that I published one on his life and miracles.'

'I am familiar with that fact,' said Postumianus. 'Indeed, that book of yours has never left my hands. If you recognize it, look: here it is!' The book had been hidden under his clothing and he opened it. 'It has been my companion on land and sea. In all my travels it has been my associate and my comforter. I shall tell you how far that book of yours has

3 The greater part of the text of *Dial.* 1 from Ch. 3 to this point is contained in Chs. 1-14 of the fourth book of the *Vitae Patrum,* edited in 1615 and 1628 by the Jesuit H. Rosweyde: *PL* 73.813-824; the conversational exchanges between the speakers are not included. While it is not known who drew up these excerpts—Rosweyde suggested a fifth-century compiler—they form a good source for the text of Sulpicius.

penetrated. There is almost no place in the whole world where the happy story it tells is not commonly known. First to bring the book to Rome was your great friend Paulinus.[1] Copies were zealously snatched up all over the city. I saw the booksellers there carried away with joy. It was their most profitable item, they said; nothing sold more readily and nothing sold at a higher price. When I crossed over the sea, it had long before preceded me. When I arrived in Africa, it was already being read throughout Carthage. Alone in not knowing it was my Cyrenian priest,[2] but I lent it to him and he copied it. What to say about Alexandria? There almost everybody knew it better than you do. It had traversed Egypt, Nitria, the Thebaid, and all the kingdom of Memphis. I once saw an old man in the desert reading it. When I told him I was a good friend of yours, he—and many of the brothers, too—charged me with this mission: if I should ever reach your country and find you safe and sound, I was to compel you to complete your book on the virtues of the blessed man, adding what you there said you had omitted. Come, then! What has already been written down is enough for the book. It is not that which I am eager to hear, but, rather, all that you left out, for fear, I suppose, of wearying your readers. Please tell us that, and so comply with a wish that many men join me in making.'

Chapter 24

'Just now, Postumianus,' I said, 'when I was listening intently to what you were saying about the miracles of those holy men, my secret thoughts kept going back to my dear Martin. I think I was justified in concluding that all those

1 See above, p. 80f., and *Life* Ch. 19 n. 2.
2 See above, Chs. 4, 5.

various deeds done by many individuals had plainly been matched by Martin singly. The acts you reported were indeed of a noble quality, yet—and may none of the saints be offended at this—I heard from you absolutely nothing which shows his inferiority.

'When I claim that there is no one whose virtue is comparable to the merits of that great man, there is one point that ought to be noticed: any comparison between him and the hermits, or even the anchorites, is not made on an equal basis. All their quite admirable deeds were performed by men unhampered by any impediment, with only heaven and the angels to witness. It was otherwise with Martin: he lived surrounded by the thronging community of men, in the midst of dissident clerics, of fanatic bishops; nearly every day scandals bore down upon him from one direction or another. Yet, he stood firm on a base of virtue which none of those things could overthrow. And the deeds he thus performed were beyond the doing even of those men who, as you told us, either live in the desert or once lived there. Even if their accomplishments were equal to his, what judge could be so unjust as not to give him the verdict of well-deserved superiority? Put it this way: Martin was a soldier who fought in an unfavorable position, but emerged victor. Liken them, also, to soldiers, but soldiers who did combat from a good position or even from high ground. What conclusion is to be drawn? All, indeed, are victors, but not all can have equal glory. Again, among the marvellous things you reported, there was no mention of anyone raising a dead man to life.[1] This one count compels us to recognize that no one is comparable to Martin.'

---

1 See *Life* Ch. 7 and n. 3 there.

Chapter 25

'The case of the Egyptian untouched by fire[1] does, indeed, win our admiration; yet Martin more than once was master over flames.[2] If you are thinking of how the anchorites could conquer and subdue the fierceness of wild beasts,[3] Martin was no stranger to restraining raging beasts and poisonous serpents.[4] Perhaps you bring forward for comparison the man who cured the victims of unclean spirits by the power of his words or even through the virtue found in the fringes of his garments.[5] There are many proofs that Martin was not inferior even in such cases.[6] If you fall back on the man whose body's hair served him for clothes and who was thought to be visited by angels,[7] angels talked every day with Martin.[8]

'Further, in the face of vanity and presumption, Martin's spirit was unconquered; no one spurned these vices more bravely than he. Even when not present, he often cured persons possessed by unclean spirits. And not only counts and prefects obeyed him, but emperors themselves.[9] This is, indeed, the least among his virtues, but I want you to realize that he resisted not only vanity as no one else did, but also the causes and occasions of vanity.

'Although what I am about to tell is only a small matter, it should not be passed over. It supplies a basis for praising

---

1 Cf. *Dial.* 1.18.
2 Cf. *Life* 14; *Epist.* 1 (*Dial.* 2.9).
3 Cf. *Dial.* 1.10; *ibid.* 14-16.
4 Cf. *Epist.* 3 (p. 155); *Dial.* 2.9, 3.3, 3.9.
5 Cf. *Dial.* 1.20.
6 For miracles worked by Martin from a considerable distance, cf. *Life* 12; *Dial.* 2.3, 3.6, 3.14; miracle worked through invocation of Martin's name: *Dial.* 3.3 (cf. 3.14); miracles worked through garments or other objects touched by Martin: *Life* 18, 19; *Dial.* 2.8, 3.5.
7 Cf. *Dial.* 1.17.
8 See *Life* Ch. 21 n. 1.
9 Cf. *Dial.* 2.5, 3.4, 3.12 (less clear example: *Life* 20).

a man endowed with high political power who nevertheless showed a pious inclination to venerate the blessed Martin. The man I have in mind is the prefect Vincentius.[10] A man of great distinction, he was unsurpassed for any kind of virtue in all the Gallic provinces. When passing through Tours, he often asked Martin to have him for dinner in his monastery. (He quoted as precedent the example of the blessed bishop Ambrose,[11] who at that time was said often to entertain consuls and prefects.) But Martin, in his deep wisdom, refused, fearing from his consent that vanity and pride might creep into his soul.

'In view of this, you must admit that there were present in Martin the virtues of all those you have named, while in them, even taken as a whole, Martin's virtues were not altogether included.'

Chapter 26

'Why deal with me like this?' said Postumianus. 'As if I am not and have not always been of your opinion. As for me, as long as I live and have my reason with me, I shall celebrate the monks of Egypt, I shall praise the anchorites, I shall admire the hermits. But Martin I shall always treat as a special case. There is no monk and surely no bishop I should dare compare with him. This is what Egypt and Syria admit, what the Ethiopian has learned, what the Indian has heard, what the Parthian and the Persian know so well; Armenia[1] is

10 *Praefectus praetorio* in Gaul in the years immediately preceding 400, according to evidence cited by Bihlmeyer 99 n. 4.

11 Sulpicius mentions the great bishop of Milan (373-397) only here and in the *Chronica* 2.48, where his hostility to the Priscillianists is referred to (*PL* 20.124; *CSEL* 1.101).

1 In his *Vita S. Antonii* 93, St. Athanasius includes a similar but shorter list of places to which the fame of his hero had spread (*PG* 26.973); cf. Babut 81f. and above, Ch. 17 n. 1.

not ignorant of it, or the Bosphorus, for all its isolation, or such inhabitants as there be of the Fortunate Isles[2] or of the glacial Ocean.[3] Is there any region more wretched than that of our own compatriots, not meriting to know so great a man, even when he was so close to them? Yet, I would not involve the laity in this charge. It is only the clergy, it is only the bishops who do not know him. And it is not without reason that, in their envy, they refuse to know him: knowledge of his virtues would make them aware of their own vices. I actually am afraid to tell you something I recently heard: that some unfortunate or other declared you had included a number of lies in your book. It is the Devil who spoke there, not a man. The speech involved not any detraction of Martin, but an outright refusal to believe in the Gospels. The Lord Himself testified that such deeds would be done by all the faithful.[4] These Martin has performed. Anyone who does not believe that Martin has done these things denies the very words of Christ. But these unfortunates, these sleepers, these degenerates are ashamed that he has done what they themselves cannot do. They deny his miracles rather than confess their own impotence.

'But, since we must hasten to other things, let us put aside all reference to those people. You are the man to speak. Tell us the rest of Martin's deeds. We have long been eager to hear them.'

'In my opinion,' I answered, 'you would have done better to put your request to Gallus. He knows more than I do—a disciple cannot fail to know the deeds of his master—and it is also his turn to speak. He owes it not only to Martin, but

---

2 The Isles of the Blessed have a tradition as old as Homer; in extant Latin writings, Plautus, *Trinummus* 549, seems to be the earliest mention.

3 Sulpicius may have had in mind Juvenal, *Satires* 2.1.

4 Cf. John 14.12.

to us. I have already published my book, and you have been telling us up to now about the deeds of the Orientals. In this conversation among friends, it is for Gallus to tell the story. As I have said, he owes it to us to take his turn at speaking. And, if I am right, he will gladly serve his dear Martin by relating his deeds.'

Chapter 27

'Unequal as I am to this burden,' said Gallus, 'the examples of obedience brought forward by Postumianus compel me not to refuse the task you impose upon me. Yet, remembering that I, a Gaul, am about to speak among Aquitanians, I am afraid that my rather rustic speech will offend your city-trained ears.[1] Yet, the language you will hear from me will be free from pretense and tragic elevation, as befits that of a man from Gourdon.[2] In assigning me a place among Martin's pupils, you must also make me a concession: that I may use

1 On Aquitanian refinement cf. Jerome, *Epist.* 125.6 (*PL* 22.1075; *CSEL* 56. 123); Ammianus Marcellinus 15.11; Salvian, *De gubernatione Dei* 7.2.8 (p. 187 of J. F. O'Sullivan's translation in this series).

2 Lat. *audietis me tamen ut Gurdonicum.* What to do with *Gurdonicum* is a problem. The *Thes. ling. Lat.* (*s. v*). reports the word only from this passage, declaring its origin unclear (possibly 'Gallic') and its meaning uncertain. It is tempting to follow Da Prato and others and see the word as a derivation from *gurdus* (assigning it then some such meaning as 'rude' or 'rustic'), but modern etymology forbids this (cf. A. Ernout-A. Meillet, *Dict. étymologique de la langue latine* [nouv. éd. Paris 1939] 438). I tentatively follow Bihlmeyer and Monceaux in making the problem-word a place-adjective, but am no surer than is the former as to where to locate an appropriate Gourdon. A likely possibility is a Gourdon near Chalon-sur-Saône (dep. Saône-et-Loire); cf. Longnon, *Géographie* 218. This Gourdon is sufficiently removed from the cultivated Aquitanian region to make the speaker's point clear. The same can be said for Jullian's suggestion, Sancerre (dep. Cher), originally named Gortona, he reports (*REA* 25.250). Sancerre is near Bourges, a fact which leads Jullian to propose re-examining the long abandoned tradition which made Sulpicius a bishop of Bourges; cf. above, p. 83.

his speech as a model and disdain all rhetorical decoration and verbal ornament.'[3]

'Speak Celtic,' said Postumianus, 'or Gallic, if you prefer so to call it,[4] provided that Martin is your subject. I think that, even if you were dumb, you would not lack for words with which to speak eloquently of Martin. The tongue of Zacharias was loosened when it came to pronouncing the name of John.[5] Anyway, you are a scholar and you use the scholar's artifice of excusing your ignorance when, actually, your mouth runs over with eloquence. Such astuteness does not befit a monk or such cunning a Gaul.[6] But, enough of that! Begin and meet your obligation. We have already wasted too much time in doing other things. The lengthening shadow of the setting sun now warns us that there is not much left of the day and that night is near.'

We kept quiet for a little while; then, Gallus began: 'Above all, as I speak of Martin's miracles, I must avoid repeating what Sulpicius here has already told in his book. Consequently, I shall pass over his early deeds, those of his military life, and I shall not touch on what he did as a layman and a monk. Further, I shall avoid all second-hand accounts and speak only of what I myself have seen.'

---

3 See *Life* 25 (end) for Sulpicius's commendation of Martin's speech.

4 Lat. *vel Celtice aut, si mavis, Gallice loquere*. J. Whatmough, in *Harvard Stud. in Class. Philol.* 55 (1944) 72 n. 151, holds that no opposition between 'Celtic' and 'Gallic' is intended.

5 Cf. Luke 1.64.

6 The Gauls had a certain reputation for dullness. Bihlmeyer appropriately cites the phrases 'stolid Gauls' and 'Gallic stolidity' from the fourth-century rhetor Firmicus Maternus, *Mathesis* 1.2.3; 1.2.4.

the speech as a model and disdain all rhetorical decoration and verbal ornament.[3]

"Speak Gallic," said Postumianus, "or Celtic if you prefer so to call it,[4] provided that Martin is your subject. I think that, even if you were dumb, you would not lack for words with which to speak eloquently of Martin. The tongue of Zachary was loosened when it came to pronouncing the name of John. Anyway, you are a scholar and you use the Scholar's practice of excusing your ignorance when, actually, your mouth overflows with eloquence. [illegible] does not need [illegible] speak or such [illegible] Gallus,[5] enough of that. Begin and [illegible] your explanation. We have already wasted too much time in doing other things. The lengthening shadow of the setting sun now warns us that there is not much left of the day and that night is near."[6]

We kept quiet for a little while, then Gallus began: "Above all, I [illegible] speak of Martin's miracles. I must avoid repeating what my companion here has already told in his book. Consequently, I shall pass over his earlier deeds, those of his military life, and I shall not touch on what he did as a layman and a monk. Further, I shall avoid all secondhand reports and speak only of what I myself have seen.

3 See I Cor. 2.4, and [illegible] communication of Martin's speech.
4 The old Gallic sort of speech [illegible] ([illegible]). J. Whitmore(?), in [illegible] 28 (1940) 75 n. 134, holds that no opposition between 'Gaul' and 'Celtic' is intended.
5 Cf. Luke 19.4.
6 The Gauls had a [illegible] reputation for [illegible]; [illegible] the phrase [illegible] with 'Gallic' [illegible] from the fourth-century [illegible] 12.1.

THE SECOND DIALOGUE[1]

Chapter 1

IT WAS THE PERIOD in which I had just left school and joined the blessed Martin. A few days after this, he went to the church and we followed him. It was winter, and a half-naked man came running up to him, begging a gift of clothing. Martin called the archdeacon and told him to supply clothing at once. He himself then went into the sacristy[2] and, as was his habit, remained alone. Even in church, Martin in this way found moments of solitude, while giving full liberty to the clerics. The priests used another sacristy, where they either had time to see visitors or kept themselves occupied listening to matters of business. Martin, however, guarded his solitude right up to the hour at which the regular public offices were to begin. (A fact worth mentioning is that, when sitting in the sacristy, Martin never used the bishop's chair. In fact, no one ever saw him use it in the church proper. In this he was unlike a certain bishop whom, to my embarrassment, I recently saw seated high on a towering throne, not unlike an emperor's tribunal. All this while, Martin sat on a rustic bench of the kind that slaves use: we unpolished Gauls call them *tripecciae,* while you

1 For the connection of *Dial.* 2 with *Dial.* 1 and 3, see above, pp. 87-89.

2 Lat. *secretarium.* The incident narrated in *Epist.* 1 also occurred in a *secretarium.* Cf. also *Dial.* 3.8 and Da Prato's remarks (*ed. Sulp.* 1. 369f).

scholars—and surely you, [Postumianus,] just back from Greece—call them *tripodes.*[3])

'That day, Martin's quiet was interrupted. The archdeacon had put off giving a tunic to the pauper and he, disappointed, invaded the sacristy. He complained that the cleric had neglected him and that he was bitterly cold. Instantly, and so that the pauper could not see him, the saint drew off his tunic from under his mantle. With this he clothed the pauper and had him go away. A little later, the archdeacon came in, giving his usual warning that the people were ready in the church and that it was time for Martin to go to the altar to celebrate the office. Martin's reply was that a pauper—and here he meant himself—had to be clothed first; he could not go into the church unless the pauper received his clothing. The archdeacon, of course, understood nothing of this. Martin, having his mantle to cover him, gave no appearance of wearing nothing under it. The archdeacon finally excused himself by saying that the pauper had disappeared. 'Let the tunic that has been made ready be brought to me,' said Martin. 'The pauper will surely be here to receive his clothing.' It was a strict[4] obligation the cleric now confronted. With his anger rising high, he went to a nearby shop, picked up a short, shaggy garment from the Bigorre,[5] and bought it for five pieces of silver. In anger, he threw it at Martin's feet. 'Here is the clothing,' he said, 'but the pauper is not here.' Martin, unmoved, told him to stay a little while outside the

---

3 The form *tripecciae* was taken over by Halm directly from the MS. *V*; *tripetiae* is the more normal spelling.

4 Reading *arta tum,* as Da Prato did; cf. Hyltén 149f.

5 Lat. *bigerricam vestem.* Cf. *Thes. ling. Lat.* (*s.v., bigerricus*). The Bigorre is a part of Gascony in the neighborhood of Tarbes. Quite possibly, the phrase used by Sulpicius had virtually lost its local reference and simply designated a garment of a certain shape or texture. For various interpretations see Du Cange, *Glossarium* and Da Prato, *ed. Sulp.* 1.99 (on line 17).

door. Using every possible device to conceal what he had done, he contrived in this way to be alone while he put on the tunic to cover his nakedness. But, when can holy men succeed in keeping such things hidden from inquirers? Whether they like it or not, everything is revealed.'

Chapter 2

'Martin was wearing this tunic[1] as he advanced toward the altar to offer the sacrifice to God. On that day, something marvellous happened which I shall tell. While he was blessing the altar in the appointed manner, we saw a globe of fire spring as if from his head. It rose in the air, leaving a long trail behind it like a fiery lock of hair.[2] This happened on a feast-day, in the midst of a great multitude of people, yet, very few saw it: one of the virgins, one of the priests, and only three of the monks. Why the others did not see it, we cannot judge.

'About this same time, my uncle Evanthius,[3] a profoundly Christian man, though much occupied in worldly business, was gravely ill. Since death seemed imminent, he called for Martin. The blessed man hastened to him without delay, but, before he had come half the way, the sick man felt the miraculous power of his approach. He instantly recovered his health and went out to meet us.

'The next day, though Martin wanted to return, he remained when Evanthius begged him to do so. A slave boy belonging to the household had been poisoned by a deadly

1 See *Life,* Ch. 3 n. 2.

2 For Sulpicius's language Da Prato (*ed.* Sulp. 1.100, on line 10) cites Virgil, *Aeneid* 5.527f., Valerius Flaccus, *Argonaut.* 1.205, and other verse parallels.

3 An Evanthius was *comes* under Constantius: PWK 6.847. Babut 202 n. 1 doubts the historicity of the Evanthius in Sulpicius.

snake bite and was already nearly dead from the powerful venom. Evanthius put him on his shoulders and laid him before the holy man's feet. He was sure that nothing was impossible to Martin. The poison had already spread through the boy's entire body: you could see all the swollen veins standing out and his vital organs tense like wineskins. Martin stretched out his hand and touched all the members of the boy's body. Then he placed his finger near the tiny wound through which the beast had poured in its poison. The effect was amazing. We saw the poison stream from every part, attracted to Martin's finger, and then, mixed with blood, ooze out of the tiny opening of the wound. (It was like the long stream of milk which flows copiously from the udder of a goat or sheep when the shepherd's hand squeezes it.) The boy rose, completely cured. Dumbfounded at this great miracle, we declared, in all truth, that there was no one under heaven who could imitate Martin.'

Chapter 3

'Some time after this, we were traveling with Martin while he visited his parishes.[1] Something or other had compelled us to stay behind, and he had gone on somewhat ahead of us. Meanwhile, a vehicle belonging to the imperial treasury,[2] packed with armed officials, was making its way along the public highway. Martin was advancing on the same side of the road, wearing his shabby tunic, covered with a flowing black pallium. The mules were startled at the sight of him

1 See *Epist.* 1 n. 12.

2 Lat. *fiscalis raeda.* Babut 318 (correction to p. 204) describes the vehicle as a *'voiture des postes impériales.'* As to the mules which drew the vehicle, Da Prato noted that there is a provision in the *Codex Theodosianus* which permitted eight mules to be yoked to a wagon in summer, twelve in winter: *Cod. Theod.* 8.5.5 (ed. Mommsen, Berlin 1905, p. 377; a law of A. D. 357).

and drew over a little to the other side. Then, the traces became tangled and the whole team was thrown into disorder, for the poor animals had been harnessed together in long lines in a way you have often seen. It was not easy to disengage the mules, and this business delayed the officials, who were in a hurry. They were angered by this, jumped to the ground and began to attack Martin with whips and clubs. He said not a word, but with incredible patience gave his back to their blows. This only aroused the madness of the unfortunate officials, who were furious that he took their lashings lightly, as if he did not feel them. When we came on the scene, we found him lying on the ground where he had fallen in a faint. He was bleeding horribly and every part of his body had been mangled. We at once set him on his donkey[3] and quickly made our departure, cursing the scene of this bloody deed.

'The officials, meanwhile, had satisfied their anger and returned to their vehicle. They gave orders to start up the mules and continue the journey. But the mules remained fixed to the ground, rigid, as if they were bronze statues. The drivers shouted louder and snapped their whips on this side and that, but the mules did not so much as budge. All the passengers then rose to join in the lashing. Gallic whips were used up in the punishment the mules received. A whole grove from nearby was pulled up and the beasts were beaten with tree trunks. This savagery accomplished nothing: the mules remained in the same spot, immobile statues still. The unfortunate men did not know what to do, yet, even their stupid heads could not prevent them from recognizing that they were being held back by divine power.

'They finally came to their senses and began asking who

3 It would appear from Gregory of Tours that St. Martin habitually journeyed on a donkey: *Gloria confessorum* 5; *De virtut. S. Martini* 4.31.

it was they had beaten on that spot just a while before. Putting the question to passers-by they learned that the victim of their cruel blows was Martin. The whole thing then became clear to them all. They could not fail to see that they were being held back because of their misuse of him. So, they all set off after us at a rapid pace. They were conscious of what they had done and what they deserved; they were ashamed and confused. Weeping and with their heads and faces covered with the dust by which they had defiled themselves, they flung themselves at Martin's knees, imploring forgiveness and begging that he let them go. They had already been punished enough, they said, by their pangs of conscience. They knew full well that the earth could have swallowed them[4] up alive, or, rather, that they ought to have had their senses snatched from them and been turned into solid rock, as, indeed, they had seen their mules nailed to the ground where they stood. They begged and besought him to pardon their crime and grant them power to go away.

'Even before they came up, the blessed Martin knew that they were held fast and had told us so. Now, he mercifully forgave them, gave them back their mules, and permitted them to go away.'

Chapter 4

'I often noticed, Sulpicius, that Martin would frequently tell you that during his episcopate he did not have that fullness of miraculous power he remembered having before. If this is so—rather, since this is so—we can conjecture the magnificence of the miracles he performed when a monk or [as a bishop] alone, without a witness, since we have seen him as a bishop working great wonders in the sight of all.

4 Reading *eosdem,* as Hyltén 150 proposes.

Of the miracles he worked earlier, many escaped suppression and are known to the world. But, it is said that there are innumerable miracles which, in avoiding vanity, he concealed and kept from men's notice. He went beyond human nature: in the knowledge he had of his own power, he scorned worldly glory, wishing no other witness than heaven. We can judge the truth of this assertion even from the miracles which could not be suppressed and are known to us. Before becoming bishop, he restored two dead men to life, as your book tells in detail.[1] In the course of his episcopate, however, there was only one case of a resurrection, an incident I am surprised you omitted. Of this event I am the witness, provided, that is, you have no doubt as to the value of my testimony. How this miracle occurred, I shall now explain to you.

'For some reason or other we had set out for the town of the Carnutes.[2] As we were passing through a certain densely populated village,[3] an enormous crowd came out to meet us. It was composed entirely of pagans, for no one in that village knew a Christian. But, at the news of the coming of so great a man, all the country for some distance around was filled with a multitude of people, streaming in from all directions. Martin perceived that he had work to do. As the Spirit brought him this prompting, he groaned in body and soul.[4] With a superhuman voice[5] he preached the word of God to the pagans, often asking in sorrow why so great a throng did not know the Lord and Saviour. An unbelievably large crowd

1 *Life* 7 and 8.
2 Chartres.
3 Probably Vendôme, as Lecoy de la Marche suggests (p. 263).
4 Lat. *totus infremuit.* I have adopted the Douay translators' version of *infremuit* at John 11.33, a passage which Sulpicius would most appropriately have had in mind here. Babut's interpretataion (p. 210 n.3) unfortunately fails to take the Biblical parallel into account.
5 Lat. *nec mortale sonans;* cf. Virgil, *Aeneid* 6.50 and Statius, *Thebaid* 4.146.

had surrounded us, when a woman approached, whose son had just died. With her arms extended, she held the dead body out to the blessed man and said: "We know you are a friend of God. Restore my son to me; he is the only one I have." The rest of the multitude joined their cries to the mother's prayers. Then Martin perceived what he later told us of: that, on behalf of the conversion of those who were waiting expectantly, he was able to perform a miracle. He took the body of the dead boy in his own hands, and knelt in the sight of all. When his prayer was done, he arose and handed to his mother the infant restored to life.

'Then the whole crowd raised a shout to heaven, proclaiming that Christ was God. Finally, they all began to come to Martin by groups, throwing themselves at the blessed man's knees and demanding with faith that he make them Christians. Without delay, in the middle of the field where they were, he placed his hand on all of them and made them catechumens. While doing so, he turned to us and said it was very right for them to become catechumens in an open field, because it was there that the consecration of martyrs occurred.'

Chapter 5

'You have conquered, Gallus, you have conquered,' said Postumianus. 'Not me, surely, for I am a champion of Martin and have always known and believed all this about the great man. But you have conquered all the anchorites and hermits. For, not one of them had the dead at his control, as had your—or rather our—Martin. It was quite proper that our friend Sulpicius compared him with the Apostles and the Prophets.[1] The power of his faith and his miraculous works shows him to be like them in every way.

1 *Epist.* 2 (above, pp. 149-151); Cf. Life Ch. 7 n. 4.

'But, please keep on, even though you can have nothing more magnificent to tell us. Keep on, Gallus, and finish the rest of your account of Martin. Our mind is eager to learn even the least and most ordinary of his deeds, having no doubt that his least deeds are greater than the greatest of others.'

'I shall do so,' said Gallus. 'But note that what I am about to tell is something I myself did not see. It happened before I joined Martin. The deed is well known; it has been spread abroad through the report of dependable brothers who were present.

'At about the time when Martin had just been made bishop, he had need to visit the court. The elder Valentinian[2] was then master of the empire. When he learned that Martin was asking for things he was unwilling to grant, he gave orders that he be kept outside the palace gates. Valentinian, besides being cruel and proud, had an Arian wife.[3] She prevented him from rendering the holy man the respect due him. When Martin had made repeated attempts to see the proud prince, he had recourse to familiar expedients: he clothed himself in sackcloth, he covered himself with ashes, he abstained from food and drink, he prayed continually night and day. On the seventh day an angel stood at his side, ordering him to go to the palace and to have no worry: its doors were closed but would open of themselves, and the emperor's proud spirit would be softened. Martin was encouraged by the presence of the angel and his words, and trusted his support. He went to the palace. The doors were open, and no one stood in the way. Finally, with no resistance from anyone, he came near

2 Valentinian I, Emperor 364-375. The incident narrated here took place at Trèves. Babut 206 n. 3 proposes a chronological difficulty, solved by Delehaye 32.

3 The emperor's second wife is meant—Justina, mother of Valentinian II, whose policy she largely inspired, especially in the field of religion.

the emperor. Valentinian saw him coming from a distance. Grinding his teeth, he asked why Martin had been admitted. When Martin stood before him, the emperor did not have the grace to rise, until fire covered the imperial throne and the emperor himself was burned in that part of his body which was resting on the chair. Then, the proud ruler shot out of his throne and, in spite of himself, stood up before Martin. The bishop, who before had been scorned, now received the emperor's lengthy embraces. The latter, chastened, said that he had felt divine power. He did not wait for Martin's petitions, but gave consent to everything before he was asked. He frequently invited him to talk and to dine. Finally, when Martin was going, he offered him many gifts, all of which the blessed man refused, keeping an ever-watchful eye on his poverty.'

Chapter 6

'Now that we have once entered the palace, I shall join to the foregoing incident another which also happened there, though at a different time. The example furnished by a Christian empress in showing admiration for Martin should not, I think, be omitted.

'The Emperor Maximus then governed the state. He was a man whose whole life would have merited praise, if only he could have repudiated the crown which a military uprising illegally offered him or if, at least, he could have abstained from civil strife.[1] But, one cannot refuse a mighty empire without peril or retain it without armed force. He would often invite Martin and receive him in the palace with honor and veneration. His conversation with Martin always turned on

1 On Maximus see *Life,* Ch. 20 n. 1. The meetings between Martin and Maximus and his wife took place at the court in Trèves around the year 385, prior, no doubt, to the condemnation of Priscillian (see *Dial.* 3.11 n. 2)

things present and things to come, the glory of the faithful and the eternal blessedness of the saints. During these conversations, the empress hung on Martin's words day and night. The example furnished by the Gospel[2] did not find her wanting: she washed the saint's feet with her tears and dried them with her hair. Martin, whom no woman had ever touched up to then, could not escape her assiduous, not to say servile, attentions. She had no thought for the wealth of the realm, for her place of honor in the empire, for the diadem, for the imperial purple. Prostrate on the floor, she refused to be torn away from Martin's feet. Finally, she asked her husband to join her in prevailing on Martin to come to a dinner which she alone would serve him, dismissing all the servants. For all his reluctance, Martin could not refuse. The simple arrangements were made by the empress with her own hands. She herself put a covering on the chair, moved up the table, brought water for his hands, and placed before him the food she herself had cooked. As he ate, she followed the practice of servants. She stood away from the table, motionless, as if fixed to the floor, showing all the modesty of a serving-maid and all the humility of a slave. It was she who mixed his drink when he was ready and handed it to him. When the little dinner was over, she gathered the fragments of the bread and the crumbs, in her intense faith preferring these leftovers to an imperial banquet.

'Blessed woman, justly to be compared in her loving devotion to that queen who came from the ends of the earth to hear Solomon.[3] This comparison is proper if we confine ourselves to the simple narrative. But we must compare the faith of the two royal women. So doing, and taking no account of the solemn dignity of the mystery, I have this to point out:

2 Luke 7.36ff. and parallel passages in the other Gospels.
3 Cf. Matt. 12.42; Luke 11.31; 3 Kings 10.1-10.

the Queen of Saba sought out the wise man only to listen to him, but our empress, not content with listening to so wise a man, also merited the opportunity of serving him.'

Chapter 7

At this point Postumianus remarked: 'For some time, as I listened to you, Gallus, I have greatly admired the faith of the empress. But, where do we stand in respect to the report that no woman ever approached Martin? Here we have the empress not only standing near him, but also serving him at table. I am afraid that this precedent will give some small comfort to those who like to get involved with women.'

'Why do you not take account,' asked Gallus, 'as our grammarians commonly urge us to, of the circumstances of place, time, and person? Try to imagine the situation: how Martin was taken by surprise in the palace, solicited by the emperor's prayers, compelled by the faith of the empress, bound by the necessities of the moment. He had prisoners to free, exiles to bring back, confiscated property to restore. How cheap must the bishop have valued all that, not to have been willing, in securing all these ends, to relax a little bit from his rigorous principles? You say that some people will take occasion to misuse Martin's example. They will be happy indeed, if they abide by the lesson this example teaches. Let them note that this happened to Martin only once in his life, when he was seventy years old;[1] that the woman who did him menial service was not a licentious widow, not a flighty virgin, but an empress and a wife, ruled by her husband, who himself joined in her request; that she simply served him as he ate and did

1 Since the year of this palace incident is known fairly closely, we have here an important datum in the vexed chronology of Martin's life; see above, p. 91.

not recline at banquet with him, not venturing to share the meal but merely showing him deference.

'This is the lesson to learn: let a matron serve you, not command you; let her serve you, not recline with you at table. It was in this way that Martha waited on the Lord,[2] without sharing the repast; in fact, preference was given over Martha, who served, to Mary, who listened to His words. In Martin's case, the empress did both things: like Martha, she served; like Mary, she listened. So, whoever wants to use this case as a model should follow it completely, being sure of the appropriateness of the cause, of the person, of the service rendered, of the meal itself, and that it happens only once in all his life.'

Chapter 8

'Admirable,' said Postumianus. 'What you have said sets the limits within which our clerics can move if they want to follow Martin's example. But, let me assure you, all this will fall on deaf ears. If we follow in Martin's path, we will never have to [defend ourselves against a charge of kissing or][1] reckon with any injuries rising from hostile opinion. But, as you yourself say, when you are reproved for heavy eating, we are Gauls.[2] So, in this matter, neither Martin's example nor your disputation will make us mend our ways. But, tell me, Sulpicius. While we have been busy with discussion for a long time, why are you so obstinately silent?'

'I am not only silent now,' I said, 'but I have for some time decided to remain silent about those things. I once reproved an elegant, capricious, and spendthrift widow for wanton liv-

2 Cf. Luke 10.40ff.

1 The bracketed clause is omitted in several MSS., among them, *V* and *D*.
2 Cf. *Dial.* 1.4.

ing. Another time, it was a virgin who had an unbecoming attachment to a young man who was dear to me, yet I often heard her upbraiding others who behaved in this way. My strictures aroused among all women and all monks such animosity that their two legions conspired and made war upon me. That is why I ask you to keep quiet. I do not want what you say to increase my own unpopularity. Let us give up recalling things like this and return, instead, to Martin. You began, Gallus; complete what you started.'

'The stories I already have told you,' he said, 'are such that your eagerness ought now to be satisfied with my recitation. But, because I am not at liberty not to comply with your wishes, I shall continue speaking for what still remains of the day. I notice that straw is being prepared for our beds, and, by this, I am reminded of a miracle which was worked through straw on which Martin had lain.[3]

'The incident happened this way. There is a village, Claudiomagus, on the common boundary of the Bituriges and the Turoni.[4] The church there is celebrated for the piety of its monks and no less renowned through the presence of a large number of consecrated virgins. Once, when passing through, Martin took up lodging in the sacristy of the church.[5] After he left, the virgins rushed into the sacristy. They covered with kisses all the places, one by one, where the blessed man had sat or stood. They even divided among themselves the straw on which he had lain. A few days later, one of them put to use the bit of straw she had collected as a relic for herself: she hung it from the neck of a possessed man who was being

3 *Epist.* 1 tells another story about Martin and a bed of straw.

4 The modern Clion (dep. Indre); Ihm in PWK 3.2662. The principal city of the Bituriges was *Avaricum,* the present-day Bourges. Similarly, it was from the Turoni that their chief city, Tours, was named.

5 As in the case narrated in *Epist.* 1.

tormented by a false spirit.[6] At once, quicker than you could say it, the demon was expelled and the person cured.'

Chapter 9

'About the same time, when Martin was returning from Trèves, he encountered a cow tormented by a demon. She had left her herd and was going about attacking people; she had already dangerously gored a number with her horns. When she came near us, the people who were following her from a distance began calling out with a loud voice that we should be careful. But the raging beast, staring savagely, came nearer to us. Martin raised his hand and ordered her to stand still. At his word the cow halted, motionless. Meanwhile, Martin spied a demon sitting on her back, and rebuked him. "Depart from the beast," he said, "and stop tormenting a harmless animal." The evil spirit obeyed and withdrew. The heifer did not fail to sense that she had been delivered. Having recovered her composure, she threw herself at the saint's feet. When Martin then told her to go back to her own herd, she rejoined the company of the other cows, quieter than a lamb.

'This was the time when Martin found himself surrounded by flames, yet felt no effect from the fire. I believe I shall not have to report this story, since Sulpicius here has related it in detail. He omitted it in his book, but dealt with it later in a letter he wrote to Eusebius,[1] who, then a priest, is now a bishop. I suspect, Postumianus, that you have already read it. If you do not know it, it is at hand in that bookcase yonder, whenever it suits you. I shall keep telling things that Sulpicius omitted.

---

6 Lat. *spiritus erroris.*

---

1 Above, pp. 141-145.

'One time, when Martin was making the round of his parishes, we met a band of hunters. The hounds were pursuing a hare. The long course had overcome the poor little beast. Nowhere in all the broad-spreading field was there any way of escape. Its death was imminent. Constantly at the point of being captured, it put off its fate by quick zigzag movements. The blessed man, in his bounty, had pity on the hare's desperate position, and ordered the hounds to give up the chase and let the fugitive escape. Instantly, at the very first word of his command, they halted: you would have thought them chained, or rather rooted in their very tracks. And so, with its pursuers immobilized, the little hare escaped unharmed.'

Chapter 10

'It is also worth while to recall some of Martin's familiar sayings, well seasoned with spiritual salt.

'It happened that he spied a sheep that had been lately shorn. "*There* is one," he said, "who has fulfilled the Gospel precept.[1] She had two tunics, and one of them she has given to one who had none. That is what you also ought to do."

'Similarly, he once saw a swineherd, chilled to the bone, ill-covered by his coat of sheepskin. "Here," he said, "we have Adam [driven from paradise,][2] dressed in a coat of sheepskin and feeding his swine.[3] But we ought to put off that old Adam, who survives in this swineherd, and put on the new Adam."[4]

'Some oxen had used up part of a meadow in their grazing, while other sections had been rooted up by swine. The rest of the meadow, which remained undamaged, had a

1 Luke 3.11.
2 This phrase, omitted in *V*, is bracketed by Halm.
3 Cf. Gen. 3.21.
4 Cf. Eph. 4.24; Col. 3.10.

springlike greenness studded with many kinds of flowers, as in a painting. "We have a symbol of marriage," he said, "in that part of the meadow which has been used by the grazing herd: it has not altogether lost the beauty of its grass, but has retained nothing of the dignity its flowers once gave it. That part which the filthy animals that are swine have uprooted supplies the ugly image of fornication. Finally, that portion which has suffered no damage shows us the glory of virginity: it abounds in luxuriating grass; there is a rich crop of hay on it; it is clothed in ornament of surpassing beauty; its flowers stand out like glistening gems. A blessed spectacle and one worthy of God, for there is nothing that can be compared with virginity. Those who compare the life of fornication to marriage are gravely in error. And, similarly, those who think that marriage measures up to virginity are wholly miserable and foolish. Here is a distinction to which the wise must hold: marriage relates to indulgence,[5] virginity tends to glory, while fornication is destined for punishment, unless satisfaction be made to cleanse it." '

Chapter 11

'A certain soldier had laid aside his sword belt in a church to enter upon monastic profession. He had built a cell for himself in a retired and distant spot, intending to live as a hermit. But, the cunning Enemy soon was disturbing his untrained heart with strange thoughts; his resolution was altered and he wanted to live again with his wife, whom Martin had instructed to join a convent.

'So, the brave hermit came to see Martin and confessed

---

5 Lat. *pertineat ad veniam.* The Vulgate at 1 Cor. 7.6 shows *secundum indulgentiam,* but a common Old Latin reading was *secundum veniam;* cf. Wordsworth and White *ad loc.*

what he had in mind. But Martin's refusal was firm: it would be improper for a woman to be joined again to a man who was now a monk and no longer her husband. The soldier insisted, affirming that this would in no way harm his earlier resolve. He only wanted to have the consolation his wife's presence could bring him; there was no need to fear they would return to their former habits. He himself was Christ's soldier, he said, and she also had taken the same oaths in the same service;[1] the bishop could well permit two holy persons who had now become ignorant of their sex through the merit of their faith to serve together.

'Then Martin said (and I am going to cite his very words): "Tell me whether you have ever been in war, whether you have ever stood on the battle line." He replied, "I have frequently stood on the battle line, and I have frequently had part in war." At that, Martin said: "Tell me this then: in any battle array—whether the armed line was being put in readiness for combat or whether the fight against the hostile army was already on, foot placed against foot and swords drawn—have you ever seen a woman standing and fighting?" Then, at last, the soldier blushed in his confusion. He thanked Martin for not having abandoned him to his error and for having used no harsh reproof in his correction, but an apt and just simile, appropriate to his character as a soldier.

'But Martin turned to us—for a considerable crowd of brothers had gathered about him—and said: "No woman should enter into the camp of men. A battle array of soldiers should hold itself apart. A woman should remain far from them and live by herself, in her own tent. An army becomes contemptible if its cohorts of men are mingled with a horde of women. It is for a soldier to fight in the battle line and on the

1 At her baptism, as it seems; cf. *Epist.* 3 n. 18.

field. A woman should keep herself within the defenses of the walls. Yet, she also has her own glory, if, in her husband's absence, she preserve her chastity. It is her first virtue and her supreme victory not to be seen." '

Chapter 12

'This, Sulpicius, I think you recall—the enthusiasm with which Martin, when you also were present, commended the austerity of a certain virgin. She kept herself so strictly removed from all men's gazes that she refused to see Martin himself when he wished to pay her the homage of a visit. He was passing near the country property in which she had lived for many years in chaste retirement. Since he had heard of her faith and virtue, he made a detour in order to give due honor, through an episcopal visit, to a virgin of such illustrious merits. We who were attending him thought the virgin would be delighted: she would take it as an evidence of her virtue that a bishop of such renown should have renounced his rigorous principle in coming to see her. But she was bound by the chains of an heroic vow and did not loosen them even in consideration of Martin. He received her praiseworthy excuses from another woman—she herself was neither to be seen nor greeted—and went away from her door joyful.

'Glorious virgin, not to let herself be seen even by Martin! Blessed Martin, not to take her refusal as an insult! On the contrary, he gave her virtue enthusiastic commendation and took joy in her example—an unusual one, at least for these parts. The coming of night forced us to remain not far from her house. Here, that same virgin sent a present to the blessed man. He did something he had never done before (for he had never accepted a gift of any kind from anyone): he refused not one of the things the venerable virgin had sent him. No bishop, he said, should refuse any blessing of hers, whose value was higher than that of many bishops.

'Let virgins pay heed to this example. If they want their doors to keep out the wicked, they should close them also to the good. To keep the impious from having free access to them, they should not fear even to exclude bishops. There also is something here for the whole world to hear. A virgin did not permit herself to be seen by Martin. It was, to be sure, no ordinary bishop that she refused. Rather, the man into whose presence she did not come was one whose very sight had been the salvation of those who saw. Yet, what bishop other than Martin would not have considered himself misused by this treatment? What sentiments of anger would his mind not have conceived against the holy virgin? He would have adjudged her a heretic and pronounced an anathema upon her. In preference to that blessed soul, he would have chosen those virgins who at every turn always contrive to meet the bishop, who set expensive banquets for him and recline at them in his company.

'But, to what is my flow of oratory leading me? My too free speech must be curbed a little, so that it will not give offense to certain persons. For those weak in faith, words of reproof will be useless; for the faithful, the example itself will be enough. When I continue to commend the virtue of that virgin, it is not because I wish to detract from those who often came from distant regions to see Martin. With like purpose, even angels often came to visit the blessed man.'

Chapter 13

'What I am now about to tell, Sulpicius, I bring forward with you as witness'—and here Gallus was looking at me. 'One day, Sulpicius and I were keeping vigil before Martin's door. We had been sitting there for some hours in silence, experiencing a sense of religious awe and trembling as if we were standing guard before the tabernacle of an angel. Since the door of Martin's cell was closed, he did not know we were there. At some point, we heard the murmur of a conversation and were at once enwrapped by a strange dread and wonderment. We could not fail to know that something divine was occurring.

'After about two hours, Martin came out and found us. Then Sulpicius (and no one spoke with Martin on more familiar terms than he) begged him to satisfy our pious curiosity and to tell us what was that divine dread we both declared we had felt, and whom he had talked with in the cell. For, the sound of conversation we had heard through the door was weak and hardly intelligible. He hesitated long and earnestly, but there was nothing Sulpicius could not extract from him, even against his will. What I am about to tell may, perhaps, be incredible, but Christ is my witness that I do not lie and surely no one is so sacrilegious as to think that Martin ever lied. "I shall tell you," he said, "but I beg you to tell no one. Agnes, Thecla, and Mary have been with me." He described to us the countenance and dress of each. He confessed that it was not only on that day that he had received a visit from them, but frequently. He also said he had often seen the Apostles Peter and Paul.

'As to demons, he would rebuke them by name as each visited him. From Mercury[1] he had to endure a particular hostility. He said Jupiter was stupid and dull. All this seemed incredible to most, even to those living in the monastery. Hence, I am far from confident that all who hear it will be-

1 For Mercury and for Jupiter (mentioned in the next sentence) cf. *Life* 22 and n. 2 there.

lieve it. In fact, if Martin's life and virtue had not been beyond men's power to judge, he would surely not have acquired such great glory among us. Still, it is small wonder that human weakness hesitates before the deeds of Martin, when, even today, as we see, many people have not believed the Gospels.

'Martin often saw angels and dealt with them as friends; this we have learned through our own experience. The fact I shall now cite is not impressive; nevertheless, I shall cite it. A synod of bishops was held at Nîmes.[2] Martin declined to attend it, but was eager to know what had occurred there. It happened that Sulpicius was traveling with him by water. But Martin, as always, was sitting away from the other passengers, in a secluded part of the ship. There, an angel announced to him what had occurred at the synod. We made careful inquiry later as to the time the council was held. We determined for certain that the very day of the voyage was that of the assembly, and that the decrees voted there were those the angel had announced to Martin.'

Chapter 14[1]

'One day, we were asking Martin about the end of the world. He said that Nero and the Antichrist would come first. Nero would subdue ten kings and rule in the regions of the West. A persecution he was to impose would go so far as to

2 Duchesne, *Fastes épiscopaux* 1.366 dates the synod 1 October 396; 394 is also a possibility (Delehaye 33). From *Dial.* 3.13 we learn that beginning with 385 Martin avoided all synods and meetings of bishops.

1 The first paragraph of this chapter is omitted in a number of MSS., doubtless because the doctrine contained in it had drawn the condemnation of St. Jerome (*In Ezech.* 11.36: *PL.* 25.339), which, in turn, was the probable reason why the *Dialogues* of Sulpicius were proscribed in the *Decretum Gelasianum;* cf. above, pp. 95-96.

require the worship of heathen idols. The Antichrist would first seize the empire of the East; he would have Jerusalem as his seat and imperial capital. Both the city and its temple were to be rebuilt by him. His persecution would require the denial of Christ's divinity (he himself pretending to be Christ) and would by law impose circumcision on all. Finally, Nero himself was to perish at the hands of the Antichrist. In this way, the whole world and all its people would be brought under the latter's yoke, until, at Christ's coming, the impious imposter[2] would be overcome. There was no doubt that the Antichrist, begotten by the evil Spirit, was already born and had now come to the years of boyhood, awaiting the legal age to assume his empire. This we heard Martin say eight years ago.[3] It is for you to judge how near to us now are those fearful events to come.'

Gallus was just saying this and had not finished what he had undertaken to relate, when a slave of the household came in, announcing that the priest Refrigerius stood at the door. We were in doubt whether it would be better to keep on listening to Gallus or to go out to meet one whose arrival was most welcome to us and who had come to honor us with a visit.

Then Gallus spoke: 'Even if we did not have to abandon our discourse because of the arrival of so holy a priest,[4] night itself would compel us to put an end to the conversation that has been extended until now. It has been quite impossible

---

2 Cf. 2 Thess. 2.4.

3 If Martin's speech on the imminent coming of Antichrist is to be dated in the period of the council of Nîmes (Ch. 13 and n. 2), i.e., about 396, the dramatic date of this dialogue can be assigned approximately to the year 404.

4 Lat. *sacerdotis.* The word *sacerdos* elsewhere in these writings of Sulpicius is used for 'bishop' (cf. Babut 124 n. 3). Refrigerius is elsewhere called *presbyter,* Sulpicius's normal word for 'priest.'

to exhaust the subject of Martin's miracles. Let it be enough that you have heard this much today. Tomorrow I shall tell the rest.'

So we accepted Gallus's promise and rose from our places.

THE THIRD DIALOGUE[1]

Chapter 1

IT IS BEGINNING to grow light,[2] Gallus: we must get up. As you see, Postumianus is coming. And the priest[3] who yesterday lost the opportunity to listen is waiting for you, who have a promise to pay off:[4] to tell us about Martin all that you postponed telling until the next day. To be sure, he already knows everything that can be told. But, even to review what is known is a pleasing and agreeable form of knowledge. Nature has so arranged it that one finds joy in knowing with greater confidence what through numerous witnesses he sees to be quite certain. This priest has been attached to Martin since his early youth; he knows everything, indeed, but is glad to relearn what he already knows. And so, Gallus, I confess it is with me. I have repeatedly heard Martin's miracles related. I have committed to writing many things about him. Yet, my admiration for his deeds always makes their telling new for me, even when people again and again bring up stories about him that I have already heard. We have an added reason to congratulate ourselves that Refrigerius has joined us as a listener: Postumianus here—who is

1 For the connection of *Dial.* 3 with *Dial.* 1 and 2, see above, pp. 87-89.
2 Lat. *Lucescit hoc,* a phrase found in Roman comedy: Plautus, *Amphitryo* 543; Terence, *Heautontimorumenos* 410.
3 Refrigerius; his arrival was mentioned in *Dial.* 2.14.
4 Cf. *Dial.* 1.12 and 2.14.

eager to transmit all this to the Orient—will all the more willingly accept from you as truth what has, as it were, been confirmed through witnesses.'

While I was saying this and Gallus was already prepared for his narration, a crowd of monks rushed in,[5] along with the priest Evagrius,[6] Aper,[7] Sabbatius,[8] and Agricola. A moment later, the priest Aetherius came in, accompanied by the deacon Calupio and the subdeacon Amator.[9] Last of all was my very dear friend, the priest Aurelius;[10] he had come a longer journey and arrived all out of breath.

'What has happened,' I asked, 'that you all arrive together, so suddenly, so unexpectedly, from so many places, and so early in the morning?'

'We learned yesterday,' they said, 'that Gallus here had related Martin's miracles all day long, and, because of nightfall, had put off telling the rest until the next day. That is why we have hastened to offer him a large company of listeners, since he is to speak of so noble a subject.'

Meanwhile, word was brought that many lay persons were standing at the door, not venturing to enter, but asking admittance. Then Aper said: 'It is not at all proper that those people be joined to our company, because what has brought

5 Probably members of the community at Primuliacum; cf. above, p. 81.

6 Probably identical with the south-Gallic priest Evagrius who, about 430, wrote an *Altercatio legis inter Simonem Iudaeum et Theophilum Christianum* (*PL* 20.1165; *CSEL* 45). See Da Prato, *ed. Sulp.* 1.377.

7 Possibly to be identified with an Aper addressed in Paulinus, *Epist.* 38, 39, 44 (*PL* 61; *CSEL* 29); see Da Prato's discussion, *ed. Sulp.* 1.377f.

8 It is not clear that this reading (that of *V*) is to be preferred to the variant, *Sebastianus*. See *Life* Ch. 23 n. 3. *Epist.* 26 of Paulinus is addressed to a Sebastianus.

9 Bihlmeyer reasonably suggests that the persons named in this sentence were clergy serving the church at Primuliacum; see above, n. 5.

10 Quite probably the Aurelius to whom Sulpicius wrote *Epist.* 2. Described as deacon there Aurelius may have been ordained priest meanwhile.

them to listen is curiosity rather than piety.' Since he did not wish them to be let in, I was embarrassed for them. Finally, and with difficulty, I gained admittance for the former *vicarius* Eucherius[11] and for Celsus,[12] a man of consular rank. The rest were sent off. Then we arranged for Gallus to sit down in the middle. And, after his well-known modesty had forced him to be silent for a long time, he finally made this beginning.

Chapter 2

'It is to listen to me that you have come together,' he said, 'you holy and eloquent men. But the ears you lend me are, I suppose, eager for matters of religion rather than for those of scholarship. You mean to listen to me as a witness of the faith, not as a copious orator.

'What I said yesterday I shall not repeat. Those who did not hear it can learn it from the transcript.[1] New matter is what Postumianus is waiting for. He is eager to announce it to the Orient, so that the Occident may not have to yield place should the Oriental solitaries be compared with Martin.

'First, I wish to relate an incident which a whisper in my ear from Refrigerius has suggested. It happened in the city of

11 Possibly to be identified, as Bihlmeyer suggests, with an uncle of the Emperor Theodosius who was consul in 381 (he is not elsewhere recorded as serving as *vicarius*) ; cf PWK 6.882.

12 A Celsus was *praefectus annonae* in Rome in 385; PWK 3.1884, art. 'Celsus (17) .

1 Lat. *ex scripturis cognoscent.* According to Babut 49 n. 2, the indication that a stenographer is at work (cf. below, Ch. 17, second paragraph, third sentence) is part of Sulpicius' *'artifice littéraire.'* (See above, p. 90) . While other arguments may support Babut's case for a literary fiction (cf. below, Ch. 5 n. 2) , none is supplied by the suggestion of a stenographer (*notarius*) occupied in taking down the conversations. According to St. Augustine, a stenographer was used to record the conversations at Cassiciacum less than twenty years before: *Contra Academicos* 1.1.4 and *De beata vita* 2.15, 3.18 (translations in this series, *Writings of St. Augustine* 1.109, 63, 66; cf. Arbesmann, *ibid.* 97) .

Chartres. A certain householder brought to Martin his twelve-year-old daughter who had been dumb from birth. He begged that the blessed man use his holy intervention to free the child's tongue from its impediment. In this, Martin yielded to the bishops Valentinus[2] and Victricius,[3] who happened to be at his side. He declared himself inadequate to such a great task, while for their superior sanctity nothing was impossible. But they joined their pious prayers to the father's request and begged Martin to do what was hoped for from him. He delayed no longer—admirable both in showing his humility and in not postponing his charity. He told the large crowd standing by to clear away. Then, in the presence only of the bishops and the girl's father, he followed his usual practice and prostrated himself in prayer. Next, he blessed a little oil, using the formula of exorcism. The sanctified liquid he then poured into the girl's mouth, holding her tongue meanwhile with his fingers. The saint was not disappointed in the miraculous outcome. He asked the girl her father's name; she instantly replied. The father shouted for joy amidst his tears. Embracing Martin's knees, he declared, to everyone's amazement, that he had just heard his daughter speak for the first time.[4]

'If anyone thinks this story incredible, here is Evagrius to give evidence of its truth, for he was present when the event occurred.'

Chapter 3

'The following incident is of minor importance, but I still

---

2 Probably the Valentinus who was Bishop of Chartres at this time: Duchesne, *Fastes épiscopaux* 2.424.

3 Doubtless the well-known Bishop of Rouen: Duchesne, *op. cit.* 2.204, 424.

4 As Babut discerned (p. 268f.), we have in this chapter another version of the miracle narrated in *Life* 16; cf. Delehaye 40.

think it should not be omitted. I recently learned of it from the report of the priest Arpagius.

'The wife of the *comes* Avitianus,[1] following a common practice, had sent to Martin, for his blessing, some oil to use in curing various diseases. The glass container was round-bellied,[2] and had a long neck. This projecting neck was empty, for it is usual in filling such vessels to leave the extreme upper part free for the stopper. The priest testified that he saw the oil increase under Martin's blessing until it overflowed and spread outside. As the vessel was being taken back to the mistress of the house, the oil seethed with the same miraculous power. While the slave carried the vessel in his hands, the overflow was so abundant as to cover all his clothing. Yet, when the matron received the vessel it was full to the very brim. Even today, as the priest testifies, there is no room in the bottle for the stopper commonly used to seal up liquids that are being kept with special care.

'This, too, is a remarkable incident that I remember happened to our friend here'—and Gallus was looking at me.[3] 'He had placed in a rather high window a glass vessel filled with oil that Martin had blessed. A slave, not knowing there was a bottle there, carelessly pulled the cloth covering it. The vessel fell upon the marble-paved floor. Everyone was terrified that the divinely blessed oil had been lost, but the bottle was found undamaged, as if it had fallen upon the softest of feathers. This outcome should be referred not to chance, but to the miraculous power of Martin, whose blessing could not be lost.

1 Claudius Avitianus. In the year 363 he was *vicarius* for Africa. After 366 he was entrusted with the conduct of criminal trials in Gaul, an office in which he showed great cruelty. See below, Ch. 4, 5, 8. Cf. Seeck in PWK 2.2394f.

2 Lat., *in ventrem cresceret*. Cf. Virgil, *Georgics* 4.122.

3 *Viz.*, at Sulpicius.

'And what, now, of this wonder? It was performed by someone whose name I shall suppress, for he is present among us and has forbidden me to betray him. Anyway, our friend Saturninus was also there at the time. A dog was barking at us with more than usual vigor. "In Martin's name," said that other companion, "I order you to be quiet." The dog ceased at once; the bark stuck in his throat—you would have thought his tongue had been cut off. It is a relatively small matter that Martin worked miracles in his own person; you can believe me that others also have worked many in his name.'

Chapter 4

'You knew the cruel temper of the former *comes* Avitianus, how savage and bloodthirsty he was.[1] One day in a rage of spirit he entered Tours, followed by ranks of captives, pitiful and all in chains. To the city's amazement he ordered various kinds of torture to be prepared for their punishment, with the next day set for beginning the gloomy executions.

'When Martin learned of this, he set out alone a little before midnight for the palace of this ferocious beast. In the deep silence of the night everyone was sleeping and the doors were barred. With no way, then, to enter, Martin prostrated himself at the tyrant's bloody threshold. While Avitianus lay buried in deep slumber, an angel broke in and struck him. "The servant of God," he said, "lies at your threshold and are you sleeping?" Troubled at hearing these words, Avitianus leaped from his bed. He called his slaves together and cried out, trembling, that Martin was at the door; they were to go at once and open it, so that the servant of God should receive no slight or injury. But they, as is the way with all slaves, hardly went farther than the inner doors, making sport of

1 See Ch. 3 n. 1.

their master for having been deluded by a dream. They said there was no one at the door, arguing from their own character that no one could be keeping vigil in the night. It was inconceivable to them that a bishop could lie prostrate before a stranger's threshold in the dread darkness. Avitianus was easily persuaded of this and again relaxed in sleep.

'But soon, struck with greater force, he cried out that Martin was standing before the door; that was why he could have no rest of mind or body. While his slaves dawdled, he himself advanced to the outer doors and there, as he suspected, found Martin. Smitten by a power so great and so manifest, he cried out: "Why, sir, have you done this to me? You do not need to speak. I know what you want; I see what you demand. Leave as quickly as possible, so that heaven's wrath may not devour me for wrong done to you. I have already paid penalty enough. Believe me, it was no slight cause that brought me here in person."

'When the saint had gone away, Avitianus called his officers and ordered all the prisoners to be released. And he himself promptly went away. With Avitianus thus put to flight, the city found both happiness and freedom.'

Chapter 5

'The foregoing facts have been learned by many people through the testimony of Avitianus. The priest Refrigerius, whom you see here, recently heard them from a reliable man, the former tribune Dagridus,[1] who called the Divine Majesty to witness his oath that the incident had been related to him by Avitianus himself.

'Do not be surprised that I am doing today what I did not

1 The MSS. vary widely in the spelling of this proper name. There is no certainty that *Dagridus* (the spelling of *V*) is correct.

do yesterday—attaching to each miracle the names of witnesses, persons still living, to whom any skeptic may have recourse. It is incredulity that forces me to do this, for I have been told that many have some hesitation about the truth of certain incidents reported yesterday. All such are free to accept the testimony of these still surviving witnesses; doubting *our* trustworthiness, they may put greater faith in *them*. But, if their skepticism has come to such a point, they will not, in my opinion, believe those others, either.

'I am amazed that a man of even the slightest religious sensibility could consent to such a sacrilege as to think that anyone could possibly lie about Martin. Anyone who lives under God's law should put aside any such suspicion, for Martin surely has no need to be glorified by lies. It is Thee, O Christ, that I call to witness for the good faith of my entire report. All I have said, all I am going to say are facts I myself have seen or have learned from dependable sources, chiefly from Martin's own report.

'True, we have adopted the dialogue form to allay boredom and lend variety to the narrative. But we conscientiously declare that it is historical truth we have used as our foundation.[2]

'I have had to introduce this digression—and it has pained me to do so—because of the incredulity of certain persons. Our conversation should now return to the theme agreed upon. Since, in dealing with it, I find myself so zealously listened to, I must confess that Aper made an appropriate judgment in sending away the incredulous and in thinking only those should hear who would believe.'

2 The words of this paragraph are hardly any words of Gallus. Sulpicius, like a careless 'ghost-writer,' has let his own voice be heard. The passage lends force to Babut's argument that the *Dialogues* are a literary artifice; cf. Ch. 2 n. 1 and, above, p. 90.

Chapter 6

'Something, believe me, which puts me quite beside myself and makes me completely insane with grief is this: that Christians disbelieve in Martin's miraculous powers, whereas demons recognize them!

'The blessed man's monastery was two miles distant from the city.[1] Yet, whenever he set foot beyond the threshold of his cell, starting for the church, you could see the demoniacs, the whole length of the church, roar and tremble like hordes of criminals at the approach of the judge. Indeed, the clergy, when not aware that the bishop was coming, would have indication of his approach from the groans of the demons. When Martin was once drawing near, I saw one demoniac lifted in mid-air and, with arms extended upwards, held there, his feet not touching the floor.

'When Martin set himself to exorcizing demons, he would not touch anyone with his hands or reprove anyone with such twisted tumultuous speech[2] as the clergy for the most part use. Rather, he would bring the demoniacs to him and order everyone else to go away. Behind locked doors, in the middle of the church, he would cover himself with sackcloth and sprinkle himself with ashes; then, he would pray, prostrate on the floor. That is when you could see the pitiful demoniacs suffering their extremities of torment, affected now in this way, now in that. Some would have their feet in the air, suspended as if from a cloud; yet, their clothing would not fall about their faces to cause shame because of their nakedness.[3] Elsewhere, you could see the tormented demons con-

---

1 See *Life* 10.

2 Lat., *rotatur turba verborum.*

3 Sulpicius is again (cf. *Epist.* 2 n. 8) drawing on Hilary, *Contra Constantium.* The borrowing here is from Ch. 8 (*PL* 10.585). Jerome, *Epist.* 108.13 (*PL* 22.889; *CSEL* 55.323) seems to have used the same source. Cf. Babut 84; Delehaye 49 finds a further parallel in Paulinus, *Carm.* 23.82-95.

names when none had asked for them. One would declare fess their crime with no one questioning them, revealing their he was Jupiter; another, Mercury.[4] Finally, you would see all the Devil's ministers in torture, and with them the Devil himself. In Martin we must grant the fulfillment of the words of Scripture: "The saints will judge the angels." '[5]

Chapter 7

'A village in the country around Sens was devastated every year by hail. The inhabitants, compelled by their great losses, asked help from Martin. A reliable delegation was sent in the person of the former prefect Auspicius, whose fields generally were ravaged by heavier storms than fell elsewhere. Martin set to praying at once, and so thoroughly freed the whole region from its scourge that, for the twenty years during which he remained alive, no one in those parts had to suffer from hail. This should not be thought a chance occurrence or anything other than a favor granted to Martin's intervention: the very year in which he died the hail storms resumed their burdensome fury. Even the world of nature felt the passing of that man of faith so keenly that, having taken a just joy in his life, it bewailed his death.

'If any hearer of weak faith should demand witnesses to confirm what I have just recounted, I shall produce not just one man but many thousands; I shall call the whole region of the Senones to give testimony to the miracle it experienced. I suspect that you, priest Refrigerius, remember we had a conversation on this matter with Auspicius's son, Romulus, a religious man of high position. He related the events to us as if we did not know them. He stood in dread, as you yourself

4 Cf. *Life* 22 and n. 2 there.
5 Cf. 1 Cor. 6.2f.

saw, of the repeated damage that might befall his crops, and experienced a great sorrow that Martin's life had not been prolonged into the present.'

Chapter 8

'I come back to Avitianus. This man who everywhere, in every city, left unspeakable monuments of his cruelty, in Tours only was incapable of doing harm. This beast who drew sustenance from human blood and from the deaths of his unhappy victims showed himself gentle and calm in the presence of the blessed Martin.

'One day, I remember, Martin visited him. On entering the audience chamber, he saw sitting on the shoulders of Avitianus a demon of extraordinary size. Whereupon Martin —to use, as I must, a word that is not good Latin—blew out upon[1] the demon from a distance, while Avitianus, thinking the breath had been directed toward himself, said: "Why, holy man, do you do that to me?" "It is not to you I do it," said Martin, "but to the foul creature that is pressing on your neck." The Devil withdrew, abandoning his familiar seat. It is well established that Avitianus was of milder temper after that day. It may be that he understood he had been doing the will of the Devil who was always hounding him, or else that the unclean spirit, driven by Martin from his seat, lost his power of violence. The servant was ashamed of the master and the master could no longer oppress the servant.

'In the village of Amboise,[2] that is, in the old fortress which is now inhabited by numerous brothers, there was, you know,

1 Lat. *exsufflans*. Bad Latin or not, the word was very useful for Christian Latin writers from Tertullian on. Du Cange, *Glossarium* (*s.v., exsufflatio*), supplies numerous examples; cf. also Da Prato, *ed. Sulp.* 1.379f.

2 Lat. *in vico Ambatiensi*. Cf. Lecoy de la Marche 204.

the sanctuary of an idol—a magnificent construction. It rose to a massive tower built of polished stones terminating in a cone high at the top.[3] The very grandeur of the construction maintained the superstitious honor paid to the locality. Orders for the destruction of the temple had often been given by the blessed Martin to Marcellus, the priest in residence. After a while, he came himself and reproached the priest for having left the sanctuary intact. The priest gave as excuse that a force of soldiers and a powerful band of public workmen would hardly serve to overturn so vast a construction; the bishop should not lightly suppose that such an operation could have been handled by feeble clerics and far from robust monks. Martin then had recourse to his familiar expedients. He spent the whole night in prayer and vigil. When morning came, a storm broke and overturned the whole temple upon its foundations. I have this story on the evidence of Marcellus.'

Chapter 9

'I have the agreement of Refrigerius concerning a further miracle, like the last, and involving similar actions. There was a massive column surmounted by an idol. This Martin was trying to overturn, but he could not do so through lack of adequate means. In his customary way he turned to prayer. There was seen to fall from heaven—the fact is certain—a sort of column of about equal dimensions, and this, striking the idol, reduced to dust the whole indomitable mass. It was not enough that heavenly powers should come to his aid unseen: those very powers had to be observed by the human eye in openly doing service for Martin.

3 Halm's reading *in conum* retained; adopted by Monceaux and favored by Chase (*Harv. Stud. in Class. Philol.* 43 [1932] 73) and Hyltén 80. Babut 209 n. 1 preferred the harder reading of *V, D, in thronum,* which was adopted by Bihlmeyer.

'Refrigerius is likewise my witness in another matter. A woman was suffering from a hemorrhage. Like the woman in the Gospel,[1] she touched Martin's clothing and was instantly healed.

'A serpent swimming in the river was cutting his way toward the bank where we had stopped. "In God's name," said Martin, "I order you to go back." At this word from the saint, the evil serpent at once reversed its course and, under our very eyes, swam across to the farther bank. As we watched this in amazement, Martin said with a deep sigh: "Serpents hear me and men do not." '

Chapter 10

'Martin had the habit of eating fish during the Easter[1] days. A little before meal time, he asked whether there was any on hand. The deacon Cato, who was charged with the administration of the monastery and was himself a capable fisherman, replied that he had not caught anything the whole day through; nor had the other fishermen, those who commonly sold fish, caught anything either. "Go, cast your net, and you shall have a catch," said Martin. We lived, as Sulpicius here has described, close to the river. Since it was a holiday, we all went out to watch the fishing. We were filled with hope that the attempt would not be in vain, since the fishing was being done at Martin's order to supply Martin's meal. At the first cast

1 Cf. Matt. 9.20 and parallel passages in Mark and Luke.

1 According to Dom Besse (p. 27), the episode here described occurred on Easter Sunday (*'le jour de Pâques'*); the Latin (*Paschae diebus*) hardly necessitates this precision. He is no doubt right in interpreting the eating of fish as a rare seasonal relaxation from the extremely simple dietary regime orinarily followed at Marmoutier. This (the traditional) interpretation goes back to the fifth century: Paulinus of Périgueux, *De vita Martini* 5.651-654 (*PL* 61.1060; *CSEL* 16.130).

of his little net, the deacon drew out a huge pike, and came running, full of joy, to the monastery: much as in the words of some poet or other[2]—I cite an author of the schools since I am speaking among scholars—"he brought in the captive boar to the amazement of the Argives."

'A true disciple of Christ, Martin rivaled the miracles which the Saviour worked and gave as an example to His saints. Martin showed Christ working in him, who glorified His saint on every occasion and showered His various graces on one man.

'The former prefect Arborius[3] states that once, when Martin was offering the Sacrifice, he saw the saint's hand, decked as it were with precious jewels, give out a gleam of purple light, and that, at each motion of the right hand, he heard the sound of the jewels striking against one another.'

Chapter 11

'I come now to something which Martin, because of the unfortunate circumstances then prevailing, always kept a secret, but could not hide from us. The miracle here is that of conversation with an angel face to face.

'The Emperor Maximus,[1] in other matters a good man, had

---

2 Statius, *Thebaid* 8.750. The line refers to the capture by Hercules of the Erymanthian boar (*sus*), but the quotation gains added point from the fact that *sus* also designated a kind of fish: Ovid, *Halieutica* 132; cf. Pliny, *Hist. Nat.* 11.112.267.

3 Cf. *Life* 19 n. 1.

---

1 See *Life* 20 n. 1; *Dial.* 2.6 n. 1.

been corrupted by the advice of certain bishops.[2] After the execution of Priscillian, he used his imperial power to protect the Bishop Ithacius (Priscillian's accuser) and the other persons allied with him, whom I need not mention by name. No one was to bring it as a charge against Ithacius that he had helped to condemn a man, no matter what his character. Meanwhile, to assist in a number of cases in which people were in grave peril, Martin had had to go to the court, and here he confronted the full force of a violent storm.

'Certain bishops who had met in Trèves were remaining there, communicating daily with Ithacius and making common cause with him. When the unexpected word was brought that Martin was coming, their courage quite collapsed and they gave themselves over to speechless fear. The day before, following their counsel, the emperor had decided to send tribunes into the Spanish provinces, armed with full power to search out the heretics, arrest them, and deprive them of life and property. There was no doubt that this storm would

2 Ch. 11-13, together with *Chronica* 2.46-51, are fundamental documents for the history of the fourth-century Spanish heretic Priscillian and for that of the early stages of the opposition aroused by the doctrines associated with his name. Priscillianism was in part a survival of older heresies. Vincent of Lerins, *Commonitorium* 25 (see below, pp. 315-318) traces its roots to Simon Magus. Chief among the bishops to press the case against Priscillian was Ithacius of Ossonuba (in Portugal), who, at the synod of Saragossa (380), had part in the first official action taken against the heresy. The events described in Ch. 11-13 of this dialogue took place five years later, when, in consequence of a trial at Trèves (385), Priscillian and certain of his adherents were condemned to death. That trial and the events immediately leading up to it are the subject of a passage in Sulpicius's *Chronica* which is translated below as an Appendix (pp. 252-254). For initial orientation in Priscillianism, see the article 'Priscillianism' in the *Catholic Encyclopedia,* but important advances achieved by more recent studies make necessary the use of such treatments as the following: G. Bardy in *DTC* 13.391-400; P. de Labriolle in the Fliche-Martin *Histoire de l'Eglise* 3 (Paris 1936) 385-392; A. D'Alès, S.J., *Priscillien et l'Espagne chrétienne à la fin du IVe siècle* (Paris 1936). On E.-Ch. Babut, *Priscillien et le Priscillianisme* (Paris 1909), see D'Alès, *op. cit.* 76.

ravage a great number of saintly men as well, for no nice distinction would be made between classes.[3] Eyes alone were judges then; a man was declared a heretic more by the pallor of his face and by his clothing than by his faith. The bishops saw this would not find favor with Martin. But what most irked them, in their evil conscience, was the fear that, on arrival, Martin would refuse to associate with them; they well knew there would be those who would be guided by his authority and imitate his courageous position. They went into consultation with the emperor. Officers of the *magister officiorum* would be sent to meet Martin, to forbid his further approach to the city unless he declared he would be in peace with the bishops there. Martin cunningly baffled the emissaries with the statement that he would come with the peace of Christ. He finally entered the city by night and went to the church, but only in order to pray there. The next day he went to the palace. Besides a number of other requests which would take too long to enumerate, his principal petitions were for the count Narses and the governor Leucadius; they had both belonged to the party of Gratian and their passionate acts of resistance had merited the anger of the victor. But Martin's chief concern was that tribunes with life-and-death powers should not be sent to the Spanish provinces. The pious Martin was anxious to preserve not only the Christians whom this would be an occasion to maltreat, but also the heretics themselves.

'The first and second day, the shrewd emperor kept Martin in suspense; possibly in order to lend more weight to the affair, possibly because he was unreconcilable to those who had

3 See *Chronica* 2.50 (below, p. 253 n. 6).

resisted him,[4] or possibly, as many thought at the time, because avarice stood in the way, the property of the future victims being the object of his cupidity. It is said that the emperor, though given to many good works, yielded easily to avarice. Perhaps this came about through political necessity. The state treasury had been exhausted by earlier emperors and Maximus always stood in constant expectancy of civil wars. It will be easy, therefore, to excuse him for having used any occasion whatever as a means of providing resources for his empire.'

Chapter 12

'Meanwhile, the bishops, with whom Martin refused to associate, were alarmed and ran to the emperor. They complained that they had been condemned in advance; that the position of all of them was already determined, if Martin's authority should strengthen the insistence of Theognitus,[1] who alone, when the sentence had been rendered, had openly condemned them; that Martin ought not to have been permitted to enter the city walls—he was now no defender of heretics, but an avenger; nothing would have been accomplished through Priscillian's death if Martin were to work vengeance for it. Finally, they prostrated themselves with tears and lamentations, and implored the emperor to exercise his imperial

4 With Bihlmeyer and Hyltén (p. 153) I adopt the emendation of Fürtner (p. 37f.): *obnixis* (or *obnisis*) *sibi* instead of Halm's *obnoxius episcopis* (the latter yielding the translation: 'because in his servility to the bishops he was implacable'). In the Fürtner reading we have a reference to Narses and Leucadius, who, as partisans of Gratian, had been opposed to Maximus. For Narses, see art. 'Narses (6)' in PWK 16.1758; Babut 149 n. 1.

1 The MSS. leave the spelling of this name uncertain. Halm drew the spelling given above from *V*, which here shows a manifestly corrupt form, but a few lines later shows *Theognitum*. Editions prior to Halm generally printed *Theognistus*, the spelling used by Ensslin in PWK, 2te Reihe 5.1985.

might against the man. Maximus, indeed, was almost forced to involve Martin in the fate of the heretics. But, while he showed excessive favor and subservience to the bishops, he still knew well that Martin was superior to them all in faith, sanctity, and virtue. He set about preparing another way in which to overcome him.

'He first summoned Martin to a private conference and addressed him with pleasant words: the heretics had been duly condemned under the procedure of the public courts and not through any persecution by the bishops; there was no reason for him to think he should condemn any association with Ithacius and the rest of his party; as for Theognitus, it was through animosity and not any just motive that he had disagreed; the same Theognitus was the only one who meanwhile had separated himself from association with the rest—no change had been made by the latter; moreover, a synod held a few days earlier had pronounced Ithacius free of guilt. When these reasons did not succeed in moving Martin, the emperor burst into a rage and instantly withdrew from his sight. Forthwith, men were dispatched to execute those persons for whom Martin had interceded.'

Chapter 13

'Although it was night when he learned this, Martin burst into the palace. He promised, if the Priscillianists should be spared, to associate with the other bishops, but only if there should be a recall of the tribunes already dispatched to the Spanish provinces for the destruction of the churches there. The effect was immediate; Maximus granted every petition.

'The next day was appointed for the consecration of Bishop Felix,[1] certainly a very holy man and worthy to have been

---

1 On Felix, Bishop of Trèves, see Duchesne, *Fastes épiscopaux* 3.36. He is commemorated in the *Roman Martyrology* (March 26).

bishop in better days. On that day, Martin entered into communion with the bishops, thinking it better to yield for an hour than to abandon those whose necks were threatened with the sword. The bishops used all their power to force Martin to set his signature in witness of that communion, but they could not wrest it from him.

'On the following day, he left Trèves in haste and began his journey home. He was sad and groaned inwardly that he had involved himself even for an hour in communion with guilty men. Not far from a village named Andethanna[2] was a place where the lonely forest opens out into a vast solitude.[3] Here, when his companions had gone forward a little, Martin sat down. As he reflected upon the cause of the deed which sorrowed him, his thoughts in turn accused and defended him.[4] Suddenly an angel appeared to him. "You have reason, Martin," said he, "to feel compunction, yet you had no other way out. Renew your courage, resume your determination; otherwise, you may incur danger not to your honor but to your salvation."

'Accordingly, from that time, Martin took great care not to be involved in association with the party of Ithacius. Afterwards, when he cured possessed persons more slowly than usual and through a diminished gift of grace, he would sometimes declare to us, weeping, that because of the evil of that communion—in which he had been involved for only a moment, and that through necessity and not from choice—he

2 While it is clear from the *Itinerarium Antonini* that Andethanna lies between Trèves and Reims, no certain identification with a modern locality has been made. Some hold for Epternach (Echternach) in the duchy of Luxembourg; others for a village named Nieder-Anwen, also in Luxembourg. Cf. Lecoy de la Marche 253f.; Ihm in PWK 1.2123f.

3 Text marked as corrupt by Halm. I have adopted Haupt's emendation, *panduntur*; cf. Hyltén 154f.

4 Cf. Rom. 2.15.

was aware of a loss of his miracle-working powers.[5] He lived thereafter sixteen years.[6] He attended no synod and kept aloof from all meetings of bishops.'[7]

Chapter 14

'The divine grace which had been diminished in him for a time Martin recovered, as we came to know, with heavy interest. I saw a possessed man being brought to the rear door[1] of the monastery and healed before he reached the threshold.

'Recently, I heard the testimony of a man who had been sailing on the Tyrrhenian Sea on his way to Rome. The sudden outbreak of a storm had put the lives of all the passengers into extreme danger. At this point, an Egyptian merchant, who was not yet a Christian, cried out in a loud voice: "God of Martin, save us." Soon, the tempest was calmed, and my witness could continue his desired course with the complete assurance of a smooth sea.

'The servants of the former *vicarius* Lycontius, a Christian, were in the grip of a severe epidemic. Throughout the house they lay sick from the effects of this strange calamity. By letter, Lycontius sought the help of Martin. The blessed man was convinced that the result asked for was difficult of attainment,[2] for he perceived in spirit that the household was being chastised by divine power. Nevertheless, for seven days and nights he prayed and fasted continuously and did not stop

5 Cf. *Dial.* 2.4.

6 Another troublesome chronological datum; cf. above, p. 91f. Sixteen years can not be fitted in between the consecration of Felix (385) and the death of Martin, if the latter event is to be dated in 397 (cf. nn. 14 and 15 on *Epist.* 3). One proposal is to emend here to 'thirteen,' but cf. Delehaye 33.

7 E.g., from a synod at Nîmes mentioned in *Dial.* 2.13.

1 Lat. *pseudoforum.*

2 Text marked as corrupt by Halm, but the meaning intended is reasonably clear; cf. Hyltén 78f.

until he had obtained what he had undertaken to beg for. Lycontius, when he had received the God-sent favors, came quickly to Martin, announcing gratefully that his household had been completely freed from danger. As an offering, he also brought a hundred pounds of silver. This the blessed man neither rejected nor accepted. Before the bullion crossed the threshold of the monastery, he at once designated it to be used in ransoming captives. Some of the brothers suggested to him that a part of the sum be reserved to meet monastery expenses: the whole community, they said, was badly off as regards food, and many lacked clothing. To this Martin replied: "It is for the Church to feed and clothe us, so long as we are seen seeking nothing for our own use."

'There here come to mind certain of Martin's great miracles which are easier to admire than relate. You surely know what I mean: there are things about Martin which cannot be explained in detail. What follows is an example. Whether I can present it just as it happened I do not know.

'One of the brothers (you know the name, but I must conceal his identity for fear of bringing embarrassment to a holy man)—a certain brother, then, had found in Martin's stove a good supply of burning coals. He brought up a little stool, spread his legs apart, bared the lower part of his body and seated himself over the fire. Martin at once sensed that his holy cell[3] was being profaned. In a loud voice he cried out, "Who is defiling our dwelling-place with his belly all bare?" The brother heard this and, conscious of his fault, recognized that the rebuke was directed against him. He at once ran to us, breathless, and, constrained by Martin's power, acknowledged his shame.'

---

3 Lat. *sacro tegmini sensit iniuriam.* The sense given for the first two words is gained from the following clause (*quis . . . nostrum incestat habitaculum?*). *Tegmen* (= covering generally) is used somewhat similarly in Statius, *Thebaid* 1.406.

Chapter 15[1]

'One day, in the tiny space which surrounded his cell, Martin was sitting on that wooden stool of his you all know.[2] Perched on the high rock which rises above the monastery, he spied two demons, who were emitting lively and joyous shouts of encouragement: "On, Brictio! Come on, Brictio!"[3] They noticed, I suppose, that that unfortunate man was approaching, and well knew what madness they had excited in him.

'Immediately, Brictio broke in, in a rage. Full of frenzy, he poured out a torrent of abuse upon Martin. The day before, Brictio had been reprimanded by Martin: when Brictio, before belonging to the clergy, had had nothing (having been reared in the monastery by Martin himself), how was he now keeping horses and buying slaves? (For he was then being accused by many of having bought not only barbarian boys but also fair-faced girls.) All this moved the unhappy wretch to insane anger, while his torment of spirit was largely due, I suppose, to the instigation of the demons. His attack upon Martin, then, was such that he could hardly restrain himself from violence. On his part, the holy Martin, with his countenance calm and his spirit unruffled, sought to check poor Brictio's frenzy with gentle words. But Brictio was so far engulfed by the Evil Spirit as even to have lost control of his mind, weak

1 This chapter and the following are omitted or displaced in a number of MSS., probably out of respect for Brictio, about whom they relate much that is unpleasant and who succeeded Martin as Bishop of Tours. Cf. Babut 301ff.; Delehaye 13f.; Chase, *op. cit.* 60f.

2 Cf. *Dial.* 2.1.

3 Also called Brice, from a variant Latin form of his name, *Brictius.* Although perhaps St. Martin's most outspoken enemy (Babut 118), Brice succeeded him in the see of Tours (although the succession was contested at the time)—cf. Duchesne, *Fastes épiscopaux* 2.303—and was subsequently venerated as a saint (*Roman Martyrology*, November 13). Babut regards the scene here described as perhaps a fiction (*loc cit.*); cf. *op. cit.* 116ff., 285ff. for his treatment of Brice.

as it was. His lips trembled, his features quivered, his face was pale from frenzy. Sinful words came rolling out: he said he was more saintly than Martin, having been brought up in the monastery from his earliest years, educated by Martin himself in the sacred disciplines of the Church; while Martin from the beginning (he himself could not deny it) had been soiled by leading the life of a soldier, and now, deranged and in his dotage, was the victim of empty superstitions and of the ridiculous phantasms of his visions.

'When he had spat out these and other bitter words which it would be better not to repeat, Brictio finally went away. His anger was sated and it was as if he had worked his full vengeance. He was returning quickly by the path by which he had come when he was brought to repentance—I believe it was because the demons had been routed from his heart through Martin's prayers. He promptly came back and prostrated himself at Martin's knees. He begged forgiveness and confessed his error. Restored at last to his senses, he admitted he had been possessed by demons. It was easy for Martin to forgive the suppliant. Then, to him and to all of us, the holy man told how he had seen Brictio incited by the demons: he had not been moved by the abuses, which were damaging only to him who uttered them.

'Later, the same Brictio was repeatedly charged in Martin's presence with many serious crimes. But Martin could never be induced to remove him from the priestly office; he wished to avoid the appearance of taking action against a personal injury, and would often say this: "If Christ put up with Judas, why should I not put up with Brictio?" '

Chapter 16[1]

At this, Postumianus said: 'I should like that example to

1 See Ch. 15 n. 1.

be heard by that neighbor of ours.[2] He is a prudent man who does not concern himself with either the present or the future, but, when he has been wronged, he goes crazy and loses control of himself. He rages against the clergy, he attacks the laity, he puts the whole world into commotion to effect his revenge. For three years now he has been constantly affected by this contentiousness; neither time nor reason can calm him. This is a grievous and pitiable condition for a man to be in, even if this were the only incurable evil which afflicts him. But you, Gallus, ought to have confronted him often with those examples of patience and serenity, so that he might come to unlearn anger and learn to forgive. Perhaps he will find out that this little speech of mine, spoken in parenthesis, was meant for him. If so, I hope he will know I have spoken not as an enemy, but as a friend. Were it possible, I should prefer to have him compared to the bishop Martin than to the tyrant Phalaris.[3]

'But, let us be done with talking about him—it can only be unpleasant—and return, Gallus, to our dear Martin.'

Chapter 17

With the sun about to set, I saw that evening had come upon us and said, 'The day has gone, Postumianus; we must get up. At the same time, such eager listeners have a dinner due them. And as for Martin, you should not expect that anyone telling about him will find an end. He is a subject of such scope that no discourse can comprehend him. However, you can carry to the Orient what you have just heard about Martin. Wherever you pass on your return, through whatever

2 Da Prato suggests (*ad loc.*) that some Aquitanian bishop is intended here; cf. *Dial.* 1.2 (with n. 1) and Introduction, p. 90.

3 The proverbially cruel tyrant of Agrigentum in the sixth century B.C.

coasts, in whatever locality, harbor, island, and city, you must spread among the people the name and glory of Martin.

'Bear it in mind, first of all, not to bypass Campania. However far off your route it may lie, do not attach such importance to even a great loss of time that you will be prevented from visiting there the illustrious Paulinus, whose fame has spread throughout the world. Read to him, first of all, the book that contains our discourse, both that of yesterday and of today. Report everything to him, tell him everything. Soon, through him, Rome will learn the praises of the holy man. Just so did he spread that first little book of ours,[1] not through Italy alone, but also through all Illyria.[2] He felt no jealousy toward Martin and could justly esteem Martin's glories and the miracles he accomplished in Christ's name. He did not refuse to compare our bishop with his own dear Felix.[3]

'If, from there, you pass over to Africa, report to Carthage what you have heard. Carthage may already know Martin, as you yourself have said;[4] yet, especially now, she should know more about him and not confine her admiration to her own martyr Cyprian, even if her soil has been consecrated through his holy blood.

---

1 The *Life of St. Martin;* cf. *Dial.* 1.23.

2 As Bihlmeyer suggests (cf. Delehaye 60), Paulinus may have been assisted in circulating the book in Illyria by his close friend St. Niceta of Remesiana (in Dacia), whose influence seems to have extended far beyond his diocese. Paulinus, *Epist.* 29.14 (*PL* 61.231; *CSEL* 29.261) is especially interesting in connection with Bihlmeyer's suggestion. The works of Niceta are translated into English elsewhere in this volume. It is a curious fact that the two friends, Paulinus and Niceta, are commemorated in the *Roman Martyrology* on the same day, June 22.

3 Priest and confessor of Nola in Campania; *Roman Martyrology* (January 14). Thirteen of the poems of Paulinus are written in honor of St. Felix—birthday pieces (*carmina natalitia*) for his feast. See the recent study of R. C. Goldschmidt, *Paulinus' Churches at Nola* (Amsterdam 1940) 7-10. In *Epist.* 17.4, Paulinus puts the merits of St. Martin side by side with those of St. Felix (*PL* 61.236; *CSEL* 29.127).

4 *Dial.* 1.23.

'If you veer somewhat to the left and enter the Achaean Gulf, make Corinth know, make Athens know, that Plato in the Academy was no wiser than Martin, Socrates in his prison no braver. Happy, indeed, is Greece to have been permitted by God to hear the preaching of the Apostle, yet Christ did not forget the Gallic provinces, since He sent them a Martin for their keeping.

'When you have gone as far as Egypt, whatever be her pride in the number of her saints and in their miracles, still she should hear how neither to her nor yet to Asia as a whole does Europe yield the palm, staking her claim on Martin alone.'

Chapter 18

'But, when you once more set sail, leaving Egypt and making for Jerusalem, there is a mission with which I charge you, a mission which concerns a sorrow of mine. If ever you come to the shores of the renowned Ptolemais,[1] inquire carefully of the place where our Pomponius[2] is buried, and do not fail to visit the spot where his bones lie in foreign soil. Shed abundant tears there; tears that spring as well from your affection as from my deep-rooted love. Scatter purple flowers and sweet-smelling grasses upon the soil, even if this be but an

1 The later Acre (Akka), in Palestine.

2 This Pomponius is probably to be identified with the freedman whose flight is discussed in *Dial.* 1.12; cf. Da Prato's remarks there and Hyltén 77f. In both passages the desertion is blamed on the influence of a person whose name is withheld. Babut identifies this abductor with a notorious opponent of St. Jerome's, the priest Vigilantius: in *Le moyen âge* 19 (1906) 205-213 (Babut's arguments are reproduced by J. Gwynn, *The Book of Armagh* [Dublin 1913] cclxxvi ff.); cf. also Babut, *Saint Martin de Tours* 48ff.

empty homage.[3] Speak to him, not harshly, not bitterly, not in the language of reproof, but in a tone of compassion. Tell him that if he had been willing to listen to you at one time or to me at all times, and had taken Martin as a model rather than that man I choose not to name,[4] he would never have been so cruelly separated from me; he would not now be covered by the sand of an unknown beach, or, like a shipwrecked pirate, have met his death in mid-sea and barely secured burial at the very edge of the shore. Let them see this as their work, all those who have sought to harm me in avenging themselves on him; let them look upon their glory, and, now at least, their vengeance done, let them cease their attacks on me.'

I spoke these words of sorrow in a plaintive voice and my grief moved all to weeping. With our great admiration for Martin was mingled an equal sadness, awakened by our tears. And so we parted.

---

3 The whole sentence is surely a reminiscence of Virgil, *Aeneid* 6.884ff. Here follow in the Dublin MS. (and only there) the following words: *simul ignosce decepto et misserere fugitivo placitum illi esse dominum et indulgens tantis obnoxio erroribus precare iudicium.* The interpretation may be as follows (with a full- or half-stop after *fugitivo* and *placidum* read for *placitum*—all as in Zellerer 48) : 'At the same time pardon that victim of deception and have mercy on the fugitive; pray that the Lord be gentle towards him and that judgment be lenient upon one who yielded to such false teachings.' The genuineness of the passage has been much disputed since Babut published it in 1906 (*Le moyen âge* as in the foregoing note; cf. Gwynn, *op. cit.* cclxxvi n. 1 and 433) . See Hyltén's careful analysis (pp. 77f.) .

4 Cf. n. 2 above.

APPENDIX

St. Martin and the Condemnation of Priscillian[1]

(Extract from the *Chronicles* of Sulpicius Severus, Book II, Chapters 49 and 50)

(49) . . . When the victorious Maximus entered Trèves, [Ithacius] pressed upon him petitions directed against Priscillian and his adherents that were full of hatred and criminal intent. This action aroused the emperor. He sent letters to the prefect of the Gallic provinces and to the *vicarius* of the Spanish provinces, directing that absolutely everyone involved in the disgraceful affair should be brought for trial to a synod at Bordeaux.[2]

When Instantius[3] and Priscillian had been brought to trial in this way, Instantius was ordered to state his case first. He was unsuccessful in exculpating himself and was pronounced unworthy of the episcopate. Priscillian, however, was unwilling to be heard by the bishops and appealed his case to the emperor. The request was granted, because of the timidity of our bishops, who ought either to have pronounced their judg-

1 See *Dial.* 3.11 n. 2, which fits this excerpt into its context. For Maximus, represented here as occupying his capital after the overthrow of Gratian, see *Life* Ch. 20 n. 1.

2 The synod was held in 384.

3 One of the two bishops—a Salvianus was the other—who, with Priscillian and another layman, were held suspect of heresy by the council of Saragossa (380); cf. Sulpicius, *Chronica* 2.47 (*PL* 20.124; *CSEL* 1.100).

ment even against a person who resisted their authority, or, if they were themselves under suspicion, to have reserved the case for a hearing before other bishops. In a matter involving such manifest crimes they ought not to have let the case pass to the emperor.

(50) Thus, all who were compromised in the affair were brought before the emperor. Following after them came their accusers, the bishops Ydacius[4] and Ithacius. I should not blame their zeal for condemning the heretics, if their efforts had not been fired by an excessive eagerness for victory. In my opinion there is as much fault to find with the accusers as with the accused. In any case, I find Ithacius to have been without principle and without scruple:[5] he was audacious, excessively talkative, impudent, a spendthrift who bestowed most of his attention on his gullet and his belly. His foolishness went even so far that he denounced as accomplices and disciples of Priscillian all men, even holy ones, who had a taste for sacred reading or a firm disposition toward frequent fasting.[6]

The wretched Ithacius even dared at this time to make an open charge of heresy against the bishop Martin, a man clearly to be compared with the Apostles. Martin was then at Trèves. He constantly upbraided Ithacius, so that he might give up the accusation; he constantly pleaded with Maximus not to shed the blood of the unfortunate defendants. It was enough and more, he urged, that these men should be declared heretics by the judgment of the bishops and dismissed from their

4 Also written *Idacius* and *Hydatius*. He was Bishop of Merida; see D'Alès, *op. cit.* (*Dial.* 3.11 n. 2) 163-166.

5 With the Lat. (*nihil pensi, nihil sancti habuisse*) cf. Sallust, *Bellum Jugurth.* 41.9 and Delehaye 57; the description which follows likewise shows Sallustian features.

6 Lat. *quibus propositum erat certare ieiuniis.* Rivalry in fasting possibly is intended, but (see Da Prato, *ad loc.*) the interpretation given above is more likely (Babut 138, Delehaye 62).

sees; it would be a monstrosity and an unheard-of impiety for an ecclesiastical case to be tried by a secular judge. Finally, as long as Martin stayed at Trèves, the hearing was deferred. When he was about to leave, he used his exceptional authority to elicit from Maximus the promise that no capital punishment would be pronounced upon the accused.

But, later, the emperor was misled by the bishops Magnus and Rufus.[7] Abandoning his counsel of clemency, he turned the case over to the prefect Evodius,[8] a man of passionate severity. Submitting Priscillian to a double interrogation, Evodius convicted him of sorcery.[9] In fact, Priscillian did not deny that he had been given to obscene doctrines,[10] that he also had conducted night-time gatherings of infamous women, that he had the habit of praying naked. When Evodius had declared Priscillian guilty, he had him imprisoned until he could refer the case to the emperor. The proceedings were brought to the palace, and the emperor decreed that Priscillian and his adherents should be condemned to death.

7 This Rufus is probably distinct from the Rufus of *Life* 24; see n. 1 there.
8 See *Life,* Ch. 20 n. 2, where Evodius is described as surpassingly just.
9 Lat. *convictum maleficii.* See D'Alès, *op cit.* 61 n. 1.
10 Lat. *obscenis . . . doctrinis.* D'Alès (p. 62) translates *'sciences occultes.'*

VINCENT OF LERINS

THE COMMONITORIES

(*Commonitoria*)

Translated

by

RUDOLPH E. MORRIS, J.U.D.

Marquette University

INTRODUCTION

THERE is a striking similarity between our age and that of Vincent of Lerins. Today as then the world is in turmoil. New forces have penetrated the historically established centers of power and are a menace to traditional order. People are living in a state of permanent insecurity. Today as then ideologies are in conflict one with another.

Vincent of Lerins' *Commonitories* captivate the modern reader with its verve, its penetrating analysis, its brilliance. It deals chiefly with one issue, the question of the historical permanence of the Catholic Church throughout the changing ages.

In Vincent's day the Visigoths were in Spain and southern France; the Vandals occupied northern Africa. Conquest and struggle darkened all horizons; there seemed little likelihood that any strong power, or even a balance of powers, could be established. The links with the past were being weakened; the path to the future was dim and uncertain. The Huns to the North were a constant menace; the people along the Mediterranean from Marseilles to Genoa were disturbed by the influx of refugees, among them Prosper of Aquitaine, Vincent's famous adversary. Those whose minds and souls were vitally interested in the spiritual heritage of Christianity devoted their full energies to preserving the doctrine of the only force that they knew was unchanging.

The Christian atmosphere of that time was charged with

explosive problems and alternatives. Four hundred years of Christian tradition had already passed, yet what we consider today as its foundation had been only recently clarified by the decisions made in famous General Councils. The Council of Nicaea (325) had taken place only about one hundred years before Vincent wrote his work; the Council of Constantinople had convened in 381; and the Council of Ephesus in 431 was, so to speak, the topic of the day. St. Augustine had just died. The discussion between his basic opposition to Pelagius and the so-called Semi-Pelagians had turned into a passionate fight for or against the role of free will and its relationship to divine grace. The region in which Vincent lived was the center of Western theology: Cassian, Vincent and Hilary of Arles favored Semi-Pelagianism, Prosper defended the Bishop of Hippo. Pope Celestine I (d. 432), in a famous letter addressed to the bishops of southern Gaul, criticized the priests of Marseilles who 'abused their preaching to confuse people's minds' by denouncing errors in the Augustinian doctrine. In short, the great power of Christianity, the only power of that era, asserted its own vitality precisely by the controversies about important issues which either had been clarified but recently, or were still open and unresolved.

St. Vincent of Lerins died about 450 A.D. He wrote the *Commonitories* probably ten or fifteen years earlier. Not very much is known about his life. In his youth he was active in worldly affairs, perhaps even in military service; he certainly knew the political problems of his time. Later he retired to the monastery of Lerins,[1] an island off the southern coast of France, known today as St. Honorat, near Cannes. It was just at its prime when Vincent entered it as a monk. There he wrote his work, which portrays him as a well-trained

1 Founded by St. Honorat in 410.

theologian and a man burning with the inner fire of Christian enthusiasm.[2]

It seems understandable, perhaps even natural, that a man with the zeal and knowledge of Vincent should retire into a monastery; no other place gave the spiritual and intellectual forces of a man a better opportunity for wrestling with, and solving, the essential issues of contemporary Christian thought. Here, the theologian could sit back, and survey calmly the pertinent and important problems of his time, and write down notes on the results of his thinking. Perhaps, at first he wrote really only to have a memorandum to which he could constantly refer in his daily studies. But whether or not this was so, he must have polished and elaborated his first notes, for his work shows correct logical development and good style.

Although the *Commonitories* were written shortly after the General Council of Ephesus (431), it is doubtful if they were published during his lifetime. At any rate, he used a pen name and wrote as 'Peregrinus' (the Pilgrim); he may have felt, just as we do today, that each of us is only a pilgrim, having no secure place on earth. He called his work *Commonitories* in the strict sense of the word. He wrote them, as he tells his reader, because he felt his memory getting weak and because he had observed that persistent reading of his notes helped him to see more clearly in matters of decisive importance. The second of these memoranda is very brief, and it is assumed by the experts that it is only a summary of a manuscript which was lost.

Everyone who approaches the *Commonitories* with this historical, spiritual and personal background in mind will from the very outset be enraptured by the transparence of

2 Cf. Ch. 20.

thought, the intensity of love, and the breadth of vision which characterize Vincent's plea for the tradition and universality of the Catholic faith and his radical opposition to heretical innovations. His point of view, recognized through the ages up to our time, is simple. Our faith is based on the authority of divine Law, which has to be understood and interpreted according to the tradition of the Church; the tradition consists of what has been believed everywhere, always, and by all. This principle, however, does not exclude progress or doctrinal development. But it must be progress in the proper sense of the word, and not a change. Progress is defined by Vincent as a growing of doctrine within its own orbit, whereas change implies that a thing is transformed into something different.

The *Commonitories* elaborate this thesis, with ample references to the various heresies, on the one hand, and to the Apostle Paul, the great Councils, and the authority of the Church, on the other. Vincent may also have had in mind to attack, as one of the 'profane innovations' which he denounces, the Augustinian position on grace and free will.[3] It is likely that some passages implicitly contain such criticism, but this point is of merely historical importance today. Thus, the reader of this translation will do well not to burden himself too much with the study of intricate problems in the history of theology. In doing so he might lose his grasp of the main thesis of the author, which, in itself, is of such vital importance in our age, an age which has brought to the fore the conflict between the theocentric and the anthropocentric philosophies of life.

But it will certainly interest the reader to learn that the

---

3 The reader who is interested in St. Augustine's teaching on grace does well to read John Courtney Murray's translation of St. Augustine's *De correptione et gratia* (Admonition and Grace) in the 4th volume of the Works of St. Augustine in this series.

Commonitories, and especially Chapter 23, which explains the problem of 'progress in faith,'[4] has played an ever-increasing role in the 19th century. Cardinal Newman quotes Vincent in his 'Essay on the Development of Christian Doctrine' (1845), where[5] he discusses the concept of genuine development and of preservation of type. More important is the reference to the *Commonitories* in the *Dogmatic Constitution of the Catholic Faith*[6] of the Vatican Council. Furthermore, Pope Pius X, in his famous Encyclical, 'Pascendi' (Against Modernism), of 1907, refers to Vincent.

The text followed in the present translation is that of G. Rauschen, *Vincentii Lerinensis Commonitoria* (Florilegium Patristicum, fasc. 5 Bonnae 1906). Some of Rauschen's invaluable notes, necessary for the better understanding of the translation, have been added.

4 Cf. Ch. 23 below.
5 Ch. 5, sec. 1.
6 Ch. 4, 'On Faith and Reason'. The passage in question reads as follows: 'Let, then, the intelligence, science, and wisdom of each and all, of individuals and of the whole Church, in all ages and all times, increase and flourish in abundance and vigor; but only in its own proper kind, that is to say, in one and the same doctrine, one and the same cause, one and the same judgment.'

Commonitorium and especially Chapter 23, which treats the problem of "progress in faith," has played an important role in the 19th century. Cardinal Newman quotes Vincent in his Essay on the Development of Christian Doctrine (1845), where he discusses the concept of genuine development and of preservation of type. More important is the reference to the Commonitorium in the [illegible]

[illegible]

The text [illegible] translation is that of [illegible] Florilegium [illegible] Rauschen [illegible] Bonn [illegible] valuable notes, necessary for the better understanding of the translation have been added.

[illegible]

CONTENTS

THE COMMONITORIES[1]

Chapter 1

HOLY SCRIPTURE admonishes us: 'ask my father, and He will declare to thee: thy elders and they will tell thee';[2] and again: 'Incline thy ear and hear the words of the wise';[3] and again: 'My son, forget not my law: and let thy heart keep my commandments.'[4] According to these words, it seems to me, Peregrinus,[5] the least of all the servants of God, that it will be rather useful for me to write down, with the help of the Lord, what I have faithfully received from the holy fathers.[6] Of this I shall certainly be in great need in my infirmity, for my memory may be refreshed by persistent reading if I have these matters down in writing. I am induced to perform this task not only for the results of the work but

1 This is the title of the work of St. Vincent in the Paris codices; but Gennadius states (*De vir. inl.* 64) that the title should be 'Of the Pilgrim, against heretics'. Also, in the codices at the end of the work we read: 'The explanation of the treatise of the Pilgrim against heretics.' In the first edition of Sichardus (Basel 1528) we read: 'In defense of the antiquity and universality of the Catholic faith, [the work] of Vincent of Lerins against the profane innovations of all heretics.'

2 Deut. 32.7.

3 Prov. 22.17.

4 Prov. 3.1.

5 We read in Gennadius that Vincent adopted this name.

6 But to this statement the *Commonitories* themselves, in so far as they are extant, give only little support, for in them does not appear the collected testimony of the Fathers, but certain notes and rules whereby Catholic doctrine may be distinguished from heresy.

also because I have the time and a suitable place to do it. As for the time element: since time snatches away all things human, we ought to snatch from it something which may profit us unto life eternal. We are moved particularly by the terrible fear of the approaching Judgment which urges us to increase our studies of religion, and by the deceitfulness of the new heretics which requires much careful attention. As for the place: far from the masses that overcrowd large cities, I am living in a very remote spot where, within the cell of a monastery with nothing to distract me, I can practice what is sung in the psalm: 'Be still and see that I am God.'[7] This way of life is well suited to the work I am planning to do. Long involved in various unstable and saddening whirpools of secular strife, I finally arrived, under Christ's inspiration, at the harbor of religion, always the safest place for everyone. There, after the storms of vanity and pride have ceased, I may propitiate God by the sacrifice of Christian humility and thus avoid not only the shipwrecks of the present life, but also the flames of the world to come.

But now it is time for me to begin, in the name of the Lord, my work, namely, to describe what our ancestors have handed down and entrusted to us. I shall do this more as an honest reporter than as a presumptuous author. I shall follow this plan in my writing. I shall not cover everything, but only the essential points; not in an embellished and meticulous form, but in easy and popular language. In this way most of the points will appear to be indicated rather than developed. Let those make use of a flowery and precise style who approach such a task either from confidence in their own ability or through a sense of duty. As for me, I shall be satisfied to compose this *Commonitory* for my own use, to aid my

7 Ps. 45. 11.

memory, or, rather, [to check] my forgetfulness. In any case, with the Lord's help, I shall do my best recalling step by step what I have learned, emending and filling out my knowledge from day to day. I have prefaced my work with this warning so that in case it slips from my hands into those of saintly persons,[8] they may not hastily censure certain passages, but remember that I have promised to correct and improve them.

Chapter 2

With great zeal and full attention I often inquired from many men, outstanding in sanctity and doctrinal knowledge, how, in a concise and, so to speak, general and ordinary way, I might be able to discern the truth of the Catholic faith from the falsity of heretical corruption. From almost all of them I always received the answer that if I or someone else wanted to expose the frauds of the heretics and to escape their snares and to remain sound in the integrity of faith, I had, with the help of the Lord, to fortify that faith in a twofold manner: first, by the authority[1] of the divine Law; second, by the tradition of the Catholic Church.

Here, perhaps, someone may ask: Since the canon of the Scripture is complete and more than sufficient in itself, why is it necessary to add to it the authority of ecclesiastical interpretation? As a matter of fact, [we must answer,] Holy Scripture, because of its depth, is not universally accepted in one and the same sense. The same text is interpreted differently by different people, so that one may almost gain the impression that it can yield as many different meanings as there are men. Novatianus, for example, expounds a passage in one way;

---

8 Of those who have forsaken the world, i.e., priests and monks.

---

1 Cf. the interesting comment of Tertullian, *De praescr.* 16-19 (Rauschen, 11).

Sabellius, in another; Donatus,[2] in another. Arius, and Eunomius and Macedonius read it differently; so do Photinus,[3] Apollinaris, and Priscillianus; in another way, Jovinianus, Pelagius, and Celestius; finally, in still another, Nestorius. Thus, because of the great distortions caused by various errors, it is, indeed, necessary that the trend of the interpretation of the prophetic and apostolic writings be directed in accordance with the rule of the ecclesiastical and Catholic meaning.

In the Catholic Church itself, every care should be taken to hold fast to what has been believed everywhere, always, and by all. This is truly and properly 'Catholic,'[4] as indicated by the force and etymology of the name itself, which comprises everything truly universal. This general rule will be truly applied if we follow the principles of universality, antiquity, and consent. We do so in regard to universality if we confess that faith alone to be true which the entire Church confesses all over the world. [We do so] in regard to antiquity if we in no way deviate from those interpretations which our

---

2 We must understand this to refer to that Donatus who was Bishop of Casae Nigrae in Numidia, 'who, coming from Numidia, and drawing to himself the bishops of his own faction against Caecilian, creating division, among the Christian people, ordained Majorinus bishop in Carthage,' or Donatus the Great, who succeeded Majorinus to the See of Carthage, 'who by his eloquence so strengthened this heresy that many thought that because of him they should rather be called Donatists' (Augustine, *De haeresibus* 69).

3 This Bishop of Sirmium (chief city of Lower Pannonia, now Mitrovica, Yugoslavia), who preached that Christ was merely a man endowed with divine virtues and adopted by God, was removed from his See by the Synod of Sirmium in 351, and died in exile in 376.

4 The fold of Christ is first called the Catholic Church (*Katholikè ecclesia*) by St. Ignatius, *Ep. ad Smyrn.* 8 (See G. G. Walsh's translation in *The Apostolic Fathers* [p. 121] in this series.)

The name is given by St. Optatus, *De schism. Donat.* 2.1: 'The proper significance of the name Catholic will be had when that is called Catholic which is in accordance with reason (*catholicus—katà lógon*? du Pin) and diffused everywhere.

ancestors and fathers[5] have manifestly proclaimed as inviolable. [We do so] in regard to consent if, in this very antiquity, we adopt the definitions and propositions of all, or almost all, the bishops[6] and doctors.

Chapter 3

What, therefore, will the Catholic Christian do if some members of the Church have broken away from the communion of universal faith? What else, but prefer the sanity of the body universal to the pestilence of the corrupt member? What if a new contagion strives to infect not only a small part but the whole of the Church? Then, he will endeavor to adhere to the antiquity which is evidently beyond the danger of being seduced by the deceit of some novelty. What if in antiquity itself an error is detected, on the part of two or three men, or even on the part of a city or a province? Then, he will take care to prefer the decrees of a previous ecumenical council (if there was one) to the temerity and ignorance of a small group. Finally, what if such an error arises and nothing like a council can be found? Then, he will take pains to consult and interrogate the opinions of his predecessors, comparing them with (one another only as regards the opinions of) those who, though they lived in various periods and at different periods and at different places, nevertheless remained in the communion and faith of the One Catholic Church, and who therefore have become reliable authorities. As he will discover, he must also believe without hesitation whatever not only one or two but all equally and with one and the same consent, openly, frequently, and persistently have held, written, and taught.

5 Cf. Ch. 28.5 and Ch. 29.4.
6 The text has *sacerdotum* (priests).

Chapter 4

To make clearer what we say, examples will be given for each instance, and we must dwell on them more extensively. For it must not be that our eagerness to be brief deprives the matters in question of their weight by an overhasty presentation.

In the time of Donatus (from whom rose the Donatists), a great part of Africa rushed[1] into the madness of his error and, forgetful of name, religion, and profession, preferred the sacrilegious rashness of a single man to the Church of Christ. Then, of all the people of Africa, only those who detested this profane schism and remained associated with the universal Church were able to keep themselves safe within the sanctuary of Catholic faith. Thus, they left an outstanding example to posterity of the way in which the soundness of the body universal ought rightly to be set above the unsoundness of a single man or even of a few individuals.

Similarly, when the poison of Arianism had infected not only a small part but nearly the entire world[2]—to such an extent that most bishops of the Latin tongue were led into error, partly by force and partly by fraud, and a kind of darkness had obscured their minds, depriving them of insight into what it was best to do in such a confused situation—then each true lover and worshiper of Christ preferred the ancient faith to the modern falsehood, and thus remained untouched by the infection of that plague. The disaster of that perilous period demonstrates abundantly what calamity is brought about by the induction of a novel dogma. Not only were matters of small moment destroyed, but also those of the

1 Cf. Possidius, *Vita S. Augustini* 7.

2 Jerome (*Dial. adv. Luciferianos* 19) complains thus of the Synod of Rimini, held in 359: 'The whole world groaned, and was amazed to find itself Arian.'

greatest import were affected.[3] Not only personal relations, kinship, friendships, homes, but even cities, peoples, provinces, nations, finally, the whole Roman Empire were rocked and shaken to their foundations. When this profane Arian novelty, like Bellona[4] or a Fury, had first of all captured the emperor[5] and then subjugated to the new laws the leaders in the imperial palace as well, it no longer avoided mixing up and disturbing everything, public and private interests, sacred and profane. It did not discriminate in favor of the good and the true; it struck down whomever it capriciously selected, as though it were superior to them. Then wives were dishonored, widows desecrated, virgins ravished, monasteries demolished, clerics thrown into panic, Levites beaten, priests exiled. Prisons, jails, and mines were overcrowded with saintly persons. Most of them, forbidden to enter the cities, hunted and exiled, exposed to life in deserts, caves, among wild beasts and amid rocks, exhausted by exposure, hunger, and thirst, perished. And all this for no other reason than that human superstitions were substituted for divine dogma; that well-founded tradition was ruined by criminal novelties; that institutions established by authority were violated; that the wisdom of the fathers was rescinded; that the teaching of the elders was thrown into confusion; that the lust for profane and novel curiosity did not contain itself within the most unpolluted bounds of a sacred and uncorrupted antiquity.

Chapter 5

Or is it that we fancy all this, because of our hatred of modernism and our love of what was established of old?

3 The allusion is to Sallust, *Jug.* 10.
4 Bellona was a goddess of the Sabines, the companion or wife of Mars.
5 Constantius.

Whoever harbors this suspicion should at least give ear to blessed Ambrose, who, in the second book of his work dedicated to Emperor Gratian, in which he deplores the rudeness of his age, has this to say: 'But by now, Almighty God, we have through our ruin and our blood sufficiently expiated the murder of confessors, the exile of priests, and the wickedness of such atrocious impiety. It is now sufficiently evident that those who violated the faith cannot live in security.'[1] And he says, in the third book of that same work: 'Let us preserve the precepts of our ancestors and not violate the stamp of tradition in a mood of reckless and daring boldness. That sealed prophetic book neither the elders nor the powers nor the angels nor the archangels have dared to open; to Christ alone is reserved the prerogative of explaining it.[2] Who among us would dare to unseal the sacerdotal book confirmed by the confessors[3] and now consecrated by the martyrdom of so many? Those who were forced to subscribe to it retracted this later on, after the fraud was denounced;[4] those who did not dare to violate it became confessors and martyrs. How, then, can we deny the faith of those whose victory we proclaim?'[5] We proclaim it, indeed, venerable Ambrose; we give them praise and admiration. For who is so foolish as not to desire (although he may not be able to reach

1 *De fide* 2.6.141.

2 Apoc. 5.1ff.

3 In the third and fourth centuries, those were called Confessors who confessed the Name of Christ before a judge, or in chains and prison (cf. Cyprian, *Ep.* 37.1). Later, all those who lived in and died for Christ were accorded the title and honor of Confessor.

4 Ambrose is speaking of the bishops, worn down by poverty and old age, whom Constantius, in 359, in the Synod of Rimini, compelled to abjure the faith, by denying them (permission) to return. When the Emperor died a short time later, almost all condemned the subscription and the Arian heresy, especially the French under the leadership of St. Hilary, in the Synod of Paris, 361 (Cf. Jerome, *Dial. adv. Luciferianos* 19).

5 *De fide* 3.15.128.

such heights) to follow those whom no force could keep from defending the faith of their ancestors—no threats, no blandishments, neither life nor death, not the palace, not the courtiers, not the emperor, not the empire, not men, not demons? These, I say, because of their tenacious attachment to the ancient faith, were deemed worthy by the Lord of so great a reward that through them He restored battered churches, brought to life peoples that were spiritually dead, and restored the stolen crowns of priests. He erased those nefarious, not letters but blots, of the new impiety with the tears shed by the faithful bishops, a fountain divinely fed. Finally, He recalled the world, which had been almost completely shaken by the furious hurricane of unexpected heresy, from the new perfidy to the old faith, from modern unreasonableness to ancient sanity, from the blindness of novelty to the ancient light.

What we have to consider above all, when admiring the quasi-divine power of the confessors, is that they took up the defense of the old tradition of the Church, not with regard to a particular group, but to a whole body. Indeed, it would not have been possible for such outstanding men to assert, with such elaborate equipment, the erroneous and self-contradictory assumptions of one or two individuals, or to fight for the cause of some impudent conspiracy that might arise in some corner of a province. No, what they actually did was to stay in line with the decrees and definitions[6] of all the priests of Holy Church as the heirs of Apostolic and Catholic Truth. They preferred to surrender themselves rather than the faith universally held from the beginning. For this reason, they deserved to rise to such a height of glory that they rightly and deservedly are regarded not as mere confessors, but rather as princes among confessors.

---

6 Especially the decrees of the Nicene Council.

Chapter 6

A great and evidently divine example that should be meditated upon and recalled again and again by every true Catholic is given by those blessed persons who, like the seven-branched candlestick radiating the sevenfold light of the Holy Spirit, manifested to posterity the clearest formula for the way in which the rashness of profane novelty, with all its boastful display of errors, is to be crushed from now on by the authority of sacred tradition. This method, to be sure, is not at all new. It has been an established custom in the Church that the more devout a person is, the more prompt he is to oppose innovations.

History offers a wealth of such examples. But, in order to be brief, we take only one, but one of exceptional weight—namely, from the Apostolic See[1]—so that it may appear clearer than daylight to all with what vigor, zeal, and fighting spirit the blessed successors of the blessed Apostles have defended the integrity of the religion that they had accepted once and for all. This is what happened. Bishop Agrippinus of Carthage,[2] of venerable memory, was the first to hold that rebaptism might be permitted—contrary to divine Law;[3] contrary to the rule of the Church Universal, contrary to the opinion of all of his fellow bishops, contrary to the customs and institutions of our forefathers. This false doctrine carried with it so much evil that it afforded not only all heretics a pattern for sacrilege, but also some Catholics an opportunity

1 The Roman See. Cf. Tertullian *De praescer.* 20.

2 Agrippinus, in a council of Africans and Numidians (at Carthage about 220) decreed that baptisms of heretics were invalid. Cf. Cyprian, *Ep.* 71.4 and 73.3. The bishops of Asia, in the Synods of Iconium and Synnada (about 230), gave the same decision, as Dionysius, Bishop of Alexandria (cf. Eusebius, *Historia ecclesiastica* 7.7) and Bishop Firmilianus (Cf. Cyprian, *Ep.* 75.7) bear witness.

3 Contrary to Sacred Scripture.

for error.[4] When, then, people everywhere protested against this novelty and priests from all corners of the world—each according to the degree of his zeal—strove against it, Pope Stephen, of blessed memory, who then held the Apostolic See, opposed it, together with his colleagues, yet more earnestly than they. He apparently considered it fitting to surpass all others in his devotion to the faith, inasmuch as he was superior to them by virtue of his office.[5] In an epistle, which he thereupon sent to Africa, he stated it as a rule that 'nothing new is to be accepted save what has been handed down by tradition.' For that saintly and prudent man realized that the principle of piety admits of only one attitude: namely, that everything be transferred to the sons in the same spirit of faith in which it was accepted by the fathers; that religion should not lead us whither we want to go, but that we must follow whither it leads; and that it is proper to Christian modesty and earnestness not to transfer to posterity one's own ideas, but to preserve those received from one's ancestors. To resume: What was the final issue of the whole problem? What else, but the rule to which we are used and accustomed? Antiquity was retained; novelty, repulsed.

But, perhaps only the necessary patronage was lacking for establishing the innovation? Quite the contrary. They had at their disposal such strength of ingenuity, such streams of eloquence, such numerous followers, so great a resemblance to the true, so many references to the divine Law obviously interpreted, however, in a new and wrong sense that—as it seems to me—the whole conspiracy could not have been crushed if it had not been overthrown by reason of terrific weight, namely, by the proclamation on its novelty, which has been accepted, defended, and so highly praised. What was

4 The custom of rebaptizing heretics flourished.
5 *Loci auctoritate* [through the authority of his See].

the final impact of this African council[6] and its decrees? Thanks be to God, there was none. The whole matter was abolished, rejected, and trodden upon[7]—like a dream, like a fable, like an empty thing.

And now, what an amazing reversal of the situation! The authors of that same opinion are adjudged to be Catholics, but the followers, heretics;[8] the masters are absolved, the disciples, condemned; the writers of the books will be children in the Kingdom, the adherents of their doctrine will be in Gehenna. For who would be so foolish as to doubt that the most blessed Cyprian, the light of all saints and bishops and martyrs, will with his other colleagues reign with Christ in eternity? Or who, on the other hand, would be so sacrilegious as to deny that the Donatists and the rest of the pests who pride themselves in rebaptism, under the authority of that council, will burn forever with the Devil?

Chapter 7

In my opinion, this judgment [of the Church on rebaptism, as discussed in the preceding chapter] has been promulgated by divine wisdom. Especially is this so because of the fraudulence of those men who try to make it seem that their heresy

6 Three Councils on the rebaptism of heretics were held at Carthage, St. Cyprian presiding: the first in 255, the second in 256, the third on Sept. 1, 256. Vincentius mentions here the third, in which the eighty-seven bishops who were present agreed with Cyprian.

7 The decree of that third African council was set aside both by the agreement of the entire Catholic Church and by the eighth canon of the Council of Arles, held in 314. Jerome (*Dial ad Luciferianos* 23) also states: 'At last these very bishops who had agreed with him [Cyprian] as to the rebaptism of heretics, when they returned to the ancient custom, issued a new decree.' But the testimony is not trustworthy.

8 I.e., the authors of rebaptism, as St. Cyprian, *remained in communion with those who did not assent to it* (Cf. Augustine *De bapt.* 3.2), but those who later embraced their opinion were adjudged heretics.

is something that has a different name; who often seize upon some of the more involved writings of an ancient author, which, merely because of their obscurity, seem to stand in agreement with the new dogma these men propose. By these means, what they profess will not make them appear as though they were the first and only ones to have sensed it. In my judgment, their wrongdoing is doubly vicious: first, because they do not shrink from making others drink the poison of heresy; second, because, with a profane hand, they scatter like ashes already quenched the memory of some holy man and, by reviving his opinions, defame what ought to remain buried in silence. They thus follow the pattern of Ham, who not only failed to cover the nakedness of the venerable Noe, but even held it up to ridicule. Because of this violation of filial piety, therefore, he was considered so guilty that even his descendants inherited the malediction he incurred for his sin. Quite differently, his blessed brothers sought neither to profane with their own eyes nor to expose to others the nakedness of their venerable father. As it is written, they turned away and covered him, that is to say, they neither approved nor betrayed the fault of the saintly man, and for this they were rewarded with a happy benediction for their children. But let us return to our subject.

We should, therefore, dread with a great fear the sacrilege of changing faith and profaning religion. We should be deterred from such a sin not only by the discipline of ecclesiastical rule, but also by the censure of apostolic authority. For it is well known to all how heavily, how severely, how vehemently the blessed Apostle Paul attacks those who, with amazing levity, 'are so quickly deserting him who called them to the grace of Christ, unto another gospel, which is not another';[1] who, 'according to their own desires had heaped

1 Gal. 1.6,7.

to themselves teachers . . . and will turn away their hearing from the truth and will be turned into fables,'[2] 'having damnation because they have made void their first faith.'[3] They deceived those about whom the same Apostle writes to his Roman brothers: 'Now I beseech you, brethren, to mark them who make dissentions and offenses contrary to the doctrine which you have learned, and avoid them. For they that are such do not serve Christ our Lord but their own belly; and by pleasing speeches and good words reduce the hearts of the innocent.'[4] 'For of these sort are they who creep into houses and lead captive silly women laden with sins who are led away by divers desires: ever learning and never attaining to the knowledge of the truth.'[5] 'For there are also . . . vain talkers and seducers . . . who subvert whole houses, teaching things which they ought not, for filthy lucre's sake,'[6] 'proud, knowing nothing, but sick about questions and strifes of words,—men corrupted in mind and who are destitute of the truth, supposing gain to be godliness.'[7] 'And withal being idle, they learn to go about from house to house, and are not only idle but tattlers also and busybodies, speaking things which they ought not';[8] 'having . . . a good conscience, which some rejecting have made shipwreck concerning their faith';[9] 'profane and vain babblings, for they grow much towards ungodliness, and their speech spreadeth like a canker.'[10] What follows about them is equally well said: 'But they shall proceed no farther, for their folly shall be manifest to all, as theirs also was.'[11]

2 2 Tim. 4.3,4.
3 1 Tim. 5.12.
4 Rom. 16.17,18.
5 2 Tim. 3.6,7.
6 Titus 1.10,11.
7 1 Tim. 6.4,5.
8 1 Tim. 5.13.
9 1 Tim. 1.19.
10 2 Tim. 2.16,17.
11 2 Tim. 3.9.

Chapter 8

Some men of this type traveling through provinces and cities, hawking their venal errors, came also to the Galatians. These, after having listened to the travelers, became lukewarm toward the truth, rejecting the manna of apostolic and Catholic doctrine and delighting in the dirt of heretical novelty. On this occasion, the authority of the apostolic power asserted itself and decreed with utmost severity: 'But though we, or an angel from heaven, preach a gospel to you besides that which we have preached to you, let him be anathema.'[1] Why does he say: 'But though we'? Why not rather: 'But though I'? Because it is his understanding that even if Peter, or Andrew, or John, even, finally, if the whole community of Apostles 'should preach a gospel to you other than that which we have preached to you, let them be anathema. What tremendous strictness! To assure firmness in the loyalty to the 'first faith,' he is ready to spare neither himself nor his fellow Apostles. But he is not satisfied with that, for his words are: Even if 'an angel from heaven should preach a gospel to you besides that which we have preached to you, let him be anathema.' For the preservation of the traditional faith it was not sufficient for him to look only on the condition of human nature; he also included the eminent angelic nature. 'Though we,' he says, 'or an angel from heaven.' Not that he thinks the holy and celestial angels could sin. What he really means is: If that happened which cannot happen, let whosoever may attempt to change the traditional faith be anathema.

But, perhaps he pronounced these words incidentally, uttering them out of a quite human impulse rather than forming them under divine inspiration? This is far from the case. He continues, and emphasizes his point with the whole weight of

Gal. 1.8.

reiterated assertion: 'As we said before, so now I say again: If anyone preach to you a gospel besides that which you have received, let him be anathema.'[2] He did not say: 'If anyone announced to you something besides that which you have received, let him be blessed, praised, welcome,' but: 'let him be anathema.' That is, let him be separated, segregated, excluded, so that the horrible contagion of a single sheep may not infect the innocent flock of Christ with its poisonous virus.

Chapter 9

Perhaps those precepts are aimed only at the Galatians? Then, other rules mentioned in later parts of the same Epistle would likewise be addressed only to the Galatians, as, for example: 'If we live in the Spirit, let us also walk in the Spirit. Let us not be made desirous of vainglory, provoking one another, envying one another,'[1] and so on. But, if this is absurd, and if the rules are aimed equally at all, then it follows that, equally with the moral commandments, those concerning faith apply to all in the same manner. Just as people are not permitted to provoke or envy one another, so no one is permitted to accept doctrines other than those the Catholic Church preaches everywhere. Or, perhaps it was an order only for that time that whosoever preached otherwise than had been taught [by the Apostles] be anathema, and that this order is now no longer valid? If this were true, then the exhortation, 'But I say to them: Walk in the Spirit: and you shall not fulfill the lusts of the flesh,'[2] would likewise have been a command only for that time, and not for afterwards. But, if it is impious as well as perilous

2 Gal. 1.9.

1 Gal. 5.25,26.
2 Gal. 5.16.

to think in this way, it follows logically that, so far as these rules are to be observed at any time, those concerning the immutability of holy faith also are orders which remain in force for all ages.

Consequently, to announce to Catholic Christians a doctrine other than that which they have received was never permitted, is nowhere permitted, and never will be permitted. It was ever necessary, is everywhere necessary, and ever will be necessary that those who announce a doctrine other than that which was received once and for all be anathema. If this be so, is there anyone alive so bold as to preach dogmas other than those taught by the Church, or so foolish as to accept doctrines besides those accepted by the Church? Crying aloud, crying aloud again and again and again, crying aloud to everyone, always and everywhere throughout his writings, is he, this 'vessel of election,'[3] this 'doctor of the Gentiles,'[4] this trumpet among the Apostles, this herald of the earth, this heaven-conscious man; he is crying aloud that whoever announces a new doctrine is anathema. Against this voice there shout certain frogs and gnats and day flies,[5] such as the Pelagians, who have this to say to Catholics: We are the leaders, the chiefs, the interpreters. We tell you: Condemn what you adhered to; adhere to what you condemned; reject the ancient faith, the paternal institutions, the ancestral inheritance, and accept . . . After all, accept what? I shudder to say. It is so presumptuous that to refute it, let alone to utter it, is almost impossible without incurring some sort of sin.

---

3 Acts 9.15.

4 1 Tim. 2.7.

5 By these names he compares the heretics to the plagues of Egypt. (Exod. 8) Eccli. 10.1: *muscae morientes,* dying flies.

Chapter 10

There are some who will say: Why, then, does Divine Providence often permit eminent persons, who are well established in the Church, to announce novel ideas to Catholics? This is a good and earnest question, and should be thoroughly and extensively discussed. To do so satisfactorily, we have to refer not to our own ingenuity, but to the authority of divine Law and to the basic documents of ecclesiastical teaching. Let us listen, therefore, to blessed Moses. He himself may teach us why learned men and those who, because of their mysterious gifts, are called Prophets by the Apostles, sometimes are permitted to advance new dogmas. These are customarily called 'strange gods' in the Old Testament, in accordance with its allegorical pattern of speech (and a very good term, incidentally, since the heretics have the same reverence for their own opinions as the Gentiles for their gods). Blessed Moses has this to say in Deuteronomy: 'If there rise in the midst of thee a prophet or one that saith he hath dreamed a dream,' that is, a doctor of the Church who, in the opinion of his disciples or listeners, is teaching by some revelation—well, what then? Moses continues: 'and he foretell a sign and a wonder: and that come to pass which he spoke . . .' Evidently, he has some outstanding master of great knowledge in mind, one who, in the eyes of his followers, is not only familiar with human affairs but also capable of a foreknowledge of transcendent matters (a master such as Valentine, Donatus, Photinus, Apollinaris, and the rest of them appeared to be in the opinion of their boasting disciples)—well, and what then? 'And he say to thee: Let us go and follow strange gods, which thou knowest not, and let us serve them . . .' (And who are the 'strange gods,' if not strange errors?) 'Which thou knowest not,' that is, novel and unheard-of ones. 'And let us serve them,' that is, let us have faith in them; let us serve them. And now, what is Moses' conclusion? 'Thou shalt not hear the words of that prophet or dreamer,' he says. And why, I ask you, does God not forbid to be taught what He forbids to be listened to? 'For the Lord your God trieth you, that it may appear whether you love Him with all your heart, and with all your soul.'[1] Clearer than daylight is the reason why Divine Providence sometimes suffers certain doctors of the Church to preach new dogmas: to the effect that 'the Lord your God trieth you.' And great is the temptation indeed when that man whom you look upon as a prophet, as a disciple of prophets, as a doctor and a defender of truth, whom you have embraced with highest veneration and love, suddenly and surreptitiously introduces noxious errors which you are unable to detect quickly so long as you still are under the spell of his former teaching, and which you do not dare to condemn easily so long as the affection for your old teacher hinders you from so doing.

Chapter 11

Here, someone perhaps may insist upon being given an illustration of the words of venerable Moses by a few examples from the history of the Church. We respond to this justifiable demand at once, and begin with most recent and well-known events. How did the latest temptation come about, that this unfortunate man, Nestorius,[1] suddenly changed from a sheep into a wolf and began to harass the flock of Christ, while most of those who were bitten by him still believed in him

---

1 Deut. 13.1-3.

---

1 Socrates (*Historia ecclesiastica* 7.29) deals more extensively with Nestorius. In 428, Nestorius, a priest of Antioch, was proclaimed, by Emperor Theodosius the Younger, Bishop of the See of Constantinople.

as a sheep and were therefore the more exposed to the effects of his teeth? For who could readily consider entangled in error that man whom he saw elected after a judicious examination by the imperial court and honored by such deep affection on the part of the clergy, who was extolled by the holy men who loved him so much and by the people who gave him all their favor when in public he daily explained Holy Scripture and disclosed all the noxious errors of the Jews and Gentiles? How, then, could he fail to make everyone believe that he was teaching, preaching, and thinking orthodox truth—he who persecuted the blasphemies of all heresies in order to open the way for one heresy, his own?[2] This is precisely what Moses said: 'The Lord your God trieth you that it may appear whether you love Him or not.'[3]

But, let us leave Nestorius, who excelled more by the admiration he created than by actual worth, more by reputation than by actual performance, and who for a time appeared great in public opinion less by divine grace than by natural cleverness. Let us rather remember those who, endowed with many outstanding qualities and great zeal, turned out to be serious temptations for Catholic people. Thus, for instance, Photinus[4] is still remembered by the older generation of Pannonia as the man who put the Church of Sirmium on trial. He had been admitted to the priesthood there with general approval, and then, having held his office for a while as a Catholic, suddenly, like that evil 'prophet or dreamer' (as Moses called them), he began to persuade

2 As Socrates (*Hist. eccles.* 1.1) bears witness, Bishop Nestorius, on the fifth day after his appointment, succeeded in his attempt to have the church of the Arians destroyed by fire. And, if we can trust Gothofredus, Nestorius was the author of that severe law enacted against the heretics by the Emperor toward the end of May in that same year (*Cod. Theod.* 16.5,65).

3 Deut. 13.3.

4 For Photinus, cf. above, Ch. 2.3.

the people of God entrusted to him to follow 'strange gods,' that is, strange errors formerly unknown to them. The case as such was not unusual. What made it particularly pernicious was the fact that he buttressed his nefarious undertaking with his extraordinary qualities: his powerful genius, his excellent education, and his outstanding eloquence. He used two languages bluntly and forcibly for disputations and writings; proof of this is the number of his books, composed partly in Greek, partly in Latin. Fortunately, the sheep of Christ entrusted to him were watching and caring for the Catholic faith and remembered in time the warnings of Moses. Thus, they were not unaware of the temptation, in spite of the admiration they had for the eloquence of their prophet and pastor. As a matter of fact, by now they began to shun as a wolf the very man they previously had followed as the ram of the flock.

Not only the example of Photinus, but that of Apollinaris[5] as well, teaches us the danger of temptation arising from churchmen; but it likewise admonishes us to guard with great care the observance of our faith. For he, too, caused his listeners great trouble and deep anxiety. Drawn toward one side by the authority of the Church and toward the other by the influence of a master wavering and fluctuating between both, they did not know how to make up their minds. Was this man, perhaps, the sort of person who could not be but despised? Not at all. He was of such worth that, in most respects, people trusted him only too readily. Who was more outstanding than he in acuteness, versatility, and erudition? How many heresies did he crush, in as many volumes! How many errors dangerous to orthodoxy did he silence—as indi-

5 Accounts of Apollinaris may be found in Voisin, *L'Apollinarisme* (Louvain 1901) and Lietzmann, *Apollinaris von Loadicea und seine Schute* 1 (Tübingen 1904).

cated by that work of no less than thirty books, that eminent and outstanding work in which he refuted with a mass of arguments the mad calumnies of Porphyry![6] It would take too long to mention all his works, by which he could have been deemed an equal of the most constructive minds in the Church, if he had not, out of impious desire for heretical curiosity, invented some new doctrine or other which infected all his labors with a kind of leprosy and caused his teaching to become more a temptation than an edification in the Church.

Chapter 12

At this point, I may be asked to explain the heresies mentioned above, namely, those of Nestorius, Apollinaris, and Photinus. This matter, to be sure, is not directly related to the problem with which I am concerned. It is my purpose not to follow up the errors of individuals, but to bring out a few examples that give clear and convincing illustration of Moses' word that, if at any time a doctor of the Church—himself a prophet interpreting the mysteries of the Prophets—make the attempt to introduce some novelty into God's Church, Divine Providence admits this to test us. It will be useful, therefore, to develop the ideas of the afore-mentioned heretics only very briefly, in the form of a digression.

First, then, the doctrine of Photinus. According to him, God is singular and unique, and one has to conceive of Him in the manner of the Jews. He denies the plenitude of the Trinity and denies that there is either the Person of the Word or the Person of the Holy Spirit. As for Christ, he asserts that, though unique, He is merely a human being, and ascribes his origin to Mary. He states dogmatically that we

6 These books against Porphyry (d. 304) have been completely destroyed.

must show reverence only to the Person of God the Father, but to Christ only as man. Thus Photinus.

Apollinaris boasts of consenting to the doctrine of the Unity of the Trinity—though not in the full purity of the faith. But he blasphemes openly with regard to the Incarnation of our Lord. He says that there was no human soul in the body of our Saviour, or, if there were one, that it had neither mind nor reason. He asserts that the flesh of our Lord was not formed from the flesh of Holy Virgin Mary, but descended from Heaven into the Virgin, and he taught, in constant wavering and doubt, sometimes that she was co-eternal with God the Word, sometimes that she was only created out of the divinity of the Word. He refused to admit two substances in Christ—one divine, the other human; one from the Father, the other from the mother. He believed that the Word's nature was itself divided, as though the one remained in God and the other had been converted into flesh. Whereas the Truth says that the One Christ consists of two substances, he—contrary to truth—asserts that from One Divinity of Christ two substances were made. This is the doctrine of Apollinaris.

Nestorius, who suffered from a disease quite contrary to that of Apollinaris, suddenly introduces two persons while pretending to distinguish two substances in Christ. In his unheard-of wickedness he assumes that there are two sons of God, two Christs—the one God, the other man; one, begotten of the Father, the other, of the mother. Thus he asserts that Holy Mary is not to be called '*Theotòkos*' [Mother of God], but Christotòkos [Mother of Christ], since she gave birth not to Christ-God, but Christ-man. But, if one believes that he speaks in his writings of *one* Christ and that he teaches *one* Person of Christ, let him be careful not to give too easy credence to such an interpretation. Nestorius contrives this wording skillfully to deceive his readers—in order to recommend evil doctrines more easily through the intermediary of good ones, according to the words of the Apostle: 'was that then which is good, made death unto me?'[1] Well, either he deceitfully overemphasizes in certain passages of his writings that he believes in *one* Christ and *one* Person of Christ, or he pretends that, only after the birth from the Virgin, both Persons were united in *one* Christ. But this statement is made in such a way that it means that at the time of the Virgin's conception or bearing, and even for some time after, two Christs existed. Thus, though Christ, as merely man, was born the first, and unique, and not joined in Unity of Person to the Word of God, afterwards the Person of the Word descended into Him, assuming Him. Although now, having been assumed (by the Word), He abides in the glory of God, yet it would seem that for a time there was no difference between Him and other men.

Chapter 13

Thus do these mad dogs—Nestorius, Apollinaris, and Photinus—bark against the Catholic faith. Photinus denies the Trinity. Apollinaris declares that the nature of the Word is convertible; he does not recognize two substances in Christ; he says that Christ either has no soul at all or at least that there is no human mind and reason in His soul, and he asserts that the Word of God takes the place of that mind. Nestorius claims that there were always two Christs, but that for a time they were separated. But the Catholic Church, which has the true doctrine about God and our Saviour, does not blaspheme against either the mystery of the Trinity or the Incarnation of Christ. For it adores one Divinity in the plenitude of the Trinity and the equality of the Trinity in one and

1 Rom. 7.13.

the same Majesty; and confesses one Jesus Christ, not two, the same Jesus Christ being at once God and man. The Church believes that there are in Him one Person, but two substances;[1] two substances, but one Person. Two substances because the Word of God is immutable so that it could not be converted into flesh; one Person, lest by acknowledging two Sons it seem to adore a quaternity instead of a trinity.

It is worth while to elaborate more distinctly and clearly on this point. In God there is one substance, but three Persons; in Christ, two substances, but one Person. In the Trinity there is distinction of Persons, but not of substance. In our Saviour there is distinction of substances, but not of Person. How is it that in the Trinity there is distinction of Persons, but not of substance? Because the Father is one Person, the Son, another, the Holy Spirit, a third. Yet, Father, Son, and Holy Spirit are not distinct in nature, but one and the same. Why in our Saviour is there a distinction of substances and not of Person? Because there is a divine substance and also a human substance. Yet, His Godhead and His humanity are not two persons, but one and the same Christ, one and the same Son of God, and one and the same Person of one and the same Christ and Son of God.

So, in man, flesh and soul are differentiated, but soul and flesh are one and the same man. In Peter or Paul there is a distinction of soul and flesh, yet flesh and soul do not form two Peters, and there are not one Paul-soul and another Paul-flesh. But there are one and the same Peter and one and the same Paul, each of them consisting of a twofold and diverse nature of soul and body. Hence, there are also two substances

1 I.e., natures. Cf. Tertullian, *Adv. Prax.* 27: Therefore is to be preserved the property of either substance, namely, that in Him the soul performed the acts proper to it, i.e., virtues, works and signs, and the body functioned in its proper passions.'

in one and the same Christ, the one is divine, the other human; one is from God the Father, the other, from the Virgin Mother; one co-eternal and co-equal with the Father, the other temporal and less than the Father; one consubstantial with the Father, the other consubstantial with the Mother; yet one and the same Christ in either substance. Therefore, there is not one Christ-God and another Christ-man; not one uncreated and another created; not one impassible, the other passible; not one equal to the Father and the other less than the Father; not one from the Father and the other from the Mother. But one and the same Christ is God and man; one and the same noncreated and created; one and the same unchangeable and impassible *and* transformed and having suffered; one and the same co-equal with and less than the Father; one and the same begotten of the Father before time and born from a Mother in time—perfect God and perfect man; as God, highest divinity, as man, fullest humanity. I say fullest humanity, since He possesses both soul and flesh—true flesh, ours, from His mother, and a soul endowed with intelligence, possessing mind and reason.

Hence, there is in Christ the Word, soul, flesh. But this whole is one Christ, one Son of God and for us one Saviour and Redeemer. He is One, not by some kind of corruptible mingling of divinity and humanity, but by an integral and unique Unity of Person. That conjunction neither converted nor changed one substance into the other—this is the characteristic error of the Arians.[2] Rather, both are united in such a way that, while singularity of one and the same Person

2 Since the Arians denied that there was a human soul in Christ, they referred His Passion to His divinity. Since this took the place of the soul or substantive form in man, they said that in some manner it had been transformed into His humanity (Cf. Hilary, *De Trinitate* 10.9 and 18: 'But that the power and the nature of the Word might not be considered as lacking to Him in the flesh,' etc.).

always remains in Christ, the property of each Nature, on the other hand, endures for all eternity. Thus, God never begins to be a body, nor does the body ever cease to be body. The human condition offers a good illustration. For—not only at present but also in the future—each individual does and will consist of body and soul. Never will either the body be converted into the soul or the soul into the body, but, in each individual destined to live without end, the differentiation of both substances will necessarily endure forever. So, also, in Christ the specific property that is characteristic for each of both substances will be retained forever, while the Unity of Person remains intact.

Chapter 14

As we rather frequently use the term 'Person' [*persona*] and declare that God became man 'in person,' we must take great care not to produce the impression that we mean that God the Word assumed our nature by mere imitation of our behavior and that He pursued His manner of life as an unreal and not as a true human being—as happens on the stage, where one individual in quick changes plays several parts without being identical with any of them. Each time that the behavior of other people is *imitated,* their reactions and actions are reproduced in such a way that those who are acting are not actually those whom they imitate. To use examples from secular plays, when an actor in a tragedy plays the part of a priest or king, he is not that priest or king; with the end of the play, the person he played ceases to exist. Far from me be such wicked and vicious mockery. We may leave madness like that to the Manichaeans, preachers of a phantasm, who declare that the Son of God, God Himself, did not exist in substance as a human person, but that He simulated it by fictitious behavior and manner of life. But the Catholic faith affirms that the Word of God was made man in such a way that He assumed our nature, not fallaciously and unreally, but in truth and reality; that He did not imitate human nature as being something different, but rather as His very own; furthermore, that He was that which He acted and whom He acted—precisely like ourselves, who, in so far as we speak, think, live, and exist, do not imitate, but actually are, human beings. Thus, Peter and John, to take such outstanding names, were men, not by imitation, but by subsistence. Similarly, Paul did not pretend to be an Apostle or feign to be Paul; he actually was the Apostle and subsisted as Paul. In the same way, also, God the Word deigned, by assuming and having a body, and by speaking, acting, and suffering through the flesh (without, however, any corruption of His own nature), to make it manifest that He did not imitate or feign, but that He actually presented, the perfect human being; so that He really was, and subsisted as, a true man, and did not merely seem nor was only believed to be such. Therefore, just as the soul united to the body (without, however, being converted into it), does not imitate man, but is man—and this not by simulation but by substance—so was God the Word (without any conversion of Himself and not by confounding Himself with, but by uniting Himself to, man) made man, not by imitation, but substantially. We must, therefore, completely reject any notion of 'Person' that is built on fiction or imitation, on a permanent difference between being and pretending, and on the assumption that the acting individual never is the individual whom he represents. Let us get rid of the idea that God the Word assumed human personality in such a fallacious way. Let us rather realize that, His substance remaining immutable, He Himself existed as flesh, as man, as a human person, when He assumed to Himself the nature of a perfect human being; that He existed so, not by simulation, but really, not by imitation, but substantially; and finally, that His existence did not cease with His acting, but remained permanently in its substance.

Chapter 15

Thus, this unity of the Person in Christ was formed and completed, not after the birth from the Virgin, but in the very womb of the Virgin. We must therefore take utmost care to be precise in our confession, so as to say that Christ is not merely *one,* but that He *always* has been *one.* It were, indeed, an intolerable blasphemy to assert that, although you admit His now being One, you contend that He once was not One but Two—One after His baptism, but Two at the time of His birth. We cannot escape this enormous sacrilege unless we assert that humanity has been united to divinity through the Unity of Person, not through the ascension or resurrection or baptism, but within the Mother, in her womb, and—even more—in the Virginal Conception itself. Because of this Unity of Person, it happens that what is proper to God is ascribed to the man, and what is proper to the flesh is ascribed to God—indifferently and without distinction. Therefore, as it is written in Holy Scripture: 'He that descended from heaven, the Son of man who is in heaven'[1] and 'crucified the Lord of glory'[2] on earth. Furthermore, since the body of the Lord was made and created, it is said that the 'Word' of God Himself was 'made,'[3] His wisdom filled up,[4] His knowledge created;[5] therefore do the prophetic writings refer to His hands and feet as 'pierced.'[6] Through this Unity of Person it

1 John 3.13.
2 1 Cor. 2.8.
3 John 1.14.
4 Eccli. 24.35.
5 Eccli. 1.4; 24.36.
6 Ps. 21.17.

also becomes perfectly clear—by reason of a similar mystery—that it is most truly Catholic to believe (and most impious to deny) that the Word of God Himself was born from the Virgin even as the flesh of the Word was born from an Immaculate Mother.

Therefore, may God forbid that anyone should attempt to defraud holy Mary of her privileges of divine grace and of her special glory. For by a unique favor of our Lord and God she is to be confessed to be the most true and most blessed Mother of God (*theotòkos*). She is truly the Mother of God, not merely in name, as a certain impious heresy claims, because she gave girth to a man who later became God, as we call the mother of priests or bishops such, because she gave birth, not to a priest or a bishop, but to a child who later became one. Not thus, I say, is holy Mary the Mother of God, but rather because, as has already been said, in her sacred womb was accomplished the mystery that, by reason of a certain singular and unique Unity of Person, even as the Word is flesh in flesh, so the man is God in God.

Chapter 16

In order to refresh our memory, let us more briefly and concisely repeat what we said about the above-mentioned heresies[1] and about the Catholic faith. By such a repetition we may acquire a fuller understanding of and gain a firmer grasp on the matters already dealt with. Anathema upon Photinus, who does not accept the plenitude of the Trinity and who teaches that Christ is merely man! Anathema upon Apollinaris, who asserts that the divinity had been transformed and corrupted in Christ and who takes away from Him the property of a perfect humanity! Anathema upon Nestorius,

1 Cf. Chapters 12-14, above.

who denies that God was born from the Virgin, and who asserts that there are two Christs, thus introducing to us the quaternity after having destroyed the faith in the Trinity! But blessed be the Catholic Church, which adores One God in the plenitude of the Trinity and the equality of the Trinity in One Divinity, so that neither the Uniqueness of the Substance confuses the individuality of the Persons, nor does the distinction of the Trinity differentiate the Unity of the Divinity![2] Blessed, I say, be the Church, which believes that there are in Christ two real and perfect substances, but only One Person, so that neither the distinction of the Natures divides the Unity of the Person nor does the Unity of the Person confuse the difference of the substances! Blessed, I say, be the Church, which confesses that Man was united to God, not after His birth, but even in the womb of His Mother, so that it thus makes clear that there always is and always was, only Christ. Blessed, I say, be the Church, which recognizes that God was made man, not by a conversion of nature, but in virtue of the Person—not of a fictitious and transitory, but of a substantial and permanent, Person! Blessed, I say, be the Church, which teaches that this Unity of the Person has such power that, because of it, by a wonderful and ineffable mystery, divine action can be ascribed to man and human action to God. For, because of that power, it does not deny that man descended from heaven as God, but also believes that on earth God was made, suffered, and was crucified as man. Finally, because of that power, she confesses the man as Son of God and God as the son of the Virgin. Blessed, therefore, and revered, praised and sacred and wholly worthy of that highest panegyric of the angels, be the confession which glorifies One Lord God in threefold sanctification! For that reason, this

[2] Many things read either in this or in the preceding chapters may be found explained most clearly in the Athanasian Creed.

confession proclaims the Unity of Christ in such wise as not to deny the mystery of the Trinity.

All these foregoing remarks were made in form of a digression. If it pleases God, these matters will be treated and explained more fully at another time. Now we return to our thesis.

Chapter 17

We said above[1] that in the Church of God the teacher's error was the people's temptation, and that the greater the erring teacher, the greater the temptation. We made this clear, first, by the authority of Holy Scripture, then, by examples taken from the history of the Church that recalled to our mind the men who had departed from their allegiance to sound faith and thus had fallen into the doctrines of a strange sect or had founded a heresy of their own. This is an important matter, indeed, a useful experience, and to be remembered again and again. We must insist on it and illustrate it by impressive examples, so that all true Catholics may realize that they should accept the teachers with the Church, and not desert the faith of the Church with the teachers.

It is easy to produce innumerable instances of this kind of temptation, but there is in my opinion scarcely a single one comparable to that created by Origen. He had such outstanding, such rare, such admirable qualities that, at first sight, everyone was ready to accept all his statements with a like trust. To judge from his way of life, great were his zeal, his chastity, his patience, his endurance. With regard to his family background and education, what can be considered more noble than his birth into a family that had become famous by martyrdom?[2] And, later on, after he had lost for

1 Ch. 10.1.
2 Leonidas suffered martyrdom in 202.

the cause of Christ not only his father but also his whole fortune, [what was more admirable] than his life in the bonds of holy poverty—a life in which he so progressed as to suffer more than once (as we are told) for having confessed the name of the Lord?[3] But these are far from being all the traits that later would stimulate the temptation. There still remain his powerful genius, so profound, so acute, so subtle that he greatly surpassed almost everyone, and his astounding knowledge and erudition, so comprehensive that there were few matters in theology and almost none in human philosophy that he did not master. When he had gone through his studies in Greek, he took up Hebrew.[4] And, what shall I say of his eloquence? His speech was so delightful, so fluid, so soft that it seems to me it is honey rather than words which flows from his lips. What difficult problems did he not clarify by the power of his persuasive speech? What difficult facts did he not present in a way easy to understand? Perhaps he built up his statements by means of abstract reasoning? Not at all; no other teacher made use of more examples taken from divine Law. Or did he write only a few works? On the contrary; no mortal ever wrote more. It is quite impossible to establish all his writings, not to speak of reading them all; moreover, he became extremely old and thus could acquire every scientific technique. Perhaps he had no influence over his disciples? Who ever had more? Innumerable were the doctors, priests, confessors, and martyrs who came from his school. Who can describe their admiration for him and the extent of his fame and influence? Who with any serious interest in religion did not rush to him from the most distant

3 Eusebius states that, in the persecution of Decius, Origen bore with fortitude imprisonment, the rack, threats of torture by fire, and other forms of suffering.

4 For Origen's extraordinary skill in Greek and his knowledge of Hebrew, cf. Jerome. *De viris illust.* 54, and Origen, *Hom. in Num.* 14.1.

corners of the world? What Christian did not venerate him almost as a prophet; what philosopher, as his master? History tells us how he was honored, not only by private persons but also by the court. The mother[5] of Emperor Alexander sent for him because of the divine wisdom with which he was endowed and with the love of which she also was burning. Another proof of his renown is the correspondence he addressed with the authority of a Christian teacher to Emperor Philip,[6] the first Christian among the Roman princes.[7] As for his almost incredible knowledge, if one does not accept our reference to Christian testimony, he may at least heed the statements made by pagan philosophers. The godless Porphyry says that, attracted by Origen's fame, he had gone as a young boy, to Alexandria, and that he saw him there—an old man of such extensive and deep wisdom that it seemed he had constructed a very fortress of universal knowledge. It would take more than a whole day to describe—even briefly—all the outstanding qualities of the man. But, the main point is that they tend not alone to the glory of religion, but also indicate the magnitude of the temptation involved. For are there many who would pass by a man of such genius, such knowledge, such influence? Would they not rather make theirs the statement: 'It is better to err with Origen than to be right with others?'[8] Why say more? The result was that not any ordinary human temptation but the exceedingly grave one of so great a personality, so prominent a doctor, so influential a prophet, turned masses of people away from the

---

5 Julia Mammaea, who summoned him to Antioch.

6 References to the letter from Origen to the Emperor Philip and to another written to his wife Severa are found in Eusebius, *Hist. eccl.* 6.36.3.

7 Cf. Eusebius, *Chronicon ad annum* 247.

8 Cf. Cicero, *Tusc. disp.* 1.17.39.

integrity of the faith, as later events made clear.[9] Hence, to the same Origen, great and outstanding as he was, should be applied the words addressed to the Church of God: 'If there rise in the midst of thee a prophet,' and a little later on, 'thou shalt not hear the words of that prophet,' and again, 'for the Lord your God trieth you, whether you love Him or not.'[10] And this, because he arrogantly abused the grace of God; because he set too much store on his own ability and relied too much on himself, neglecting the old simplicity of the Christian religion; because he presumed to know more than all the others; because he despised ecclesiastical traditions and the teachings of the fathers and interpreted some passages of Holy Scripture in a novel manner.[12] Indeed, it is not an ordinary, it is a very great trial that the Church which was devoted to and depended upon him out of admiration for his genius, his knowledge, his eloquence, his manner of life and his influence—that the Church which had no suspicion and feared nothing for itself—was suddenly endangered by being gradually turned away from the old religion to a modern heresy. Someone may object and say that Origen's writings were falsified.[12] I do not oppose this idea; I would prefer that it were so. Indeed, several people, Catholics as well as heretics, have orally and in writing asserted the truth of this conjecture. But the point we must emphasize is that the books published under his name, even if he were not their author, are the cause of serious temptation. Abounding in deadly blasphemies, they are read and loved, not as books by some-

---

9 As to the disputes about Origen which arose at the end of the fourth century between the bishops and the monks of Egypt, we have, as it were, an eye-witness in Sulpicius Severus, *Dial.* 1.6.

10 Deut. 13.1-3.

11 Origen emphasized unduly the allegorical interpretation.

12 Origen himself complained that his writings had been falsified by the heretics, and later many made a similar charge, e.g., Sulpicius Severus, *Dial.* 1.6.

one else, but as his writings, so that on Origen's authority they have the power to persuade their readers to error, even if this were not his intention.

Chapter 18

Quite similar, also, is the case of Tertullian. For, as Origen among the Greeks, so must Tertullian among the Latins clearly be considered as supreme. Who was more scholarly than this man, and who better trained in divine and human matters? With his amazing mental capacity he actually embraced the entire range of philosophy, including all particular schools, their heads, disciples, and systems, as well as the manifold forms of historical and natural sciences. Did his outstanding genius not possess such vigor and impetus that whatever he was attacking was either caught by the keenness or crushed by the weight of his mind? No one is able adequately to evaluate and to praise his eloquence. The logical nexus of his argumentation was so closely knit that he forced those whom he could not persuade to adhere to his point of view.[1] Almost each word of his is a thought, and each sentence a victory. They all experienced it—the followers of Marcion, Apelles, Praxias, Hermogenes, the Jews, the Gentiles, the Gnostics, and so many others whose blasphemies he demolished with many and weighty books, as though by lightning. Yet, this same Tertullian was, after all, not steadfast enough in Catholic dogma, the universal and traditional faith. He was more eloquent than faithful,[2] and thus ended in changing his position, precisely as the blessed confessor Hilary said of him: 'By his subsequent error he deprived his com-

1 Cf. Augustine, *De haer.* 86, Lactantius, *Inst. div.* 5.1.23, and Jerome, *Epist.* 58.10; 48.13.

2 The text in the four codices (*Parisenis* and *apud Pithoeum*) reads *fidelior;* but all later editors, with Sichardus and Costerius, have *felicior.*

mendable writings of their authority.'[3] So, too, he turned out to be a great temptation to the Church. But I do not wish to say more about this case. Only one point may be added. When the modern madness of Montanus and the foolish imaginings of ridiculous women[4] about a new dogma arose in the Church, he declared them to be true prophecies—contrary to Moses' advice. Hence, he richly deserved that it also ought to be said of him and his writings: 'If there rise in the midst of thee a prophet thou shalt not hear the words of that prophet.' And why not? 'For,' it is said, 'the Lord your God trieth you whether you love Him or not.'[5]

Chapter 19

By virtue of these many convincing examples from Church history, and others of the same kind, we must clearly perceive and, according to the rules of Deuteronomy, fully understand that, if at any time a teacher of the Church deviates from the faith, Divine Providence permits this to happen in order to test and to try us, 'whether we love God, or not, with all our heart and all our soul.'[1]

Chapter 20

Since this is so, we may say that a true and genuine Catholic is the man who loves the Truth of God, the Church, and the Body of Christ;[1] who does not put anything above divine religion and the Catholic faith—neither the authority, nor the affection, nor the genius, nor the eloquence, nor the philo-

---

3 *Commentary on St. Matthew* 5.1.
4 Priscilla and Maximilla.
5 Deut. 13.1-3.

---

1 Deut. 13.3.

---

1 Eph. 1.23.

sophy of any other human being. He despises all that and, being firmly founded in the faith, is determined to hold and believe nothing but what the Catholic Church, as he has perceived, has held universally and from ancient times. He is one who comprehends that any kind of modern and sensational doctrine, introduced by someone outside of and contrary to the position taken by the saints, does not pertain to religion, but rather constitutes a temptation, according to the words he has learned from the blessed Apostle Paul, who has this to say: 'For there must be also heresies, that they also who are approved may be made manifest among you.'[2] It is as if the Apostle meant: The authors of heresies are not instantly rooted out by God, in order to make manifest those who are approved, that is, in order to make evident to what degree each one is a steadfast, faithful, and firm lover of the Catholic faith.

Indeed, as soon as some novelty is stirred up, the wheat and the chaff are immediately separated from each other by their respective heaviness and lightness;[3] what for lack of weight cannot be held within the threshing floor is then easily fanned away. Some fly off instantly; others, only shaken up, fear to perish and are ashamed to return—hurt, half-dead and half-alive, since they have devoured a quantity of poison (not enough to kill, but too much to be digested), a quantity that does not necessarily bring with it death, yet does not permit them really to live. What a miserable situation! In what anxieties do they linger! By what whirlwinds are they harassed! Sometimes, stirred up by an error, they are tossed wherever the wind drives them; sometimes they turn back on themselves as though driven by counter currents. Now they

2 1 Cor. 11.19.
3 Matt. 3.12

approve with arbitrary presumption what seems to be uncertain; now, under the pressure of an irrational fear, they are in dread of even the most certain truths—never being sure where to go, where to return, what to desire, what to avoid, what to hold, what to give up. If only they would understand that what they are suffering in their wavering and unbalanced hearts is the medicine which the divine compassion has prepared for them! As a matter of fact, being outside the completely secure harbor of the Catholic faith, they are harassed, beaten, and, as it were, slain, by the onslaughts of opposing ideas. Under their impact, they may furl the sails of their puffed-up minds which they had guiltily spread in the wind of novelty; they may return to and stay within that most trustworthy resting place of their gentle and kind mother; they may disgorge those bitter and stormy floods of error, and, finally, be able to drink of the streams of 'living water springing up (into life everlasting).'[4] They may well unlearn what they had badly learned; they may grasp as much of the whole dogma of the Church as can be intellectually understood, and accept in faith[5] what cannot be understood.

Chapter 21

Since this is so, I am moved to reflect and ponder again and again. I cannot help wondering about such madness in certain people, the dreadful impiety of their blinded minds, their insatiable lust for error that they are not content with the traditional rule of faith as once and for all received from antiquity, but are driven to seek another novelty daily. They are possessed by a permanent desire to change religion, to add something and to take something away—as though the dogma

4 John 4.10,14.
5 Cf. Augustine, *De Trinitate* 7, end.

were not divine, so that it has to be revealed only once. But they take it for a merely human institution, which cannot be perfected except by constant emendations, rather, by constant corrections. Yet, the divine prophecies say: 'Pass not beyond the ancient bounds which thy fathers have set,'[1] and 'Judge not against a judge,'[2] and 'he that breaketh a hedge, a serpent shall bite him.'[3] And we have this word of the Apostle that like a spiritual sword has often slaughtered and will forever slaughter all the vicious novelties of all the heretics: 'O Timothy, keep that which is committed to thy trust avoiding the profane novelties[4] of words and oppositions of knowledge falsely so called which some promising have erred concerning the faith.'[5] Are there really people who can listen to such adjurations and then remain in such hardened and shameless stubbornness, such stony impudence, such adamant obstinacy, as not to yield to the mighty weight of these divine words and to weaken under such a load, as not to be shattered by these hammer strokes, as not to be crushed by such powerful thunderbolts? 'Avoiding,' he says, 'profane novelties of words.' He did not say 'antiquities' or 'the old traditions.' No, he clearly shows the positive implications of this negative statement: Novelty is to be avoided, hence, antiquity has to be respected; novelty is profane, hence, the old tradition is sacred. 'And,' he continues, 'the oppositions of knowledge falsely so called.' A misnomer indeed for the doctrines of the heretics—ignorance beautified by the name of knowledge, darkness by that of clarity, night by that of light! 'Which some promising have erred concerning the faith.' What did they

1 Prov. 22.28.
2 Eccli. 8.17.
3 Eccle. 10.8.
4 In Greek, *kenophonias.*
5 1 Tim. 6.20,21.

promise, and in what did they err, if not in regard to a hitherto unknown doctrine?

You may hear it said by some of these modernists: 'Come, you poor ignorant people, commonly called Catholics, and learn the true faith which no one knows except ourselves, which was concealed for many centuries, but which lately has been revealed and made manifest. But learn it furtively and secretly; it will delight you. And when you have learned it, teach it covertly, lest the world hear it or the Church find out about it. For it is given only to a few to receive the secret of so great a mystery.' Are not these the words of that harlot, who, in the Proverbs of Solomon, 'calls them that pass by the way and go on their journey'? 'He,' she says, 'that is a little one, let him turn to me.' And she invites fools, in the words: 'Stolen waters are sweeter, and hidden bread is more pleasant.' And how does the author continue? He says: 'But he did not know that her guests are in the depths of hell.'[6] Who are these guests? Let the Apostle explain it to us: they are those 'who have erred concerning the faith.'[7]

Chapter 22

It is worth while to study the whole text of the Apostle more thoroughly. 'O Timothy,' he says, 'keep that which is committed to thy trust, avoiding the profane novelties of words.'[1] The exclamation 'O' is at one and the same time an expression of foreknowledge and of love. He foresaw future errors and suffered pain in advance over their coming. The Timothy of today is either, speaking generally, the Universal Church, or, in particular, the whole body of ecclesiastical superiors who

6 Prov. 9.15-18.
7 1 Tim. 6.21.

1 1 Tim. 6.20.

ought to have for themselves and to administer to the people an integral knowledge of divine worship. What, then, does 'keep that which is committed to thee' mean? 'Keep it,' he says, in the face of thieves and enemies, lest, while men are asleep, they oversow cockle among the good wheat which the Son of man had sown in His field.[2] 'Keep that which is committed.' What is 'committed'? It is that which has been entrusted to you, not that which you have invented; what you have received, not what you have devised; not a matter of ingenuity, but of doctrine; not of private acquisition, but of public tradition; a matter brought to you, not created by you; a matter you are not the author of, but the keeper of; not the teacher, but the learner; not the leader, but the follower. This deposit, he says, guard. Preserve the 'talent'[3] of the Catholic faith unviolated and unimpaired. What has been entrusted to you may remain with you and may be handed down by you. You received gold; hand it down as gold. I do not want you to substitute one thing for another; I do not want you shamelessly to put lead in the place of gold, or, deceitfully, copper. I do not want something that resembles gold, but real gold. O Timothy, O priest, O interpreter,[4] O doctor, if a gift of heaven has prepared you by mental power, experience, and knowledge, to be the Beseleel[5] of the spiritual Tabernacle, to cut the precious gems of divine dogma, to put them together faithfully, to adorn them judiciously, to add glamor, grace, and loveliness, may that which was formerly believed with difficulty be made, through your interpretation, more understandable in the light. May posterity, through

2 Matt. 13.24ff.

3 Matt. 25.15.

4 This term, which was introduced by the writers of that time, means one who explains, or a teacher (Cf. Ch. 28.7).

5 Beseleel was chosen by God above all others to construct the tabernacle, the Ark of the Covenant, and the sacred vessels (Cf. Exod. 31.2ff).

your aid, rejoice in the understanding of things which in old times were venerated without understanding. Yet, teach precisely what you have learned; do not say new things even if you say them in a new manner.

Chapter 23

At this point, the question may be asked: If this is right, then is no progress of religion possible within the Church of Christ? To be sure, there has to be progress, even exceedingly great progress. For who is so grudging toward his fellow men and so full of hatred toward God as to try to prohibit it? But it must be progress in the proper sense of the word, and not a change in faith. Progress means that each thing grows within itself,[1] whereas change implies that one thing is transformed into another. Hence, it must be that understanding, knowledge, and wisdom grow and advance mightily and strongly in individuals as well as in the community, in a single person as well as in the Church as a whole, and this gradually according to age and history. But they must progress within their own limits, that is, in accordance with the same kind of dogma, frame of mind, and intellectual approach.

The growth of religion in the soul should be like the growth of the body, which in the course of years develops and unfolds, yet remains the same as it was. Much happens between the prime of childhood and the maturity of old age. But—the old men of today who were the adolescents of yesterday, although the figure and appearance of one and the same person have changed, are identical. There remains one and the same nature and one and the same person. The limbs of infants are small, those of young men large—yet they are

1 The term *in semetipsum* seems to have supplanted adverbially the *in idipsum* of the Vulgate version.

the same. The joints of adult men are as many as those of young children; though some are developed only in maturity, they already existed virtually in the embryo. Hence, nothing new is later produced in old men that has not previously been latent in children. Therefore, without any doubt, this is the legitimate and correct rule of progress and the established and most impressive order of growth: The course of the years always completes in adults the parts and forms with which the wisdom of the Creator had previously imbued infants. If, on the other hand, the human form were turned into a shape of another kind, or if the number of members of the body were increased or decreased, then the whole body would necessarily perish, or become a monstrosity, or be in some way disabled. In the same way, the dogma of the Christian religion ought to follow these laws of progress, so that it may be consolidated in the course of years, developed in the sequence of time, and sublimated by age—yet remain incorrupt and unimpaired, complete and perfect in all the proportions of its parts and in all its essentials (let us call them members and senses), so that it does not allow of any change, or any loss of its specific character, or any variation of its inherent form.

To give an example. In ancient times, our forefathers sowed the seeds of the wheat of faith in that field which is the Church. It would be quite unjust and improper if we, their descendants, gathered, instead of the genuine truth of wheat, the false tares of error. On the contrary, it is logically correct that the beginning and the end be in agreement, that we reap from the planting of the wheat of doctrine the harvest of the wheat of dogma. In this way, none of the characteristics of the seed is changed, although something evolved in the course of time from those first seeds and has now expanded under careful cultivation. What may be added is merely appearance, beauty, and distinction, but the proper nature of each kind remains. May it never happen that the rose garden of the Catholic spirit be turned into a field of thistles and thorns. May it never happen that in this spiritual paradise darnel and poison ivy suddenly appear from growths of cinnamon and balsam. Whatever has been planted in the husbandry of God's Church by the faith of the fathers should, therefore, be cultivated and guarded by the zeal of their children; it should flourish and ripen; it should develop and become perfect. For it is right that those ancient dogmas of heavenly philosophy should in the course of time be thoroughly cared for, filed, and polished; but it is sinful to change them, sinful to behead them or mutilate them. They may take on more evidence, clarity, and distinctness, but it is absolutely necessary that they retain their plenitude, integrity, and basic character.

If such a license for impious fraud be granted only once, what terrible danger—I am afraid even to speak of it—would result, with religion being destroyed and abolished. If one tenet of Catholic dogma were renounced, another, then another, and finally one after the other would be abandoned, first by custom, and then as though by right. When, one segment after the other had been rejected, what else would the final result be, except that the whole would be likewise rejected? On the other hand, once there is a beginning of mixing the new with the old, foreign ideas with genuine, and profane elements with sacred, this habit will creep in everywhere, without check. At the end, nothing in the Church will be left untouched, unimpaired, unhurt, and unstained. Where formerly there was the sanctuary of chaste and uncorrupted truth, there will be a brothel of impious and filthy errors. May divine compassion divert such shocking impiety from the minds of its children; instead, may the impious crowd itself be left in its madness!

The Church of Christ, zealous and cautious guardian of the dogmas deposited with it, never changes any phase of them. It does not diminish them or add to them; it neither trims what seems necessary nor grafts things superfluous; it neither gives up its own nor usurps what does not belong to it. But it devotes all its diligence to one aim: to treat tradition faithfully and wisely; to nurse and polish what from old times may have remained unshaped and unfinished; to consolidate and to strengthen what already was clear and plain; and to guard what already was confirmed and defined. After all, what have the councils brought forth in their decrees but that what before was believed plainly and simply might from now on be believed more diligently; that what before was preached rather unconcernedly might be preached from now on more eagerly; that what before was practiced with less concern might from now on be cultivated with more care? This, I say, and nothing but this, has the Catholic Church, aroused over the novelties of the heretics, again and again accomplished by the decrees of its councils, i.e., what it earlier received from our forefathers by tradition alone, it has handed down to posterity by authoritative decisions, condensing weighty matters in a few words, and particularly for the enlightenment of the mind, by presenting in new words the old interpretation of the faith.

Chapter 24

But let us return to the Apostle. 'O Timothy,' he says, 'keep that which is committed to thy trust, avoiding the profane novelties of words.' 'Avoiding,'[1] he says, as you would avoid

1 1 Tim. 6.20.

a viper, a scorpion, or a basilisk, lest they strike you not only with their touch, but even with their look and breath. What does 'avoiding' mean? 'With such a one, not so much as to eat.'[2] What does 'avoiding' mean? 'If any man come to you and bring not this doctrine.'[3] Of course, this means the Catholic and universal doctrine, which remains one and the same through all successive ages in the uncorrupted tradition of truth, and which will remain so without end for ever and ever. What then? 'Receive him not,' St. John continues, 'into the house, nor say to him, God speed you. For he that saith to him, God speed you, communicated with his wicked works.'[4] 'Profane novelties of words,' he says. What is 'profane'? That which has nothing sacred, nothing religious, which is completely outside the inner sanctuary of the Church, God's Temple.[5] 'Profane novelties of words,' he says. 'Of words,' i.e., novelties of dogma, subject matter, and opinions, contrary to tradition and antiquity which, should they be accepted, would of necessity defile the faith of the blessed fathers either entirely or to a great extent. If they are accepted, then it must be stated that all the faithful of all ages—all the saints, all the chaste and continent virgins, all the clerics, levites, and priests, the many thousands of confessors and the vast armies of martyrs, many cities and great masses of people, innumerable islands, provinces, kings, races, kingdoms, and nations, finally, almost the whole world, incorporated through the Catholic Church in Christ as Head—that all of them have for so many centuries been ignorant, have erred, have blasphemed, have not known what ought to be believed.

'Avoiding profane novelties of words,' he says, novelties

2 1 Cor. 5.11.
3 2 John 10.
4 2 John 10,11.
5 1 Cor. 3.16.

which were never accepted and followed by Catholics, but always by heretics. Indeed, when did a heresy ever boil up except under a definite name, at a definite place, and at a definite time? Who ever introduced a heresy who had not first separated from the common agreement prevailing in the universal and traditional Catholic Church? A few examples will support these statements by clearer evidence. Who, before the profane Pelagius, ever dared to attribute such power to free will as not to believe in the indispensable help of God's grace for our good deeds in every act? Who, before his monstrous[6] disciple, Celestius, denied that the entire human race was bound by the guilt of Adam's transgression? Who, before the sacrilegious Arius, was audacious enough to split the Unity of the Trinity, or, before the wicked Sabellius, to confuse the Trinity of the Unity? Who, before the most cruel Novatianus, called God cruel, on the ground that He preferred the death of a dying person to his conversion and life?[7] Who, before Simon Magus[8]—whom the Apostle's wrath had attacked[9] and from whom that old stream of disgrace has flown on in uninterrupted and secret succession down to the most recent heretic, Priscillian[10]—dared to say that God the Creator was the author of evil, that is, of our crimes, impieties, and infamies? He actually makes the statement that God with His own hand created such a nature in man that he, by his own initiative and by his entirely determined will, neither can do

6 Rauschen is not certain whether *prodigiosus* or *monstrosus* is here deservedly used by Vincent.

7 Ezech. 33.11. The Novatians held that deadly sins, such as murder, fornication, and denying the faith, could not be remitted by the Church, but were reserved to God alone.

8 St. Irenaeus (*Adv. haer.* 1.23.2f.) states of Simon the Samaritan that he taught that good works were unnecessary, and further, that by the Commandments of God men were reduced to slavery.

9 Acts 8.20.

10 Bishop of Gallaecia (now Gallizia). This heresy had been founded on the teaching of the Manichaeans and the Gnostics.

nor want to do anything but sin, because he is driven and inflamed by the furies of all the vices and dragged down by unquenchable lust into the abyss of depravity.

Innumerable are the examples we must omit, since we wish to be brief. But all of them make it sufficiently clear that the customary method of most heresies consists in rejoicing in 'profane novelties,' in loathing traditional knowledge, which some rejecting have made shipwreck concerning the faith.[11] Conversely, it is proper for Catholics to guard the 'deposit' handed down by the holy fathers, to condemn profane novelties, and, as the Apostle said 'before and now I say again,' let him be anathema 'if any one preach to you a gospel besides that which you have received.'[12]

Chapter 25

At this point one may ask me: Do the heretics also make use of the testimonies of Holy Scripture? Indeed they do; and to a great degree. They go through each and every book of the Bible: Moses and the Books of Kings, the Psalms, the Apostles, the Gospels, the Prophets. They utter almost nothing of their own that they do not try to support with passages from the Scripture—whether they are among their own disciples or among strangers, in private or in public, whether in sermons or in writings, in private meetings or in forums. Read the treatises of Paul of Samosata, of Priscillian, of Eunomius, of Jovinian,[1] and of the rest of these pests, and you will discover an abundance of examples; there is scarcely a page that is not painted and illumined with texts from the

11 1 Tim. 1.19; 6.20.
12 Gal. 1.9.

1 For the extant works of these heretics, cf. Rauschen, *Vincentii Lerinensis Commonitoria* 54, nn. 3ff.

Old and New Testaments. One must be on guard and fear them all the more because they are concealed under the protective shade of divine Law. They know well that their putrid products would not easily please anyone if their vapors were emitted undisguised; therefore, they sprinkle them with the perfume of divine words, knowing too well that anyone who readily despises human errors would hesitate to set aside divine prophecies. Thus, they behave like those who have to prepare a bitter drink for their infants and first smear some honey around the rim of the cup so that the unsuspecting child may not be averse to the bitterness when he has first sipped the sweet taste, or like those who take great pains to embellish poisonous herbs and noxious juices with high-sounding medical names, so that no one suspects the poison while reading the labels on the mixture.

After all, that is why the Saviour exclaimed: 'Beware of false prophets, who come to you in the clothing of sheep, but inwardly they are ravening wolves.'[2] What does 'the clothing of sheep' mean save the words of the Prophets and Apostles, which these men in their pretended lamb-like simplicity put on as a fleece, imitating the lamb unspotted[3] 'who taketh away the sin of the world?'[4] What are 'ravening wolves'? What but the fierce and insane doctrines of the heretics who invade the sheepfold of the Church, wherever they can, and harass the flock of Christ. To approach the trusting sheep more deceitfully, they discard their wolf-like appearance, though keeping their wolfish ferocity, and cover themselves with quotations from the Bible as though these were fleece. Thus, no one who has first felt the softness of the wool will fear the sharpness of their teeth. How does the Saviour

2 Matt. 7.15.
3 1 Pet. 1.19.
4 John 1.29.

continue? 'By their fruits you shall know them.'[5] This means: Once they begin not only to use the divine expressions but also to explain them, not only to present them but also to interpret them, then people will realize how bitter, how sharp, how fierce they are. Then will the poisonous breath of their new ideas be exhaled, then will 'profane novelties' appear in the open, then will you see that 'the hedge is broken,'[6] that the ancient bounds have been passed,[7] that the dogma of the Church is lacerated, that the Catholic faith is harmed.

Such were those whom the Apostle Paul attacked in the Second Epistle to the Corinthians, when he says: 'For they are false apostles, deceitful workmen, transforming themselves into the apostles of Christ.'[8] What does 'transforming themselves into the apostles of Christ' mean? The Apostles quoted the divine Law; so did the heretics. The Apostles adduced the authority of the Psalms; so did they. The Apostles invoked texts from the Prophets; so did they. But, when they began to interpret in an inaccurate way what they had accurately quoted, it became easy to distinguish the simple-minded from the deceitful, the unsophisticated from the sophisticated, the upright from those of perverted mind; in short, the true apostles from the false. 'And no wonder, for Satan himself transformeth himself into an angel of light. Therefore it is no great thing if his ministers be transformed as the ministers of justice.'[9] Hence, according to the teaching of the Apostle Paul, whenever false apostles, false prophets, or false doctors quote passages from the Bible—in an attempt to support their errors with the aid of wrong interpretations—they are obvi-

5 Matt. 7.16.
6 Eccle. 10.8.
7 Prov. 22.28.
8 2 Cor. 11.13.
9 2 Cor. 11.14,15.

ously imitating the cunning machinations of their master.[10] Satan certainly would never have invented them if he had not known that there was no easier way to deceive people than by pretending to the authority of the Bible when wicked errors were to be fraudulently introduced.

Chapter 26

Some one may offer the objection: Where is the proof that Satan is accustomed to make use of examples taken from the Bible? Let him who asks such a question read the Gospel in which it is written: 'Then the devil took him' (the Saviour, our Lord) 'up into the holy city and set him upon the pinnacle of the Temple, and said to him, If thou be the Son of God, cast thyself down; for it is written, that He hath given His angels charge over thee; and in their hands they shall bear thee up, lest thou dash thy foot against a stone.'[1] What can he not do to wretched human beings—he who assailed the 'Lord of Glory'[2] Himself with quotations from the Bible? 'If thou be the Son of God,' he said, 'cast thyself down.' Why? 'For it is written.' We should give particular attention to the lesson to be drawn from this passage. In the face of such an outstanding example of evangelical authority, we should never doubt that, every time we see people offering texts of the Apostles and Prophets against the Catholic faith, Satan is speaking through them. For, just as at that time the head (of the devils) spoke to the head (of the Church-to-be), so now do members speak to members, namely, members of the Devil's body to members of Christ's Body, perfidious men to the faithful, sacrilegious ones to the religious; in short, here-

10 Of the Devil.

1 Matt. 4.5,6.
2 1 Cor. 2.8.

tics to Catholics. What do they say? 'If thou be the Son of God, cast thyself down.' This means: If you want to be a son of God and possess the inheritance of the heavenly kingdom, cast yourself down, that is, separate yourself from the doctrine and tradition of that sublime Church which is God's Temple. But if you ask one of the heretics who is about to persuade you to such ideas: 'What are the foundations of your arguments and teachings, according to which I have to give up the universal and traditional faith of the Catholic Church?' he will immediately say: 'For it is written.' He will then present you with thousands of testimonies, examples, and authorities—from the Law, the Psalms, the Apostles, the Prophets—which in his new and wrong interpretation precipitate your unhappy soul from the Catholic fortress into the abyss of heresy. Here are the promises by which the heretics usually mislead those who are wanting in foresight. They[3] dare to promise in their teaching that in *their* church—that is, in their own small circle, is to be found a great and special and entirely personal form of divine grace; that it is divinely administered, without any pain, zeal, or effort on their part, to all persons belonging to their group, even if they do not ask or seek or knock. Thus, borne up by angels' hands—that is, preserved by angelic protection, they can never 'dash their foot against a stone,' they never can be scandalized.

Chapter 27

We now deal with the following question: If it is true that Satan and his disciples, of whom some are false apostles, some, false prophets, and some, false teachers, but all entirely heretical, make use of Scriptural passages, texts, and promises —what should Catholics, children of Holy Mother Church,

3 The followers of Semi-Pelagianism. Cf. Rauschen, *op. cit.* 56.

do? How shall they discern in Holy Scripture truth from falsehood? Here is the answer as we gave it at the beginning of this Commonitory,[1] in accordance with what holy and scholarly men have handed on to us. They will devote all their care and attention to interpreting the divine Canon according to the traditions of the Universal Church and the rules of Catholic dogma; within the Catholic and Apostolic Church they must follow the principles of universality, antiquity, and consent. If, at any time, a part is in rebellion against the whole [*universitatem*], or some novelty against tradition [*vetustatem*], or if there is a dissension of one or a few involved in error against the consent of all or the vast majority of Catholics, then they should prefer the integrity of the whole to the corruption of a part. Further, within the same universality, they should place traditional religion [*antiquitatis religionem*] before profane novelty. Likewise, within tradition, before the inconsiderate attitude of a very few they should place, first, the general decrees (if there are any) of a universal council, and, then, if this is less important, they should follow the concordant opinions of great and outstanding teachers. If, with God's help, these rules are cautiously and carefully observed, then we may with little difficulty control all the noxious errors of rebellious heretics.

Chapter 28

Following up the preceding considerations, I have now to show by examples how the profane novelties of the heretics can be detected and condemned by quoting from, and collating with each other, the concordant opinions of the ancient teachers. However, we must carefully investigate and follow this traditional consent of the holy fathers, not in every

1 Chapter 2.3, above.

minor problem concerning the divine Law, but certainly and particularly for the basis and for the rules of faith. Moreover, we need not always fight in this way against all heresies, but only against those which are new and recent; but, in the latter case, as soon as they appear, before they have time to falsify the rules of traditional faith, and before they spread their poison any farther to spoil what our forefathers have written. Inveterate and widespread heresies are in nowise to be attacked by this method, because in the course of their long histories they had ample opportunity to plagiarize the truth. Thus, those older abominations of schisms or heresies cannot be overcome save by refuting[1] them (if necessary) on the authority of Holy Scripture alone, or by avoiding them if they formerly have been refuted and condemned by universal councils of the Catholic bishops. Therefore, as soon as the foulness of some evil error begins to break out and its defenders abuse passages of Holy Scripture and explain them deceitfully and fraudulently, the opinions of our ancestors must immediately be collected for the interpretation of the Canon. Each novelty, hence, each abomination that may arise will thus be brought to light without ambiguity and be condemned outright. But, only those opinions of the fathers are to be brought forward which were expressed by those who lived, taught, and persevered in the holy Catholic faith and communion, and who deserved either to die faithfully in Christ or to be martyred gloriously for Him. Those men are to be believed, moreover, in accordance with the following rule: Only that is to be held as certain, valid and beyond doubt, which either all or most of them have confirmed in one and the same sense—manifestly, frequently, and persistently, as though a council of masters stood in agreement—and which

1 On this matter, Tertullian (*De praescr.* 19) disagreed.

they have accepted, kept, and handed on. On the other hand, what some saint, learned man, bishop, confessor, or martyr has individually thought outside of, or even contrary to, the general opinion—must be considered his personal, particular, and quite private opinion, entirely removed from the common, public, and general opinion. If we respect such a rule, we shall not fall into the sacrilegious custom of the heretics and schismatics, who reject the ancient truth of universal dogma and follow the error of one man, and we shall thus escape the very grave danger of losing our eternal salvation.

Lest anyone think that the holy and Catholic consent of those blessed fathers can arbitrarily be despised, the Apostle says in his First Epistle to the Corinthians: 'And God indeed hath set some in the church, first apostles' (of whom he was one), 'secondly prophets' (as Agabus, mentioned in the Acts), 'thirdly doctors'[2] (who are now called *'tractatores'* — interpreters, also called Prophets by the same Apostle because the mysteries of the Prophets were made plain by them to the people). Everyone, therefore, who disregards these men whom God has given to His Church in all times and in all places, who disregards them when they agree in Christ about the interpretation of Catholic dogma, does not disregard man, but God Himself. Lest anyone cease to adhere to their true unity, the same Apostle urgently implores him: 'Now I beseech you, brethren . . . that you all speak the same thing; and that there be no schisms among you, but that you be perfect in the same mind and in the same judgment.'[3] But, if someone has departed from the general opinion, let him listen further to the same Apostle: 'God is not the god of dissension, but of peace,' i.e., not the God of men who revolt against the common

2 1 Cor. 12.28.
3 1 Cor. 1.10.

consent, but of those who maintain the peace of agreement, 'as also I teach in all the churches of the saints.'[4] This further means: In the churches of Catholics, which are holy because they persevere in the communion of faith. And lest anyone arrogantly claim that he alone should be heard and believed, all the rest being set aside, the Apostle continues a little later: 'Or did the word of God come out from you? Or came it only unto you?' In order to be more emphatic, he adds: 'If any seem to be a prophet or spiritual, let him know that the things that I write to you are the commandments of the Lord.'[5] What other commandments than that he who is 'a prophet or spiritual'—a teacher of spiritual matter—cultivate to the utmost the principles of harmony and unity, and, therefore, never prefer his personal opinions to those of all the others or depart from the general opinion? If any man, the Apostle concludes, 'know not' these commandments, 'he shall not be known.'[6] This means that he who does not learn what he does not know, or who disregards what he does know, 'shall not be known,' that is, shall be considered unworthy to be counted by God among those who are united in faith and made equal by humility. Is there any greater disaster imaginable than that? But, in accordance with the Apostle's threat, precisely this occurred, as we saw only recently, to the Pelagian Julian,[7] who did not care to belong to the united body of his brethren, and had the self-conceit to exclude himself from that body.

But now it is time to present the example[8] I promised and

---

4 1 Cor. 14.33.

5 1 Cor. 14.36,37.

6 1 Cor. 14.38.

7 Julian, Bishop of Eclana, a city in Apulia, a man much skilled in Greek and Latin, and always ready for a fight, upheld the Pelagian heresy against St. Augustine, who answered him in the six books *Contra Julianum.*

8 Cf. the beginning of this Chapter.

to show where and how the opinions of the holy fathers have been collected so that, in accordance with them, the Church's rule of faith may be fixed by the decree and authority of a council. To accomplish my plan more conveniently, it is best to close this Commonitory here and to start anew on what I still have to say.

The second Commonitory has been lost. There remains of it nothing more than the final fragment. That is, only the recapitulation, which is here appended.[9]

Chapter 29

The time has come to recapitulate here, at the end of the Second Commonitory, the content of both. As we said in earlier sections, it always was, and is today, the usual practice of Catholics to test the true faith by two methods: first, by the authority of the divine Canon, and then, by the tradition of the Catholic Church.[1] Not that the Canon is insufficient in itself in each case. But, because most [false] interpreters of the Divine Word make use of their own arbitrary judgment and thus fall into various opinions and errors, the understanding of Holy Scripture must conform to the single rule of Catholic teaching—and this especially in regard to those questions upon which the foundations of all Catholic dogma are laid. We also said that within the Church itself an agreement of universality and antiquity must be observed, lest we either

9 These words, which are found in all the codices and early editions, cannot be those of Vincent. In regard to the second *Commonitory*, Gennadius (*De vir. ill.* 64) states: 'Since, by theft, he lost the major portion of his work, written on scrolls, having briefly recapitulated the meaning, he first assembled, and then produced it in one volume.

1 Origen, Irenaeus, and Tertullian agree with Vincent that, in deciding questions concerning the faith, tradition is reasonably to be adhered to. Cf. especially the preface of Origen, *De principiis*.

are drawn away from integral unity into the separatism of schism or precipitated from traditional belief into the novelties of heresy. Moreover, we said that, with regard to the tradition of the Church, two precautions had to be rigorously and thoroughly observed, adhered to by everyone who does not wish to become a heretic: first, it must be ascertained whether there exists from ancient times a decree established by all the bishops of the Catholic Church with the authority of a universal council, and second, should a new question arise for which no decree can be found, one must revert to the opinions of the holy fathers;—to be more precise, of those fathers who remained in their own times and places in the unity of communion and of faith and who were therefore held as teaching 'probable' doctrine. If we can discover what they held in full agreement and consent, then we can conclude without hesitation that this is the true and Catholic doctrine of the Church.

Since we sought to avoid the impression that we set forth these principles more by our own presumption than by the authority of the Church, we chose the example of that holy council which took place about three years ago at Ephesus in Asia, while the illustrious Bassus and Antiochus[2] were consuls. When a debate arose on what rules of faith should be sanctioned in order to avoid new and profane novelties from creeping in as if by chance, as had happened disastrously at the Council of Rimini,[3] the nearly two hundred

2 The year 431.

3 At Rimini in 359, about four hundred bishops, 'some overcome by weakness of intellect, some worn out by traveling' (Sulpicius Severus, *Chron.* 2.43), subscribed to a formula which decreed that the Son was like (*hómoion*) to the Father.

members[4] of the hierarchy who were present declared the following procedure to be the most Catholic and truly the best in the interests of the faith. [It was agreed] by the assembled bishops that there should be presented the opinions of the holy fathers, some of whom were martyrs, others confessors, but all of them Catholic bishops[5] who, as was well known, had remained so; and that what they had unanimously accepted should be duly and solemnly confirmed as the dogma of the ancient faith, and thus, vice versa, the blasphemy of profane novelty condemned. They actually proceeded in this way. The impious Nestorius was formally and correctly judged as opposing ancient Catholic belief, while, on the other hand, blessed Cyril was declared to be in agreement with that most sacred tradition. Moreover, to make our report on the facts fully trustworthy, we also indicated the names and number—we had forgotten their rank—of those fathers according to whose unanimous and concordant opinion the words of the divine Law were explained and the rule of divine dogma established. To refresh our memory, it is worth while to recall their names here once more.

Chapter 30

These are the men whose writings were quoted at that council, either as judges or as witnesses: St. Peter, Bishop of Alexandria, an outstanding doctor and most blessed martyr;[1]

4 At the first session of the Council of Ephesus, held on June 22, one hundred ninety-eight bishops, joined a short time later by some others, deposed Nestorius. Prosper (*Chron. ad annum 431*) states as follows: 'At the synod of more than two hundred bishops, convened at Ephesus, Nestorius was condemned, as was the heresy bearing his name; so also were many Pelagians who were supporting very similar doctrines.'

5 *episcopoi* (in the text, *sacerdotes*).

1 Peter was Bishop of Alexandria from the year 300, and suffered martyrdom in 311 (Cf. Eusebius, *Hist. eccl.* 9.6.2).

St. Athanasius, Bishop of that same city, a most faithful teacher and most eminent confessor; and St. Theophilus,[2] also Bishop of that city, a man famous for his faith, knowledge, and whole life, whose successor is the venerable Cyril, now an honor to the Church in Alexandria. But it would be wrong to conclude that this doctrine came only from one city and province. There were, in addition, those stars of Cappadocia: St. Gregory of Nazianzus, bishop and confessor; St. Basil, confessor and Bishop of Caesarea in Cappadocia; and that other Gregory, Bishop of Nyssa, who, through the merits of his faith, integrity, wisdom, and manner of life, was of equal worth with his brother Basil. Furthermore, to prove that the Western and Latin world, no less than Greece and the East, had always been in agreement, letters addressed to various persons were read at that council, letters written by St. Felix the Martyr and St. Julius,[3] both Bishops of the city of Rome. And since witnesses should come not only from the center, but also from the outposts of the world, the meeting was also joined by the most blessed Cyprian, Bishop of Carthage and martyr, from the South, and by St. Ambrose, Bishop of Milan, from the North. All these men, of a number[4] made sacred by the Decalogue, were brought before the assembly at Ephesus as teachers, counselors, witnesses, and judges, and that holy council clung fast to their teaching, followed their advice, believed in their testimony, obeyed their judgment, and thus decided upon the rule of faith without any preconceived prejudice or favor. To

2 Theophilus, Bishop of Alexandria, 385-412, was an opponent of St. John Chrysostom.

3 Felix I was Bishop of Rome, 269-274; Julius I, 337-352.

4 Vincent forgot not only the rank, as he himself admits (Ch. 29.10), but also the number. For besides the ten whom he mentions, two others are brought forward as witnesses to the truth: Atticus, who succeeded St. Chrysostom at Constantinople, and Amphilochius, Bishop of Iconium (d. about 394).

be sure, a far greater number of fathers could have been added to this list, but there was no need. Too many witnesses would have prolonged unnecessarily the time of the debate; besides, no one had the least doubt that the opinions of these ten men were, by and large, identical with those of all their colleagues.

Chapter 31

After we had related all these facts, we specifically quoted a sentence from blessed Cyril which is included in the council's record. When the letter of St. Capreolus,[1] Bishop of Carthage, had been read—and he intended no more than to request that novelty be destroyed and tradition defended—Bishop Cyril spoke, and concluded with a remark which it is apposite to quote once more: 'This letter of the venerable and most pious Bishop of Carthage, Capreolus, which was just read to us, may be introduced into the record. Its meaning is obvious: he wishes that the dogma of traditional faith be confirmed and that the novelties—useless inventions as they are, propagated by impious hangers-on, be disapproved and condemned.' All the bishops acclaimed, and cried: 'These are the words of us all; this is what we all mean; this is what all of us desire.'[2] To what purpose this unanimous voice and vote? That the ancient tradition ought to be adhered to, and recent novelties rejected.

After that, we emphatically expressed our admiration for the great humility and sanctity of that council. There were assembled so many members of the hierarchy—almost all Metropolitans—of such high attainments in scholarship and doctrinal knowledge, that almost all of them were qualified

1 Capreolus succeeded Aurelius in the See of Carthage. This letter is extant in both Greek and Latin (Cf. Migne, *PL* 53.843ff.).

2 Cf. Harduinus, *Acta conciliorum* 1.1.1422

to participate in discussions on dogmatic problems. Yet, although their meeting obviously might have tempted them to take the initiative in setting up additional rules of their own, they invented nothing new, they conjectured nothing, they claimed no privilege for themselves. On the contrary, they cared for only one thing: that they should by no means hand on to posterity anything which they themselves had not received from the fathers. In this way they not only settled effectively the problems with which they were faced at that time, but also set an example for future generations. These, too, should honor the doctrines of sacred tradition and condemn the fancies of profane novelty.

We also assailed the vicious presumption of Nestorius, who had boasted that he was the first and only one to understand the Scriptures and that all the others who had interpreted the divine Word before him were ignorant, even though they were truly gifted teachers—all the priests, confessors, and martyrs, some of whom had explained the divine Law, while others accepted or believed in their explanations. He even asserted that the entire Church was now involved in error and always had been so, because it had, in his opinion, followed and still was following ignorant and misguided doctors.

Chapter 32

All this material that we have accumulated should be more than sufficient to crush and eliminate every kind of 'profane novelty.' Yet, to make the evidence more complete, we still referred at the close—in addition to all other testimony—to two utterances made by authority of the Holy See: one by the holy Pope Sixtus III, that venerable man who at present does honor to the Roman Church; the other by his predecessor of happy memory, Pope Celestine I. We consider it necessary to repeat them here. The holy Pope Sixtus said in a letter[1] which he sent to the Bishop of Antioch in the Nestorian affair: 'Hence, because, as the Apostle said, there is "one Faith,"[2] which he victoriously kept, let us believe in the things to be said, and speak the things to be maintained.' But which are the things to be believed in and to be taught? The Pope continues: 'Let no further advance of novelty be permitted, because it is unbecoming to add anything to ancient tradition; the transparent faith and belief of our forefathers should not be soiled by contact with dirt.' It is truly apostolic to compare the riches of belief that our ancestors possessed to the transparence of light and to describe profane novelties as a mixture of dirt. The holy Pope Celestine wrote in the same manner and the same spirit. In a letter which he addressed to the bishops of Gaul and in which he accused them of passive collaboration, because by their silence they were forsaking the old faith and permitting 'profane novelties' to arise, he said: 'Rightly we have to bear the responsibility, if by our silence we encourage error. Therefore, those who behave in this way should be rebuked! They should have no right to free speech.'[3] One may perhaps doubt whether those whom he wishes to deprive of the right to 'free speech' are the preachers who have remained in keeping with tradition or the inventors of novelties. He himself answers this objection and dissipates such doubts, for he continues: 'If that be so'— and he means: If it be true, as some men complain to me, that in your cities and provinces you encourage them by your harmful dissimulation to consent to some of those novel-

1 This letter, the sixth in the letters of Pope Sixtus III, was sent in 433 to John of Antioch, after the latter, who had previously favored Nestorius, had made his peace with St. Cyril (Migne *PL* 50.609).
2 Eph. 4.5.
3 *PL* 50.528.

ties—'if it be so,' he says, 'then stop such novelties from assailing tradition!' Thus, it was the sound opinion of blessed Celestine not that tradition should cease to crush novelties, but, on the contrary, that novelties should refrain from attacking tradition.

Chapter 33

Everyone who is opposed to these apostolic and Catholic decrees first deliberately insults the memory of St. Celestine, who made the point that novelties should cease from attacking tradition; secondly, derides the definitions of St. Sixtus, who was of the opinion that 'no further advance should be permitted to novelties, because it is unbecoming to add anything to the ancient tradition'; and lastly, disregards the statements of St. Cyril, who in a fine sermon praised the zeal of the venerable Capreolus, because the latter desired that the 'dogmas of the traditional faith be confirmed and that novel inventions be condemned.' Further, such an opponent also rejects the Synod of Ephesus, that is, the judgments of the bishops of almost the entire East, whom it pleased under divine inspiration to decree that posterity should believe only what the sacred tradition, represented by the holy fathers, had unanimously maintained in Christ—the same synod whose members by unanimous vote attested that all of them agreed, with regard to wording, intention, and conviction, on the following decision: Precisely as almost every heretic before Nestorius who disregarded tradition and adhered to novelty was condemned, so Nestorius himself, as the author of novelties and the assailant of tradition, should be condemned. If this sacred consent inspired by the gift of heavenly grace should displease anyone, what conclusion follows, save that, in the opinion of such persons, the condemnation of Nestorius' blasphemy was unjust? Finally, they can have nothing but disregard for the entire Church of Christ, for its teachers, apostles, and prophets, and above all for the blessed Apostle Paul, as though all of these were despicable; contempt for the Church, since it has never abandoned its awe-inspired respect for the faith that was once and for all handed over to it and that it has ever practised and revered. It is also contempt for the Apostle, who wrote: 'O Timothy, keep that which is committed to thy trust, avoiding the profane novelties of words,'[1] and again: 'If anyone preach to you a gospel besides that which you have received, let him be anathema.'[2] Therefore, it is not lawful to despise the apostolic definitions and ecclesiastical decrees, in which, in accordance with the sacred common consent and tradition, all heretics always have justly been condemned (as, of late, Pelagius, Celestius, and Nestorius were). It is, therefore, an indispensable obligation for all Catholics who are eager to prove that they are true sons of Holy Mother Church to adhere to the holy faith of the holy fathers, to preserve it, to die for it, and, on the other hand, to detest the profane novelties of profane men, to dread them, to harass and attack them.

This is more or less the subject matter which I discussed somewhat briefly in the two Commonitories, and a condensation of which I presented just now in the form of a recapitulation, in order to refresh my memory for the support of which I wrote this book by persistent recollection, without, however, overburdening it by unpleasant prolixity.

1 1 Tim. 6.20.
2 Gal. 1.9.

PROSPER OF AQUITAINE

GRACE AND FREE WILL

(*De gratia Dei*)

Translated

by

J. REGINALD O'DONNELL, C.S.B., Ph.D.

Pontifical Institute of Mediaeval Studies (Toronto)

IMPRIMI POTEST
Very Rev. E. J. McCORKELL, C.S.B.
Superior General

Toronto
June 15, 1949

INTRODUCTION

FROM THE MEAGER DETAILS at our disposal, it is almost impossible to write a biography of St. Tiro Prosper of Aquitaine. Historical documents are annoyingly silent on the events of the life of this great champion of St. Augustine's teaching on grace and predestination. Scholars have been content to quote the findings of Abbé L. Valentin,[1] who closes the chapter on the biography of Prosper with a discouraging note: 'In sum, to all the questions that can be asked concerning the biography of Saint Prosper science replies only with conjectures more or less plausible. He was born in Aquitaine around the end of the fourth century and died in the last third of the fifth century. That is all. Was he layman, priest or bishop? He was probably a layman. Is he a saint? The testimony of the martyrology lends considerable strength to the opinion that he is. More we cannot say. St. Prosper, however, is much more famous for what he wrote than for what he did, and his real biography is found in a historical study of his works.'[2] Abbé Valentin places the date of birth somewhat after the year 390 and, regarding the date of death, ventures nothing further than to say that he was still living in 455.

Sometime before the year 428, Prosper must have come to Marseilles; in his letter to St. Augustine, written in that

1 *Saint Prosper d'Aquitaine* (Paris 1900).
2 *Ibid.*, p. 154.

year, he speaks specifically of the monks of Marseilles.[3] Not only was he aware of the public furor caused by the attacks on the teaching of St. Augustine, but he was also familiar with the discussions carried on in private.[4]

Although the historical data on Prosper's life are few, nevertheless he holds an undisputed place in the ranks of the moulders of theological understanding of the doctrine of grace. From the year 397, the date of completion of the *De diversis quaestionibus VII ad Simplicianum*,[5] St. Augustine's position on the question of the relations of grace and the free will was firmly established. He tells us in the *Rectractations*[6] that he did his best to defend a triumphant free will, but the grace of God won out. Henceforth, he was to teach the complete incapability of the free will, unaided by grace, to fulfill the Commandments, that every act which is not a fruit of grace is useless, and that, as a result of the sin of Adam, the whole human race has become a damnable mass, curable only by the grace of the Redeemer. Likewise, he expressed the opinion that there were a certain number of elect already determined by God to show forth His mercy, and a certain number predestined to eternal death to show the justice of the penalty.[7]

In his reply to St. Prosper and Hilary of Arles, St. Augustine makes his position very clear regarding the dispute with Cassian. To no one is given the sufficiency either to begin or complete any good work. The Semi-Pelagians were not essentially different from the Pelagians.[8] St. Augustine admits

---

3 *'Multi ergo servorum Christi qui in Massiliensi urbe consistunt'—Epistola ad Sanctum Augustinum* (*PL* 51.67B).
4 Cf. Chapter 14.2, below.
5 *PL* 40.170ff. Chapter 1 n. 2, below.
6 *Retractationes* II 2 (*PL* 32.629).
7 *De civitate Dei* 21.12 (*PL* 41.727).
8 *De praedestinatione sanctorum* 2 (*PL* 44.961).

frankly that he had once been in error on this point, since he thought that the faith whereby we believe in God is not God's gift, but that it is in us of ourselves, and by it we obtain the gifts of God. He goes on to say that in his error he did not think that faith was 'prevented' by God's grace; rather, that the assent to the Gospel, when it was preached to us, was our own doing, and came to us from ourselves.[9] Faith, then, both in its beginning and completion, is God's gift. Let no one doubt that this gift is given to some, and not to others. We ought not be disturbed by the fact that all do not attain it; even if no one at all were delivered from sin, there would be no reason whatsoever to blame God.[10]

As far as I can see, Prosper of Aquitaine quite faithfully reproduced the teaching of St. Augustine. Prosper's *Liber contra Collatorem* represents, I think, the final opinion of its author on the problem of the necessity of grace. It was written while Pope Sixtus (432-440) occupied the Chair of Peter. It was evidently very early in the reign of Sixtus, since Prosper was not quite sure what position he would take in the anti-Augustinian dispute.[11] Consequently, it seems safe to conjecture that the work in question was written within the first two or three years of Sixtus' pontificate.

The *Liber contra Collatorem* contains a step-by-step refutation of Conference XIII of the *Conlationes* of Cassian, entitled *On the protection of God*.[12] The doctrine advanced by Cassian in this Conference was gaining more and more ground in Gaul, until, in Prosper's opinion, the problem had

9 *Ibid.* 3.7 (*PL* 44.964).
10 *Ibid.* 8.16 (*PL* 44.972).
11 Cf. Chapter 22.4, below.
12 For the method, cf. pp. 406-411, below.

become acute. He had already appealed to both St. Augustine and Pope Celestine (422-432) for a clarification of the problem.[13] Finally, he set out to attack and refute once and for all the Semi-Pelagianism of Cassian.[14] To one with the mental outlook of Prosper, the term Semi-Pelagian would have been meaningless; there was no middle term; either you took a Pelagian or a Christian stand in the dispute concerning the necessity of grace even to begin a good work. I do not know how far it is safe to suggest that a considerable part of Prosper's interest in the dispute was due to the deep admiration in which he held St. Augustine. He was delighted with Pope Celestine's praise of his hero, even though it did not contribute very much to the solution of the problem at hand.

The teaching of St. Augustine had been found a difficult doctrine to accept. The first call by a purely gratuitous grace seemed to be a guarantee of salvation; without this gift of grace, man was helpless. St. Augustine had no explanation for the choice, as it were, made by God, but in the final analysis asserted that the ways of God are unsearchable.[15] It would be difficult to preach effectively a rigid monastic observance, if the full doctrine of St. Augustine were not well understood; a difficult task, since much of the teaching of

13 Prosper and Hilary of Arles journeyed to Rome to discuss with Pope Celestine the validity of the doctrine of St. Augustine (See Valentin, *op. cit.*, p. 132). St. Celestine then wrote a letter to the bishops of Gaul in praise of St. Augustine, *Epistola XXI ad episcopos Galliarum* (*PL* 50.528ff).

14 Cf. M. Jacquin, O.P., 'A quelle date apparait le terme semipélagien?' *Revue des sciences philosophiques et théologiques* 1 (1907) 506ff. According to Fr. Jacquin, the term came into use at the beginning of the seventeenth century.

15 Cf. n. 10, above. Cf. for Augustine's teaching on grace his work *Grace and Freedom of Choice* (*De gratia et libero arbitrio*—*PL* 44. 881-912), in which Augustine reaffirms his teaching that grace is a free gift of God but also tries to show that this does not need

St. Augustine had to be picked out of a mass of controversial works on grace, written against Origenists and Pelagians. To spur on his monks to the pursuit of perfection, Cassian had endeavored to lay as much responsibility as possible on the individual himself. But, as Prosper has emphasized, two wrongs do not make a right.[16] Grace does not destroy free will or take away moral responsibility. Cassian tried to prove from Sacred Scripture that grace is the reward given us for good beginnings which spring from the will's own natural powers. Grace is only necessary in order to carry to completion or to facilitate the carrying out of these good first intentions. God can, of course, choose and draw to salvation anyone He pleases, but there hardly seems to be any merit for such a one; certainly, he has expended no efforts which are properly his own. Such, in brief, is the position which Prosper seeks to disprove in the work which is here translated.

Dom Cappuyns[17] has indicated that it is possible to discern a gradual relaxation of the original position taken by St. Prosper of Aquitaine. He singles out three different periods: a period of no compromise; a period of some concessions; finally, a period of greater concessions. The first period is marked by a literal defense of St. Augustine; here, the bitter problem of predestination plays a considerable role, if not a

---

to entail a denial of free will in man (V. J. Bourke, p. 288). For the most complete exposition (according to A. M. Jacquin, 'La prédestination d'aprés S. Augustin,' *Miscel. Agost.* 2 855-858) of Augustine's views on grace and predestination one should read his *Admonition and Grace,* translated in Vol. 2 of the *Writings of St. Augustine* in this series, and also A. C. Pegis's Introduction to Vol. 3 of the *Writings of St. Augustine* in this series, containing "*The Freedom of Choice*" etc.

16 Cf. Chapter 5.2, below.

17 Cf. Dom D. M. Cappuyns, 'Le Premier représentant de l'Augustinisme médiéval. Prosper d'Aquitaine,' *Récherches de théologie ancienne et médiévale* 1 (1929) 308-337.

capital one. The second period, to which the *Liber contra Collatorem* belongs, sees no mention of predestination. The final period coincided with Prosper's stay at Rome; far from the field of battle, the controversies of a corner of Gaul are seen in a new perspective and consequently appear less important. Besides, Pope Leo (440-461), a prudent ruler, was able to exercise a considerable influence on Prosper. It was during this period that he began his calm commentary on the Psalms.

It is certainly not necessary to conclude that Prosper changed his opinion on grace simply because he withdrew from the field of controversy. I think the *Liber contra Collatorem* represents his final position on the problem. At any rate, the Council of Orange in 529 justified his stand.[18] That, I think, is reason enough to affirm that the *Liber contra Collatorem* is the most representative of Prosper's works and, historically speaking, the most significant.

It is written in a turgid, although generally correct, style of Latin, reminiscent of fifth-century Gallic schools of rhetoric. Long Scripture quotations, sometimes complete sentences in themselves, are woven into the fabric of his Latin period. There is no documentary evidence that Prosper attended any school, but his degree of erudition makes it a reasonable presumption.[19]

A single method of controversy prevails throughout the work, namely, to argue from authority and to reduce the opponent to the dilemma of either self-contradiction or to a position contrary to authority. The Semi-Pelagians had used much the same tactic. They had said: Either give up your doctrine on grace or deny free will. They had also claimed that St. Augustine had divided the body of Chris-

18 Cf. Hefele-Leclercq, *Histoire des conciles* II.2 (1086) n.3.

19 Cf. M. Roger, *L'Enseignement des lettres classiques* (Paris 1905) 83.

tians into two camps: those predestined to glory and those predestined to damnation. Prosper answers what he calls the calumnies of the heretics by citing the condemnations of the Popes and Councils against the Pelagians. He quotes text after text of Sacred Scripture. The conclusion to be drawn, therefore, is that doctrines contrary to the decisions and statements of Scripture, Popes and Councils are to be rejected with horror. The heretics, too, had divided the Christian body into two classes: into a class which gets along on its own strength, and a class which God saves by a purely gratuitous gift of His grace. Moreover, in Prosper's opinion, Cassian is somewhat dishonest; in the hope of deceiving the easy-going reader he begins his discourse with a very definitely Catholic statement of doctrine, but the later development finds him contradicting himself. We could qualify the arguments used by Prosper against Cassian as follows: *argumentum ad hominem; argumentum ex auctoritate; reductio ad absurdum.* They are the arguments of a man trained in rhetoric.

If we hope to find an analysis or an exposition of the nature and essence of grace, we shall be disappointed; such was not Prosper's aim. He was primarily interested in the exigencies of the historical circumstances of his own time. We need not be surprised at the strong terms used by Prosper both in attacking his adversary and in describing the lamentable state in which man finds himself without grace. The Latin Fathers were trained, not in metaphysics, but in the school of Cicero and Quintilian, in the school of rhetoric. Although Prosper describes man's miserable conditions after the Fall in vehement terms, he is very careful to make it unequivocally clear that grace can heal man's wounded nature; there is still a nature to be cured.[20]

---

20 Cf. Chapters 9.3 and 10.3, below.

Prosper's influence on the Middle Ages was not negligible. In addition to the rather numerous extant manuscripts of his works, many authors quote him.[21] A series of *Capitula* aimed at Semi-Pelagianism, if not certainly from the pen of Prosper, are undoubtedly based upon his works.[22]

The works of St. Prosper, which are generally accepted as authentic, run to more than 700 columns of Migne's *Latin Patrology*. In the translation of the *Liber contra Collatorum,* I have had at my disposal the texts of Migne and a Venice edition of 1782. Except for a rare typographical difference, the texts are identical. Migne lists thirteen columns of the various editions of Prosper's works throughout the centuries.[23]

As far as the present translator has been able to ascertain, no previous English translation of the present work exists.

---

21 Cf. Cappuyns, *op. cit.* 335.

22 Cf. Cappuyns, 'L'Origine des Capitula Pseudo-célestiniens contre le semipélagianisme,' *Revue Bénédictine* 41 (1929) 156-170.

23 *PL* 51.49ff.

GRACE AND FREE WILL

A Defence of St. Augustine against Cassian[1]

Chapter 1

There are some bold enough to assert that the grace of God, by which we are Christians, was not correctly defended by Bishop Augustine of holy memory; nor do they cease to attack with unbridled calumnies his books composed against the Pelagian heresy.[2] Their own internal discord and malice within would be as much an object of scorn as their heretical and ranting verbosity without, even if they did not support the wolves which have been cast from the Lord's fold, and which are of the fold in name, and even if they were not such that neither their rank in the Church nor their talents were to appear despicable. Since, indeed, they possess an appearance of piety in their devotion, the virtue of which is denied by their frame of mind, they attract to themselves many unlearned, and disturb hearts which have no

---

1 The full title, as listed in Migne's *Latin Patrology*, is: *Sancti Prosperi Aquitani de Gratia Dei et Libero Arbitrio Liber contra Collatorem, id est, Pro Defensione Sancti Aurelii Augustini Hipponensis Episcòpi contra Cassiani Presbyteri Librum qui Titulo de Protectione Dei Praenotatur.*

2 For a list of the Anti-Pelagian writings, see Otto Bardenhewer, *Patrology. The Lives and Works of the Fathers of the Church,* trans. by Thomas J. Shahan (St. Louis 1908) 486-488. Cf. also, Vernon J. Bourke, *Augustine's Quest of Wisdom* (Milwaukee 1945) 175-200. These writings will be published in this series.

discernment of spirits. Besides, they strive to reduce the cause of the Church to such a pass that, when they assert that those of our side have not spoken truly about grace, they insinuate that the enemies of grace were unjustly condemned. There must be, therefore, no overlooking this evil, which from hidden and tiny seeds is daily increasing and spreading far and wide from its beginning. Rather, care must be exercised to the extent of God's help, that the hypocrisy of the deceitful slanderers be uncovered, who from the very magnitude of the injury they brought as one against all, and especially against the pontiffs of the Apostolic See, are judged by the untutored and incautious to be men of lofty knowledge, and who with lamentable and perverse success gain through lies a ready assent, because they have presumptuously created an awe of themselves. Since they are men of good reputation, they are not considered to have been capable, through any slowness of wit or rashness of judgment, of having voiced in unison vain complaints, instead of having labored with great skill and tireless zeal in order that, once the discussions of the subtle compiler were understood, a presently more rigid examination and sharper scrutiny would discover what a previously unconcerned indulgence and careless benevolence had not seen.

(2) Whence, then, has arisen the painstaking effort of so strict an examination? Wherefore has the countenance assumed for this serious task a lean and hungry look in order that the crafty inquisitor might scrutinize the measures of the lines, the balance of the sentences and the quantity of the syllables, and presume that he was accomplishing something great, if he could tag the Catholic preacher with the label of error? Just as if he were assailing some unknown work hitherto hidden! But, that doctrine is not rent by these malicious attacks, a doctrine which dislodged the commen-

taries of the heretics and dashed to pieces the devilish ferment of Pelagian pride. It is now twenty years and more that the Catholic battle line under his [Augustine's] leadership is fighting against and conquering the enemies of grace. Conquering, I say, because those whom it conquers it does not permit to revive, and toward whose downfall it wrote the single opinion of all priests. Put to rout by the popes and deprived of communion, they who have preferred to be strangers to the truth rather than citizens of the Church complain about the good fortune of our victory. Why do those of our side, who are of one body and partake in common of the grace of Christ, debate about the arms with which the common faith is defended? Why do they take up again a war that is finished, and weaken the bulwarks of a long and tranquil peace? Are the victors uneasy and the vanquished finding favor? Are the condemned errors so impudently encouraged that, with depraved ill-will, both our writers and judges are placed on trial? Has, in fact, the more demanding rule of the new censors so modified itself that it asserts none of the things which have been extirpated, and rejects some of the things which have been held? With due regard of the tranquillity of a Catholic victory and the indissolubility of the decrees: behold, we are ready to hear the advocates of an emended doctrine and to acknowledge the outlines of an acute discernment, when cleared of all error. Let the golden mean be kept in the products of new inventions.

Chapter 2

(1) That we may not appear to belabor what the common herd and the brazen verbosity of the incompetent have advanced in order to obscure the knowledge of the more learned, let us set forth the propositions of the one person especially

who doubtless excels all of them in the study of Sacred Scripture. It is necessary to take these up now for discussion, since there can be no doubt whether they are as described. For they are written and promulgated in the publications of their author. The question, however, is not now whether they are; rather, what they teach must be elucidated. So, in a book entitled *On the Protection of God,*[1] a certain priest, who excelled in the art of disputation those with whom he lived, invented an abbot who treated the problem of the grace of God and the free will. The former made clear that he approved and accepted the opinion of the latter, and so now we have naught to do with the latter, who would casually refute such opinions of his own either by denying them or removing them by correction. Rather, our affair is with him who has endeavored to advance such a doctrine as a tool in the hands of the enemies of grace.

(2) This doctrine, however, was not at the outset of the discussion at variance with true piety, and would have deserved a just and honorable commendation, had it not, in its dangerous and pernicious progress, deviated from its initial correctness. For, after the comparison of the farmer, to whom he likened the example of one living under grace and faith, and whose work he said was fruitless unless he were aided in all things by the divine succor, he introduced the very Catholic proposition, saying: 'From which it is clearly deduced that the beginning not only of our acts, but also of our good thoughts, is from God; He it is who inspires in us the beginnings of a holy will and gives us the power and capacity to carry out those things which we rightly desire.

1 Edited by Michael Petschenig, in *Corpus Scriptorum Ecclesiasticorum Latinorum* 13.2 (Vienna 1886) 361-397. According to L. Christiani, *Jean Cassien* (S. Wandrille 1946) I 252, this work of Cassian was written, at the latest, shortly after 426.

"Every best gift and every perfect gift is from above, coming down from the Father of lights."[2] He it is who begins in us what is good and likewise accomplishes and fulfills it. In the words of the Apostle: "And He that ministereth seed to the sower, will both give you bread to eat and will multiply your seed, and increase the growth of the fruits of your justice."[3] Lest anyone think that there was nothing left for the free will to do, he added quite reasonably as proof that it was not taken away, but rather strengthened, by these gifts, unless, bent upon its own iniquities, it preferred to turn away from the divine aid.'[4] It is in our power, he says, each day to comply humbly with the grace of God which attracts us, or certainly, as it is written,[5] by resisting it with a stiff neck and uncircumcised ears we deserve to hear through Jeremias: 'Shall not he that falleth rise again? Or he that is turned away, shall he not turn again? Why then is this people in Jerusalem turned away with stubborn revolting? They have hardened their necks and would not return.'[6] Again later on, when he had taught that all zeal for virtue required the grace of God, he aptly added: 'Just as all these things cannot continually be desired by us without the divine inspiration, likewise without His help they can in no way be brought to completion.'[7]

(3) In the seventh chapter, when he wanted to show that the grace of Christ, which neglects no man and deserts not even the rebellious and perverse, is universal, he said: 'The divine protection is inseparably with us, and so great is the love of the Creator toward His creature, that not only does

---

2 James 1.17.
3 2 Cor. 9.10.
4 Cf. Johannis Cassiani, *Conlatio XIII* 3.5 (*CSEL,* p. 364).
5 Acts 7.51.
6 Jer. 8.4.
7 Cassian, *op. cit.* 6.3 (*CSEL,* p. 367).

His providence accompany it, but even unceasingly goes before it.'[8] Here it can be seen that he called providence a companion for this reason, that it generally does not desert its deserters, or because all whom it precedes it likewise follows. But he continues with these words: 'And when He sees in us any beginning of a good will, He illumines it, strengthens it, and directs it to salvation, giving increase to that which either He planted or which He saw come forth from our own efforts.'[9] Here he can still say that he meant that the origin of a good will is from that, whose beginnings have been planted or inspired by God, because salutary efforts can proceed from hearts already illumined. These, therefore, can be said to be of man himself, because he has already received the power of the good endeavors, and their seeds are referred to their author.

(4) And also in the ninth chapter he added: 'Wherefore it is not easily discernible by human reason how the Lord gives to those who ask, is found by those who seek, and opens to those who knock,[10] and likewise how He is found by those who do not seek, and how he openly appears among those who did not ask after Him, and how "All the day long He spread His hands to a people that believeth not and contradicteth,"[11] how He calls them resisting and from afar, how He calls them to salvation unwilling, how He takes away from those who desire to sin the capacity of carrying out their will, how He stands in the way of those who hasten towards evil.'[12] At this point, by a sort of inscrutable contradiction, there is introduced a proposition in which it is taught that many come to grace without grace, and that some also, from

8 *Ibid.* 8.3 (*CSEL,* p. 371).
9 *Ibid.*
10 Cf. Matt. 7.7.
11 Rom. 10.20.
12 Cassian, *op. cit.* 9.1 (*CSEL,* p. 372).

the endowments of the free will, have this desire to seek, to ask and to knock; yet in other things this free will is marked by so blind an aversion that no inducements lead it back, unless it is unwillingly recalled by the strength of Him who draws it. As if this were not wholly brought about in the souls of all by the work of a multiform grace, so that, being unwilling, they become willing! Or as if anyone from among those who use the judgment of reason could receive faith except by the will! Wherefore, it is as foolish to say that anyone can willingly strive toward a sharing in grace as it is to assert that anyone can come to it when not impelled by the Spirit of God.

(5) Quickly, then, did this disputant forget the foregoing proposition; quickly and with capricious instability did he dissent from his own statement. For he had correctly stated that 'the beginning not only of our acts, but also of our good thoughts, is from God.' Lest this should be understood as irrelevant to the stated doctrine, he was careful to add: 'He it is who inspires in us the beginnings of a holy will and gives the power and capacity to carry out those things which we rightly desire. For "every best gift, and every perfect gift, is from above, coming down from the Father of lights."[13] He it is who begins in us what is good and likewise accomplishes and fulfills it.'[14] O Catholic teacher, why do you forsake your profession, why do you turn to the cloudy darkness of falsity and depart from the light of the clearest truth? Why do you not ascribe to the same grace, which is lacking, what you are in amazement at in those who seek, ask and knock? You see the good endeavors, the holy zeal; do you doubt that they are the gifts of God? The work of grace will have remained hidden as long as the implanted faith is enclosed

---

13 James 1.17.

14 Cassian, *op. cit.* 3.5 (*CSEL*, p. 364).

within the mystery of thought. But where there is supplication and diligent searching, where there is manifest and frequent knocking, why do you not understand from the quality of the work the supply of the One who incites it?

Chapter 3

(1) You think you guard sufficiently against the Pelagian fallacies if you grant to us in part what is to be held in the whole body of those called. On your part, however, there is complete agreement with neither the heretics nor the Catholics. The former regard the beginnings in every just work of man as belonging to the free will; we constantly believe that the beginnings of good thoughts spring from God. You have found some indescribable third alternative, unacceptable to both sides, by which you neither find agreement with the enemies nor retain an understanding with us. How is it that you do not realize that you fall willy-nilly into that condemned position, since you incontestedly assert that the grace of God is given according to our merits, in that you affirm that some good works proceed from man himself, for which he receives grace? For the faith of him who seeks, the piety of him who asks, the constancy of him who knocks cannot be regarded as of no merit, especially when all the so-described are said to receive, find and enter. And in this case it is vain, even impious, to want to make a place for merits existing before grace, so that what the Lord says may not be wholly true: 'No man can come to Me, except the Father, who hath sent Me, draw him.'[1] This he would not have said at all, were the conversion of anyone to be thought to be without the illumination of God, or if in any way the will of man could tend toward God without God, who attracts him who

1 John 6.44.

is called to the Son. He does not compel him who resists and is unwilling, but makes him, who was unwilling, willing and in various ways disposes the lack of faith of him who resists, so that the heart of him who hears and obeys, because of the delight begotten within itself, rises whence it was pressed down, finds knowledge where it was ignorant, places its trust where it lacked confidence, becomes willing, whence it was unwilling. 'For the Lord will give goodness, and our earth shall yield her fruit.'[2]

Let us examine the nature of what follows: 'But to whom is it readily evident how the whole of salvation is attributed to our will, and how "it is not of him that willeth or of him that runneth, but of God that sheweth mercy"?[3] Anent this there are the words: "If you be willing and will hearken to Me, you shall eat the good things of the land."[4] Likewise, what is it that "God will render to every man according to his works,"[5] and "It is God who worketh in you both to will and to accomplish, according to his good will";[6] and "that not of yourselves, for it is the gift of God: not of works, that no man may glory" '?[7] And the other things which were gathered from the Scriptures, he arranged as though they were contradicting each other, so that he might assign to human energy the desire for the gifts of grace. All men are divided into classes: some there are whom the grace of God saves; others whom the Law and nature justifies. The Law, however, can command that we do no evil, but it cannot free from evil; it makes the commandment known, but it does not bestow a love of obedience, unless what kills through

2 Ps. 84.13.
3 Rom. 9.16.
4 Isa. 1.19.
5 Matt. 16.27.
6 Phil. 2.13.
7 Eph. 2.13.

the rule of the letter is made life-giving through the spirit of grace.

(2) Thereupon he concludes, saying [what are we being told] 'Except that in all these [Scriptural texts] both the grace of God and the liberty of our will are proclaimed, and also that man can sometime by his own activity reach out to a desire of the virtues; but he always needs the Lord's help'?[8] What has become of what was premissed in the correct proposition: 'The beginning not only of our good acts, but also of our good thoughts, is from God. He it is who begins in us what is good and likewise accomplishes and fulfills it'?[9] Behold here also, even if you do admit that the help of God is necessary for good undertakings, nevertheless you ascribe to the bare liberty of the will, without the grace of God, the very praiseworthy activity and desire of the virtues! Consequently, good and salutary endeavors cannot progress unless God help; they can, however, make a beginning even without the divine inspiration.

Chapter 4

(1) Whereupon, the more clearly to define what man has from his free will and what from grace, you add: 'For nobody enjoys health whenever he wishes, nor is he freed from sickness by the desire of his will.'[1] You teach, therefore, that man of himself cannot, indeed, gain health, but that he has of himself the desire of health; also, that he approaches the physician of his own free will; and the very fact that he does

8 Cassian, *op. cit.* 9.4 (*CSEL*, p. 373). It has been necessary to add *quid sit quod ad nos dicitur* from the text of Cassian to complete the sense.

9 *Ibid.* 3.5 (*CSEL*, p. 364).

1 Cassian, *op. cit.* 9.5 (*CSEL*, p. 374).

approach him is in no way attributable to the physician. Just as if the soul itself were not sick, and, being healthy, were to seek out a cure for the body! But the whole man through it and along with it falls into the depths of his misery. And before receiving from the physician a knowledge of its disaster, he delights that the soul linger there, even enamored of its errors and embracing the false for the true. Its first salvation is to begin being dissatisfied with itself and to note its *old* debility; next, that it long to be cured and know the author of the cure. These so precede its cure that they are placed there by Him who will operate the cure, in order that, since they cannot at all be there in vain, it may appear to have been saved by grace, not merit.

(2) Then you add:[2] 'In order that it may be the more evident that the beginnings of a good will sometimes emanate from a good will, through the bounty of nature bestowed by the beneficence of the Creator, the Apostle is also the witness that, unless these beginnings are directed by God, they cannot come to the perfection of virtues, he says: "For to will is present with me; but to accomplish that which is good, I find not." '[3] According to this proposition, therefore, you spoke falsely before: 'The beginning not only of our acts, but also of our good thoughts, is from God. He it is who begins in us what is good and likewise accomplishes and fulfills it.'[4] But this cannot in any way or from any angle be false, and what is contrary to it should not have been advanced in such a way that what you correctly professed to begin from grace you afterwards affirm us to have through the gift of nature and the free will. In fact, the blessed Apostle said: 'For to will is present with me; but to accomplish that which

2 *Ibid.*
3 Rom. 7.18.
4 Cassian, *op. cit.* 33.5 (*CSEL*, p. 364).

is good, I find not.'[5] And the same Apostle said: 'Not that we are sufficient to think anything of ourselves, as of ourselves; but our sufficiency is from God.'[6] Likewise, he said: 'For it is God who worketh in you, both to will and to accomplish, according to His good will.'[7] The Apostle, therefore, does not contradict himself. But when the good will has been given us, we do not immediately find its accomplishment, unless He who gave the will also grant its accomplishment to those who seek, ask and knock. For the words of him who says: 'For to will is present with me; but to accomplish that which is good, I find not,'[8] are the words of one who has been called and already possessed of grace. In fact, he is delighted with 'the Law of God, according to the inward man,' but sees 'another law in (his) members, fighting against the law of (his) mind, and captivating (him) in the law of sin.'[9] Although he has received the knowledge of right willing, nevertheless he does not find in himself the power to do what he wills, until he merit, because of the good will which is his, to find the power for the virtues which he seeks.

Chapter 5

(1) After this, you tender several proofs to demonstrate that the free will is now strong, now weak; as if there were some who accomplish by their own strength what others cannot do without God's help; or as if man receives a commandment for another purpose than to seek the divine aid! You conclude, therefore, and say: 'And so these are somewhat indiscriminately mixed up and confused; consequently,

5 Rom. 7.18.
6 Phil 2.13.
7 *Ibid.*
8 Rom. 7.18.
9 Rom. 7.22.

which depends on which is a considerable problem: namely, whether God is merciful to us because we have presented the beginning of a good will, or we receive the beginning of a good will because God is merciful. Many, believing these individually and affirming more than is right, are caught in many and self-contradictory errors.'[1] Behold, what, as it seems to you, were confused are distinct, and what could not be explained is settled! You propose two contradictory errors in which are implicated those who do not know what must be held between free will and grace. In one class you place those who say that God is merciful to us because we present of ourselves the beginnings of a good will; doubtless, you mean the followers of the Pelagian doctrine, who assert that the grace of God is given according to our merits. In the other class you place those who say that the beginnings of a good will come from the mercy of God, intending those to be understood who fight against the enemies of grace. If, therefore, it is wrong to ascribe the beginning of a good will to man not divinely aided, and it is an error to admit that the will is prepared by the Lord, whither must we go to avoid both?

(2) If we follow both, you say, we subscribe to no error. You expose us to two, and, according to your way of thinking, you condemn the double distortion by dividing and justify it by combining the two. According to this law, this rule, you were able to preach that both are wrong: those who say that one must always deceive, and those who declare that one must never deceive; but there is sin in neither in following both, because neither is falsehood always to be avoided nor truth always to be neglected.[2] You are completely wrong in

---

1 Cassian, *op. cit.* 11.1 (*CSEL,* p. 375).
2 Cf. Cassian, *Conlatio XVII* 20 (*CSEL,* pp. 480ff.).

your opinion. Of two evils, one cannot become good. Two vices do not beget one virtue; two falsehoods do not make one truth. What are equal in merit are not diminished by joining; rather, they increase. And so, they who asserted that the beginnings of good will are generated by a divine inspiration should not be indicted in the same judgment in which they are condemned who think that the free will without the strength of grace can suffice for these beginnings. One of these propositions has been attacked by the Church, the other defended; nor do the stipulations of this new invention in any way agree with those propositions, so that, the more corrupt the Catholic one is, the more correct is the Pelagian.

(3) 'Many,' you say, 'believing these individually, and affirming more than is right, are caught in numerous and self-contradictory errors.'[3] It is your intention, therefore, to condemn the Catholics along with the heretics, the victors with the vanquished, and to brand with the stamp of error those who have driven error from the Church. According to your opinion, wherein you propose that the source of holy and faithful wills is not from God in the case of all men—as if you would make a considerable concession to grace, if you were thereby to admit that it is operative in the minds of some!—Pope Innocent, most worthy of the See of Peter, was wrong when he said of those who gloried in the free will: 'What shall we henceforth think of the understanding of those who believe it is due to themselves that they are good?' And again, when he wrote about the fall of the first man, he said: 'For he once tested his free will, when he imprudently made use of his goods. And falling into the depths of sin, he was buried there; nor did he find anything whereby he might rise thence. Eternally deceived by his liberty, he would have

3 Cassian, *Conlatio XIII* 11.1 (*CSEL*, p. 375).

been prostrate under the weight of this ruin, if afterwards the coming of Christ had not raised him up again by His grace.'[4] The Eastern bishops were wrong, at whose investigation Pelagius, to appear Catholic, was compelled to anathematize those who say that the grace of God is given according to our merits.[5] The African councils of bishops were wrong, which established in their decrees that to know what we ought to do and to have the love to do it are both gifts of God, so that through the edification of charity knowledge may not be puffed up.[6] For, just as it has been written of God: 'He that teacheth man knowledge,'[7] so also is it written: 'Charity is of God.'[8] The two hundred and fourteen priests were wrong, who, in the letter which they sent in advance of their constitutions to the blessed Zozimus, bishop of the Apostolic See, had this to say: 'We have decided that the pronouncement, made against Pelagius and Celestius by the venerable Bishop Innocent of the See of the most blessed Apostle Peter, stand until, with a very clear confession, they admit that we are in our every act aided by the grace of God through Jesus Christ our Lord, not only to know but also to accomplish justice, so that without it we have, think or perform no true and holy piety.'[9] The most holy See of the blessed Peter was wrong, which spoke thus to the whole world through the mouth of Pope Zozimus: 'We have, by the divine inspiration (for all good things must be referred to the Author

4 Cf. Hefele-LeClercq, *Histoire des conciles* II.1 168ff., for a history of the conciliar decisions on Pelagianism. For the particular passage referred to here, cf. H. Denzinger, *Enchiridion Symbolorum Definitionum et Declarationum de Rebus Fidei et Morum* (Freiburg i. Br. 1932) no. 130.
5 Hefele-LeClercq, *op. cit.* 177, n. 1.
6 Cf. 1 Cor. 8.1.
7 Ps. 93.10.
8 1 John 4.7.
9 Cf. Hefele-LeClercq, *op. cit.* 189, n. 3.

whence they were given birth) referred everything to the combined knowledge of our brethren and fellow bishops.'[10] The African bishops erred when they wrote back to the same Pope Zozimus and commended him for the soundness of his decision in these words: 'What you have written in your letters, which you took care to have sent to all the provinces, saying: "We have, by the divine inspiration (for all good things must be referred to the Author whence they were given birth) referred everything to the combined knowledge of our brethren and fellow bishops."—we have understood your statement thus, that you have unsheathed the sword of truth and as though with a quick thrust have cut off those who extol the liberty of the free will at the expense of the divine help. For what have you done with a will so free but refer everything to our humble and combined knowledge. Nevertheless, you have faithfully and wisely seen, and truthfully and confidently said, that it was done under a divine impulse. Therefore, since the Lord prepares the will, He also, indeed, touches the hearts of His children with fatherly inspirations in order that they may do good. 'For whosoever are led by the Spirit of God, they are the sons of God.'[11] Consequently, neither do we think that our free will is lacking, nor do we doubt that, in each and every motion of man's free will, His aid is the stronger. Do you see that your canons, broken upon the solid and irrefutable decrees, as also your perverted and perforated fabrications against the edifice of the faith, are fallen down like the walls of Jericho before the sound of the priests' trumpet?[12]

---

10 Denzinger, *op. cit.*, no. 134.
11 Rom. 8.14.
12 Cf. Josue 6.20.

Chapter 6

(1) When the question about the beginnings of holy wills and the principles of faith and charity was raised between our side and the Pelagians, the struggle ended in a positive victory and a clear-cut finish. Consequently, we now must treat of the nefarious peace of this compact of yours. The battle line of the enemy is flattened; the war is finished; we are the victors through Him who 'has shown might in His arm'; 'has scattered the proud in the deceit of their heart'; 'has put down the mighty from their seat and has exalted the humble'; 'has filled the hungry with good things and sent the rich empty away.'[1] Through Him who, performing 'mercy to our fathers,' remembered 'His holy testament,' and 'the oath, which He swore to Abraham our father, that He would grant to us, that being delivered of the fear of our enemies, we may serve Him without fear, in holiness and justice before Him, all our days.'[2] Through Him 'Who hath given us the victory through Jesus Christ our Lord.'[3] Through Him from whom 'we have received, not the spirit of this world, but the Spirit, that is of God, that we may know the things, that are given us from God.'[4] Why do you strive to gather together the shattered weapons of the petty reasonings of broken arguments? Why do you attempt to kindle into a revived flame the glow of a failing smoke by stirring the ashes of a burned-out doctrine? There is no danger for the free will from the grace of God, nor is the will taken away, since there is generated in it to will well. If, therefore our doctrine is not to be considered, because the will is fashioned, directed, ordered and inspired, the children of God, 'who are led by the

1 Luke 1.51-53.
2 Luke 1.72-75.
3 1 Cor. 15.57.
4 1 Cor. 2.12.

Spirit of God,'[5] are despoiled of their liberty. They lose the strength of the rational soul and are deprived of all praise for free devotion; to them is given the Spirit of wisdom and understanding, counsel and fortitude, knowledge and piety and fear of the Lord.[6] In fact, they who think they have no need of these transformations have turned from the habitude of the old malady to madness; they reject the remedy, they declaim, rage and struggle. But, if they are children of promise, they will be at rest and healed.

Chapter 7

(1) Let us now examine what the soberness of the disputant has to offer. By a new art he jumbles together self-contradictory propositions to dispel vice with vice and to cure error with error. And in order to drink to the health of unsuspecting hearers, he planned to color with a mixture of examples this cup of his own concoction. He says: 'For, if we say that the beginning of a good will is ours, what was it in Paul the persecutor? What was it in the tax collector Matthew? One of whom by the blood and torture of innocent people, the other by brooding upon violence and public robbery, are drawn to salvation. But if, indeed, we say that the beginnings of a good will are always inspired by the grace of God, what about the faith of Zachaeus? What do we say about the piety of that thief upon the cross? They, bringing violence to bear upon the Kingdom of Heaven by their desire, anticipated the explicit admonitions of their vocation.'[1]

(2) Through that dissimilarity of good beginnings, he attempts to prove that some, through their free will, without

5 Rom. 8.14.
6 Isa. 11.2.

1 *Cassian, op. cit.* 11.2 (*CSEL*, p. 376).

the help of God, can do what some cannot without divine co-operation. It is this he wants understood concerning the rather slothful obedience of some, and the more eager consent of others. Just as if, when a stern infidelity is subject to God and suddenly succumbs to the Gospel which it had long fought against, there the right hand of the Most High would bring about a change in man;[2] but where the docile hearer embraces without reluctant hesitation a quiet urging or mere murmur, the good of such a conversion belongs to the human will alone! Just as if the divine power attracted only those to the Son whom He has either verbally blamed, or chastised by a penalty, or terrified by fear, but brings to bear nothing of his power upon the minds of those who rush to the promises of their Redeemer with ready hope and avid longing! But Truth says: 'No man comes to Me except the Father who hath sent Me draw him.'[3] If, therefore, no one comes unless drawn, all who in any manner whatsoever come, are drawn. Contemplation of the elements and the ordered beauty of everything which is in them leads to God. 'For the visible things of Him, from the creation of the world, are clearly seen, being understood by the things that are made.'[4] The narrators of events draw; those 'declaring the praises of the Lord, and His powers, and His wonders, which He hath done'[5] enflame the soul of him who hears. Fear draws, for 'the fear of the Lord is the beginning of wisdom.'[6] Joy draws, because 'I rejoiced at the things that were said to me: We shall go into the house of the Lord.'[7] Desire draws, because

2 Ps. 76.11.
3 John 6.44.
4 Rom. 1.20.
5 Ps. 77.4.
6 Ps. 110.10.
7 Ps. 121.1.

'my soul longeth and fainteth for the courts of the Lord.'[8] Delights draw, for 'how sweet are the words to my palate! More than honey and the honey-comb to my mouth.'[9] And who can perceive or relate through what longings the divine visitation leads the human soul to follow what it fled, to love what it hated, to hunger after what was distasteful; and suddenly, with wondrous change, what had been closed becomes open, what was burthensome is light, what was bitter is sweet, what was obscure is lightsome? 'But all these things one and the same Spirit worketh, dividing to everyone according as He will.'[10] 'God, who commanded the light to shine out of darkness, hath shined in our hearts, to give the light of knowledge of the glory of God, in the face of Christ Jesus,'[11] that is, in the manifestation of His Son, who is in the glory of the Father.

(3) He who illumined the heart of Matthew the tax collector, and Paul when he was persecuting the Church, also enlightened the heart of the thief crucified with the Lord. Unless, perchance, the words of the Lord were vain when he deigned to address Zachaeus, who 'sought to see Jesus, Who He was,'[12] saying: 'Zachaeus make haste and come down; for this day I must abide in thy house,'[13] and He did not prepare for Himself the soul of him whose hospitality He chose. Finally, when all murmured, asking why He betook Himself to a sinful man for hospitality, and when Zachaeus was already doing penance by giving half of his goods to the poor and promising to restore fourfold his ill-gotten gains, the Lord said: 'This day is salvation come to this house, because

---

8 Ps. 83.3.
9 Ps. 118.103.
10 1 Cor. 12.11.
11 2 Cor. 4.6.
12 Luke 19.3.
13 Luke 19.5.

he also is a son of Abraham.'[14] And lest the cause of his salvation be hidden, He added: 'For the Son of man is come to seek and to save that which was lost,'[15] so that we should know that he whom we acknowledge as saved had been 'prevented' by the one seeking. Also, in the justification of the thief, even if no indications of the operation of grace were perceptible, should we, along with all the faithful, not consider him drawn, when the Lord said: 'all things are delivered to Me by My Father,'[16] and I, when 'I shall be lifted up, will draw all things to Myself?'[17] But, amid everything, his confession also teaches that this man was either delivered or drawn; who, when he had for a time blasphemed against Jesus Christ, was suddenly changed, and said: 'Lord remember me when Thou hast come into Thy kingdom.'[18] The blessed Apostle teaches us in these words, whence has arisen so great a diversity of contradictory words in one man: 'No man speaking by the Spirit of God saith anathema to Jesus. And no man can say the Lord Jesus, but by the Holy Ghost.'[19] As a consequence, we do not doubt that it was in the will of the same man and of his strength that he blasphemed, and of the Holy Spirit that he believed. In vain, therefore, has that disputant tried to adapt the content of his proposition to the inscrutable variety of the one grace, so that a part of the justified be thought to come to Christ by the impulses of their wills alone, and a part to be drawn reluctantly and unwillingly compelled, since it is God 'Who worketh all in all,'[20] whether He wish to draw some in one way, others in another, to whom nobody comes unless in some way drawn.

14 Luke 19.9.
15 Luke 19.10.
16 Luke 10.22.
17 John 12.32.
18 Luke 23.42.
19 1 Cor. 12.3.
20 1 Cor. 12.6.

Chapter 8

(1) Afterwards, he adds the testimonies of sacred history,[1] whereby he shows that the observance of the commandments of God and the accomplishment of the virtues are to be attributed to divine grace. And this we also may readily admit. After he had recalled the examples of Balaam, whom, when he intended to utter curses against Israel, God transformed to an utterance of blessings;[2] and of Abimelech, who was not permitted to sin against Rebecca;[3] and of Joseph, sold by his brothers whose ill will God turned into good;[4] he turns once more to a confirmation of his proposition, to take away, as far as he can, from part of the human race, and to confirm in a part, the free will which, he says, is joined to grace. He says: 'For these two, that is, both grace and free will, seem indeed to be contrary to each other; but both are in harmony. And we conclude that, because of piety, we should accept both, lest, taking one of these away from man, we appear to violate the Church's rule of faith.'[5]

(2) The rule of faith of the Church is, according to the preaching of the Apostle: 'No man can say the Lord Jesus, but by the Holy Ghost.'[6] The rule of the Church is: 'What hast thou that thou hast not received? And if thou hast received why dost thou glory as if thou hadst not received?'[7] The rule of the Church is: 'By the grace of God I am what I am, and His grace in me hath not been void, but I have labored more abundantly than all they; yet not I but the

1 Cassian, *op. cit.* 11.2 (*CSEL*, pp. 376ff.).
2 Num. 23.
3 Gen. 26.
4 Gen. 37.
5 Cassian, *op. cit.* 11.4 (*CSEL*, p. 377).
6 1 Cor. 12.3.
7 1 Cor. 4.7.

grace of God with me.'[8] And: 'having obtained mercy, to be faithful.'[9] The rule of the Church is: 'But we have this treasure in earthen vessels, that the excellency may be of the power of God, and not of us.'[10] The rule of the Church is: 'By grace you are saved through faith, and that not of yourselves, for it is the gift of God.'[11] The rule of the Church is: 'And in nothing be ye terrified by the adversaries, which to them is a cause of perdition, but to you of salvation and this is from God: For unto you it is given for Christ, not only to believe in Him but also to suffer for Him.'[12] The rule of the Church is: 'With fear and trembling work out your salvation. For it is God Who worketh in you both to will and to accomplish according to His good will.'[13] The rule of the Church is: 'Not that we are sufficient to think anything of ourselves, as of ourselves, but our sufficiency is from God.'[14] The Lord confirms this rule, saying: 'No man can come to Me, unless it be given him by My Father.'[15] And: 'All that the Father giveth Me shall come to Me.'[16] And: 'Without Me you can do nothing,'[17] and: 'You have not chosen Me, but I have chosen you,'[18] and: 'No one knoweth the Son, but the Father, neither doth anyone know the Father, but the Son, and he to whom it shall please the Son to reveal Him.'[19] And: 'As the Father raiseth up the dead, and giveth

---

8 1 Cor. 15.10.
9 1 Cor. 7.25.
10 2 Cor. 4.7.
11 Eph. 2.8.
12 Phil. 1.28.
13 Phil. 2.12.
14 2 Cor. 3.5.
15 John 6.66.
16 John 6.37.
17 John 15.5.
18 John 15.16.
19 Matt. 11.27.

life, so the Son also giveth life to whom He will.'[20] And: 'Blessed art thou, Simon Bar-Jona, because flesh and blood hath not revealed it to thee, but My Father, Who is in heaven.'[21]

(3) By this rule the will is taken away from no man, because the power of grace does not destroy wills; rather, it makes bad wills good, and faithless ones faithful; and brings it about that those things which were of themselves darkness become light in the Lord,[22] that what was dead be given life, that what was prostrate be raised up, that what was lost be found. In fact, we believe that the grace of the Saviour operates in all men, without any exception of person, who are delivered from the power of darkness into the kingdom of the love of the Son of God; because, just as this same man correctly, but without conviction, declared, so do we assert and defend that 'the beginning, not only of our acts, but also of our good thoughts is from God. He it is who inspires in us the beginnings of a holy will, and gives us the power and capacity to carry out those things which we rightly desire. "For every best gift, and every perfect gift is from above, coming down from the Father of lights."[23] He it is who begins in us what is good and likewise accomplishes and fulfills in us those things which are good.'[24] But, if its author were to continue in that opinion, he would not violate the rule of the Church. He would neither have attacked the free will nor, at the same time, have been ungrateful to the grace of God. And when he intimates that one of these was at work in Paul and Matthew, another in Zachaeus and the thief, he

20 John 5.21.
21 Matt. 16.17.
22 Eph. 5.8.
23 James 1.17.
24 2 Cor. 9.10.

does not understand that he upheld the free will in the former and grace in the latter.

Chapter 9

(1) Then he added: 'For, when God sees us turn to a good will, He comes to meet us, directs and strengthens us. "At the voice of thy cry, as soon as He shall hear, He will answer thee."[1] And: "Call upon me (He said) in the day of trouble; I will deliver thee, and thou shalt glorify Me." '[2] Who does not see that this doctrine gives merit to the free will, by which grace is 'prevented,' and that this latter is servant to the former and performs its duty, and does not confer a gift upon it? Moreover, this proposition was condemned during the synod of the bishops of Palestine, as well as being denounced by Pelagius.'[3] For we profess that it is the grace of God that brings it about in him who begins to will the good, and desires to quit iniquity and error, since 'with the Lord shall the steps of a man be directed, and he shall like well His way.'[4] And: 'Every way of man seemeth right to himself; but the Lord weigheth the hearts.'[5] And: 'the steps of man are guided by the Lord, but who is the man that can understand his own way?'[6] And the Apostle also says: 'For you have not received the spirit of bondage again in fear, but you have received the spirit of adoption of sons, whereby we cry: Abba, Father.'[7]

(2) Thereupon, he continues and says: 'For God must not be thought to have created man such that he could never

1 Isa. 30.19.
2 Ps. 49.15; cf. Cassian, *op. cit.* (*CSEL*, p. 377).
3 Cf. Hefele-LeClercq, *op. cit.* 182.
4 Ps. 36.23.
5 Prov. 21.2.
6 Prov. 20.24.
7 Rom. 8.15.

either will or perform the good. Moreover, He has not bestowed upon him a free will, if He granted him only the will and capacity for evil, but not the will and the capacity for good. And how will that statement of the Lord stand, after the sin of the first man: "Behold Adam is become like one of us, knowing good and evil,"[8] for he must not be thought to have been such before the sin that he was wholly ignorant of good. Otherwise, it must be admitted that he was created like an irrational and senseless animal; and this is quite absurd and foreign to the Catholic faith. Nay, rather, according to the pronouncement of the most wise Solomon, "God made man right,"[9] that is, to enjoy continually the knowledge of good alone. But they sought many thoughts. So they were made, as it was said, "Knowing good and evil."[10] After the fall, therefore, Adam conceived a knowledge of evil, which he did not have; but he did not lose the knowledge of good, which he did have.'[11]

(3) It is unspeakable to doubt that the first man, in whom the nature of all men was concreated, was created right and devoid of every defect. It is also wrong to doubt that he received such a free will that, if he were not to desert the helping hand of God, he could persevere if he wished in the goods which he had received, and through the merit of a voluntary perseverance come to such a happiness that he could neither wish nor settle for the meaner things. But, by the very free will through which he remained good, as long as he wished, he transgressed the law established for him. When he turned from God and followed the Devil, when he was insubordinate to the Lord, the deliverer, and subservient

8 Gen. 3.22.
9 Eccle. 7.30.
10 Gen. 3.22.
11 Cassian, *op. cit.* 12.2 (*CSEL,* p. 378).

to his enemy, the destroyer, he did not fear the condemnation of death pronounced upon himself. Thus the blessed Ambrose was not wrong in saying: 'Adam was, and in him were all of us; Adam perished and we all perished in him,'[12] just as Truth itself was not wrong in asserting: 'For the Son of Man is come to seek and to save that which was lost.'[13] Neither the substance nor the will of human nature was taken away in the ruin of the universal sin, but the illumination and splendor of the virtues, of which the deceit of the envier despoiled them. Once it had lost those things, through which it could come to the eternal and inamissible incorruption of body and soul, what was left to it except what belongs to the temporal life, which is completely under condemnation and penalty? Wherefore, those born in Adam must be reborn in Christ, lest there be found anyone in that generation which was lost. For, if the descendants of Adam were naturally to act in those virtues in which Adam was before the sin, they would not be 'by nature children of wrath';[14] they would not 'be darkness'[15] nor under the 'power of darkness.'[16] They would, in fine, have no need of the grace of the Saviour, because they would not be good in vain, nor be cheated of the reward of justice; and this because they would be in possession of the good, for losing which our first parents deserved to be driven from Paradise. Now, however, since no one can escape eternal death without the sacrament of rebirth, is it not clearly manifest, from the singleness of the remedy itself, into how deep an evil the nature of the whole human race has been plunged by the sin of him in whom all have sinned, and have lost whatever he lost? First of all he lost faith; he lost continence; he lost charity; he was despoiled

12 St. Ambrose, *Commentary on St. Luke* 7.15 (*PL* 15.1852B).
13 Luke 19.10.
14 Eph. 2.3.

of wisdom and understanding; he was without counsel and fortitude; and, because he blasphemously pursued what was higher, he was cut off from the knowledge of truth and the piety of obedience. Not even fear was left to him, so that he who would not refrain out of love for justice might avoid what was forbidden from fear of the penalty. The free will, therefore, that is, the spontaneous appetite of what pleases it, when it grew tired of the use of the goods which it had received, and when the bulwarks of its happiness became worthless, directed its insane desire to a trial of sin; it drank the poison of every vice and besot the whole nature of man with the drunkenness of its own intemperance. Thereupon, before eating the Flesh of the Son of Man and drinking His Blood, human nature swallows a deadly mass, is weak in memory, errant in judgment, staggering in step; it is quite incapable of choosing and desiring that good of which it was of its own free will deprived, because the fact is not thus that, since human nature was able to fall without a divine impulse, it can arise without God's raising it up.

(4) Therefore, it was incorrectly said: 'God must not be thought to have created man such that he can never either will or do good.'[15] Just as if we were to say that that weakness was established by the Creator, and not contracted through the deserts of sin! Whoever thinks it to follow that, if the free will is called blind, the blindness must be referred to the Author of nature, intends to imply that the free will in the descendants of Adam is as sound as it was in Adam prior to his sin. This we consider quite foreign to the Catholic faith. For, what has been injured by sin, if not that whence sin is? Unless by chance it be said that the penalty passed to Adam's descendants, and not the sin. This is a completely false

15 Eph. 5.8.

statement and consequently not made by chance. It is exceedingly blasphemous to think that the divine justice wishes to condemn those free from sin along with the guilty. Sin, therefore, is manifest when the penalty is not hidden, and fellowship in sin is argued from the commonness of the penalty. Consequently, what human misery there is comes not from a disposition of the Creator, but from the retribution of the Judge.

(5) What he added to prove the soundness of the free will is foolish and contrary to the thought of all writers. He says:[16] 'And how will that pronouncement of the Lord stand, after the sin: "Behold Adam is become as one of us, knowing good and evil"?'[17] As if the Devil promised what is true to Adam, and Adam, by violating the divine command, became more godlike. And as if God declared that this was conferred upon him when, rather, there was indicated what he would not attain; who, once he had walked the way of pride, lost what he had, when he desired what he had not received! The error in the conclusion of this sentence is as great, when it is said: 'After the sin, therefore, Adam conceived a knowledge of evil which he did not have; but he did not lose the knowledge of good which he had received.'[18] Adam did have a knowledge of good while he kept with faithful heart the good and holy command of God, and he was just while he persevered in the image of God and was not unmindful of His Law. But, afterwards, he sold himself, the image and temple of God, to his deceiver; he lost the knowledge of good because he lost a good conscience. Iniquity drove out justice, pride destroyed humility, concupiscence crushed continence, infidelity stole away faith, captivity took away liberty; nor

16 Col. 1.13.
17 Gen. 3.22.
18 Cassian, *op. cit.* 12.2 (*CSEL,* p. 378).

could any part of the virtues dwell there, wherein so great a swarm of vices had entered. For no one 'can serve two masters.'[19] And: 'whoever committeth sin is the servant of sin.'[20] And: 'by whom a man is overcome, of the same also he is the slave.'[21] But no one serves without some liberty, and, according to the words of the Apostle, no one is free without some servitude. 'For when you were the servants of sin, you were free men to justice; what fruit therefore had you then in those things, of which you are now ashamed? For the end of them is death. But now being made free from sin, and become servants of God, you have your fruit unto sanctification, and the end life everlasting.'[22] He, therefore, who serves the Devil is free from God; but he who, being freed, serves God is free from the Devil. As a result, it is apparent that an evil liberty could have been had from a defect of the human will, but that a good liberty could not have been received without the aid of the liberator.

Chapter 10

(1) But, in order that his calamity may not appear to have passed to Adam's descendants, this teacher endeavors from the example of the pagans to prove how perfect the nature of all men is in judgment. He adds, saying: 'Finally, it is also very clearly declared in the statement of St. Paul that the human race did not lose the knowledge of good after the Fall: "For when the gentiles, who have not the law, do by nature those things that are of the law, those having not the law are a law unto themselves; who show the work of the law written in their hearts, their conscience bearing witness

19 Luke 16.13.
20 John 8.34.
21 2 Pet. 2.19.
22 Rom. 6.20.

to them, and their thoughts between themselves accusing, or also defending one another, in the day when God shall judge the secrets of men." '[1]

(2) If the Apostle is speaking of those who are called from uncircumcision, even though 'they were afar off, (they) are made nigh,'[2] believing in Him who now has mercy upon those upon whom He once had no mercy; and justifying 'circumcision by faith, and uncircumcision through faith,'[3] He made the two one in Himself; having broken the wall of enmity[4] of Jew and Gentile, He established the peace in the one new man, 'concluding all under sin, that the promise by the faith of Jesus Christ might be given to them that believe.'[5] If, I say, the Apostle is speaking of them in whose hearts God, with His finger, that is by the Holy Spirit, writes the new covenant, so that they naturally fulfill the plenitude of the Law and the works of charity, that is, with a reformed and renewed nature, what help, then, is the newness of the very proud power, since reconciliation of enemies can only be ascribed to the grace of the mediator? 'For all have sinned, and do need the glory of God, being justified freely by His grace.'[6] Grace, therefore, is the glory of God, not the merit of him who has been freed. 'For who has first given to him, and recompense shall be made him?'[7] No good work comes from the dead; nothing just, from the impious. Their whole salvation is gratuitous, and is, therefore, the glory of God, so that he who glories may glory in Him of whose glory he has stood in need.

---

1 Rom. 2.14.
2 Eph. 2.11.
3 Rom. 3.30.
4 Eph. 2.14.
5 Gal. 3.22.
6 Rom. 3.23.
7 Rom. 11.35.

(3) But, if those words are spoken of those who, strangers to the grace of Christ (which this disputer prefers to be understood), established by means of their own judgment certain things as sacred, resembling legal precepts, and if they thought that the morals of cities and concord of peoples could not otherwise be obtained, except rewards be decreed for what was rightly done, and penalties for misdemeanors, in accord with what Divine Wisdom itself said: 'I came out of the mouth of the most high, and I have held first place among every race; I have sought rest in Jacob and have found it,'[8] then who doubts that this wisdom, coming from the remnants of the nature established by God, is sufficient unto the human race for use in the temporal life? For, if the power of the rational soul were not capable of ordering those earthly things, nature would not be vitiated, but extinct. Moreover, it cannot, even if endowed with the most excellent arts and all the sciences of mortal learning, be justified of itself, because it uses badly its goods, in which, without the worship of the true God, it is convinced of impiety and uncleanness; and he is accused whence he thinks he is sustained. Since, therefore, Paul declares that 'from the works of the Law, no flesh shall be justified,'[9] and since 'in Christ neither circumcision availeth anything, nor uncircumcision, but the new creature,'[10] why does that man construct the impious liberty of the unfaithful upon natural goods, and endeavor to justify it from its own beginnings? Why does he declare that a bare and sinful knowledge is apt for a renewal of the injured '*oldness*'?[11] As if that knowledge, whether possessed as a remnant of the resources of nature, or sought

8 Eccli. 24.5.
9 Rom. 3.20.
10 Gal. 6.15.
11 Rom. 7.6.

from a learning in the teaching of the Law, could grant from its own discernment that we know what must be done and love to do it! Or as if there were any motion of a good will except what the inspiration of charity, poured forth by the Holy Spirit, [12] has created! 'Without faith it is impossible to please.'[13] And: 'For all that is not faith is sin.'[14] And: 'in Christ Jesus neither circumcision availeth anything, nor uncircumcision; but faith that worketh by charity.'[15]

Chapter 11

(1) Thereafter, at the end of the witnesses, with which he tried to prove that these who in the Prophet's rebuke are called deaf and blind[1] can from the capacity of nature both open their ears to hear and their eyes to see—as if the Lord does not speak of those same ones: 'And I will give them [another] heart, and [I will give] them a new spirit; and I will take away the stony heart out of their flesh, and will give them a heart of flesh, that they may walk in My commandments, and keep My judgments, and do them—'[2] he adds: 'And then to signify that the power for good was in them, he rebuked them: "And," he said, "why even of yourselves, do you not judge that which is just?"[3] He would not have said this to them unless he had known that they could discern by a natural judgment what is right.'[4] In fact, he ascribes to the free will not only the will of, but also the

12 Rom. 5.5.
13 Heb. 11.6.
14 Rom. 14.23.
15 Gal. 5.6.

1 Isa. 42.18.
2 Ezech. 11.19.
3 Luke 12.57.
4 Cassian, *op. cit.* 12.5 (*CSEL*, p. 379).

power for, good: just as understanding, therefore, is required of them, justice is also demanded, because they can produce these from the goods of nature without the gifts of God. But man was charged with those things, so that, from the very precept by which what he received was imposed upon him, he might acknowledge it to have been lost by his own sin, and that it is not, therefore, an iniquitous requirement that he is not capable of rendering what he owes. Rather, let him flee from the letter which kills to the spirit which gives life, and let him seek from grace the capacity which he does not find in nature. If he does this, great is God's mercy; if not, the penalty of sin is just.

(2) Then, to complete the foregoing discussion, in a statement according to his rule, he makes this assertion: 'Wherefore, we must beware lest we refer all the merits of the saints to God in such a way that we ascribe only what is evil and perverse to human nature.'[5] What could be stated more clearly, more expressly in accordance with the invention of Pelagius and Celestius by any of their disciples? They say that the grace of God is given according to our merits; likewise, they say that the grace of God is not given for individual acts. This man has included within one statement both blasphemies, saying: 'Wherefore, we must beware lest we refer all the merits of the saints to God in such a way that we ascribe only what is evil and perverse to human nature.' He means, therefore, that there are many of man's own merits which are not conferred by the bounty of grace, to which are owed the gifts from above, for the increase of natural riches. He means that we do not receive the grace of God for individual acts; hence, that we do not always pray for every good work. Thus, as a consequence, we need

5 *Ibid.*

not believe that in the gifts of God there is no merit, seeing that he is without merit whom God always aids in all things; or even if in those things which God bestows some merits are obtained, it is also clear that they could have been acquired by his own power, and that, therefore, it is necessary that we be aided in some things, so that what was not impossible by nature may be more ably done by grace. Lo and behold, then, there is in those few words a manifold combination of not only two, but of many, impieties, which, if treated with the discernment of a more painstaking care, it would be shown to be in no way free from the chain of the condemned error!

Chapter 12

(1) Lest we appear to act on suspicion, and to dig into hidden meanings not warranted by the words, let the sequence elucidate the content of what is known. He who, in the beginning of his disputation, had said: 'The beginning not only of our acts, but also of our good thoughts, is from God. He it is who inspires in us the beginnings of a holy will and gives us the power and capacity to carry out those things which we rightly desire,[1] now intending to prove that religious thoughts and holy counsels can come from natural wisdom without divine inspiration, sets down the words of Solomon, who said: 'And David my Father would have built a house to the name of the Lord, the God of Israel. And the Lord said to David my Father: Whereas thou hast thought in thy heart to build a house to My name, thou hast done well in having this same thing in mind. Nevertheless, thou shalt not build Me a house.'[2] Then: 'Must it be said therefore

1 Cf. Chapter 2, n. 6, above.
2 3 Kings 8.17.

that this thought and consideration of David was good and from God, or evil and from himself? For, if that thought was good and from God, why is its execution denied by Him who inspired it? If, however, it was evil and from man, why did the Lord praise it? It remains, therefore, that it be believed to have been both good and from man. And in this way also we can judge daily our thoughts. For it was not conceded to David alone to think good from himself, nor is it denied to us ever to be able naturally to savor or think anything good.'[3]

(2) It cannot in any way be proved by this testimony and argument that pious thoughts are begotten of the free will alone, and not of divine inspiration. For the will of David, which was good, must not be considered as not from God, because the Lord desired a temple built for himself, not by David, but by his son. We must ask, therefore, from what Spirit that affection of the will proceeded, namely, in that divine pronouncement in which he said: 'If I shall enter into the tabernacle of my house; if I shall go up into the bed wherein I lie: if I shall give sleep to my eyes, or slumber to my eyelids, or rest to my temples: until I find out a place for the Lord, a tabernacle for the God of Jacob.'[4] Although the Prophet desired it, he was well aware that the true and perfect temple was to be built by Him who, although He was the Son of God, became also the Son of David. And He, when He saw the temple built by Solomon, said: 'Destroy this temple, and in three days I will raise it up. But He spoke of the temple of His body.'[5] That this temple, therefore, formed in Christ and in the Church, be prefigured, it was fitting that David was not chosen to build it, but rather his

3 Cassian, *op. cit.* 12.6 (*CSEL,* p. 380).
4 Ps. 139.3.
5 John 2.19.

son, in order that the Son of God and man might be signified through the son of man, and that the incorruptible tabernacle be indicated through the destructible temple. The will of David was approved to establish this figure, and the execution was transferred to him whose person was better fitted for the figure. Thus, both the will of David to build was from God, and it was from God that Solomon did the building.

(3) That this may be more apparent by examples, let us examine where God did not want done what men wished to do, if God were willing. The Lord commanded the Apostles, saying: 'Going therefore, teach ye all nations; baptizing them in the name of the Father, and of the Son, and of the Holy Ghost. Teaching them to observe all things, whatsoever I have commanded you.'[6] When the Apostles heard this, they doubtless did not receive the bare words through the bodily sounds on external ears only, but by virtue of the living word an inextinguishable flame of charity was enkindled in their hearts, by which they most ardently desired to preach the Gospel of Christ to all peoples. But when 'they were forbidden to preach the word in Asia,' and when 'they attempted to go into Bithynia,'[7] they were prevented by the Spirit of Jesus, did they not have this will from God that they also desired to convert to the faith the hearts of those whom by a hidden judgment God was unwilling at that time to hear the Gospel? Or the fact that the Church daily prays for its enemies, that is, for those who have not yet believed in God, does she not do this from the Spirit of God? Who would say this except he who does not do so, or he who thinks that faith is not a gift of God? Yet, what is sought for all is not obtained for all.

6 John 28.19.
7 Acts 16.6.

There is no injustice in God, who does not always grant the things asked, for which He has given the power to ask.

(4) We must not deny that the good will, by which one adheres to God, belongs to man, but we must admit that it is received by divine inspiration. For since 'none is good but God alone,'[8] what kind of good will there be, which does not have a good author? To human nature, indeed, whose Creator is God, even after the Fall there remain the substance, form, life, senses and reason and the other goods of body and soul, which not even the evil and the vicious lack; but in these it does not have the attainment of the true good, which can make mortal life upright, but cannot bestow eternal life. For it is well known how Grecian schools and Roman eloquence and the search of the whole world in the quest of the supreme good, with the most penetrating study and outstanding ability, accomplished nothing by their labor except to become 'vain in their thoughts and their foolish heart was darkened';[9] who to know the truth used themselves as guides. If, therefore, anyone, ashamed of the wretched vanities and foolish deceptions, understands that whatever is embraced in place of the light and the life is darkness and death, and endeavors to withdraw himself from them, that conversion is not of himself, although not without himself. Neither does he strive toward the sources of salvation by his own strength; rather, the hidden and powerful grace of God does this. And, once the embers of earthly opinions and dead works are removed, it awakens the torch of the buried heart and enflames it with the desire of truth; not to make man subject unwillingly, but to make him desirous of subjection; not to draw him in ignorance, but to precede him who understands

8 Luke 18.19.
9 Rom. 1.21.

and follows. The abiding free will, which, indeed, God established with man himself, is turned by the Creator, not himself, from its vanities and cupidities into which it had fallen once it neglected the Law of God. Consequently, whatever is bettered in him is not without him who is healed, but is from Him alone who heals, whose new creature and new creation we are, 'created in Christ Jesus in good works, which God has prepared, that we should walk in them.'[10]

Chapter 13

(1) Now let us see whither the efforts of the disputant are leading. He says: 'It cannot, therefore, be doubted that the seeds of virtue are naturally in every soul, placed there by the Creator's favor. But, unless these are aroused by the help of God, they will not come to the increase of perfection, since, according to the blessed Apostle: "Neither he that planteth is anything nor he that watereth; but God that giveth the increase."[1] But even the book of the so-called Shepherd[2] very openly teaches that freedom of the will in man is found on every side. In this book, two angels are said to be attached to each one of us; namely, one good and one bad. The free will is said to consist in man's choice to elect which one to follow. For this reason, the free will always remains in man, because he can either despise or cherish the grace of God.'[3] If it cannot be doubted that the seeds of virtue are naturally in every soul, placed there by the Creator's favor, then only Adam sinned, and in his sin, no one sinned; we were not

10 Eph. 2.10.

1 1 Cor. 3.7.
2 Shepherd of Hermas, Mandate 6.2, in *The Fathers of the Church* (New York 1947) I 268.
3 Cassian, *op. cit.* 12.7 (*CSEL*, p. 381).

conceived in iniquity and our mothers did not bear us in sin;[4] we were not by nature children of wrath, nor were we under the power of darkness; rather, are we born children of light and peace, with the virtues naturally abiding in us. God forbid that the insidious deception of a fallacious doctrine beset pious souls! Virtues cannot dwell with vices. The Apostle says: 'For what participation hath justice with injustice? Or what fellowship hath light with darkness?'[5] Virtue is, indeed, in its source God, for whom to have virtue is nothing else than to be Virtue. When we share in it, Christ dwells in us, who is "the power of God, and the wisdom of God."[6] Faith, hope, charity, continence, understanding, counsel, fortitude and the other virtues dwell in us, and, when we depart from this good, all things arise contrariwise for us from ourselves. For, when beauty departs, what save ugliness takes its place? When wisdom leaves, what save folly finds a home? When justice does not reign, what save injustice rules?

(2) And so the seeds of the virtues, which were inserted by the favor of the Creator, have been lost by the sin of the first parent and they cannot be had unless He who gave them restore them. For human nature is transformable by its Maker and is capable of those things which it had; consequently, through the Mediator between God and man, the man Jesus Christ, he can recover, in that very thing which is left to him, what he lost. There is left to him a rational soul, which is not virtue, but the dwelling place of virtue. From a participation in wisdom and justice and mercy, we are not wisdom, or justice or mercy, but wise, just and merciful. Although what is rational in us is possessed by vices and the unclean spirit enters the temple of God when we sin, nevertheless

4 Cf. Ps. 50.7.
5 2 Cor. 6.14.
6 1 Cor. 1.24.

these goods can flow again into what is rational, through Him who 'casts out the prince of this world,'[7] and, binding the strong man, seizes his vessels and, having put to flight the spirit of this world, gives the Spirit, which is from God, 'that we may know the things that are given us from God.'[8] Now, he who has 'not the Spirit of Christ, he is none of his.'[9]

(3) I think man is deceived by a likeness of truth and is led astray into the appearance of false virtues, when he imagines that those goods, which could be had only from the divine bounty, are also found in the souls of the impious. Since, indeed, many of them pursue justice, temperance, continence and benevolence, all of which they neither vainly nor uselessly possess, they attain from those virtues much honor and glory in this life; but, because of their zeal for them they serve not God, but the Devil; although they do have the temporal reward of an empty praise, nevertheless, these false virtues do not lead to that truth which belongs to the blessed virtues. Thus, it is very evident that virtue does not dwell in the souls of the impious, but all their works are unclean and polluted, not having a spiritual but an animal wisdom, not a heavenly but an earthly wisdom, not Christian wisdom but diabolic, not from the Father of lights but from the Prince of darkness; whereas they do not have those things unless God give them, they are subject to him who first deserted God.

(4) What, then, does he who says that the seeds of the virtues are naturally in every soul, without any question of grace, strive to show except that from those seeds the sprouts of preceding merits give birth to the grace of God? Then, to appear to grant something to grace, he says: 'These seeds cannot reach the increase of perfection unless aroused by

7 John 12.31.
8 1 Cor. 2.12.
9 Rom. 8.9.

the help of God';[10] consequently, the help of God is an exhortation and teaching; the mind, however, which is rich with the seeds of virtues, uses the faculty which it possesses only to be aided to attain the heights of those virtues whose beginning it knows to be in itself. Therefore, according to him, the human soul is so built into a temple of God that it may not receive a foundation than which 'no man can lay another, which is Christ Jesus.'[11] But, when is this foundation begun except when faith is generated in the heart of him who listens? And if this was naturally in it, nothing is begun there; rather, it is a superstructure. He, who had faith before he believed, wrongly appeared as an unbeliever. And this also must be said concerning the sources of the other virtues which grace must increase, since they already exist, not give, because they are lacking. But, all the texts of Sacred Scripture teach us something else. We read that the beginning of wisdom is fear of the Lord;[12] we also read that this virtue is a gift of God.[13] 'The fear of God,' he says, 'hath set itself above all things. Blessed is the man to whom it is given to have the fear of God.'[14] Since, therefore, the fear of God is the beginning of wisdom, and this virtue can be had without wisdom, to whom belongs the beginning of fear? The blessed Apostle Peter says: 'Grace to you and peace be accomplished in the knowledge of God, and of Christ Jesus our Lord,' who has now given 'us all things of his divine power, which appertain to life and godliness.'[15] Does he say: 'who has excited in us by His help the seeds of virtues which we had naturally implanted'? Rather, he says:

10 Cassian, *op. cit.* 12.7 (*CSEL*, p. 380).
11 1 Cor. 3.11.
12 Cf. Prov. 1.7.
13 Cf. Prov. 9.10.
14 Eccli. 25.14.
15 2 Pet. 1.2.

'Who now has given us all things which pertain to life and godliness.'[16] And in saying this, of what virtue has he placed the beginning in nature, which was not conferred by Him who gave all things?[17] Wherefore, St. Paul also says: 'For what hast thou that thou hast not received? And if thou hast received, why dost thou glory as if thou hadst not received?'[18]

(5) We have, therefore, everything pertaining to life and godliness, not through nature, which is vitiated, but we have received it through grace by which nature is healed. We ought not think, therefore, that the beginnings of virtue are in our natural treasury, because many praiseworthy things are also found in the endowments of the impious. And those, indeed, come from nature; but, because they have departed from Him who made nature, they cannot be virtues. For, what is illumined by light is light, and what lacks the same light is night. 'For the wisdom of this world is foolishness with God.'[19] Thus, what is thought to be virtue is vice, since that which is thought to be wisdom is folly. But, how is it possible that they who glory in the seeds of the natural virtues, which he extols, will subject those very virtues of theirs, which are to be promoted, to that doctrine which says: 'if any man among you seem to be wise, let him become a fool that he may be wise,'[20] and: 'Seeing that in the wisdom of God the world by wisdom knew not God, it pleased God, by the foolishness of our preaching, to save them that believe'?[21]

What would that presumption of knowledge and wisdom consider more foolish and ridiculous, if the Spirit of God did not subdue the snobbery of the proud, and did not destroy

16 *Ibid.*
17 Cf. 1 Cor. 12.6.
18 1 Cor. 4.7.
19 1 Cor. 3.19.
20 1 Cor. 3.18.
21 1 Cor. 1.21.

by the power of His grace those reasons which, along with the abusive flow of language, are contrary to the truth which is unknown to them, so that the seed of the Word might conceive in the cultivated earth of the heart, and bring forth by the divine husbandry fruits worthy of the eternal granaries?

(6) Following after that unauthoritative testimony inserted into his discussions from the book of the Shepherd, by which he wanted to show, notwithstanding the contrary persuasions of the good and bad angel, that every man was so entrusted to his own judgment and discernment that there was no more protection for him from God than danger from the Devil, he added the rule of his proposition, saying: 'And, therefore, there always remains in man his free will, which can either despise or cherish the grace of God? In this statement, even what he says to the effect that the free will always remains in man is not clear from some angles, since many thousands of infants taken into the Kingdom of God or excluded from the Kingdom of God either receive or lose the grace of God without any choice of their will, and many, completely senseless in every regard and fools, are freed by the sacrament of regeneration from the chains of eternal death. But, let us understand this statement thus, that the proposition may properly apply to those who can use the free will. Is that liberty so free that it has as much pleasure in cherishing the grace of God as it has distastefulness in spurning it? Thus, has no breath of noonday heat melted the icy hardness of the old faithlessness and has the sluggishness of the mind, benumbed by its coldness, grown warm? In the words of the Lord: 'I came to cast fire on the earth,'[22] has no spark come to the cold heart and the dead ashes of themselves burst into a flame of charity? No such thing has hap-

22 Luke 12.49.

pened in those lovers of grace, as they have experienced who said: 'Was not our heart burning within us' while we were with Him 'in the way, and He opened to us the Scriptures?'[23] But, neither did there take place in them what happened in Lydia, to the seller of purple of the city of Thyatira, who, among the women to whom the Apostle preached there, alone at that time is evinced to have believed; 'whose heart,' he said, 'the Lord opened to attend to those things which were said by Paul.'[24] According to him [Cassian], so great is the soundness and capability of the free will that charity, which is at the summit of all virtues, is possessed not from the divine bounty, but from the will alone. What, then, has been repaired in the soul by its builder? Or by what boon of grace will it become more beautiful, if those things are its own, without which the gifts can be of no advantage? But the Apostle, who asserts that, without charity, the working of miracles, knowledge, faith, prophecy, the distribution of riches, the bearing of the most cruel of torments, are of no avail,[25] does not refrain from telling whence comes charity. He says: 'Because the charity of God is poured forth in our hearts, by the Holy Ghost, Who is given us.'[26] And, he says: 'Peace be to the brethren and charity with faith, from God the Father, and the Lord Jesus Christ.'[27] St. John the Apostle also instructs us on the beginnings of our participation in this good. He says: 'Dearly beloved, let us love one another, for charity is of God.'[28] And, lest we might therefore think that love is said to be from God, because this seed was planted in

23 Luke 24.32.
24 Acts 16.14.
25 Cf. 1 Cor. 13.2.
26 Rom. 5.5.
27 Eph. 6.23.
28 1 John 4.7.

the nature of man, a little later he says: 'Not as though we had loved God, because God hath first loved us.'[29] And again: 'Let us love God, because God hath first loved us.'[30] Let human poverty admit that what is rightly said of any good whatsoever is much more rightly said of Him without whom all good things are of no avail. 'What hast thou, that thou hast not received? And if thou hast received, why dost thou glory, as if thou hadst not received?'[31]

Chapter 14

(1) Since he had attributed as much to man before grace as he can profitably have through grace, he afterwards added some vague and confused statements to demonstrate the strength of the free will. And, along with those things which he now commits to the energies given to it, he endeavors to strengthen those which he declares are naturally in it; so that to have perfected it is through the help of God; to have begun it is from the liberty of the free will. But let us pass over these as tolerable, since we also say that the free will has conceived, through the operation of grace, the affection for a good will and the beginning of faith, so that, through what is given to it without any previous merit, it merits those things which have been promised to the one who will carry them into effect; always seeking the ability to do anything good from Him who says: 'without Me you can do nothing.'[1]

With this preface, let us examine what he claims concerning the sufferings of the holy Job. He says: 'And we read that the divine justice made provision for this even in the case of the most upright Job, His champion, when the Devil sought him out for single combat. For, if he had fought

29 1 John 4.10.
30 1 John 4.19.
31 1 Cor. 4.7.

1 John 15.5.

against the Enemy, not with his own strength but under the protection of the grace of God alone, and supported by the divine help alone, without any virtue of his patience, he would have borne those multiple burdens of temptations demanded with the full cruelty of the enemy, and the injuries; how is it that the Devil did not repeat quite justly against him those slanderous words which he had previously uttered? "Does Job (worship) God in vain? Hast not Thou made a fence for him, and his house, and all his substance round about? But stretch forth Thy hand a little," that is, permit him to pit his strength against me, "and see if he blesseth Thee not to Thy face."[2] But, since the slanderous enemy dared not repeat such an accusation, he confesses that he was beaten, not by the strength of God but of Job. But it must also be believed that the grace of God was not totally lacking to him, which gave as much power to the tempter as He knew Job had the power of resisting him; He did not protect him from the Devil's onslaughts in such a way that no place was left for human strength; rather, He looked after him only to this extent that the very violent enemy, by taking away reason from his soul and rendering him powerless to sense, might not overpower him with an unequal and unjust weight in battle.'[3]

(2) Who would believe that this was preached by Catholics among Catholics, if what is often maintained, even written, in private conversations were not read? Is the vision of the intelligence in all men so darkened, and has the spirit of knowledge and piety deserted every son of the Church, that they are not ashamed to impose such dishonest lies upon the judgment of readers? Outstanding man, wise teacher, truth-

---

2 Job 1.9ff.

3 Cassian, *op. cit.* 14.1 (*CSEL,* p. 384).

ful master, give us the Catholic definition with which you laid claim to our ears and minds at the beginning of your disputation. You stated the faith of the Church in Christian words: 'The beginning, not only of our acts, but also of our good thoughts, is from God, who inspires within us both the beginnings of a holy will and gives us the power and capacity to carry out those things which we rightly desire. "Every best gift and every perfect gift is from above, coming down from the Father of lights." He it is who begins in us what is good and likewise accomplishes and fulfills it.'[4] You shattered with the soundness of this statement every device of the hostile remnants. Why, after changing your profession, do you build up what you have demolished, impugn what you maintained? Why, having deserted the citadel of unconquerable truth, do you hasten apace to the Pelagian precipice? For you, who have declared that neither the beginnings of holy thoughts, nor pious wills, nor good acts are from us, but that all good things in us are generated and made to progress and come to perfection by the inspiration of God and the help of His grace, a little afterwards begin to equate the endeavors of the free will to the gifts of grace. Consequently, you showed that man can have of himself the beginnings, which you have attributed to God. You say: 'Man can sometimes by his own activity reach out to a desire of the virtues, but he always needs the Lord's help.'[5] And again: 'Also, the beginnings of a good will sometimes come forth through the bounty of nature bestowed by the beneficence of the Creator, and, unless they are directed by God, they cannot come to the perfection of virtues.'[6] Later, to show that some are 'prevented' by grace, and to place the grace to be

4 *Ibid.* 3.5 (*CSEL,* p. 364).
5 *Ibid.* 9.4 (*CSEL,* p. 373).
6 *Ibid.*

received in the preceding merits of some, you said: 'Which depends on which is a considerable problem: namely, whether God is merciful to us because we have presented the beginning of a good will, or we receive the beginning of a good will because God is merciful.'[7] Not to leave these two rules in doubt, you took the trouble to confirm both with examples, suitable as they appeared to you, establishing one by the constrained conversion of Paul and Matthew, fortifying the other by the voluntary faith of Zachaeus and the thief, whose desire, you say, was so strong that they anticipated the explicit admonitions of their vocation to enter the kingdom of heaven.'[8] Then, in the course of the disputation, to make clear the wholeness of the interior man, you certify that Adam, in fact, conceived a knowledge of evil which he did not have, but did not lose the knowledge of good which he had received. Because you tried to prove this from a comparison of the impious, you have fallen to such lengths as to proclaim: 'We must be careful not to refer all the merits of the saints to God in such a way that we ascribe to human nature only what is evil.'[9] And in order that we might not think that this nature had lost any virtues in the sin of Adam, you declared that the souls of all men are naturally as sound as before the sin of the first man, by saying: 'It cannot therefore be doubted that the seeds of the virtues are naturally in every soul, planted there by the favor of the Creator.'[10] Once these definitions of yours have been examined, there is no dissembling how much you have deviated from the soundness of that declaration in which, by preaching falsely what was to be ascribed to grace, you attempted to win for

7 Cassian, *op. cit.* 11.1 (*CSEL,* p. 375).
8 *Ibid.* (*CSEL,* p. 376).
9 *Ibid.* 12.5 (*CSEL,* p. 379).
10 *Ibid.* 9.5 (*CSEL,* p. 374).

yourself the decision of Catholic ears, which the later passages would easily deceive, because of the negligence begotten of the outward appearance of the foregoing profession.

Chapter 15

(1) Hitherto, not to appear in complete disagreement with the foregoing rule, you transferred the beginnings of virtues and merits from the free will to grace, so as to admit that the voluntary movements themselves of good desires can neither be advanced nor perfected without the help of God. Now, however, God has been moved afar and taken away from the support of man, and you attribute so much power to the free will that he [Job] not only accepts calmly and with equanimity the loss of his many resources and a bitter end to the whole family and relatives at once; but by the determination of the bare will he also overcomes the unspeakable torments of his own body. In order that there be no doubt on your side of the discussion, you set up the example of holy Job, who fought against that extraordinary cruelty of diabolical ferocity without the support of God, and you endeavor to prove by argument that the exceedingly cruel enemy admitted that he was overcome, not by the power of the Lord, but of Job, from the fact that the Devil did not say that the grace of God opposed him in the unusually severe battle. As if that man needed to be protected in his losses and deprivations by the divine protection, but in the torments of his body and soul he did not need to be helped! If, therefore, nothing among the psalms of the saints is found more worthy or more illustrious, this greatness of soul, which the penalty imposed by each and every pressure of so many forms of death does not conquer—and you state that it comes from human strength alone—what praise and merit will there

be which the liberty of the will cannot obtain amid peaceful and quiet studies? And this liberty you have crowned at the end of so great a struggle with its own powers.

(2) I ask you, therefore, does that man seem to you to have had within him the Holy Spirit, when he was tested by those tortures about which we have read? If you say that he had, it is certain that God helps him, from whom he has not departed; if, however, you say that the Holy Spirit deserted him, the prophetic speech of the same man accuses you. It reads: 'For I know that my Redeemer liveth, and in the last day I shall rise out of the earth. And I shall be clothed again with my skin, and in my flesh I shall see my God. Whom I myself shall see, and my eyes shall behold, and not another; this my hope is laid up in my bosom.'[1] If what was foretold concerning the Incarnation of our Lord Jesus Christ, and the Resurrection of Him who is the 'first fruits of them that sleep,'[2] and the hope of Redemption, which is placed in Him for all the saints, is rightly understood, it is manifestly clear that the grace of God did not desert His people and that the Lord performed in His holy one already at that time what He promised to do afterwards in His apostles and martyrs, saying: 'But when they shall deliver you up, take no thought how or what you speak, for it shall be given to you in that hour what to speak. For it is not you who speak, but the Spirit of your Father that speaketh in you.'[3] And, what about the reply of the holy one to the foolish comforters? Was he not trusting in the help of God, when he says: 'He that is mocked by his friends as I, shall call upon God and He will hear him'?[4] Or was he unaware that what he had, he had

1 Job 19.25.
2 1 Cor. 15.20.
3 Matt. 10.19.
4 Job 12.4.

from Him, of whom he says: 'With Him is wisdom and strength, He hath counsel and understanding'?[5] And of whom he says: 'In whose hand is the soul of every living thing and the spirit of all flesh of man'?[6] And again he says: 'I expect until my change come. Thou shalt call me, and I will answer Thee; to the work of thy hands Thou shalt reach out Thy right hand. Thou indeed hast numbered my steps, but spare my sins, Thou hast sealed up my offences, as it were in a bag, but thou hast cured my iniquity.'[7] The Lord, therefore, did not desert him whom He was looking after; nor did He withdraw His bounty from him, to whom he brought the purifying remedies, by which he might shine with greater splendor.

(3) For this endurance of sufferings by which the holy man distinguished himself, he was also prepared by the Lord, who said: 'For though I should walk in the midst of the shadow of death, I will fear no evils, for Thou art with me.'[8] And also: 'But the salvation of the just is from the Lord, and He is their protector in the time of trouble.'[9] For this endurance he was also prepared by the Lord; and he referred both belief in Christ and suffering for Christ to Christ, saying: 'Being justified therefore by faith, let us have peace with God, through Our Lord Jesus Christ: By Whom also we have access through faith into this grace, wherein we stand, and glory in the hope of the glory of the sons of God. And not only so; but we glory also in tribulations, knowing that tribulation worketh patience; and patience trial; and trial hope; and hope confoundeth not: because the charity of God is poured forth in our hearts, by the Holy Ghost, Who is given

5 Job 12.13.
6 Job 12.10.
7 Job 14.14ff.
8 Ps. 22.4.
9 Ps. 36.39.

to us.'[10] And again: 'Who then shall separate us from the love of Christ? Shall tribulations? or distress? or famine? or nakedness? or danger? or persecution? or the sword? (As it is written:) For Thy sake we are put to death all the day long. We are accounted as sheep for the slaughter.'[11] 'But in all these things we overcome, because of Him that hath loved us.'[12] The sources of the fortitude and the forbearance blessed Peter, and in him the whole Church, learned by the words of Truth itself, saying: 'Behold Satan hath desired to have you, that he may sift you as wheat. But I have prayed for thee, that thy faith fail not.'[13] Whoever does not fail in tribulations, therefore, should not doubt that he is aided by Him to whom the hearts of all the faithful cry out daily: 'Lead us not into temptation, but deliver us from evil,'[14] since 'the Lord preserveth the souls of His saints, He will deliver them out of the hand of the sinner.'[15]

(4) But, regarding what you say: 'That it must be understood thereby that the grace of God wholly departed from Job, because God gave to the tempter as much power to tempt as He knew he had power to resist,'[16] would you not have more correctly and truly spoken, if, when you said: 'as He knew he had the power to resist,' you had rather said: as He knew He had given him power to resist? For, in the correction of those words, you would soberly measure that whole glory which you wished. to attribute to human strength, so that the marvellous patience in so great an affliction would have been attributed to both the help of God and the free

10 Rom. 5.1ff.
11 Ps. 47.32.
12 Rom. 8.35ff.
13 Luke 22.31.
14 Matt. 6.13.
15 Ps. 96.10.
16 Cassian, *op. cit.* 14.2 (*CSEL*, p. 385).

will. But you feared to lessen the praise of human nature, if you admitted that the strength was given him by God. Therefore, you do not wish it believed that God was a co-operator at Job's battle and victory, but rather only a spectator. Consequently, he whom you are able to persuade that so a severe battle was won through the natural capability of the free will dares not doubt that in less severe cases the effects of the good will are much more free; thus, he falls into the pit of that condemned statement which asserts that the grace of justification is given us, so that what we are ordered to do through the free will we may the more easily accomplish through grace. As though, even if grace were not given, we could, nevertheless, even without it, fulfill the divine commandments, although not easily! Because the Catholic pontiffs deemed this worthy of condemnation, we must use the testimony they used. They said:[17] 'The Lord was speaking of the fruits of the commandments, where He does not say: without Me you can do something with difficulty; rather, He says: 'Without Me you can do nothing.'[18]

Chapter 16

(1) To these propositions of yours, which you believed to be fortified with suitable authority, as though sure of the consent of the readers, you add that God, in order to demonstrate our faith, sometimes is wont to offer more than is sufficient, so that it may be acknowledged how strong the faith of believers is. And you show this by the example of the centurion, who, when he asked for a cure of his servant and the Lord promised that He would go to his home, replied: 'I am not worthy that Thou shouldst enter under my roof;

17 Denzinger, *op. cit.,* no. 105.
18 John 15.5.

but only say the word, and my servant shall be healed.'[1] The Lord praised him for this with such admiration that He claimed that He had not 'found so great faith in Israel.'[2] And you confirm, by means of a trifling conclusion, almost the whole Pelagian opinion, by saying: 'For he would have had neither praise nor merit, if Christ had revealed in him what He Himself gave.'[3] Therefore, it was falsely written that man can be continent, except God give it.[4] The Apostle preached falsely when he spoke of the same virtue, saying: 'For I would that all men were even as myself; but every one hath his proper gift from God; one after this manner, and another after that.'[5] He also taught falsely, who said: 'But if any of you want wisdom, let him ask of God; and it shall be given him.'[6] And it was not truthfully spoken: 'Every best gift, and every perfect gift, is from above, coming down from the Father of lights.'[7] And: 'A man cannot receive anything, unless it be given him from heaven.'[8] Perhaps it must be said that all the virtues are to be numbered among the gifts of God, but that man is praiseworthy in those which he had of his own, and that there are merits there, where the gifts of God were not. Therefore, according to your rule, those to whom it was given not only to believe in Christ, but also to suffer for Him, have lost both praise and merit; nor do they have true glory, who glory not in themselves, but in the Lord. But we hear the Prophet, who says more correctly: 'Cursed be the man that trusteth in man, and maketh flesh his arm,

1 Matt. 8.8.
2 Matt. 8.10.
3 Cassian, *op. cit.* 14.4 (*CSEL,* p. 385).
4 Cf. Wisd. 8.21.
5 1 Cor. 7.7.
6 James 1.5.
7 James 1.17.
8 John 3.27.

and whose heart departeth from the Lord.'[9] And him who says: 'I will love Thee, O Lord, my strength.'[10] And: 'In the Lord shall my soul be praised,'[11] and 'The Lord is my strength and my praise.'[12] This is said that we may know very clearly that they have neither praise nor merit, in whom is not found what is had only by the gift of the Lord.

(2) And so, you thought you could engender from the testimony of a lauded faith a disadvantage for the gifts of grace; as if, where faith is held up for praise, it were not taught that the faith is given! The Apostle praises the faith of the Romans and gives thanks to God for this good, saying: 'First I give thanks to my God, through Jesus Christ, for you all, because your faith is spoken of in the whole world.'[13] He writes to the Corinthians in like vein, saying: 'I give thanks to my God always for you, for the grace of God that is given you in Christ Jesus, that in all things you are made rich in Him, in all utterance and in all knowledge.'[14] Did he, by giving thanks to God, take away praise from the believers? Or did he, by praising the believers, deny the Author of merit? Let us hear what he thought about the faith of the Ephesians. He says: 'Wherefore I also, hearing of your faith that is in the Lord Jesus, and your love towards all the Saints, cease not to give thanks for you, making commemoration of you in my prayers, that the God of our Lord Jesus Christ, the Father of Glory, may give unto you the spirit of wisdom and of revelation in the knowledge of Him; the eyes of your heart enlightened.'[15] Therefore,

9 Jer. 17.5.
10 Ps. 17.1.
11 Ps. 33.3.
12 Ps. 117.14.
13 Rom. 1.8.
14 1 Cor. 1.4.
15 Eph. 1.15ff.

they had faith; they also had the works of charity, which could lack neither praise nor merit; but the Apostle does not cease to give thanks to God for these virtues, knowing that these gifts came from the Father of lights. And from Him he declares that he also asks that to whom He gave faith, which works through charity, He give the spirit of wisdom and understanding. Thence, the Ephesians might know that they received what they have; and from Him they learn to hope for what they do not have. He gives like thanks for the Philippians, and does not remain silent concerning their merit and praise. He says: 'I give thanks to my God in every remembrance of you, always in all my prayers making supplication for you all with joy; for your communication in the Gospel of Christ from the first day until now. Being confident of this very thing, that He, Who hath begun a good work in you, will perfect it unto the day of Christ Jesus.'[16] And is the cause of this human praise and merit here and now discontinued in God? What virtue or piety has been received, which has not flowed from the fountain of grace, when both the beginning and the fulfillment of the good work from the start to finish is attributed to the Lord? Concerning whose holy ones there is sung: 'They shall walk, O Lord, in the light of Thy countenance, and in Thy name they shall rejoice all the day, and in Thy justice they shall be exalted. For Thou art the glory of their strength.'[17]

Chapter 17

(1) In this declaration of yours, there must be taken carefully into consideration how much you help those who say

---

16 Phil. 1.3ff.
17 Ps. 88.16ff.

that the grace of God is given according to our merits;[1] nevertheless, in order to find shelter under the shadow of the Catholic faith, you claim these to be irreligious in their opinion. You say: 'But let no one think that these things have been uttered by us in an attempt to teach that the sum total of salvation consists in the endowments of our faith in accordance with the impious opinion of some, who ascribe all to the free will and declare that the grace of God is dispensed according to the merit of each one.'[2] I am quite in wonder how you do not see or think that it is not seen by others, because you condemn yourself from your own mouth. For, by saying that 'the centurion, whose faith was praised by the Lord's words, would have had neither praise nor merit if he excelled in that which God Himself had given,' you declared that the centurion had a faith that was not given, but, rather, was his own. As if nothing had been conferred upon its beginnings through grace, but that he was the cause of both praise and merit in the same faith; neither of which he would have had if the Lord had not conferred that, to which there is due both praise and merit! To avoid the perniciousness of the condemned error, you vainly deny that the whole of salvation consists in the endowments of our faith, since in no way can there be salvation except from faith. For 'the just man liveth by faith.'[3] Truth says: 'Amen, amen, I say unto you, that he who heareth My word and believeth Him that sent Me, hath life everlasting; and cometh not into judgment, but is passed from death to life.'[4] And again: 'This is the will of My Father that sent Me: that every one who seeth the Son, and believeth in Him, may

1 *Epistola I Pelagii ad Demetriadem* 3 (*PL* 30.18D).
2 Cf. St. Augustine, *De haeresibus* 87 (*PL* 42.48).
3 Rom. 1.17.
4 John 5.24.

have life everlasting, and I will raise him up on the last day.'[5] And again: 'now this is eternal life: that they may know Thee, the only true God, and Jesus Christ, Whom Thou hast sent.'[6] Since it is clear, then, that the eternal and happy life is prepared for this faith, which you have accordingly honored with merits and praises, because you prefer that it be numbered among the goods of the free will rather than among the gifts of God, how do you avoid this wound with which you are transfixed when you say that they are impious who declare that grace is dispensed according to human merits, and when you affirm that it is clear that they have neither praise nor merit who are faithful from the gift of grace? Wherever you betake yourself, therefore, you are conquered and ensnared by your own efforts. For, if merits do not precede grace, and if faith cannot be without merits, then, faith does not precede grace. Whatever the source of merit, it is totally from grace; and this is not had anterior to grace.

Chapter 18

(1) Therefore, to avoid the appearance of self-contradiction in your absurd declaration, you endeavor to intrude what is incongruous and (with a new boldness) divide the unity of the members of the body of Christ into two kinds of faithful. In one, namely, to whom belongs what you said in the beginning: 'the beginning, not only of our acts, but also of our good thoughts, is from God. He it is who begins in us what is good and likewise fulfills and accomplishes it.'[1] And in another, those whom that rule fits, in which you say

5 John 6.40.
6 John 17.3.

1 Cassian, *op. cit.* 3.5 (*CSEL,* p. 364).

that 'the centurion would have had neither praise nor merit, if he excelled in that which God Himself had given.'[2] Although you conduct the whole text of your discussion toward these two formulae, which can in no way be reconciled, now, however, you more clearly and expressly state what you wanted to establish, saying: 'through these examples, therefore, which we have set forth from the Gospel monuments, we have been able to observe very clearly in diverse, innumberable and inscrutable ways that God procures the salvation of the human race and that He incites to greater fervor the course of some who are willing and eager, and, indeed, even compels some who are unwilling and resisting. Now, also, He gives the help to accomplish those things which He has seen us desire with utility. Again, He also inspires the principles of the holy desire itself, and gives either the beginning of the good work or perseverance in it. Hence it is that, when we pray, we proclaim that the Lord is not only Protector and Saviour, but also helper and susceptor. For, in that He first gives the call and attracts us to salvation, even though we are ignorant and unwilling, He is protector and saviour; and in that He is accustomed to give His resources to us while striving, and to take us up and fortify us, He is called susceptor and refuge.'[3]

(2) By this separation, that diversity in one Church will have been ordered, as you state, so that our Lord Jesus Christ, of whom it is said: 'And thou shalt call His name Jesus. For He shall save His people from their sins,'[4] and of whom it was said: 'For there is no other name under heaven given to men, whereby we must be saved,'[5] is not the saviour of all

---

2 *Ibid.* 14.4 (*CSEL,* p. 385).
3 *Ibid.* 17.1-2 (*CSEL,* p. 393).
4 Matt. 1.21.
5 Acts 4.12.

Christians, but of some, and the susceptor of some. Thus, only those are saved whom, turned away and resisting, God had compelled to receive grace. And those are taken up who anticipated their vocation with a fervor and alacrity for the course; upon the former there is conferred a gratuitous gift; to the latter a due reward is paid. The former have neither praise nor merit, who have nothing good except what they have received; but the latter abound in glory and are enriched with a reward, who devoutly of their own strength have offered what they had not received. Thus, Jesus Christ will have found some liberated, and others He will have liberated. Thus, what He says does not pertain to all: 'You have not chosen Me; but I have chosen you,'[6] if there are some by whom He was chosen, although He had not chosen them. Nor does it apply to all: 'No man can come to Me, unless it be given him by My Father,'[7] if there are some who, without the Father giving it, have been able to come to the Son. What the Evangelist says does not apply to all: 'That was the true light, which enlighteneth every man that cometh into this world,'[8] if there are some who either come into this world thus that they were not darkness, or so began to be light that they did not need the illumination of the true light. Again, what the Apostle says is not to be understood of all the adopted: 'Who hath delivered us from the power of darkness, and hath translated us into the kingdom of the Son of His love,'[9] if, indeed, they break their bonds, and, when the yoke of the old captivity has been cast off, they freely and eagerly go out from the sway of the Devil into the Kingdom of God. If these things can be preached within the

6 John 15.16.
7 John 6.66.
8 John 1.9.
9 Col. 1.13.

one Church, so that neither opinion gives way to the other, but each in turn surrenders, it can happen that we accept what the Pelagians hold and the Pelagians accept what we hold. But in this way they will not be as Catholic as we, which God forbid, will be Pelagians. The mixture of contraries is a defection of better things, because, when virtue accepts vice, it departs not from vice, but from virtue.

(3) Therefore, Christian hearts in no way accept what you have attempted to advocate, namely, that they who are what they are by the grace of God have neither praise nor merit, and that a portion of the Christians were saved by Him who came to save what was lost, and part have been taken up. For, the disciples of the evangelical and apostolic teaching, 'not minding high things, but consenting to the humble,'[10] abominated that aberration of haughty pride. In the whole body of the Church and in the individual members, what had been dead was given life; what had been captive was redeemed; what had been blind was illumined; what had been lost was sought; what was wandering was found. But there is not a saviour of some and susceptor of others in accordance with that new division of yours; rather, Christ is both saviour and susceptor of all the faithful, without exception. And they are not deprived of merit and praise who know whence they merit eternal goods, and the happier they become, the less they have of their own, and the more they have of God's. The stupid complaint of the proud does not disturb us, whereby they pretend that the free will is taken away, if the beginnings, the progress and perseverance in good until the end are said to be gifts of God; whereas the help of divine grace is the support of the human will. We pray when we wish; nevertheless, God sent His Spirit into

10 Rom. 12.16.

our hearts, crying 'Abba Father.'[11] We speak when we will; nevertheless, if what we speak is pious, it is not we who speak, but the Spirit of our Father who speaks in us.[12] Willingly we work out our salvation, 'yet it is God Who worketh in us both to will and to accomplish.'[13] We love God and our neighbor willingly, yet 'charity is from God, poured forth into our hearts through the Holy Ghost Who is given us.'[14] This we profess regarding the faith, tolerance of sufferings, conjugal modesty, virginal continence, and all virtues without exception; namely, that, unless they were given us, they would not be found in us; and that the free will, naturally placed in man, remains, but with its quality and circumstances changed through the mediator of God and men, the man Christ Jesus, who turned that very will from what it willed perversely and converted it to what was good for it to will. Thus, when its delight was transformed, its faith purified, its hope raised, its charity enkindled, it took on a free servitude and put off the servile freedom.

Chapter 19

From these propositions hitherto discussed, with some omissions, it is neither hidden nor doubtful what they think about the grace of God, who contradict its most authentic defenders and disturb the peace of the victorious Church, when they resume the petty questions of the condemned school of thought. And if we relate them, as they have come to our ears, our speech will become immoderately long, since, from these which are known to be from their pen, the pious reader may easily understand to what precipices these path-

11 Gal. 4.6.
12 Cf. Matt. 10.20.
13 Phil. 2.13.
14 1 John 4.7; Rom. 5.5.

ways lead, and into what a dirty marsh of muddy banks, whence an abysmal fog exudes. Indeed, I deem it necessary to arrange briefly in order before the end of the volume, and gather together those things which we have shown to be out of conformity with Catholic truth; thus, with our replies interjected, those things which could escape the reader's memory may be more easily recalled when treated together.

First Proposition

You said in your first proposition: 'that the beginning not only of our acts, but also of our good thoughts, is from God; He it is who inspires in us the beginning of a holy will and gives us the power and capacity to carry out those things which we rightly desire. For "every best gift and every perfect gift is from above, coming down from the Father of lights." He it is who begins in us what is good, and likewise accomplishes and fulfills it.'[1] We, too, heartily accept and profess this to be Catholic.

Second Proposition

It was said in the second proposition: 'The divine protection is inseparably with us, and so great is the love of the Creator for His creature that not only does His providence accompany it, but even unceasingly goes before it, and the Prophet admits this from experience. He says: "My God, His mercy shall prevent me."[2] And when He sees in us any beginning of a good will, He illumines it, strengthens it and directs it to salvation, giving increase to that which either He Himself planted, or which He saw come forth from our efforts.'[3]

1 Cassian, *op. cit.* 3.5 (*CSEL,* p. 364).
2 Ps. 58.11.
3 Cassian, *op. cit.* 8.4 (*CSEL,* p. 371).

Here, there already is a departure from the foregoing proposition; what had been attributed wholly to grace is now partially imputed to the free will.

Third Proposition

In the third proposition you asserted: 'What else are we being told except that in all these both the grace of God and the liberty of our will are proclaimed, and also that man can sometimes by his own activity reach out to a desire of the virtues; but he always needs the Lord's help'?[4] As if our physician does not also grant that the sick desire true health!

Fourth Proposition

You asserted in the fourth definition: 'In order that it may be the more evident that the beginnings of a good will sometimes emanate from a good will, through the bounty of nature bestowed by the beneficence of the Creator, and the Apostle is the witness that, unless these beginnings are directed by God, they cannot come to the perfection of virtues, he says: "For to will is present with me; but to accomplish that which is good, I find not." '[5] As if the Apostle, who professes that his sufficiency, even to think, is from God, had a good will from a natural inclination and not from the gift of grace!

Fifth Proposition

In the fifth proposition you state: 'And so these are somewhat indiscriminately mixed up and confused; consequently, which depends on which is a considerable problem: namely, whether God is merciful to us because we have presented the beginning of a good will, or we receive the beginning of

4 *Ibid.* 9.4 (*CSEL,* p. 373).
5 *Ibid.* 9.5 (*CSEL,* p. 374).

a good will because God is merciful. Many, believing these individually, and affirming more than is right, are caught in many and self-contradictory errors. . . . For, if we say that the beginning of a good will is ours, what was it in Paul the persecutor? What was it in the tax collector Matthew? One of whom by the blood and torture of innocent people, the other by brooding upon violence and public robbery, are drawn to salvation. But if, indeed, we say that the beginnings of a good will are always inspired by the grace of God, what about the faith of Zachaeus? What do we say about the piety of that thief upon the cross? They, bringing violence to bear upon the Kingdom of Heaven by their desire, anticipated the explicit admonitions of their vocation.'[6]

Both he who affirms that a good will is born of grace, and he who says that grace depends upon a good will are declared to be in error; yet, both opinions are judged acceptable, whereas the figure of the one in Paul and Matthew, of the other in Zachaeus and the thief, are condemned.

Sixth Proposition

It is said in the sixth proposition: 'For these two, that is, both grace and free will, seem indeed to be contrary to each other; but both are in harmony. And we conclude that because of piety we should accept both, lest, in taking away one of these from man, we appear to violate the Church's rule of faith.'[7]

As if each is to be so understood that in some men the will comes before grace, in others grace precedes the will, and not that in all the will follows grace! For, according to them, if the free will is taken away, when 'prevented' by grace, grace is taken away when it is 'prevented' by the free will.

6 *Ibid.* 11.1-2 (*CSEL,* pp. 375-376).
7 *Ibid.* 11.4 (*CSEL,* p. 377).

Seventh Proposition

You said in the seventh proposition: 'After the Fall, therefore, Adam conceived a knowledge of evil which he did not have; but he did not lose the knowledge of good which he did have.'[8]

Both are false, because Adam by a divine admonition knew in advance how great an evil he must be on guard against, and, when he believed the Devil, he forgot in how great a good he was established. For, just as to be evil is a very bad knowledge of evil, so not to be good is a very bad ignorance of good.

Eighth Proposition

In the eighth definition it was said: 'Wherefore, we must beware lest we refer all the merits of the saints to God in such a way that we ascribe only what is evil and perverse to human nature.'[9]

As if nature were not damned before grace, were not in blindness, not wounded; or as if they whose merits are thence, whence justice, were not gratuitously justified!

Ninth Proposition

'It cannot, therefore, be doubted that the seeds of the virtues are naturally in every soul, placed there by the Creator's favor. But, unless these are aroused by the help of God, they will not come to the increase of perfection.'[10]

Just as if Adam lost none of his spiritual goods by sinning and as if virtues were not given as a possession but as an incitement towards a more ready attainment of perfection!

8 *Ibid.* 12.2 (*CSEL,* p. 378).
9 *Ibid.* 12.5 (*CSEL,* p. 379).
10 *Ibid.* 12.7 (*CSEL,* p. 380).

Tentn Proposition

In the tenth proposition it was asserted: 'And we read that the divine justice made provision for this even in the case of the most upright Job, His champion, when the Devil sought him out for single combat. For, if he had fought against the Enemy, not with his own strength, but under the protection of the grace of God alone, and supported by the divine help alone, without any virtue of his patience, he would have borne those multiple burdens of temptations demanded with the full cruelty of the Enemy, and the injuries; how is it that the Devil did not repeat quite justly against him those slanderous words which he had previously uttered? "Does Job (worship) God in vain? Hast not Thou made a fence for him and his house, and all his substance round about? But stretch forth Thy hand a little," that is, permit him to pit his strength against me, "and see if he blesseth Thee not to Thy face."[11] But, since the slanderous enemy dared not repeat such an accusation, he confesses that he was beaten, not by the strength of God, but of Job. But it must also be believed that the grace of God was not totally lacking to him, which gave as much power to the tempter as He knew Job had the power of resisting him.'[12]

If God only knew what Job could do, and did not also give him the ability, He was a witness, not a helper of his patience. And wherein was the help of grace necessary, if so great a victory was accomplished by human strength alone?

Eleventh Proposition

In the eleventh proposition the faith of the centurion is discussed: 'The Lord marvelled at him and praised him

11 Job 1.9ff.
12 Cassian, *op. cit.* 14.1 (*CSEL,* p. 385).

and extolled him above all those of the people of Israel who believed, saying: I have not "found so great faith in Israel."[13] For he would have had neither praise nor merit, if Christ had revealed in him what He Himself gave.'[14]

It is an impious thought to consider the man to whom God gave nothing happier than him upon whom He has conferred everything.

Twelfth Proposition

In the twelfth proposition it was stated: 'Hence it is that, when we pray, we proclaim that the Lord is not only protector, but also helper and susceptor. For, in that He first gives the call and attracts us to salvation, even though we are ignorant and unwilling, He is protector and saviour; and in that He is accustomed to give His resources to us while striving, and to take up and fortify us, He is called susceptor and refuge.'[15]

Whoever does not wish to have been saved by Christ can give consent to this opinion.

Chapter 20

(1) Accordingly, by these propositions, this is taught, this is written, this is preached in the discussion set forth, that with Adam's sin his soul was not injured, and the source of his sin remained whole in him. If, indeed, he did not lose the knowledge of good which he had received, neither has his posterity lost it, nor did he suffer any loss of it. That the seeds of the virtues are naturally in every soul, placed there by the favor of the Creator, so that he who shall have wished

13 Matt. 8.10.
14 Cassian, *op. cit.* 14.4 (*CSEL,* p. 385).
15 *Ibid.* 17.2 (*CSEL,* p. 393).

can by a natural judgment anticipate the grace of God and merit in advance His help, the more easily to arrive at perfection. That he has neither praise nor merit who is adorned by goods which are not his own but bestowed upon him. That we also must be careful that all the merits of the saints be not referred to God in such a way that human nature itself can do nothing good of itself, since, so great is the integrity of his strength, that he is able to fight against the Devil himself and his ferocity, even to the extremities of torture, without the help of God. And that this power is natural in all men, but not all wish to use the virtues implanted in themselves. That so great is the goodness of the Creator toward all men that He takes up some with praise because they come of their own free will; others, because they resist, are drawn unwillingly; therefore, He is the susceptor of those who come willingly, but the saviour of those who come unwillingly. And, although part of the Church is justified by grace, and part by the free will, they whom nature has carried along are more glorious than those whom grace has freed, because the will is as free for every good work in the posterity of Adam as it was in Adam before the Fall.

Chapter 21

(1) Behold what opinion they teach! In order to corrupt the purity of Catholic minds by calumniating the defenders of grace, they revile with impassioned speech the men of our time who are outstanding in the teaching of the Church. They think that they can tear down every authoritative support, if they shall have beaten down this very strong tower of the pastoral lookout with frequent strokes of the Pelagian battering ram. Indeed, 'the foundation of God stand-

eth firm.'[1] But they do not serve well their factions, for it is fitting that they imitate the madness of those whose opinion they follow. They can only utter what is spread about by the complaints of the condemned and the revilings of the most insolent Julian.[2] The sprouts of one seed are identical; what is hidden in the roots is made manifest in the fruits. Therefore, we must not fight them on a new line of battle, nor are particular engagements to be entered upon as though against an unknown enemy. Then were their engines of war broken, then did they fall to the ground among their proud comrades and leaders, when Innocent of blessed memory struck the heads of the unspeakable errors with the apostolic sword,[3] when the synod of bishops of Palestine constrained Pelagius to pronounce sentence against himself and his followers,[4] when Pope Zozimus of blessed memory joined the weight of his pronouncement to the decrees of the African councils and armed the right hands of all the bishops with the sword of Peter to cut down the impious,[5] when Pope Boniface of holy memory rejoiced in the Catholic devotion of the most pious emperors and used against the enemies of the grace of God, not only the apostolic, but also the royal, decrees,[6] and likewise, although he was most learned, he nevertheless requested the replies of the blessed Bishop Augustine against the books of the Pelagians.[7]

(2) Wherefore, Celestine, also a pontiff of venerable memory, upon whom the Lord bestowed many gifts of His grace for

1 2 Tim. 2.19.
2 Cf. A. Bruckner, Julian von Eclanum, sein Leben und seine Lehre, *Texte und Untersuchungen zur Geschichte der Altchristlichen Literatur* (Leipzig 1897) XV 5.
3 Cf. *Epistola XXIX* (*PL* 20.582ff.).
4 Cf. Hefele-LeClercq, *op. cit.* 2.1 177 n. 1.
5 Cf. *Epistolae II et III* (*PL* 20.649).
6 Cf. *Epistola VII* (*PL* 20.766).
7 Cf. St. Augustine, *Contra duas epistolas Pelagianorum* (*PL* 44.549ff).

the protection of the Catholic Church, knowing that not the weight of a judgment but only the remedy of penance ought to be given to the condemned, ordered Celestius, who was demanding an audience, to be expelled, without any discussicn of business, from every section of Italy. And he thought that the Synodal Statutes and decrees of his predecessors ought to be kept; consequently, he never allowed a revision of what had once deserved extirpation. With no less diligence did he free Britain of this disease, when he excluded some of the enemies of grace from occupying the land of their origin,[8] even in that hidden part of the ocean;[9] he also ordained a bishop for the Irish;[10] whereas he was zealous to keep the Roman island [Britain] Catholic, he also made the barbarous one [Ireland] Christian. Through this man, the Eastern Churches were also cleansed of twin plagues, when he aided with the apostolic sword Cyril, Bishop of Alexandria, the glorious defender of the Catholic faith, to cut down the Nestorian impiety.[11] By this sword, the Pelagians, since they were kin and comrades in error, were once again brought low. Through this man, the liberty to slander was taken away from those very persons who attack the writings of Augustine of holy memory. When he took the action advised by his counselors, and when he praised the piety of the books which displeased those in error, he made it clear with a holy eloquence what was to be thought of their authority. He clearly stated how much that novel presumption displeased him, whereby some impudently dared to rise against the ancient teachers and to clamor with ignorant calumny against the preaching of truth. He said: 'We have always held Au-

8 Cf. Prosper of Aquitaine, *Chronicon integrum* (*PL* 51.595A).
9 Cf. Virgil, *Eclogues* 1.67.
10 Cf. Prosper of Aquitaine, *Chronicon integrum* (*PL* 51.595B).
11 Cf. Denzinger, *op. cit.,* no. 111ff.

gustine a man of holy memory, because of his life and merits in our communion; never has the least rumor of sinister suspicion bespattered him, whom we remember once to have been of so great learning that he was always held even by my predecessors as among the best teachers. Therefore, everyone in general has thought well of him, as one considered everywhere and by all as deserving of love and honor.'[12]

(3) Does anyone dare to emit a murmur of malicious interpretation against that triumph of highly renowned praise, against that worthy and holy testimony? That is a murmur based on the fact that, since the title of the books in question was not expressed in the pope's letter, it might also appear that they were not approved and that the praise of St. Augustine was bestowed on the basis of the merits of earlier writings. The stipulation that the late date of these books makes them appear repudiable would stand, if antiquity were at variance with this same man and concerning the same problem. Likewise, what was found not in conformity with his compositions against the Pelagians would be judged either useless or beside the point. That we may omit those volumes in which he carried on a controversy in defense of grace from the beginning of his episcopacy and long before the enemies of grace lifted their heads, let the three letters of the book to Marcellinus be read.[13] Let the letter to the holy Bishop Paulinus of Nola be reviewed.[14] Let the pages of the letter sent to the Blessed Sixtus, then priest of the Apostolic See, and now Pontiff,[15] be read through. Let the

12 *Ibid.*, no. 128.

13 *De peccatorum meritis et remissione* (*PL* 44.109ff.). The best list of the works of St. Augustine, with dates and editions, is given by Vernon J. Bourke, *op. cit.*, pp. 303-308.

14 *Epistola CLXXXVI* (*PL* 33.815ff.).

15 *Epistola CXCIV* (*PL* 33.874ff.). Pope Sixtus reigned from 432 to 440.

volumes written to the holy Pinian,[16] to Count Valerius,[17] and to the servants of Christ, Timasius[18] and James,[19] be unrolled. Let the first six books against Julian[20] be reviewed. And the one to holy Aurelius, Bishop of Carthage, on the events in Palestine,[21] and the second one to the priests Paul and Eutropius[22] against the questions of Pelagius and Celestius; likewise, the four volumes to Pope Boniface, of blessed memory.[23] And if in all these works, and in many others too numerous to mention, the same spirit of doctrine and form of presentation prevail, let the slanderers admit that their objections are vain. For, no exceptional or divided testimony is presented in books, whose rule of faith throughout all the volumes is praised. The Apostolic See approves, along with what was known in advance, that which was not at variance with what was known in advance; and what it joins in judgment, it does not divide in praise. Therefore, let those who reject the recently published books give assent to the earlier ones, and agree to what was previously written on behalf of the grace of Christ. But they fail to do so, for they know that everything is against the Pelagians, and that nothing can be of use to them in solving what follows, if they admit that there is truth in the previous works.

(4) Therefore, the depravity of men of this kind must be resisted; not so much their zeal in discussion as the prerogatives of authority, so that no disciple of their sect, long ago crushed, may be permitted to rise up again. For, it is well

16 *De gratia Christi et de peccato originali* (*PL* 44.359ff.).
17 *De nuptiis et concupiscentia* (*PL* 44.413ff.).
18 *De natura et gratia* (*PL* 44.247ff.).
19 *Ibid.*
20 *Contra Julianum haeresis Pelagianae defensorem* (*PL* 44.641ff.).
21 *De gestis Pelagii* (*PL* 44.319ff.).
22 *De perfectione justitiae hominis* (*PL* 44.319ff.).
23 *Contra duas epistolas Pelagianorum* (*PL* 44.549ff.).

known that the subtleties of that error are upheld in such a way that it would strive to rebuild itself completely, even from its smallest part, once it became apparent that an offshoot is again growing forth, due to some indulgence on its behalf, after the semblance of a correction was made. When the highest degree is only a part, it is not a sign of devotion to have given up almost the whole, but of fraud to have retained even the smallest amount. In order that the snares of the hypocrites may not prevail, we trust that, with the Lord's protection, God may bring about in Sixtus what He did in Innocent, Zozimus, Boniface and Celestine. Thus, may part of the glory reserved for this shepherd of the Lord's flock be that he drive out the hidden wolves, as they have cast out the visible ones. May there ring in his ears the speech of the learned old man, by which he exhorted his collaborator, saying: 'For there are some who think they are quite at liberty to defend the justly condemned impieties, and there are some who covertly enter homes; and they do not cease to disseminate in secret what they fear to proclaim aloud. There are some who have wholly gone into silence, overcome by a strong fear, but still retaining in their hearts what they do not now dare profess with their mouth; nevertheless, they are well known to the brethren from an earlier defense of that doctrine. Thus, some are to be coerced severely, some to be quite vigilantly watched, others are to be treated kindly, but not carelessly instructed, so that, if they do not fear to bring ruin, nevertheless, they be not unconcerned to perish.'[24]

Chapter 22

(1) It has been sufficiently demonstrated, I think, that

24 St. Augustine, *Epistola CXCIV* (1,2) *ad Sixtum* (*PL* 33.875). This letter was written fourteen years before Sixtus became Pope.

those who blame St. Augustine make empty objections, attack what is right and defend what is wrong; that, when they bring about internal strife with assassin's arms, they rebel against the divine sayings and human constitutions. But, as long as they are not separated from the society of the brotherhood, we must tolerate their intention rather than despair of their correction. Thus, while the Lord, through the princes of the Church and the legitimate ministers of His judgments allays what has been stirred up by the pride of a few and the ignorance of some, may it be our task, with God's help, quietly, moderately and patiently to return love for hatred, to avoid conflict with the foolish, not to desert the truth nor to fight with the weapons of falsity, always to seek from God that, in all our thoughts, in all our wills, in all our speech and activity, He hold first place, who says that He is the beginning: 'For of Him, and by Him, and in Him, are all things: to Him be glory forever. Amen.'[1]

1 Rom. 11.36.

INDEX

INDEX

DATE DUE
